Torstein Kvamme

**Christmas in Song and Story**

Torstein Kvamme

**Christmas in Song and Story**

ISBN/EAN: 9783743438194

Printed in Europe, USA, Canada, Australia, Japan

Cover: Foto ©Thomas Meinert / pixelio.de

Manufactured and distributed by brebook publishing software (www.brebook.com)

Torstein Kvamme

**Christmas in Song and Story**

# CHRISTMAS

## IN

# SONG, SKETCH, AND STORY

NEARLY THREE HUNDRED

### CHRISTMAS SONGS, HYMNS, AND CAROLS

WITH SELECTIONS FROM

### BEECHER, WALLACE, AUERBACH, ABBOTT, WARREN AND DICKENS

ILLUSTRATIONS BY

RAPHAEL, MURILLO, BOUGUEREAU, HOFMANN, DEFREGGER, STORY
SHEPHERD, DARLEY, MEADE, NAST, AND OTHERS

SELECTED BY

## J. P. McCASKEY

COMPILER OF "HARPER'S FRANKLIN SQUARE SONG COLLECTION," ETC.

*"CHRISTUS NATUS HODIE"*

NEW YORK
HARPER & BROTHERS, FRANKLIN SQUARE
1891

*And thou Child shalt be called the Prophet of the Highest: for thou shalt go before the face of the Lord to prepare his ways, to give knowledge of salvation unto his people, by the remission of their sins, through the tender mercy of our God, whereby the Day-spring from on high hath visited us, to give Light to them that sit in darkness, and in the shadow of death, to guide our feet in the way of Peace.*

OLD VERSION.

# Christmas * in * Song.

# CONTENTS.

# Index • of • First • Lines.

No war, or battle's sound,
Was heard the world around;
The idle spear and shield were high up hung;
The hookéd chariot stood
Unstained with hostile blood;
The trumpet spake not to the arméd throng;
And Kings sat still with awful eye,
As if they surely knew their sovereign Lord was by.

*John Milton.*

From " Hymn to the Nativity."

---

"There are many things from which I might have derived good, by which I have not profited, I dare say," returned Scrooge's nephew, "Christmas among the rest. But I am sure I have always thought of Christmas time, when it has come round—apart from the veneration due to its sacred name and origin, if anything belonging to it can be apart from that—as a good time; a kind, forgiving, charitable, pleasant time; the only time I know of in the long calendar of the year, when men and women seem by one consent to open their shut-up hearts freely, and to think of people below them as if they really were fellow-passengers to the grave, and not another race of creatures bound on other journeys. And therefore, uncle, though it has never put a scrap of gold or silver in my pocket, I believe that it *has* done me good, and will do me good; and I say, God bless it!"—*Christmas Carol.*

# Christmas ✳ in ✳ Story.

But hark ! The Waits are playing, and they break my childish sleep ! What images do I associate with the Christmas music as I see them set forth on the Christmas Tree? Known before all the others, keeping far apart from all the others, they gather round my little bed. An angel speaking to a group of shepherds in a field ; some travelers with eyes uplifted, following a star ; a baby in a manger ; a child in a spacious temple, talking with grave men ; a solemn figure, with a mild and beautiful face, raising a dead girl by the hand ; again, near a city gate calling back the son of a widow, on his bier, to life ; a crowd of people looking through the open roof of a chamber where he sits, and letting down a sick person on a bed, with ropes ; the same in a tempest, walking on the water to a ship ; again, on a seashore, teaching a great multitude ; again, with a child upon his knee, and other children round ; again, restoring sight to the blind, speech to the dumb, hearing to the deaf, health to the sick, strength to the lame, knowledge to the ignorant ; again, dying upon a Cross, watched by armed soldiers, a thick darkness coming on, the earth beginning to shake, and only one voice heard, "Forgive them, for they know not what they do !"

*Charles Dickens.*

# Illustrations.

# THE CHARMER.

*Socrates.* "However, you and Simmias appear to me as if you wished to sift this subject more thoroughly, and to be afraid, like children, lest, on the soul's departure from the body, winds should blow it away.". . .

Upon this Cebes said : "Endeavor to teach us better, Socrates. . . . Perhaps there is a childish spirit in our breast that has such a dread. Let us endeavor to persuade him not to be afraid of death, as of hobgoblins."

"But you must *charm* him every day," said Socrates, "until you have quieted his fears."

"But whence, O Socrates," he said, "can we procure a skillful charmer for such a case, now *you* are about to leave us ?"

"Greece is wide, Cebes," he replied ; "and in it surely there are skillful men, there are also many barbarous nations, all of which you should search, seeking such a charmer, sparing neither money nor toil, as there is nothing on which you can more reasonably expend your money."—*Plato.*

> "*We need that Charmer, for our hearts are sore*
> *With longing for the things that may not be;*
> *Faint for the friends that shall return no more;*
> *Dark with distrust, or wrung with agony.*
>
> "*What is this life? and what to us is death?*
> *Whence came we? whither go? and where are those*
> *Who, in a moment stricken from our side,*
> *Passed to that land of shadow and repose?*
>
> "*Are they all dust? and dust must we become?*
> *Or are they living in some unknown clime?*
> *Shall we regain them in that far-off home,*
> *And live anew beyond the waves of time?*
>
> "*O man divine! on thee our souls have hung;*
> *Thou wert our teacher in these questions high;*
> *But, ah! this day divides thee from our side,*
> *And veils in dust thy kindly-guiding eye.*
>
> "*Where is that Charmer whom thou bid'st us seek?*
> *On what far shores may his sweet voice be heard?*
> *When shall these questions of our yearning souls*
> *Be answered by the bright eternal word?*"
>
> *So spake the youth of Athens, weeping round,*
> *When Socrates lay calmly down to die ;*
> *So spake the sage, prophetic of the hour*
> *When earth's fair Morning Star should rise on high.*

*They found him not, those youths of soul divine,*
  *Long seeking, wandering, watching on life's shore—*
*Reasoning, aspiring, yearning for the light,*
  *Death came and found them—doubting as before.*

*But years passed on; and lo! the Charmer came—*
  *Pure, simple, sweet, as comes the silver dew;*
*And the world knew him not—he walked alone,*
  *Encircled only by his trusting few.*

*Like the Athenian sage rejected, scorned,*
  *Betrayed, condemned, his day of doom drew nigh;*
*He drew his faithful few more closely round,*
  *And told them that his hour was come to die.*

*"Let not your heart be troubled," then he said;*
  *"My Father's house hath mansions large and fair;*
*I go before you to prepare your place;*
  *'I will return to take you with me there."*

*And since that hour the awful foe is charmed,*
  *And life and death are glorified and fair.*
*Whither He went we know—the way we know—*
  *And with firm step press on to meet Him there.*

HARRIET BEECHER STOWE.

THE MOTHER IN EGYPT REPOSING.

# THE OVERTURE OF ANGELS.

HAD it been the design of Divine Providence that the Gospels should be wrought up like a poem for literary and artistic effect, surely the narrative of the angelic appearances would have glowed in all the colors of an Oriental morning. They are, indeed, to those who have an eye to discern, a wonderful and exquisitely-tinted prelude to the dawn of a glorious day. It is not to be supposed that the earth and its dull inhabitants knew what was approaching. But heavenly spirits knew it. There was movement and holy ecstasy in the Upper Air, and angels seem, as birds when new-come in spring, to have flown hither and thither, in songful mood, dipping their white wings into our atmosphere, just touching the earth or glancing along its surface, as sea-birds skim the surface of the sea. And yet birds are far too rude, and wings too burdensome, to express adequately that feeling of unlabored angelic motion which the narrative produces upon the imagination. Their airy and gentle coming would perhaps be better compared to the glow of colors flung by the sun upon morning clouds that seem to be born just where they appear. Like a beam of light striking through some orifice, they shine upon Zacharias in the Temple. As the morning light finds the flowers, so found they the mother of Jesus. To the shepherds' eyes they filled the midnight arch like auroral beams of light; but not as silently, for they sang, and more marvellously than when "the morning stars sang together and all the sons of God shouted for joy."

The new era opens at Jerusalem. The pride with which a devout Jew looked upon Jerusalem can scarcely be imagined in our prosaic times. Men loved that city with such passionate devotion as we are accustomed to see bestowed only on a living person. When the doctrine of immortality grew more distinctly into the belief of holy men, no name could be found which would make the invisible world so attractive as that of the beloved city. New Jerusalem was the chosen name for Heaven. Upon this city broke the morning rays of the Advent. A venerable priest, Zacharias, belonging to the retinue of the Temple, had spent his whole life in the quiet offices of religion. He was married, but childless. To him happened a surprising thing. It was his turn to burn incense—the most honorable function of the priestly office. Upon the great altar of sacrifice, outside the holy of holies, the burnt-offering was placed. At a signal the priest came forth, and, taking fire from this altar, he entered the inner and most sacred place of the Temple, and there, before the altar of incense, putting the fragrant gum upon the coals, he swung the censer, filling the air with wreaths of smoke. The people who had gathered on the outside, as soon as the smoke ascended silently sent up their prayers, of which the incense was the symbol. "And there appeared unto him an angel of the Lord, standing on the right side of the altar." That he trembled with fear and awe is apparent from the angel's address—"Fear not!" The key-note of the new dispensation was sounded! Hereafter, God was to be brought nearer, to seem less terrible; and a religion of the spirit and of love was soon to dispossess a religion of ceremonials and of fear. "Fear not, Zacharias:" said the angel. "for thy prayer is heard; and thy wife Elisabeth shall bear thee a son, and thou shalt call his name John. And thou shalt have joy and gladness; and many shall rejoice at his birth. For he shall be great in the sight of the Lord, and shall drink neither wine nor strong drink; and he shall be filled with the Holy Ghost, even from his mother's womb. And many of the children of Israel shall he turn to the Lord their God. And he shall go before him in the spirit and power of Elias, to turn the hearts of the parents to the children, and the disobedient to the wisdom of the just; to make ready a people prepared for the Lord."

If this address, to our modern ears, seems stately and formal, it is to be remembered that no other language would seem so fit for a heavenly message to a Jewish priest as that which breathed the spirit of the Old Testament writings; and that to us it savors of the sermon because it has since been so often used for the purposes of the sermon.

But the laws of the material world seemed to the doubting priest more powerful than the promise of that God who made all physical laws. To this distinct promise of a son who should become a great reformer, and renew the power and grandeur of the prophetic office, he could only say, "Whereby shall I know this?" His doubts should have begun earlier, or not at all. He should have rejected the whole vision, or should have accepted the promise implicitly; for what sign could be given so assuring as the very presence of the angel? But the sign which he asked was given in a way that he

## COME, ALL YE FAITHFUL.

J. READING, 1692.

could never forget. His speech departed; silence was the sign;—as if the priest of the Old was to teach no more until the coming of the New. When Zacharias came forth to the people, who were already impatient at his long delay, they perceived by his altered manner that some great experience had befallen him. He could not speak, and could dismiss them only by a gesture. We have no certainty whether this scene occurred at a morning or an evening service, but it is supposed to have been at the evening sacrifice. In that case the event was an impressive symbol. The people beheld

their priest standing against the setting sun, dumb, while they dispersed in the twilight, the shadow of the Temple having already fallen upon them. The Old was passing into darkness; to-morrow another sun must rise!

Elisabeth, the wife of Zacharias, returned to the "hill-country," or that region lying west and south of Jerusalem. The promise had begun to be fulfilled. All the promises made to Israel were pointing to their fulfillment through her. These promises, accumulating through ages, were ample enough, even in the letter, to fill a devout soul with ardent expectancy. But falling upon the imagination of a greatly distressed people, they had been magnified or refracted until the public mind was filled with inordinate and even fantastic expectations of the Messianic reign. It is not probable that any were altogether free from this delusion, not even the soberest and most spiritual natures. We can therefore imagine but faintly the ecstatic hopes of Zacharias and Elisabeth during the six months in which they were hidden in their home among the hills before the history again finds them. They are next introduced through the story of another memorable actor in this drama, the mother of our Lord. It is difficult to speak of Mary, the mother of Jesus, both because so little is known of her and because so much has been imagined. Around no other name in history has the imagination thrown its witching light in so great a volume. In art she has divided honors with her divine Son. For a thousand years her name has excited the profoundest reverence and worship. A mother's love and forbearance with her children, as it is a universal experience, so is it the nearest image of the divine tenderness which the soul can form. In attempting to present the Divine Being

## ADESTE, FIDELES.

J. Reading, 1692.

1. A - des - te, fi - de - les, Læ - ti tri - um-phan-tes, Ve - ni - te, ve - ni - te in
2. Can - tet nunc I - o Cho-rus an - ge - lo - rum, Can - tet nunc au - la cœ
3. Er - go qui na - tus Di - e ho-di - er - na, Je - su, ti - bi sit

Beth - le - hem, Na - tum vi - de - te, Regem an - ge - lo - rum, Ve - ni - te, a - do -
les - ti - um Glo - ri - a, glo - ria in ex - cel - sis De - o Ve - ni - te, a - do -
glo - ri - a. Pa - tris æ - ter - nie verbum ca - ro fac - tum, Ve - ni - te, a - do -

re - mus, Ve - ni - te, a - do - re - mus, Ve - ni - te, a - do - re - mus Do - mi - num.

in his relations to universal government, men have well-nigh lost his personality in a sublime abstraction. Those traits of personal tenderness and generous love which alone will ever draw the human heart to God, it has too often been obliged to seek elsewhere. And, however mistaken the endeavor to find in the Virgin Mary the sympathy and fond familiarity of a divine fostering love, it is an error into which men have been drawn by the profoundest needs of the human soul. It is an error of the heart. The cure will be found by revealing, in the Divine nature, the longed-for traits in greater beauty and force than are given them in the legends of the mother of Jesus. Meanwhile, if the doctors of theology have long hesitated to deify the Virgin, art has unconsciously raised her to the highest place. There is nothing in attitude, expression, or motion which has been left untried. The earlier Christian painters were content to express her pure fervor, without relying upon the element of beauty. But as, age by age, imagination kindled, the canvas has given forth this divine mother in more and more glowing beauty, borrowing from the Grecian spirit all that was charming in the highest ideals of Venus, adding to them an element of transcendent purity and devotion which has no parallel in ancient art.

It is difficult for one whose eye has been steeped in the colors of art to go back from its enchantment to the barrenness of actual history. By Luke alone is the place even of her residence mentioned. It is only inferred that she was of the royal house of David. She was already espoused to a man named Joseph, but not as yet married. This is the sum of our knowledge of Mary at the point where her history is introduced. Legends abound, many of them charming, but like the innumerable faces which artists have painted, they gratify the imagination without adding anything to historic truth. The scene of the Annunciation will always be admirable in literature, even to those who are not disposed to accord it any historic value. To announce to an espoused virgin that she was to be the mother of a child, out of wedlock, by the unconscious working in her of the Divine power, would,

## BRIGHTEST AND BEST.

SAMUEL WEBBE.
REGINALD HEBER, 1811.

1. Bright-est and best of the sons of the morn-ing, Dawn on our darkness, and lend us Thine aid; Star of the East, the hor-i-zon a-dorn-ing, Guide where our in-fant Re-deem-er is laid.
2. Cold on His cra-dle the dew-drops are shin-ing, Low lies His head with the beasts of the stall; An-gels a-dore Him in slum-ber re-clin-ing, Ma-ker and Mon-arch and Sa-viour of all.
3. Say, shall we yield Him, in cost-ly de-vo-tion O-dors of E-dom and off'rings di-vine? Gems of the moun-tain and pearls of the o-cean, Myrrh from the for-est, and gold from the mine? A-MEN.

Vainly we offer each ample oblation,
Vainly with gifts would His favor secure;
Richer by far is the heart's adoration,
Dearer to God are the prayers of the poor.

Brightest and best of the sons of the morning,
Dawn on our darkness, and lend us Thine aid;
Star of the East, the horizon adorning,
Guide where our infant Redeemer is laid.

beforehand, seem inconsistent with delicacy. But no person of poetic sensibility can read the scene as it is narrated by Luke without admiring its sublime purity and serenity. It is not a transaction of the lower world of passion. Things most difficult to a lower sphere are both easy and beautiful in that atmosphere which, as it were, the angel brought down with him. "And the angel came in unto her and said, Hail! thou that art highly favored! The Lord is with thee!" Then was announced the birth of Jesus, and that he should inherit and prolong endlessly the glories promised to Israel of old. To her inquiry, "How shall this be?" the angel replied: "The Holy Ghost shall come upon thee, and the power of the Highest shall overshadow thee; therefore also that holy thing which shall be born of thee shall be called the Son of God." It was also made known to Mary that her cousin Elisabeth had conceived a son. And Mary said: Behold the handmaid of the Lord! Be it unto me according to thy word.

Many have brought to this history the associations of a later day, of a different civilization, and of habits of thought foreign to the whole cast of the Oriental mind. Out of a process so unphilosophical they have evolved the most serious doubts and difficulties. But no one is fitted to appreciate either the beauty or the truthfulness to nature of such a scene, who cannot in some degree carry himself back in sympathy to that Jewish maiden's life. The education of a Hebrew woman was far freer than that of women of other Oriental nations. She had more personal liberty, a wider scope of intelligence, than obtained among the Greeks or even among the Romans. But above all, she received a moral education which placed her high above her sisters in other lands. It is plain that Mary was imbued with the spirit of the Hebrew Scriptures. Not only was the history of her people familiar to her, but her language shows that the poetry of the Old Testament had filled her soul. She was fitted to re-

## WITH GLADNESS MEN OF OLD.

W. H. Monk.
Wm. C. Dix, 1860.

1. As with glad-ness men of old Did the guid-ing star be-hold,
2. As with joy-ful steps they sped, Sav-iour, to Thy man-ger bed,
3. As they of-fered gifts most rare At Thy cra-dle rude and bare,
4. Ho-ly Je-sus, ev-'ry day Keep us in the nar-row way;

As with joy they hailed its light, Lead-ing on-ward, beam-ing bright,
There to bend the knee be-fore Thee, whom heaven and earth a-dore;
So may we with ho-ly joy, Pure and free from sin's al-loy,
And when earth-ly things are past, Bring our ran-somed souls at last

So, most grac-ious Lord, may we Ev-er-more be led to Thee.
So may we with wil-ling feet Ev-er seek the mer-cy-seat.
All our cost-liest treas-ures bring, Christ, to Thee, our heaven-ly King.
Where they need no star to guide, Where no clouds Thy glo-ry hide.

ceive her people's history in its most romantic and spiritual aspects. They were God's peculiar people. Their history unrolled before her as a series of wonderful providences. The path glowed with divine manifestations. Miracles blossomed out of every natural law. But to her there were no laws of nature. Such ideas had not yet been born. The earth was "the Lord's." All its phenomena were direct manifestations of his will. Clouds and storms came on errands from God. Light and darkness were the shining or the hiding of his face. Calamities were punishments. Harvests were divine gifts; famines were immediate divine penalties. To us God acts through instruments; to the Hebrew he acted immediately by his will. "He spake, and it was done; he commanded, and it stood fast." To such a one as Mary there would be no incredulity as to the reality of this angelic manifestation. Her only surprise would be that *she* should be chosen for a renewal of those divine interpositions in behalf of her people of which their history was so full. The very reason which would lead us to suspect a miracle in our day gave it credibility in other days. It is simply a question of adaptation. A miracle as a blind appeal to the moral sense, without the use of the reason, was adapted to the earlier periods of human life. Its usefulness ceases when the moral sense is so developed that it can find its own way through the ministration of the reason. A miracle is a substitute for moral demonstration, and is peculiarly adapted to the early conditions of mankind. Of all miracles, there was none more sacred, congruous, and grateful to a Hebrew than an angelic visitation. A devout Jew, in looking back, saw angels flying thick between the heavenly throne and the throne of his fathers. The greatest events of national history had been made illustrious by their presence. Their work began with the primitive pair. They had come at evening to Abraham's tent. They had waited upon Jacob's footsteps. They had communed with Moses, with the judges, with priests and magistrates, with prophets and holy men. All the way down from the beginning of history, the pious Jew saw the

## WHILE SHEPHERDS WATCHED.

Nahum Tate, 1703.
Old English Melody.

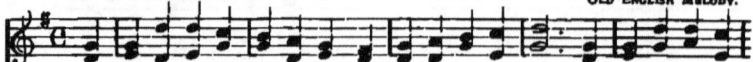

1. While shepherds watch'd their flocks by night, All seated on the ground, The an-gel of the
2. "To you, in David's town, this day Is born of Dav-id's line, The Saviour, who is
3. Thus spake the ser-aph, and forthwith Appeared a shin-ing throng Of angels, praising

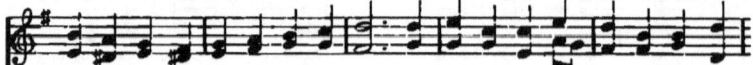

Lord came down, And glo - ry shone a - round. "Fear not," said he, for might - y dread Had
Christ the Lord, And this shall be the sign: "The heavenly Babe you there shall find, To
God, who thus Addressed their joy-ful song: "All glo - ry be to God on high, And

seized their troubled mind; "Glad tidings of great joy I bring, To you and all man - kind.
hu - man view displayed, All meanly wrapt in swathing bands, And in a man - ger laid."
to the 'earth be' peace; Good-will henceforth from Heaven to men Begin, and nev - er cease."

shining footsteps of these heavenly messengers. Nor had the faith died out in the long interval through which their visits had been withheld. Mary could not, therefore, be surprised at the coming of angels, but only that they should come to her. It may seem strange that Zacharias should be struck dumb for doubting the heavenly messenger, while Mary went unrebuked. But it is plain that there was a wide difference in the nature of the relative experiences. To Zacharias was promised an event external to himself, not involving his own sensibility. But to a woman's heart there can be no other announcement possible that shall so stir every feeling and sensibility of the soul, as the promise and prospect of her first child. Motherhood is the very centre of womanhood. The first awakening in her soul of the reality that she bears a double life — herself within herself — brings a sweet bewilderment of wonder and joy. The more sure her faith of the fact, the more tremulous must her soul become. Such an announcement can never mean to a father's what it does to a mother's heart.

And it is one of the exquisite shades of subtle truth, and of beauty as well, that the angel who rebuked Zacharias for doubt saw nothing in the trembling hesitancy and wonder of Mary inconsistent with childlike faith. If the heart swells with the hope of a new life in the common lot of mortals, with what profound feeling must Mary have pondered the angel's promise to her son! "He shall be great, and shall be called the Son of the Highest; and the Lord God shall give him the throne of his father David; and he shall reign over the house of Jacob forever, and of his kingdom there shall be no end."

It is expressly stated that Joseph was of the "house of David," but there is no evidence that Mary was of the same, except this implication, "The Lord God shall give him the throne of his father David." Since Joseph was not his father, it could only be through his mother that he could trace his lineage to David. There is no reason to suppose that Mary was more enlightened than those among whom she dwelt, or that she gave to these words that spiritual sense in which alone they have proved true. To her, it may be supposed, there arose a vague idea that her son was destined to be an emi-

## CRADLED ALL LOWLY.

Charles Gounod.
Geo. Wm. Warren arr.

Allegretto.

1. Cra-dled all low-ly, Be-hold the Saviour Child, A Being
2. No lon-ger sor-row As without hope, O earth! A brighter
( *Play these two bars before each verse.* ) 3. Babe, weak and wail-ing, In low-ly vil-lage stall Thy glory

*mp*

*cres.*

ho-ly In dwelling rude and wild, Ne'er yet was re-gal state Of monarch proud and
morrow, Dawn'd with that Infant's birth! Our sins were great and sore, But these the Saviour
veil-ing, Thou cam'st to die for all! The sac-ri-fice is done, The world's atonement

'cres

*ff*

great, Who grasped a nation's fate, So glorious as the manger bed of Beth-le-hem.
bore, And God was wroth no more, His own Son was the Child that lay in Bethle-hem.
won, Till time its course hath run, O Jesus, Saviour! Morning Star of Bethle-hem.

nent teacher and deliverer. She would naturally go back in her mind to the instances, in the history of her own people, of eminent men and women who had been raised up in dark times to deliver their people. She lived in the very region which Deborah and Barak had made famous. Almost before her eyes lay the plains on which great deliverances had been wrought by heroes raised up by the God of Israel. But that other glory, of spiritual deliverance, was hidden from her. Or, if that influence which overshadowed her awakened in her

the spiritual vision, it was doubtless to reveal that her son was to be something more than a mere worldly conqueror. But it was not for her to discern the glorious reality. It hung in the future as a dim brightness, whose particular form and substance could not be discerned. For it is not to be supposed that Mary—prophet as every woman is—could discern that spiritual truth of the promises of the Old Testament which his own disciples did not understand after having companied with Jesus for a period of three years, nor yet after his ascension, nor until the fire of the pentecostal day had kindled in them the eye of flame that pierces all things and discerns the spirit.

"And Mary arose in those days, and went into the hill-country with haste, into a city of Juda, and entered into the house of Zacharias and saluted Elisabeth." The overshadowing Spirit had breathed upon her the new life. What woman of deep soul was ever unthrilled at the mystery of life beating within life? And what Jewish woman, devoutly believing that in her child were to be fulfilled the hopes of Israel, could hold this faith without excitement almost too great to be borne? She could not tarry. With haste she trod that way which she had doubtless often trod before in her annual ascent to the Temple. Every village, every brook, every hill, must have awakened in her some sad recollection of

## HIS REIGN ON EARTH BEGUN.

Geo. J. Webb.
James Montgomery.

1. Hail to the Lord's Anoint - ed, Great David's great-er Son; Hail, in the time ap-
2. He comes with succor speed - y, To those who suffer wrong; To help the poor and
3. He shall descend like show-ers Up - on the fruitful earth; And love and joy, like

point - ed, His reign on earth be - gun! He comes to break op - pres - sion, To
need - y, And bid the weak be strong; To give them songs for sigh - ing, Their
flow - ers, Spring in His path to birth: Be - fore Him, on the moun - tains, Shall

set the cap - tive free, To take a - way transgres - sion, And rule in e - qui - ty.
dark-ness turn to light, Whose souls, condemned and dying, Were precious in His sight.
Peace, the her - ald, go; And righteousness, in foun - tains, From hill to val - ley flow.

Arabia's desert-ranger
　To Him shall bow the knee,
The Ethiopian stranger
　His glory come to see;
With offerings of devotion,
　Ships from the Isles shall meet,
To pour the wealth of ocean
　In tribute at His feet.

Kings shall fall down before Him,
　And gold and incense bring,
All nations shall adore Him,
　His praise all people sing;
For He shall have dominion
　O'er river, sea, and shore,
Far as the eagle's pinion
　Or dove's light wing can soar.

To Him shall prayer unceasing,
　And daily vows ascend,
His kingdom, still increasing,
　A kingdom without end;
The tide of time shall never
　His covenant remove;
His Name shall stand for ever;
　That Name to us is Love.

the olden days of her people. There was Tabor, from which came down Barak and his men. And in the great plain of Esdraelon he fought Sisera. The waters of Kishon, murmuring at her feet, must have recalled the song of Deborah. Here, too, Josiah was slain at Megiddo, and "the mourning of Hadad-Rimmon in the valley of Megiddon" became the by-word of grief. Mount Gilboa rose upon her from the east. Ebal and Gerizim stood forth in remembrance of the sublime drama of blessings and cursings. Then came Shechem, the paradise of Palestine, in whose neighborhood Joseph was buried. This pilgrim may have quenched her thirst at noon-day, as afterwards her son did, at the well of Jacob; and farther to the south it might be that the oak of Mamre, under which the patriarch dwelt, cast its great shadow upon her. It is plain from the song of Mary, of which we shall speak in a moment, that she bore in mind the history of the mother of Samuel, wife of Elkanah, who dwelt in this region, and whose song, at the presentation of Samuel to the priest at Shiloh, seems to have been the mould in which Mary unconsciously cast her own. Thus, one after another, Mary must have passed the most memorable spots in her people's history. Even if not sensi-

tive to patriotic influences,—still more if she was alive to such sacred and poetic associations,—she must have come to her relative Elisabeth with flaming heart. Well she might! What other mystery in human life is so profound as the beginning of life? From the earliest days women have called themselves blessed of God when life begins to palpitate within their bosom. It is not education, but nature, that inspires such

## SALUTE THE HAPPY MORN.

JOHN BYROM.

1. Christians, a - wake, sa - lute the happy morn, Whereon the Saviour of mankind was born,
2. Then to the watchful shepherds it was told, Who heard th'angelic herald's voice: "Behold,
3. He spake, and straightway the ce - les - tial choir In hymns of joy, unknown before, con - spire:
4. To Bethlehem straight the happy shepherds run, To see the wonder God had wrought for man:

Rise to a - dore the mys - te - ry of love, Which hosts of angels chanted from a - bove;
I bring good tid - ings of a Saviour's birth To you and all the nations up - on earth:
The praises of re - deeming love they sang, And Heaven's whole arch with alleluias rang:
And found with Jo - seph and the blessed maid, Her Son, the Saviour, in a man - ger laid;

With them the joy - ful tidings first be - gun Of God In - carnate and the Virgin's Son.
This day hath God fulfill'd His promised word, This day is born a Saviour, Christ the Lord.
God's highest glo - ry was their anthem still, Peace up - on earth, and unto men good - will.
Amazed, the wondrous story they proclaim, The earliest heralds of the Saviour's Name.

Let us, like these good shepherds, then employ
Our grateful voices to proclaim the joy;
Trace we the Babe, who hath retrieved our loss,
From His poor manger to His bitter Cross;
Treading His steps, assisted by His grace,
Till man's first heavenly state again takes place.

Then may we hope, the angelic thrones among,
To sing, redeemed, a glad triumphal song;
He, that was born upon this joyful day,
Around us all His glory shall display;
Saved by His love, incessant we shall sing
Eternal praise to Heaven's Almighty King.

tender amazement. Doubtless even the Indian woman in such periods dwells consciously near to the Great Spirit! Every one of a deep nature seems to herself more sacred and more especially under the divine care while a new life, moulded by the divine hand, is springing into being. For, of all creative acts, none is so sovereign and divine. Who shall reveal the endless musings, the perpetual prophecies, of the

mother's soul? Her thoughts dwell upon the unknown child,—thoughts more in number than the ripples of the sea upon some undiscovered shore. To others, in such hours, woman should seem more sacred than the most solemn temple; and to herself she must needs seem as if overshadowed by the Holy Ghost! To this natural elevation were added, in the instance of Mary and Elisabeth, those vague but exalted expectations arising from the angelic annunciations. Both of them believed that the whole future condition of their nation was to be intimately affected by the lives of their sons. And Mary said: "My soul doth magnify the Lord, and my spirit hath rejoiced in God my Saviour. For he hath regarded the low estate of his handmaiden ; for behold, from henceforth all generations shall call me blessed. For He that is mighty hath done to me great things; and holy is his name. And his mercy is on them that fear him from generation to generation. He hath shewed strength with his arm ; He hath scattered the proud in the imagination of their hearts. He hath put down the mighty from their seats, and exalted them of low degree. He hath filled the hungry with good things ; and the rich he hath sent empty away. He hath holpen his servant Israel, in remembrance of his mercy ; as he spake to our fathers, to Abraham, and to his seed forever." Unsympathizing critics remark upon the similarity of this chant of Mary's with the song of Hannah, the mother of Samuel. Inspira-

## O SANCTISSIMA.

LATIN HYMN.—A. D. 1500.
FOLK-SONG OF SICILIAN SEAS.

```
1. O sanc-tis-si-ma,   O pi-is-si-ma,   Dul-cis Vir-go Ma-ri-a.   O sanc-
2. To-ta pulchra es,   O Ma-ri-a,      Et ma-cu-la non est in te.  To-ta
3. Si-cut li-li-um    in-ter spi-nas,  Sic Ma-ri-a in-ter fi-lias. Si-cut
4. In mi-se-ri-a,     in an-gus-ti-a,  O-ra, Vir-go, pro no-bis.   In mi-
```

```
tis-si-ma,   O pi-is-si-ma, Dul-cis Vir-go Ma-ri-a.    Ma-ter a-
pul-chra es, O Ma-ri-a,     Et ma-cu-la non est in te.  Ma-ter a-
li-li-um    in-ter spi-nas, Sic Ma-ri-a in-ter fi-lias. Ma-ter a-
se-ri-a,    in an-gus-ti-a, O-ra, Vir-go, pro no-bis.   Pro no-bis
```

```
ma-ta,  in-te-me-ra-ta,  O-ra,  o-ra pro no-bis.
ma-ta,  in-te-me-ra-ta,  O-ra,  o-ra pro no-bis.
ma-ta,  in-te-me-ra-ta,  O-ra,  o-ra pro no-bis.
o-ra,   in mor-tis ho-ra, O-ra,  o-ra pro no-bis.
```

tion served to kindle the materials already in possession of the mind. This Hebrew maiden had stored her imagination with the poetic elements of the Old Testament. But, of all the treasures at command, only a devout and grateful nature would have made so unselfish a selection. For it is not upon her own blessedness that Mary chiefly dwells, but upon the sovereignty, the goodness and the glory of God. To be exalted by the joy of our personal prosperity above self-consciousness into the atmosphere of thanksgiving and adoration, is a sure sign of nobility of soul. For three months these sweet and noble women dwelt together, performing, doubtless, the simple labors of the household. Their thoughts, their converse, their employments, must be left wholly to the imagination. And yet, it is impossible not to be curious in regard to these hidden days of Judæa, when the mother of our Lord was already fashioning that sacred form which, in due time. not far from her residence, perhaps within the very sight of it, was to be lifted up upon the cross. But it is a research which we have

## CHRISTMAS CAROL.

J. M. NEALE.
THOMAS HELMORE.

1. Christ was born on Christmas day, Wreathe the holly, twine the bay, Light and life and joy is He, The Babe, the
2. He is born to set us free; He is born our Lord to be; Carol, Christians, joyfully; The God, the Lord, by
3. Let the bright red berries glow Ev'rywhere in goodly show, Light and life and joy is he, The Babe, the Son, the

Holy One of Ma-ry.
all adored for ev-er. } Christian men, rejoice and sing; 'Tis the birth-day of our King. Carol, Christians,
Holy One of Ma-ry.

joyfully; The God, the Lord, By all adored For-ev-er. Night of sadness, Morn of gladness Evermore:

Ev-er, Ev-er, Af-ter many troubles sore, Morn of gladness ever-more, and ever-more.

Midnight scarcely passed and over, Drawing to the holy morn; Very early, Very early, Christ was born.

Sing out with bliss, His name is this: Emmanuel! As 'twas foretold, In days of old, By Gabriel.

no means of pursuing. Her thoughts must be impossible to us, as our thoughts of her son were impossible to her. No one can look forward, even in the spirit of prophecy, to see after-things in all their fulness as they shall be ; nor can one who has known go back again to see as if he had not known.

After Mary's return to Nazareth, Elisabeth was delivered of a son. Following the custom of their people, her friends would have named him after his father, but the mother, mindful of the name given by the angel, called him John. An appeal was made to the priest—who probably was deaf as well as dumb, for they made signs to him—how the child should be named. Calling for writing-materials, he surprised them all by naming him as his wife had, —John. At once the sign ceased. His lips were unsealed, and he broke forth into thanksgiving and praise. All the circumstances conspired to awaken wonder and to spread throughout the neighborhood mysterious expectations, men saying,

## SONG OF THE ANGELS.

GIARDINI, 1760.
E. H. SEARS, 1860.

1. It came up-on the midnight clear, That glo-rious song of old, From angels bending near the earth To touch their harps of gold: "Peace to the earth, good-will to man, From Heaven's all-gracious King:" The earth in solemn stillness lay, To hear the an-gels sing.

2. Still thro' the cloven skies they come, With peaceful wings un-furled; And still ce-les-tial mu-sic floats O'er all the wea-ry world; A-bove its sad and low-ly plains They bend on heavenly wing, And ev-er o'er its Babel sounds, The bless-ed an-gels sing!

3. O ye, beneath life's crushing load, Whose forms are bending low, Who toil a-long the climbing way, With pain-ful steps and slow, Look up! for glad and gold-en hours Come swift-ly on the wing: Oh, rest beside the wea-ry road, And hear the an-gels sing!

4. For lo, the days are hastening on, By proph-et-bards fore-told, When with the ev-er-cir-cling years Comes round the age of gold! When peace shall o-ver all the earth Its fin-al splendors fling, And the whole world send back the song Which now the angels sing!

"What manner of child shall this be?" The first chapter of Luke may be considered as the last leaf of the Old Testament, so saturated is it with the heart and spirit of the olden times. And the song of Zacharias clearly reveals the state of feeling among the best Jews of that day. Their nation was grievously pressed down by foreign despotism. Their people were scattered through the world. The time was exceedingly dark, and the promises of the old prophets served by contrast to make their present distress yet darker. We are not surprised, therefore, to find the first portion of Zacharias's chant sensitively recognizing the degradations and sufferings of his people : "Blessed be the Lord God of Israel ; for he has visited and redeemed his people, and hath raised up an horn of salvation for us in the house of his servant David, (as he spake by the mouth of his holy prophets, which have been since the world began ;) that we should be saved from our enemies, and from the hand of all that hate us ; to perform the mercy prom- ised to our fathers, and to remember his holy covenant, the oath which he sware to our father Abraham, that he would grant unto us, that we being delivered out of the hand of our enemies might serve him with- out fear, in holiness and righteousness be- fore him, all the days of our life." Then, as if seized with a spirit of prophecy, and beholding the relations and offices of his son, in language as poetically beautiful as it is spiritually triumphant, he exclaims:

"And thou, Child, shalt be called the pro- phet of the Highest: for thou shalt go be- fore the face of the Lord to prepare His ways; to give knowledge of salvation unto His peo- ple by the remission of their sins, through the tender mercy of our God; whereby the Day-spring from on high hath visited us, to give light to them that sit in darkness and in the shadow of death, to guide our feet in- to the way of peace." Even in his childhood John manifested that fullness of nature and that earnestness which afterwards fitted him

## JOY TO THE WORLD.

ISAAC WATTS, 1709.
G. F. HANDEL. "ANTIOCH."

1. Joy to the world, the Lord is come! Let earth re - ceive her King; Let
2. Joy to the world, the Sav - iour reigns, Let men their songs em - ploy; While

ev - 'ry heart pre - pare Him room, And Heav'n and nature sing, And
fields and floods—rocks, hills and plains Re - peat the sounding joy, Re -

And Heav'n and na - ture
Re - peat the sounding

Heav'n and na - ture sing, And Heav'n and na - ture sing.
peat the sounding joy, Re - peat the sound - ing joy.
sing, joy,

sing, And Heav'n and na - ture sing.
joy, Re - peat the sounding joy.

No more let sin and sorrow grow,
Nor thorns infest the ground;
He comes to make His blessings flow
Far as the curse is found.

He rules the world with truth and grace,
And makes the nations prove
The glories of His righteousness,
And wonders of His love.

for his mission. He "waxed strong in spirit." He did not mingle in the ordinary pursuits of men. As one who bears a sensitive con- science and refuses to mingle in the throng of men of low morality, he stood apart and was solitary. He "was in the deserts un- til the day of his showing unto Israel."

Mary had returned to Nazareth, of which, as it appears to-day, this striking view is given by W. H. Dixon, in *The Holy Land:* "Four miles south of the strong Greek city of Saphoris, hidden away among gentle

hills, then covered from the base to the crown with vineyards and fig-trees, lay a natural nest, or basin, of rich red and white earth, star-like in shape, about a mile in width, and wondrously fertile. Along the scarred and chalky slope of the highest of these hills spread a small and lovely vil- lage, which, in a land where every stone seemed to have a story, is remarkable as having had no public history and no dis- tinguishable native name. No great road led up to this sunny nook. No traffic came into it. Trade, war, adventure, pleasure, pomp, passed by it, flowing from west to east, from east to west, along the Roman road. But the meadows were aglow with wheat and barley. Near the low ground ran a belt of gardens fenced with loose stones, in which myriads of green figs, red pomegranates, and golden citrons ripened in the summer sun. High up the slopes, which are lined and planted like the Rhine at Bingen, hung vintages of purple grapes. In the plain among the corn, and beneath the mulberry-trees and figs, shone daisies, poppies, tulips, lilies, anemones, endless in their profusion, brilliant in their dyes. Low down on the hillside sprang a well of water, bubbling, plentiful, and sweet; and above this fountain of life, in a long street straggling from the fountain to the synagogue, rose the homesteads of many shepherds, craftsmen, and vine-dressers. It was a lovely and humble place, of which no poet, no ruler, no historian of Israel, had ever taken note." It need scarcely be said that,

## ONCE AGAIN, O BLESSED TIME.

WM. BRIGHT.
ARTHUR SULLIVAN.

1. Once a-gain, O blessed time, Thankful hearts embrace thee; If we lost thy fes-tal chime, What could e'er re-place thee? Change will dark-en many a day, Many a bond dis-sev-er: Many a joy shall pass a-way, But the "Great Joy" nev-er.

2. Once a-gain the Ho-ly Night Breathes its blessing ten-der; Once a-gain the Man-ger Light Sheds its gen-tle splen-dor; O could tongues by an-gels taught Speak our ex-ul-ta-tion, In the Virgin's Child that brought All man-kind sal-va-tion!

3. Welcome Thou to souls a-thirst, Fount of end-less pleas-ure; Gates of hell may do their worst, While we clasp our treas-ure: Wel-come, though an age like this Puts Thy name on tri-al, And the truth that makes our bliss Pleads against de-ni-al.

4. Yea, if oth-ers stand a-part, We will press the near-er; Yea, O best fra-ter-nal Heart, We will hold Thee dear-er; Faith-ful lips shall an-swer thus To all faithless scorn-ing, "Je-sus Christ is God with us, Born on Christmas morn-ing.

5. So we yield Thee all we can, Wor-ship, thanks, and blessing; Thee true God, and Thee true Man, On our knees con-fess-ing; While Thy birth-day morn we greet With our best de-vo-tion, Bathe us, O most true and sweet! In Thy mercy's o-cean.

except the hills and terraces and the fountain, there is nothing now in or about Nazareth that could have been there in Christ's youth. The legends that abound respecting his infancy and youth are unworthy of a moment's consideration. Over the youth of Christ, in Nazareth, there rests a silence far more impressive than anything which the imagination can frame, and on which the puerile legends break with impertinent intrusion. Although Joseph, to whom she was betrothed, was descended from David, every sign of royalty had died out. He earned his livelihood by working in wood. probably as a carpenter, though the word applied to his trade admits of much larger application. Tradition has uniformly represented him as a carpenter, and art has conformed to tradition. He appears but on the threshold of the history. He goes to Egypt, returns to Nazareth, and is faintly recognized as present when Jesus was twelve years of age. But nothing more is heard of him. If alive when his reputed son entered upon his public ministry, there is no sign of it. And as Mary is often mentioned in the history of the Lord's mission, it is probable that Joseph died before Jesus entered upon his public life. He is called a just man, and we know that he was humane. For when he perceived the condition of his betrothed wife, instead of pressing to its full rigor the Jewish law against her, he meant quietly and without harm to set her aside. When in a vision he learned the truth, he took Mary as his wife. In the thousand pictures of the Holy Family, Joseph is represented as a venerable man, standing a little apart, lost in contemplation, while Mary and Elisabeth caress the child Jesus. In this respect, Christian art has, it is probable, rightly represented the character of Joseph. He was but a shadow on the canvas. Such men are found in every community,—gentle, blameless, mildly active, but exerting no positive influence.

## THE LORD'S ANOINTED.

LOWELL MASON.
J. MONTGOMERY, 1822.

1. Hail to the Lord's A-noint-ed, Great David's greater Son! Hail, in the time ap-
2. He comes with suc-cor speed-y To those who suf-fer wrong, To help the poor and
3. He shall descend like show-ers Up-on the fruit-ful earth; And love, and joy, like
4. O'er ev-'ry foe vic-to-rious, He on His throne shall rest, From age to age more

point-ed, His reign on earth be-gun! He comes to break op-pres-sion, To
need-y, And bid the weak be strong; To give them songs for sigh-ing, Their
flow-ers, Spring in His path to birth; Be-fore Him, on the moun-tains, Shall
glo-rious, All-bless-ing and all-blest; The tide of time shall nev-er His

set the cap-tive free; To take a-way transgres-sion, And rule in e-qui-ty.
darkness turn to light, Whose souls condemned and dy-ing, Were precious in His sight.
Peace, the her-ald, go; And Righteousness, in foun-tains From hill to val-ley flow.
cov-e-nant re-move; His name shall stand for-ev-er, That name to us is Love.

Except in one or two vague implications, he early disappears from sight. No mention is made of his death, though he must have deceased long before Mary, who in all our Lord's ministry appears alone. He reappears in the ecclesiastical calendar as St. Joseph, simply because he was the husband of Mary,—a harmless saint, mild and silent.

An imperial order having issued for the taxing of the whole nation, it became necessary for every one, according to the custom of the Jews, to repair to the city where he belonged, for registration. From Nazareth to Bethlehem was about eighty miles. Traveling slowly, as the condition of Mary required, they would probably occupy about four days in reaching their destination. Already the place was crowded with others brought thither on the same errand. They probably sought shelter in a cottage, for "the inn was full," and there Mary gave birth to her child. It is said by Luke that the child was laid in a manger, from which it has been inferred that his parents had taken refuge in a stable. But tradition asserts that it was a *cave*, such as abound in the limestone rock of that region, and are used both for sheltering herds and, sometimes, for human residences. The precipitous sides of the rock are often pierced in such a way that a cottage built near might easily convert an adjoining cave to the uses of an outbuilding. Caves are not rare in Palestine, as with us. On the contrary, the whole land seems to be honeycombed with them. They are, and have been for ages, used for almost every purpose which architecture supplies in other lands,—as dwellings for the living and sepulchres for the dead, as shelter for the household and for cattle and herds, as hidden retreats for robbers, and as defensive positions or rock-

castles for soldiers. Travellers make them a refuge when no better inn is at hand. They are shaped into reservoirs for water, or, if dry, they are employed as granaries. The limestone of the region is so porous and soft that but a little labor is required to enlarge, refashion, and adapt caves to any desirable purpose. Of the "manger," or "crib," Thomson, long a missionary in Palestine, says: "It is common to find two sides of the one room, where the native farmer resides with his cattle, fitted up with these mangers, and the remainder elevated about two feet higher for the accommodation of the family. The mangers are built of small stones and mortar, in the shape of a box, or, rather, of a kneading-trough, and when cleaned up and whitewashed, as they often

## HOPE OF THE WORLD.

CHARLES WESLEY.

1. Hail! thou long - ex - pect - ed Je - sus, Born to set Thy peo - ple free;
2. Is - rael's strength and con - so - la - tion, Hope of all the saints Thou art;
3. Born Thy peo - ple to de - liv - er, Born a child, yet God our King,
4. By Thine own e - ter - nal Spir - it, Rule in all our hearts a - lone;

From our sins and fears re - lease us, Let us find our rest in Thee.
Long de - sired of ev - 'ry na - tion, Joy of ev - 'ry wait - ing heart.
Born to reign in us for - ev - er, Now Thy gra - cious king - dom bring,
By Thine all - suf - fi - cient mer - it, Raise us to Thy glo - rious throne.

are in summer, they do very well to lay little babes in. Indeed, our own children have slept there in our rude summer retreats on the mountains." The laying of the little babe in the manger is not to be regarded then as an extraordinary thing, or a positive hardship. It was merely subjecting the child to a custom which peasants frequently practised with their children. Jesus began his life with and as the lowest. About five miles south of Jerusalem, and crowning the top and sides of a narrow ridge or spur which shoots out eastwardly from the central mass of the Judæan hills, was the village of Bethlehem. On every side but the western, the hill breaks down abruptly into deep valleys. The steep slopes were terraced and

cultivated from top to bottom. A little to the eastward is a kind of plain, where it is supposed the shepherds, of all shepherds that ever lived now the most famous, tended their flocks. The great fruitfulness of its fields is supposed to have given to Bethlehem its name, which signifies the "House of Bread." Famous as it has become, it was but a hamlet at the birth of Jesus. Here King David was born, but there is nothing to indicate that he retained any special attachment to the place. In the rugged valleys and gorges which abound on every side, he had watched his father's flocks and had become inured to danger and to toil, defending his charge on the one hand against wild beasts, and on the other against the scarcely

ALMA PARENS.

less savage predatory tribes that infested the region south and east. From Bethlehem one may look out upon the very fields made beautiful forever to the imagination by the charming idyl of David's ancestress, Ruth the Moabitess. Changed as Bethlehem itself is, which, from holding a mere handful then, has a population now of some four thousand, customs and the face of nature remain the same. The hills are terraced, the fields are tilled, flocks are tended by laborers unchanged in garb, working with the same kinds of implements, having the same manners, and employing the same salutations as in the days of the patriarchs. Were Boaz to return to-day, he would hardly see an unfamiliar thing in his old fields,—the barley harvest, the reapers, the gleaners, the threshing floors, and the rude threshing, — all are there as they were thousands of years ago.

At the season of our Saviour's advent, the nights were soft and genial. It was no hardship for rugged shepherds to spend the night in the fields with their flocks. By day, as the sheep fed, their keepers might

## HEILIGE NACHT.

MICHAEL HAYDN.

1. Stil - le Nacht, hei - li - ge Nacht! Al - les schläft, ein - sam wacht,
2. Stil - le Nacht, hei - li - ge Nacht! Hir - ten erst kund ge - macht;
3. Stil - le Nacht, hei - li - ge Nacht! Gott - es Sohn, o wie lacht,

Nur das traute hoch hei - li - ge Paar, Hol - der Kna - be im lo - ckigen Haar,
Durch der En - gel Hal - le - lu - ja! Tönt es laut von fern und nah;
Lieb aus dei - nem gött - li - chen Mund. Da uns schlägt dir ret - ten - de Stund',

Schlaf in himm - li - scher Ruh! Schlaf in himm - li - scher Ruh!
Christ, der Ret - ter, ist da! Christ, der Ret - ter, ist da!
Christ, in dei - ner Ge - burt, Christ, in dein - er Ge - burt.

while away their time with sights and sounds along the earth. When darkness shut in the scene, the heavens would naturally attract their attention. Their eyes had so long kept company with the mysterious stars, that, doubtless, like shepherds of more ancient times, they were rude astronomers, and had grown familiar with the planets, and knew them in all their courses. But there came to them a night surpassing all nights in wonders. Of a sudden the whole heavens were filled with light; as if morning were come upon midnight. Out of this splendor a single voice issued, as of a choral leader,— "Behold, I bring you glad tidings of great joy." The shepherds were told of the Saviour's birth, and of the place where the babe might be found. Then no longer a single voice, but a host in heaven, was heard celebrating the event. "Suddenly there was with the angel a multitude of the heavenly host, praising God, and saying, "Glory to God in the highest, and on earth peace, good-will toward men."

Raised to a fervor of wonder, these children of the field made haste to find the babe, and to make known on every side the marvellous vision. Moved by this faith to worship and to glorify God, they were thus unconsciously the earliest disciples and the first evangelists, for "they made known abroad the saying which was told them concerning this child." In beautiful contrast with these rude exclamatory worshippers, the mother is dscribed as silent and thoughtful. "Mary kept all these things and pondered them in her heart." If no woman comes to herself until she loves, so, it may be said, she knows not how to love until her first-born is in her arms. Sad is it for her who does not feel herself made sacred by motherhood. That heart-pondering! Who may tell the thoughts which rise from the deep places of an inspired love, more in number and more beautiful than the particles of vapor which the sun draws from the surface of the sea? Intimately as a mother must feel that her babe is connected with her own body, even more she is wont to feel that her child comes direct from God. *God-given* is a familiar name in every language. Not

## HOLY NIGHT.

MICHAEL HAYDN.

1. Si - lent night! Ho - ly night! All is calm, all is bright
2. Si - lent night! Ho - ly night! Shep - herds quake at the sight!
3. Si - lent night! Ho - ly night! Son of God, love's pure light,

Round yon vir - gin moth - er and Child! Ho - ly In - fant, so ten - der and mild,
Glo - ries stream from Heav - en a - far, Heav'n - ly hosts sing Al - le - lu - ia,
Ra - diant beams from Thy ho - ly face, With the dawn of re - deem - ing grace,

Sleep in heav - en - ly peace, Sleep in heav - en - ly peace,
Christ, the Sav - iour, is born! Christ, the Sav - iour, is born!
Je - sus, Lord, at Thy birth, Je - sus, Lord, at Thy birth.

from her Lord came this child to Mary. It was her Lord himself that came. A sweet and trusting faith in God, childlike simplicity, and profound love seemed to have formed the nature of Mary. She may be accepted as the type of Christian motherhood. In this view, and excluding the dogma of her immaculate nature, and still more emphatically that of any other participation in divinity than that which is common to all, we may receive with pleasure the stores of exquisite pictures with which Christian art has filled its realm. The "Madonnas" are so many tributes to the beauty and dignity of motherhood; and they may stand so interpreted, now that the superstitious associations which they have had are so wholly worn away. At any rate, the Protestant reaction from Mary has gone far enough, and, on our own grounds, we may well have our share also in the memory of this sweet and noble woman.

The same reason which led our Lord to clothe himself with flesh made it proper, when he was born, to have fulfilled upon him all the customs of his people. He was therefore circumcised when eight days old, and presented in the Temple on the fortieth day, at which period his mother had completed the time appointed for her purification. The offering required was a lamb and a dove; but if the parents were poor, then two doves. Mary's humble condition was indicated by the offering of two doves. And yet, if she had heard the exclamation of John after the Lord's baptism, years afterwards, she might have perceived that, in spite of her poverty, she had brought the Lamb, divine and precious! Surprise upon surprise awaited Mary. There dwelt at Jerusalem, wrapped in his own devout and longing thoughts, a great nature, living contentedly in obscurity, Simeon by name. This venerable man seized the child with

## BRIGHTEST AND BEST.

E. KIALLMARK.
REGINALD HEBER, 1811.

1. Bright - est and best of the sons of the morn - ing, Dawn on our
   Star of the East, the ho - ri - zon a - dorn - ing, Guide where our
2. Say, shall we yield him, in cost - ly de - vo - tion, O - dors of
   Gems of the moun - tain, and pearls of the o - cean, Myrrh from the

dark - ness, and lend us thine aid!
in - fant Re - deem - er is laid.
E - dom, and off - 'rings di - vine?
for - est, or gold from the mine?

Cold on his cra - dle the dewdrops are
Vain - ly we of - fer each am - ple ob -

shin - ing, Low lies his head with the beasts of the stall; An - gels a -
la - tion; Vain - ly with gifts would his fa - vor se - cure; Rich - er by

dore him in slum - ber re - clin - ing, Mak - er, and Monarch, and Saviour of all.
far is the heart's ad - o - ra - tion; Dear - er to God are the prayers of the poor.

holy rapture, when it was presented in the Temple, and broke forth in the very spirit of a prophet: "Lord, now lettest thou Thy servant depart in peace, according to Thy word: For mine eyes have seen Thy salvation, which Thou hast prepared before the face of all people; a light to lighten the Gentiles, and the glory of Thy people Israel." Both Mary and Joseph were amazed, but there was something in Mary's appearance that drew this inspired old man specially to her. "Behold, this child is set for the fall and rising again of many in Israel. . . . Yea, a sword shall pierce through thine own soul also." As the asters, among plants, go all summer long unbeautiful, their flowers hidden within, and burst into bloom in the late summer and autumn, with the frosts upon their heads, so this aged saint had blossomed, at the close of a long life, into this noble ecstasy of joy. In a stormy time, when outward life moves wholly against one's wishes, he is truly great whose soul becomes a sanctuary in which patience dwells with hope. In one hour Simeon received full satisfaction for the yearnings of many years! Among the Jews, woman was permitted to develop naturally, and liberty was accorded her to participate in things which other people reserved with zealous seclusion for men. Hebrew women were prophetesses and teachers (2 Kings xxii. 14), judges and queens. The advent of our Saviour was hailed appropriately by

## CAROL FOR CHRISTMAS EVE.

*Moderato.*    ROBERT HERRICK.

1. The sun sets brightly in the sea, Foreknowing what his morn shall be, And dreams throughout the dawning night Of rising on the Source of Light. The day has ended mild and calm, The sea-wind scarcely sways the palm, The olive trees beneath the hill Sleep, in its folding, hushed and still.

2. A bove, the tow'rs of Beth-le-hem Fade in the night that falls on them, Yet hold in guard the rock-y steep, That Re-ho-bo-am bade them keep. O ci-ty small, 'mid Ju-dah's host, Now growing to her crown and boast, How high at morn thy head shall be, For Earth shall bow to hal-low thee!

3. No place for those of low de-gree Could in that crowded ci-ty be; And ev-en at the low-ly inn No room could they, no wel-come, win. So where the cat-tle rest at night, Oh, hap-py they to see such sight!—Poor in all else but love and grace, The Vir-gin had her dwell-ing-place.

4. She sits beside the porch of stone,;
With golden blue the evening shone;
The timid stars come, one by one,
Incredulous that day was done.
Well Mary knew their forms on high,
And loved their gentle company,
When Joseph led the nightly way
From Nazareth, and shunned the day.

5. While Mary watches by the door,
Behold! a star unknown before
Mounts slowly up the western sky
And then she knows her hour is nigh.
The Virgin lifts her hands above,
Her eyes are tears, her heart is love;
She sees the joy she could believe
And prays the prayer of Christmas Eve.

woman,—Anna, the prophetess, joining with Simeon in praise and thanksgiving.

But other witnesses were preparing. Already the footsteps of strangers afar off were advancing toward Judæa. Erelong Jerusalem was thrown into an excitement by the arrival of certain sages, probably from Persia. The city, like an uneasy volcano, was always on the eve of an eruption. When it was known that these pilgrims had come to inquire about a king, who, they believed, had been born, a king of the Jews, the news excited both the city and the palace,—hope in one, fear in the other. Herod dreaded a rival. The Jews longed for a native prince whose arm should expel the intrusive government. No wonder that "Herod was troubled, and all Jerusalem with him." He first summoned the Jewish scholars, to know where, according to their prophets, the Messiah was to be born. Bethlehem was the place of prediction. Next, he summoned the Magi, secretly, to learn of them at what time the revealing star had appeared to them, and then, craftily veiling his cruel purposes with an assumed interest, he charges them, when the child was found, to let him be a worship-

## PEACE ON EARTH.

DONIZETTI.
J. R. LOWELL.

*Moderato.*

1. "What means this glory round our feet," The Magi mused, "more bright than morn!" And voices chanted clear and sweet, "To-day the Prince of Peace is born!" "What means this star," the shepherds said, "That brightens thro' the rocky glen?" And angels answering, overhead, Sang, "Peace on earth, good-will to men!"

2. 'Tis eighteen hundred years, and more, Since those sweet oracles were dumb; We wait for Him, like them of yore; A - las! He seems so slow to come! But it was said, in words of gold, No time or sorrow e'er shall dim, That little children might be bold, In perfect trust to come to Him.

3. All round a - bout our feet shall shine A light like that the wise men saw, If we our lov - ing wills in - cline To that sweet Life which is the Law. So shall we learn to un - derstand The simple faith of shepherds, then, And kindly clasping hand in hand, Sing, " Peace on earth, good-will to men!"

per too! The same star which had drawn their footsteps to Jerusalem now guided the wise men to the very place of Jesus' birth. What was this star? All that can be known is, that it was some appearance of light in the sky, which by these Oriental philosophers was supposed to indicate a great event. Ingenuity has unnecessarily been exercised to prove that at about this time there was a conjunction of three planets. But did the same thing happen again, after their arrival at Jerusalem? For it is stated that, on their leaving the city to go to Bethlehem, "lo, the star which they saw in the east went before them till it came and stood over where the young child was." How could a planetary conjunction stand over a particular house? It is evident that the sidereal guide was a globe of light, divinely ordered and appointed for this work. It was a miracle. That nature is but an organized outworking of the divine will, that God is not limited to ordinary law in the production of results, that he can, and that he does, produce events by the direct force of his will without the ordinary instruments of nature, is the very spirit of the whole Bible. These gleams of immediate power flash through in every age. The superiority of spiritual power over sensuous, is the illuminating truth of the New Testament. The gospel should be taken or rejected unmutilated. The disciples plucked the wheat-heads, and, rubbing them in their hands, they ate the grain. But our sceptical believers take from the New Testament its supernatural element,—rub out the wheat,—and eat the chaff. There is consistency in one who sets the gospels aside on the ground that they are not inspired, that they are not even historical, that they are growths of the imagination, and covered all over with the parasites of superstition; but in one who professes to accept the record as an inspired history, the disposition to pare miracles down to a scientific shape, to find their roots in natural laws, is neither reverent nor sagacious. Miracles are to be accepted boldly or not at all. They are jewels and sparkle with a divine light, or they are nothing. This guide of the Magi was a light kindled in the heavens to instruct and lead those whose eyes were prepared to receive it. If the vision of angels and the extraordinary conception of the Virgin are received as miraculous, it ought not

## OVER THE GREEN DOWNS.

JEAN INGELOW.

Semplice.

1. O - ver the green downs when I do wan - der, Af - ter the ewes and lambs,
2. When thro' the dark night deep the snow drift - eth, And ma - ny lambs are lost
3. Oft as the day comes, each drear De - cem - ber, How shepherds sat of old

thus oft I pon - der: When comes the Shepherd that is full ten - der, He will of
ere the storm lift - eth, Then comes the Shepherd; tho' the dark blind me, Lord, 'twill be
still I re - mem - ber, How Thou didst send them news from Thy ci - ty, All of Thy

all His own true reck'ning ren-der. Praise to the dear Lord, His Name be prais-ed. prais-ed.
light to Thee; straight Thou wilt find me. Praise to the dear Lord, His Name be prais-ed. prais-ed.
good - will and ten-der pi - ty. Praise to the dear Lord, His Name be prais-ed. prais-ed.

to be difficult to accept the star which was seen from the east as a miracle also.

The situation of the child ill befitted Oriental notions of a king's dignity. But under the divine influence which rested upon the Magi, they doubtless saw more than the outward circumstances. Humble as the place was, poor as his parents evidently were, and he a mere babe, they fell down before him in worship, and presented princely gifts, "gold, frankincense. and myrrh." Instead of returning to Herod, they went back to their own country. And now it was time for Joseph to look well to his safety. If there was to be a king in Israel, he was to come from the house of David, and Joseph was of that stock, and his child, Jesus, was royal too. Herod's jealousy was aroused. He was not a man wont to miss the fulfilment of any desire on account of humane or moral scruples. The return of the Magi without giving him the knowledge which he sought seemed doubtless to the king like another step in a plot to subvert his throne. He determined to make thorough work of this nascent peril, "and sent forth and slew all the children that were in Bethlehem, and in all the coasts thereof, from two years old and under." He put the limit of age at a period which would make it sure that the new-born king of the Jews would be included. It has been objected to the probable truth of this statement, that such an event could hardly fail to be recorded by secular historians, and especially by Josephus, who narrates the contemporaneous history with much minuteness. But this event is far more striking upon our imagination now, than it was likely to be upon the attention of men then. For, as Bethlehem was a mere hamlet, with but a handful of people, it has been computed that not more than ten or fifteen children could have perished by this merciless edict. Besides, what was such an act as this, in a life stored full of abominable cruelties? "He who had immolated a cherished wife, a brother, and three sons to his jealous suspicions, and who ordered a general massacre for the day of his funeral, so that his body should not be borne to the earth amidst general rejoicings," may easily be supposed to have filled up the spaces with minor cruelties which escaped record. But here *is* an historical record. It is no impeachment of its truth to aver that there is no other history of it. Until some disproof is alleged, it must stand. Stirred by a divine impulse, Joseph had already removed the child from danger. Whither shall he flee? Egypt was not distant, and the roads thither were easy and

## BORN OF MAIDEN FAIR.

GAUNTLET.

1. Christ is born of maid - en fair; Hark the her - alds in the air, Thus a-
2. Shep-herds saw those an - gels bright, Caroll-ing in glo - ri - ous light; "God the
2. Christ is come to save man-kind; As in ho - ly page we find; There-fore

dor - ing hear them there, "In ex - cel - sis glo - ri - a!"
Son is born to - night, In ex - cel - sis glo - ri - a!"
sing with rev' - rent mind, "In ex - cel - sis glo - ri - a!"

much frequented. Thither too, from time to time, exiled for various reasons, had resorted numbers of Jews, so that, though in a foreign land, he would be among his own countrymen, all interested alike in hating the despotic cruelty of Herod. There is no record of the place of Joseph's sojourn in Egypt. Tradition, always uncertain, places it at Matarea, near Leontopolis, where subsequently the Jewish temple of Onias stood. His stay was probably brief. For, within a few weeks of the foregoing events, Herod died. Joseph did not return to Bethlehem, though he desired to do so, but was warned of God in a dream of his danger. It was probable that Archelaus, who succeeded to Herod in Judæa, would be as suspicious of danger from an heir royal of the house of David as his father had been; so Joseph passed—it may be, by way of the sea-coast—northward to Nazareth, whence a few months before he had removed.

Before closing this chapter we shall revert to one of the most striking features of the period thus far passed over, namely, *the ministration of angels.* The belief in the existence of heavenly beings who in some manner are concerned in the affairs of men, has existed from the earliest periods of which we have a history. This faith is peculiarly grateful to the human heart, and, though it has never been received with favor by men addicted to purely physical studies, it has been entertained by the Church with fond faith and by the common people with the enthusiasm of sympathy.

## CAROL, BROTHERS, CAROL.

W. A. MUHLENBERG.

*Semi-Chorus.*

Ca - rol, brothers, ca - rol, Ca - rol joy-ful - ly, Ca - rol the good tidings, Ca - rol mer - ri - ly.

*Chorus (Forte) Animated.* *Unison.*

Ca - rol, brothers, ca - rol, Ca - rol joy-ful - ly, Ca - rol the good tidings, Ca - rol mer-ri - ly; And

*Fine.*

pray a gladsome Christmas For all good Christian men, Carol, brothers, ca - rol, Christmas day a - gain.

*Semi-Chorus.*

1. Ca - rol, but in glad - ness, Not in songs of earth, On the Saviour's
2. At the mer - ry ta - ble Think of those who've none, The orphan and
3. List - 'ning an - gel mu - sic, Dis - cord sure must cease, Who dare hate his
4. Let our hearts re - spond - ing, To the ser - aph band, Wish this morning's

birth - day, Hal - lowed be our mirth; While a thous - and bless - ings
the widow Hun - gry and a - lone; Boun - ti - ful your off - 'rings
broth - er, On this day of peace? While the heav'ns are tell - ing
sun - shine Bright in ev - 'ry land; Word and deed and pray - er

*D. C. Chorus.*

Fill our hearts with glee, Christmas day will keep The feast of char - i - ty.
To the al - tar bring, Let the poor and need - y Christmas ca - rols sing.
To man - kind good-will, On - ly love and kind - ness Ev - 'ry bo - som fill.
Speed the grate - ful sound, Wish - ing "Mer - ry Christmas!" All the world a - round.

It is scarcely possible to follow the line of development in the animal kingdom, and to witness the gradations on the ascending scale, unfolding steadily, rank above rank, until man is reached, without having the presumption awakened that there are intelligences above man,—creatures which rise as much above him as he above the inferior animals. When the word of God announces the ministration of angels, records their early visits to this planet, represents them as bending over the race in benevolent sympathy, bearing warnings, consolations, and messages of wisdom, the heart receives the doctrine even against the cautions of a sceptical reason. Our faith might be put to shame if the scriptural angels bore any analogy to those of the rude and puerile histories contained in apocryphal books. But the long line of heavenly visitants shines in unsullied brightness as high above the beliefs and prejudices of an early age as the stars are above the vapors and dust of earth. While patriarchs, prophets, and apostles show all the deficiencies of their own period and are stained with human passions, the angelic beings, judged by the most fastidious requirements of these later

## WHILE TO BETHL'EM GOING.

J. J. ROUSSEAU.
SIR JOHN BOWRING.

ages, are without spot or blemish. They are not made up of human traits idealized. They are unworldly,—of a different type, of nobler presence, and of far grander and sweeter natures than any living on earth. The angels of the oldest records are like the angels of the latest. The Hebrew thought had moved through a vast arc of the infinite cycle of truth between the days when Abraham came from Ur of Chaldæa and the times of our Lord's stay on earth. But there is no development in angels of later over those of an earlier date. They were as beautiful, as spiritual, as pure and noble, at the beginning as at the close of the old dispensation. Can such creatures, transcending earthly experience, and far outrunning anything in the life of man, be creations of the rude ages of the human understanding? We could not imagine the Advent stripped of its angelic lore. The dawn without a twilight, the sun without clouds of silver and gold, the morning on the fields without dew-diamonds,—but not the Saviour without his angels! They shine within the temple, they bear to the matchless mother a message which would have been disgrace from mortal lips, but which from theirs fell upon her as pure as dew-drops upon the lilies of the plain of Esdraelon. They communed with the Saviour in his glory of transfiguration, sustained him in the anguish of the garden, watched at the tomb ; and as they had thronged the earth at his coming, so they seem to have hovered in the air in multitudes at the hour of his ascension. Beautiful as they seem, they are never mere poetic adornments. The occasions of their appearing are grand. The reasons are weighty. Their demeanor suggests and befits the highest conception of superior beings. These are the very elements that a rude age could not fashion. Could a sensuous age invent an order of beings, which, touching the earth from a heavenly height on its most momentous occasions, could still, after ages of culture had refined the human taste and moral appreciation, remain ineffably superior in delicacy, in pure spirituality, to the demands of criticism ? Their very coming and going is not with earthly movement. They suddenly are seen in the air as one sees white clouds round out from

## O NIGHT OF NIGHTS!

JEAN INGELOW.

1. O night of nights! O night De-sired of man so long! When the ancient heav'ns fled
2. All on the hill-side grass That ful-gent ra-diance fell; And so close those in - no -
3. It was so long a - go; But He can make it *now*, And, as with that sweet

forth in light, To sing thee thy new song; And shooting down the steep, To shepherd folk of
cents did pass, Their words were heard right well; Among the sheep, their wings Some folding walked the
o - ver-flow, Our emp-ty hearts en - dow. Take, Lord, those words outworn, Oh, make them new for

old, Lo! an an - gel while they watch'd their sheep, Set foot be - side the fold.
sod An or-dered throng of shining things, White with the smile of God.
aye, Speak—"Un - to you a Child is born," To - day, to - day, to - day.

the blue sky, in a summer's day, that melt back even while one looks upon them. They vibrate between the visible and the invisible. They come without motion. They go without flight. They dawn and disappear. Their words are few, but the Advent Chorus yet is sounding its music through the world.

A part of the angelic ministration is to be looked for in what men are by it incited to do. It helps the mind to populate Heaven with spiritual inhabitants. The imagination no longer translates thither the gross corporeity of this life. We suspect that few of us are aware how much our definite conceptions of spirit-life are the product of the angel-lore of the Bible. It is to be noticed that only in Luke is the history of the angelic annunciation given. It is to Luke also that we are indebted for the record of the angels at the tomb on the morning of the resurrection. Luke has been called the Evangelist of Greece. He was Paul's companion of travel, and particularly among the Greek cities of Asia Minor. This suggests the fact that the angelic ministration commemorated in the New Testament would greatly facilitate among Greeks the reception of monotheism. Comforting to us as is the doctrine of angels, it can hardly be of the same help as it was to a Greek or to a Roman when he first accepted the Christian faith. The rejection of so many divinities must have left the fields, the mountains, the cities and temples very bare to all who had been accustomed to heathen mythology. The ancients seem to have striven to express universal divine presence by multiplying their gods. This at least had the effect of giving life to every part of nature. The imaginative Greek had grown familiar with the thought of gods innumerable. Every stream, each grove, the caves, the fields, the clouds, suggested some divine person. It would be almost impossible to strip such a one of those fertile suggestions and tie him to the simple

## HARK! THE HERALD ANGELS.

MENDELSSOHN.
CHAS. WESLEY, 1793.

1. Hark! the her-ald an-gels sing, "Glo-ry to the new-born King! Peace on earth, and
2. Christ, by highest heav'n a - dored; Christ, the ev - er - last-ing Lord; Late in time be-
3. Hail! the heav'n-born Prince of peace! Hail! the Son of Righteousness! Light and life to

mer - cy mild, God and sin - ners re - con-ciled." Joy - ful, all ye na-tions, rise,
hold him come, Offspring of the favored one. Veil'd in flesh, the Godhead see;
all he brings, Risen with healing in his wings. Mild he lays his glo - ry by,

Join the triumph of the skies; With th'angel - ic host proclaim, "Christ is born in
Hail th' incarnate De - i - ty: Pleased, as man, with men to dwell, Je - sus, our Im -
Born that man no more may die: Born to raise the sons of earth, Born to give them

Beth-le - hem."
man - u - el! } Hark! the herald an-gels sing, "Glo - ry to the new-born King!"
se - cond birth.

doctrine of One God, without producing a sense of cheerlessness and solitude. Angels come in to make for him an easy transition from polytheism to monotheism. The air might still be populous, his imagination yet be full of teeming suggestions, but no longer with false gods. Now there was to him but one God, but he was served by multitudes of blessed spirits, children of light and glory. Instead of a realm of conflicting divinities there was a household, the Father looking in benignity upon his radiant family. Thus, again, to the Greek, as to the Patriarch, angels ascended and descended the steps that lead from earth to Heaven.—*Henry Ward Beecher.*

## STORY OF THE SHEPHERD.

Joseph Barnby.
Spanish of Gongora.

*Con express.*

1. It was the very noon of night, the stars above the fold, More sure than clock or chiming bell, the
2. Oh, ne'er could nightingale at dawn salute the rising day With sweetness like that bird of song in
3. I roused me at the piercing strain, but shrunk as from the ray Of summer lightning; all around so
4. When once the happy trance was past, that so my sense did bind, I left my sheep to Him whose care was
5. I hasted to a low-roofed shed, for so the Angel bade; And bowed before the lowly rack where

hour of midnight told: When from the heavens there came a voice, and forms were seen to
his im-mor-tal lay: Oh, ne'er were wood-notes heard at eve by banks with poplar
bright the splendor lay. For oh, it mastered sight and sense, to see that glo-ry
in the western wind; I left them, for in-stead of snow, I trod on blade and
Love Divine was laid: A new-born Babe, like tender Lamb, with Lion's strength there

shine, Still bright'ning as the music rose with light and love divine. With love di-vine the
shade So thrilling as the concert sweet by heav'nly harpings made; For love di-vine was
shine, To hear that minstrel in the clouds, who sang of Love Divine, To see that form with
flower, And ice dissolved in starry rays at morning's gracious hour, Re-vealing where on
smiled, For Lion's strength, immortal might, was in that new-born Child; That Love Divine in

song be-gan; there shone a light se-rene: Oh, who hath heard what I have heard, or
in each chord, and filled each pause be-tween: Oh, who hath heard what I have heard, or
bird-like wings, of more than mor-tal mein: Oh, who hath heard what I have heard, or
earth the steps of Love Di-vine had been: Oh, who hath heard what I have heard, or
child-like form had God for ev-er been: Oh, who hath heard what I have heard, or

seen what I have seen? Oh, who hath heard what I have heard, or seen what I have seen!

## HALLELUJAH CHORUS.

G. F. Handel.
From "The Messiah."

and Lord of lords,....................
lu-jah! for-ev-er and ev-er, Halle-lu-jah! Halle-lujah! King of kings, and Lords of
lords! and he shall reign for ever and ever, and he shall reign for - ev-er and ev - - er, King of
and he shall reign for-ev-er and ev-er,
for-ev-er and ev-er, Hal-le-lu-jah! Halle-lujah! and he shall reign for-ever, for
kings,.................... and Lord of lords!............................
kings, for-ev-er and ev-er, Halle-lu-jah! Halle-lu-jah!
and
ev-er and ev - er, King of kings, and Lords of lords! King of kings, and Lord of lords! and he shall
he shall reign for - ev-er and ev - er, King of kings, and Lord of
reign for-ev-er and ev-er and ev - er, for-ev-er and ev-er, for-ev-er and
lords!
Adagio. ff
ev-er, Hal-le-lu-jah! Hal-le-lu-jah! Hal-le-lu-jah! Hal-le-lu-jah! Hal-le-lu-jah!

## BELLS ACROSS THE SNOW.

E. E. Lassen.
Frances R. Havergal.

*Slow, with feeling.*

1. O Christ-mas, mer-ry Christ-mas, Is with us once a - gain, With
2. O Christ-mas, mer-ry Christ-mas, 'T's not so ver - y long Since
3. O Christ-mas, mer-ry Christ-mas, This nev - er more can be, We

mem - o - ries and greet - ings, With joy and with its pain. A
oth - er voi - ces blend - ed With the carol and the song! Could
can - not bring again the days Of our un - shadowed glee. But

min - or in the car - ol, A shad - ow in the light, A
we but hear them sing - ing, As they are sing - ing now,— Could
Christ - mas, hap - py Christ - mas, Sweet her - ald of good - will. With

spray of cy - press twin - ing With hol - ly wreath to - night. And the
we but see the ra - diance Of the crown on each dear brow, There
ho - ly songs of glo - ry Brings ho - ly glad - ness still, For

hush is nev - er brok - en, By the laugh - ter light and low As we
were no sigh to smoth - er, No hid - den tear to flow, As we
peace and hope may bright - en, And pa - tient love may glow, As we

lis - ten in the star - light To the bells a - cross the snow!

# IN EXCELSIS GLORIA.

*Allegretto.*

WELSH AIR.

1. Not in halls of reg - al splendor, Not to princes of the earth, Did the her - ald
2. Not by world - ly wealth or wisdom, Not by power of law or sword, But by ser - vice
3. Bid the new-born Monarch welcome; Pay him homage, ev - 'ry heart! Hal - le - lu - jah!

an - gels ren - der Tid - ings of His birth. Not to statesman, priest, or sage,
to win freedom, Ser - vice of the Lord. Born to pov - er - ty and pain,
let His kingdom Come and ne'er de - part. Jus - tice hath on Mer - cy smiled,

They proclaimed the golden age 'Twas the poor man's heritage! In ex - cel - sis glo - ri - a!
Born to die and thus to reign, Freeing men from death's domain, In excel - sis glo - ri - a!
God and men are recon - ciled Thro' Emmanuel, wondrous Child. In excel - sis glo - ri - a!

For on shepherds low - ly Burst the an - them ho - ly! In ex - cel - sis
Lo! from earth as Heaven Praise shall aye be giv - en: In ex - cel - sis
Blend we then our voices, Earth with Heaven rejoic - es, In ex - cel - sis

glo - ri - a! War and blood-shed now shall cease, Selfishness its slaves re - lease,

Love shall reign and white-robed Peace! In excelsis glo - ri - a! In ex - cel - sis glo - ri - a!

4

THE MOTHER AND CHILD.

# THE STORY OF THE STAR.

HE turned to the camel, saying low, and in a tongue strange to the desert, "We are far from home, O racer with the swiftest winds—we are far from home, but God is with us. Let us be patient." Then he took some beans from a pocket in the saddle, and put them in a bag made to hang below the animal's nose ; and when he saw the relish with which the good servant took to the food, he turned and again scanned the world of sand, dim with the glow of the vertical sun. "They will come," he said, calmly. "He that led me is leading them. I will make ready." From the pouches which lined the interior of the cot, and from a willow basket which was part of its furniture, he brought forth materials for a meal ; platters close-woven of the fibres of palms ; wine in small gurglets of skin ; mutton dried and smoked ; stoneless *shami*, or Syrian pomegranates ; dates of El Shelebi, wondrous rich and grown in the *nakhil*, or palm orchards, of Central Arabia ; cheese, like David's "slices of milk ;" and leavened bread from the city bakery—all which he carried and set upon the carpet under the tent. As the final preparation, about the provisions he laid three pieces of silk cloth, used among refined people of the East to cover the knees of guests while at table—a circumstance significant of the number of persons who were to partake of his entertainment—the number he was awaiting.

All was now ready. He stepped out : lo ! in the east a dark speck on the face of the desert. He stood as if rooted to the ground ; his eyes dilated ; his flesh crept chilly, as if touched by something supernatural. The speck grew ; became large as a hand ; at length assumed defined proportions. A little later, full into view swung a duplication of his own dromedary, tall and white, and bearing a *houdah*, the travelling litter of Hindostan. Then the Egyptian crossed

his hands upon his breast, and looked to heaven. "God only is great !" he exclaimed, his eyes full of tears, his soul in awe. The stranger drew nigh—at last stopped. Then he, too, seemed just waking. He beheld the kneeling camel, the tent, and the man standing prayerfully at the door. He crossed his hands, bent his head, and prayed silently ; after which, in a little while, he stepped from his camel's neck to the sand, and advanced towards the Egyptian, as did the Egyptian towards him. A moment they looked at each other ; then they embraced —that is, each threw his right arm over the other's shoulder, and the left round the side, placing his chin first upon the left, then upon the right breast. "Peace be with thee, O servant of the true God !" the stranger said. "And to thee, O brother of the true faith !—to thee peace and welcome," the Egyptian replied, with fervor.

The new-comer was tall and gaunt, with lean face, sunken eyes, white hair and beard, and a complexion between the hue of cinnamon and bronze. He, too, was unarmed. His costume was Hindostani ; over the skullcap a shawl was wound in great folds, forming a turban ; his body garments were in the style of the Egyptian's, except that the *aba* was shorter, exposing wide flowing breeches gathered at the ankles. In place of sandals, his feet were clad in half-slippers of red leather, pointed at the toes. Save the slippers, the costume from head to foot was of white linen. The air of the man was high, stately, severe. Visvamitra, the greatest of the ascetic heroes of the Iliad of the East, had in him a perfect representative. He might have been called a Life drenched with the wisdom of Brahma—Devotion Incarnate. Only in his eyes was there proof of humanity ; when he lifted his face from the Egyptian's breast, they were glistening with tears. "God only is great !" he exclaimed, when the embrace was finished. "And blessed are they that serve him!" the Egyptian answered, wondering at the paraphrase of his own exclamation. "But let us wait," he added, "let us wait; for see, the other comes yonder!" They looked to the north, where, already plain to view, a third camel, of the whiteness of the others, came careening like a ship. They waited, standing together—waited until the newcomer arrived, dismounted, and advanced towards them. Peace to you, O my brother! he said, embracing the Hindoo. And the

Hindoo answered, "God's will be done!" The last comer was all unlike his friends : his frame was slighter ; his complexion white ; a mass of waving light hair was a perfect crown for his small but beautiful head ; the warmth of his dark-blue eyes certified a delicate mind, and a cordial, brave nature. He was bareheaded and unarmed. Under the folds of the Tyrian blanket which he wore with unconscious grace appeared a tunic, short-sleeved and low-necked, gathered to the waist by a band, and reaching nearly to the knee;

## GLORY, LAUD, AND HONOR.

M. TESCHNER, 1613.
9TH CENTURY. J. M. NEALE tr.

1. All glo - ry, laud, and hon - or To Thee, Redeemer, King! To whom the lips of
2. The com - pa - ny of an - gels Are praising Thee on high; And mortal men, and
3. To Thee be - fore Thy pas - sion They sang their hymns of praise: To Thee now high ex -

*Fine.*

chil - dren Made sweet ho - san - nas ring. Thou art the King of Is - rael, Thou
all things Cre - a - ted, make re - ply. The peo - ple of the He - brews With
alt - ed Our mel - o - dy we raise. Thou didst ac - cept their prais - es; Ac -

*D.C. 1st lines, 1st verse.*

Dav - id's roy - al Son, Who in the Lord's name com - est, The King and Blessed One.
palms be - fore Thee went: Our praise and prayer and an - thems Be - fore Thee we pre - sent.
cept the prayers we bring, Who in all good de - light - est, Thou good and gracious King.

leaving the neck, arms, and legs bare. Sandals guarded his feet. Fifty years, probably more, had spent themselves upon him, with no other effect, apparently, than to tinge his demeanor with gravity and temper his words with forethought. The physical organization and the brightness of soul were untouched. No need to tell the student from what kindred he was sprung ; if he came not himself from the groves of Athené, his ancestry did. When his arms fell from the Egyptian, the latter said, with

a tremulous voice, "The Spirit brought me first ; wherefore I know myself chosen to be the servant of my brethren. The tent is set, and the bread is ready for the breaking. Let me perform my office." Taking each by the hand, he led them within, and removed their sandals and washed their feet, and he poured water upon their hands, and dried them with napkins. Then, when he had laved his own hands, he said, "Let us take care of ourselves, brethren, as our service requires, and eat, that we may be strong for what remains of the day's duty. While we eat, we will each learn who the others are, and whence they come, and how they are called." He took them to the repast, and seated them so that they faced each other. Simultaneously their heads bent forward, their hands crossed upon their breasts, and, speaking together, they said aloud this simple grace : " Father of all—God !—what we have here is of thee ; take our thanks and bless us, that we may continue to do thy will." With the last word they raised their eyes, and looked at each other in wonder.

Each had spoken in a language never before heard by the others; yet each understood perfectly what was said. Their souls thrilled with divine emotion ; for by the miracle they recognized the Divine Presence. * *

There was silence, broken by sighs and sanctified with tears ; for the joy that filled them might not be stayed. It was the unspeakable joy of souls on the shores of the River of Life, resting with the Redeemed in God's presence. Together they went out of the tent. The desert was still as the sky. The sun was sinking fast. The camels

## RISE, CROWNED WITH LIGHT.

ALEXANDER POPE.
A. LVOFF. RUSSIAN HYMN.

1. Rise, crown'd with light, . . im-pe-rial Sa-lem, rise; Ex-alt thy
2. See a long race . . thy spa-cious courts a-dorn, See fu-ture
3. See barbarous na . . tions at thy gates at-tend, Walk in thy
4. The seas shall waste, . . the skies to smoke de-cay, Rocks fall to

tow'r-ing head and lift thine eyes; See Heav'n its spark-ling por-tals
sons, and daugh-ters yet un-born, In crowding ranks on ev-'ry
light, and in thy tem-ple bend: See thy bright al-tars throng'd with
dust, and mountains melt a-way; But fix'd His word, His sav-ing

wide . . . dis-play, And break up-on thee in a flood of day.
side . . . a-rise, De-mand-ing life, im-pa-tient for the skies.
pros . . . trate kings, While ev-'ry land its joy-ous tri-bute brings.
pow'r . . . re-main, Thy realm shall last, thy own Mes-si-ah reign.

slept. A little while after, the tent was struck, and, with the remains of the repast, restored to the cot ; then the friends mounted, and set out single file, led by the Egyptian. Their course was due west, into the chilly night. The camels swung forward in steady trot, keeping the line and the intervals so exactly that those following seemed to tread in the tracks of the leader. The riders spoke not once. By-and-by the moon came up. And as the three tall white figures sped, with soundless tread, through

the opalescent light, they appeared like spectres flying from hateful shadows. Suddenly, in the air before them, not farther up than a low hill-top, flared a lambent flame ; as they looked at it, the apparition contracted into a focus of dazzling lustre. Their hearts beat fast ; their souls thrilled ; and they shouted as with one voice, " The Star ! the Star ! God is with us !" * *

Wherever on the land men go, and on the sea ships, the face and figure of the Jew are familiar. The physical type of the race has always been the same; yet there have been some individual variations. "Now he was ruddy, and withal of a beautiful countenance, and goodly to look to." Such was the son of Jesse when brought before Samuel. The fancies of men have been ever since ruled by the description. Poetic license has extended the peculiarities of the ancestor to his notable descendants. So all our ideal Solomons have fair faces, and hair and beard chestnut in the shade, and of the tint of gold in the sun. Such, we are also made believe, were the locks of Absalom the beloved. And, in the absence of authentic history, tradition has dealt no less lovingly by her whom we are now following down to the native city of the ruddy king. Her form, voice, and manner belonged to the period of transition from girlhood. Her face was perfectly oval, her complexion more pale than fair. The nose was faultless; the lips, slightly parted, were full and ripe, giving to the lines of the mouth warmth, tenderness, and trust; the eyes were blue and large, and shaded by drooping lids and long lashes; and, in harmony with all, a flood of golden hair, in the style permitted to Jewish brides, fell unconfined

## O THOU JOYFUL DAY.
### (O DU FRÖHLICHE.)

B. M. SMUCKER *tr.*

1. O thou joyful day, O thou bless-ed day, Ho-ly, peace-ful Christmas-tide! O thou joyful day, O thou bless-ed day, Ho-ly, peace-ful Christmas-tide! Earth's hopes a-wak-en, Christ life has tak-en, Laud Him, O laud Him on ev-'ry side!

2. O thou joyful day, O thou bless-ed day, Ho-ly, peace-ful Christmas-tide! O thou joyful day, O thou bless-ed day, Ho-ly, peace-ful Christmas-tide! Christ's light is beam-ing, Our souls re-deem-ing, Laud Him, O laud Him on ev-'ry side!

3. O thou joyful day, O thou bless-ed day, Ho-ly, peace-ful Christmas-tide! O thou joyful day, O thou bless-ed day, Ho-ly, peace-ful Christmas-tide! King of all glo-ry, We bow be-fore Thee, Laud Him, O laud Him on ev-'ry side!

down her back to the pillion on which she sat. The throat and neck had the downy softness sometimes seen which leaves the artist in doubt whether it is an effect of contour or color. To these charms of feature and person were added others more indefinable—an air of purity which only the soul can impart, and of abstraction natural to such as think much of things impalpable. Often, with trembling lips, she raised her eyes to heaven, itself not more deeply blue; often she crossed her hands upon her breast, as in adoration and prayer; often she raised her head like one listening eagerly for a calling voice. Now and then, midst his slow utterances, Joseph turned to look at her, and, catching the expression kindling her face as with light, forgot his theme, and with bowed head, wondering, plodded on. So they skirted the great plain, and at length reached the elevation Mar Elias; from which, across a valley, they beheld Bethlehem, the old, old House of Bread, its white walls crowning a ridge, and shining above the brown scumbling of leafless orchards. They paused there, and rested, while Joseph pointed out the places of sacred renown; then they went down into the valley to the well which was the scene of one of the marvellous exploits of David's strong men. The narrow space was crowded with people and animals. A fear came upon Joseph—a fear lest, if the town were so thronged, there might not be house-room for the gentle Mary. Without delay, he hurried on, past the pillar of stone marking the tomb of Rachel, up the gardened slope, saluting none of the many persons he met on the way, until he stopped before the portal of the khan that then stood outside the village gates, near a junction of roads. The khan at Bethlehem was a good specimen of its class, being neither very primitive nor very princely. The building was purely Oriental; that is to say, a quadrangular block of rough stones, one story high, flat-roofed, externally unbroken by a window, and with but one principal entrance—a doorway, which was also a gateway, on the eastern side, or front. The road ran by the door so near that the chalk dust half covered the lintel. A fence of flat rocks, beginning at the northeastern corner of the pile, extended many yards down the slope to a point from whence it swept westwardly to a limestone bluff; making what was in the

## O DU FRÖHLICHE.

JOHANNES FALK, 1816.

1. O du fröh-li-che, O du se-li-ge, Gnaden-bringende Weih-nacht-zeit! O du
2. O du fröh-li-che, O du se-li-ge, Gnaden-bringende Os-ter-zeit! O du
3. O du fröh-li-che, O du se-li-ge, Gnaden-bringende Pfingsten-zeit! O du

fröh-li-che, O du se-li-ge, Gnaden-bringende Weih-nacht-zeit! Welt ging ver-
fröh-li-che, O du se-li-ge, Gnaden-bringende Os-ter-zeit! Welt lag in
fröh-li-che, O du se-li-ge, Gnaden-bringende Pfings-ten-zeit! Christ un-ser

lo-ren, Christ ward ge-bo-ren, Freu-e, freu-e dich, O Chris-ten-heit!
Ban-den, Christ ist er-stan-den, Freu-e, freu-e dich, O Chris-ten-heit!
Meis-ter, Heil-icht die Geis-ter Freu-e, freu-e dich, O Chris-ten-heit!

highest degree essential to a respectable khan—a safe enclosure for animals. In a village like Bethlehem, as there was but one sheik, there could not well be more than one khan; and, though born in the place, the Nazarene, from long residence elsewhere, had no claim to hospitality in the town. Moreover, the enumeration for which he was coming might be the work of weeks or months; Roman deputies in the provinces were proverbially slow; and to impose himself and wife for a period so uncertain upon acquaintances or relations was out of the question. So, before he drew nigh the great house, while he was yet climbing the slope, in the steep places toiling to hasten the donkey, the fear that he might not find accommodations in the khan became a painful anxiety; for he found the road thronged with men and boys who, with great ado, were taking their cattle, horses, and camels to and from the valley, some to water, some to the neighboring caves. And when he was come close by, his alarm was not allayed by the discovery of a crowd investing the door of the establishment, while the enclosure adjoining, broad as it was, seemed already full. * *

Mary's veil was raised. "Blue eyes and hair of gold," muttered the steward to himself, seeing but her. "So looked the young king when he went to sing before Saul." Then he took the leading-strap from Joseph and said to Mary, "Peace to you, O daughter of David!" Then to the others, "Peace to you all!" Then to Joseph, "Rabbi, follow me." The party were conducted into a wide passage paved with stone, from which they entered the court of the khan. To a stranger the scene would have been curious; but they noticed the lewens that yawned darkly upon them from all sides, and the court itself, only to remark how crowded they were. By a lane reserved in the stowage of the cargoes, and thence by a passage similar to the one at the entrance, they emerged into the enclosure adjoining the house, and came upon camels, horses, and donkeys, tethered and dozing in close groups; among them were the keepers, men of many lands; and they, too, slept or kept silent watch. They went down the slope of the crowded yard slowly, for the dull carriers of the women had wills of their own. At length they turned into a path running towards the gray limestone bluff overlooking the khan on the west. "We are going to the cave," said Joseph, laconically. The

## THE CHILD IS BORN.

GARDINER, 1760.

1. While an - gels thus, O Lord, rejoice, Shall men no an - them raise? Oh, may we lose these
2. Good-will to sin - ful dust is shown, And peace on earth is given; For lo! th' incarnate

useless tongues When we for - get to praise! Then let us swell re - spon - sive notes, And
Saviour comes With news of joy from Heav'n. Mer - cy and truth, with sweet ac - cord, His

join the heavenly throng; For angels no such love have known, As we, to wake their song.
ris - ing beams a - dorn; Let Heav'n and earth in concert sing, "The promised Child is born."

guide lingered till Mary came to his side. "The cave to which we are going," he said to her, "must have been a resort of your ancestor David. From the field below us, and from the well down in the valley, he used to drive his flocks to it for safety; and afterwards, when he was king, he came back to the old house here for rest and health, bringing great trains of animals. The mangers yet remain as they were in his day. Better a bed upon the floor where he has slept than one in the court-yard or out by the roadside. Ah, here is the house before the cave!" This speech must not be taken as an apology for the lodging offered. There was no need of apology. The place was the best then at disposal. The guests were simple folks, by habits of life easily satisfied. To the Jew of that period, moreover, abode in caverns was a familiar idea, made so by every-day occurrences, and by what he heard of Sabbaths in the synagogues. How much of Jewish history, how many of the most exciting incidents in that history, had transpired in caves! Yet further, these people were Jews of Bethlehem, with whom the idea was especially commonplace; for their locality abounded with caves great and small, some of which had been dwelling-places from the time of the

Emin and Horites. No more was there offence to them in the fact that the cavern to which they were being taken had been, or was, a stable. They were the descendants of a race of herdsmen, whose flocks habitually shared both their habitations and wanderings. In keeping with a custom derived from Abraham, the tent of the Bedawin yet shelters his horses and children alike. So they obeyed the keeper cheerfully, and gazed at the house, feeling only a natural curiosity. Everything associated with the history of David was interesting to them. The building was low and narrow, projecting but a little from the rock to which it was joined at the rear, and wholly without a window. In its blank front there was a door, swung on enormous hinges, and thickly daubed with ocherous clay. While the wooden bolt of the lock was being pushed back, the women were assisted from their pillions. Upon the opening of the door, the keeper called out, "Come in!" The guests entered, and stared about them. It became apparent immediately that the house was but a mask or covering for the mouth of a natural cave or grotto, probably forty feet long, nine or ten high, and twelve or fifteen in width. The light streamed through the doorway, over an un-

## THE HOLY FAMILY.

GOETHE.
A. RANDEGGER.

1. Child of beau-ty rare! Oh, mother chaste and fair,— How hap-py seem they
2. Child of beau-ty rare! Oh, mother chaste and fair,— What joy that sight might

both, So far beyond com-pare! She in her In-fant blest, And
bear To him who sees them there, If with un-trou-bled eye He

rit.

He in con-scious rest Nestling soft and warm, His cra-dle her fond breast.
looked up-on the twain, Like Joseph standing by, Like Joseph standing by.

even floor, falling upon piles of grain and fodder, and earthenware and household property, occupying the centre of the chamber. Along the sides were mangers, low enough for sheep, and built of stones laid in cement. There were no stalls or partitions of any kind. Dust and chaff yellowed the floor, filled all the crevices and hollows, and thickened the spider-webs, which dropped from the ceiling like bits of dirty linen; otherwise the place was cleanly, and, to appearance, as comfortable as any of the arched lewens of the khan proper. In fact, a cave was the model and first suggestion of the lewen. "Come in!" said the guide. "These piles upon the floor are for travellers like yourselves. Take what of them you need." Then he spoke to Mary. "Can you rest here?" "The place is sanctified," she answered. "I leave you then. Peace be with you all!" When he was gone, they busied themselves making the cave habitable. At a certain hour in the evening the shouting and stir of the people in and about the khan ceased; at the same time, every Israelite, if not already upon his feet, arose, solemnized his face, looked towards Jerusalem, crossed his hands upon his breast, and prayed; for it was the sacred ninth hour, when sacrifices were offered in the temple on Moriah, and God was supposed to be there. When the hands of the worshippers fell down, the commotion broke forth again; everybody hastened to bread, or to make his pallet. A little later, the lights were put out. there was silence, and then sleep.

About midnight some one on the roof cried out, "What light is that in the sky? Awake, brethren, awake and see!" The people, half asleep, sat up and looked; then they became wide-awake, though wonderstruck. And the stir spread to the court below, and into the lewens; soon the entire tenantry of the house and court and enclosure were out gazing at the sky. And this was what they saw. A ray of light, beginning at a height immeasurably beyond the nearest stars, and dropping obliquely to the earth; at its top, a diminishing point; at its base, many furlongs in width; its sides blending softly with the darkness of the night; its core a roseate electrical splendor. The apparition seemed to rest on the nearest mountain southeast

## REJOICE, YE CHRISTIANS.

1. Re - joice, re - joice, ye Christians, With all your hearts this morn! O hear the bless-ed tid - ings, "The Lord, the Christ is born!" Come sing with ho - ly glad - ness High Al - le - lu - ias sing, Up - lift your loud ho - san - nas To Je - sus, Lord and King.

2. What great and mighty won - der This Christmas Fes - tal brings! On earth a low - ly In - fant, Be - hold the King of kings. Since all He comes to ran - som, By all be He a - dored; The In - fant born in Bethl'em, The Sa - viour and the Lord.

3. The Word is made in - car - nate, Descend - ing from on high; And cher - u - bim sing an - thems, To shep - herds from the sky; And we with them tri - um - phant Re - peat the hymn a - gain: "To God on high be glo - ry, And peace on earth to men.

4. Sin, death, and hell, and Sa - tan, Have lost the vic - to - ry; This Child shall over - throw them, As ye shall sure - ly see. All i - dol forms shall per - ish, All er - ror shall de - cay, And Christ shall wield His sceptre, Our Lord and God, for aye.

of the town, making a pale corona along the line of the summit. The khan was touched luminously, so that those upon the roof saw each other's faces, all filled with wonder. Steadily, through minutes, the ray lingered, and then the wonder changed to awe and fear; the timid trembled; the boldest spoke in whispers. "Saw you ever the like?" asked one. "It seems just over the mountain there. I cannot tell what it is, nor did I ever see anything like it," was the answer. "Can it be that a star has burst and fallen?" asked another, his tongue faltering. "When a star falls, its light goes out." "I have it!" cried one, confidently. "The shepherds have seen a lion, and made fires to keep him from the flocks." The men next the speaker drew a breath of relief, and said, "Yes, that is it! The flocks were grazing in the valley over there to-day." A bystander dispelled the comfort. "No, no! Though all the wood in all the valleys of Judah was brought together in one pile and fired, the blaze would not throw a light so strong and high." After that there was silence on the house-top, broken but once again while the mystery continued. "Brethren!" exclaimed a Jew of venerable mien, "what we see is the ladder our father Jacob saw in his dream. Blessed be the Lord God of our fathers!"

A mile and a half, it may be two miles, southeast of Bethlehem, there is a plain separated from the town by an intervening swell of the mountain. Besides being well sheltered from the north winds, the vale was covered with a growth of sycamore, dwarf-oak, and pine trees, while in the glens and ravines adjoining there were thickets of olive and mulberry ; all at this season of the year invaluable for the support of sheep, goats, and cattle, of which the wandering flocks consisted. At the side farthest from the town, close under a bluff, there was an extensive *mârâh*, or sheepcot, ages old. In some long-forgotten

## SHOUT THE GLAD TIDINGS.

W. A. Muhlenburg, 1823.

*Chorus.*

Shout the glad tidings, ex-ult-ing-ly sing, Je-ru-salem triumphs, Messi-ah is King!

*Semi-chorus or Chorus.*

1. Si-on the marvelous sto-ry be telling, The Son of the Highest, how lowly His birth! The
2. Tell how He cometh ; from nation to nation, The heart-cheering news let the earth echo round : How
3. Mortals, your homage be grate-ful-ly bringing, And sweet let the gladsome Hosanna a-rise; Ye

*Repeat 1st chorus.*

brightest archangel in glo-ry ex-celling, He stoops to redeem thee, He reigns upon earth:
free to the faithful He of-fers sal-vation; His people with joy ever-last-ing are crowned:
an-gels, the full Al-le-lu-ia be singing; One chorus resound thro' the earth and the skies:

*Chorus after last verse.*

Shout the glad tidings, ex-ult-ing-ly sing, Je-ru-sa-lem triumphs, Mes-

si-ah is King, Mes-si-ah is King, Mes-si-ah is King. A-men.

foray, the building had been unroofed and almost demolished. The enclosure attached to it remained intact, however, and that was of more importance to the shepherds who drove their charges thither than the house itself. The stone wall around the lot was high as a man's head, yet not so high but that sometimes a panther or a lion, hungering from the wilderness, leaped boldly in. On the inner side of the wall, and as an additional security against the constant danger, a hedge of the rhamnus had been planted, an invention so successful that now a sparrow could hardly penetrate the overtopping branches, armed as they were with great clusters of thorns hard as spikes. The day of the occurrences which occupy the preceding chapters, a number of shep-

## JOYOUS ANTHEM SWELLING.

Von Flotow.
Agnes L. Pratt.

1. Hark! the Christmas bells are ring - ing; Hear their chime so sweet and clear, Would you know the song they're re sing - ing, Sing - ing to my list - 'ning ear? "Peace on earth!" the tale they're tell - ing, "And good-will to - ward all men." Loud the joy - ous an - them swell - ing, O - ver all the earth a - gain, O - ver all the earth a - gain.

2. Hark! they tell an - oth - er sto - ry! Low and sweet it sounds to me, 'Neath tri - umph - ant strains of glo - ry, As they ring so wild and free; Like soft chords, full, rich, and thrill - ing, Is its mu - sic rare to me, While me - lo - dious thoughts are fill - ing All my soul with har - mo - ny, All my soul with har - mo - ny.

3. To my heart, in language old - en, Has the blest command been sung, In the rule we call the "Gold-en," A - ges have the an - them rung; "Make the Christmas for men bright - er, Than they ev - er yet have known, Make their heav - y bur - dens light - er, Ere the Christmas - tide has flown, Ere the Christ-mas - tide has flown.

herds, seeking fresh walks for their flocks, led them up to this plain ; and from early morning the groves had been made ring with calls, and the blows of axes, the bleating of sheep and goats, the tinkling of bells, the lowing of cattle, and the barking of dogs. When the sun went down, they led the way to the *mårâh*, and by nightfall had everything safe in the field ; then they kindled a fire down by the gate, partook of their humble supper, and sat down to rest and talk, leaving one on watch. There were six of these men, omitting the watchman ; and afterwhile they assembled in a group near the fire, some sitting, some lying prone. As they went bareheaded habitually, their hair stood out in thick, coarse, sunburnt shocks; their beard covered their throats, and fell in mats down the breast; mantles of the skin of kids and lambs, with the fleece on, wrapped them from neck to knee, leaving their arms exposed; broad belts girthed the rude garments to their waists; their sandals were of the coarsest quality; from their right shoulders hung scrips containing food and selected stones for slings, with which they were armed; on the ground near each one lay his crook, a symbol of his calling and a weapon of offence. Such were the shepherds of Judea! In appearance, rough and savage as the gaunt dogs sitting with them around the blaze; in fact, simple-minded, tender-hearted: effects due, in part, to the primi-

## CHRISTMAS DAWN.

BELLINI.
CELIA THAXTER.

Andantino.

1. Shin-ing ones with drooping eyes, At the gates of Par - a - dise, Wait-ing
2. See the del - i - cate white light Sil - ver - ing the edge of night! Spread your

for the word of joy That shall sin and 'death de-stroy: Quench your tapers, burn-ing
pinions half un - furled! Shafts of splendor smite the world! An - gels twain that watch and

dim, For the tender Christ-mas Hymn Ri - ses faint - ly thro' the hush, Her-ald -
pray For the dawn of Christmas day; Lift your eyes and look a - broad, Lo! the

ing the morn-ing's blush, Ri-ses faint - ly thro' the hush, Her-ald - ing the morning's blush.
glo-ry of the Lord! Lift your eyes and look a - broad, Lo! the glo-ry of the Lord!

tive life they led, but chiefly to their constant care of things lovable and helpless. They rested and talked; and their talk was all about their flocks, a dull theme to the world, yet a theme which was all the world to them. If in narrative they dwelt long upon affairs of trifling moment; if one of them omitted nothing of detail in recount-ing the loss of a lamb, the relation between him and the unfortunate should be remembered: at birth it became his charge, his to keep all its days, to help over the floods, to carry down the hollows, to name and train; it was to be his companion, his object of thought and interest, the subject of his will; it was to enliven and share his wanderings;

in its defence he might be called on to face the lion or robber—to die. The great events, such as blotted out nations and changed the mastery of the world, were trifles to them, if perchance they came to their knowledge. Of what Herod was doing in this city or that, building palaces and gymnasia, and indulging forbidden practices, they occasionally heard. As was her habit in those days, Rome did not wait for people slow to inquire about her; she came to them. Over the hills along which he was leading his lagging herd, or in the fastnesses in which he was hiding them, not unfrequently the shepherd was startled by the blare of trumpets, and, peering out, beheld a cohort, sometimes a legion, in march; and when the glittering crests were gone, and the excitement incident to the intrusion over, he bent himself to evolve the meaning of the eagles and gilded globes of the soldiery, and the charm of a life so the opposite of his own. Yet these men, rude and simple as they were, had a knowledge and a wisdom of their own. On Sabbaths they were accustomed to purify them-

## WHAT SAID THE SHEPHERDS?

ANNA M. LIBBEY.
WM. M. HUTCHINSON.

1. What said the shep-herds when they saw the Star Rise in the East? "The night is chill and cold On Judah's hills; why should we journey far, Leav-ing our ten-der flocks in lone-ly fold,

2. But lo! the won-drous arch of heav-en's blue Is o-pened wide and an-gels fill the space; While glo-ry from the throne comes flooding thro', Il-lum-ing all that waste and dreary place!

3. The shepherds heard the song, re-membered they The wea-ry night up-on the mountain wild, When in the ro-sy flush of breaking day, They knelt be-fore the manger and the Child,

4. Oh, blind-ed eyes! for thee still shines the Star, To dull closed ears at-tendant an-gels sing, Yet flee, faint heart, the hills of doubt that bar Thy way, and lo! thou, too shalt find the King,

Leav-ing our ten-der flocks in lone-ly fold?"
Il-lum-ing all that waste and dreary place!
They knelt be-fore the manger and the Child?
Thy way, and lo! thou too shalt find the King.

selves, and go up into the synagogues, and sit on the benches farthest from the ark. When the chazzan bore the *Torah* round, none kissed it with greater zest; when the sheliach read the text, none listened to the interpreter with more absolute faith; and none took away with them more of the elder's sermon, or gave it more thought afterwards. In a verse of the Shema they found all the learning and all the law of their simple lives—that their Lord was One God, and that they must love him with all their souls. And they loved him, and such was their wisdom, surpassing that of kings.

While they talked, and before the first watch was over, one by one the shepherds went to sleep, each lying where he had sat. The night, like most nights of the winter season in the hill country, was clear, crisp, and sparkling with stars. There was no wind. The atmosphere seemed never so pure, and the stillness was more than silence; it was a holy hush, a warning that heaven was stooping low to whisper some good thing to the listening earth. By the gate, hugging his mantle close, the watchman walked ; at times he stopped, attracted by a stir among the sleeping herds, or by a jackal's cry off on the mountain-side. The midnight was slow coming to him ; but at last it came. His task was done ; now for the dreamless sleep with which labor blesses its wearied children ! He moved towards the fire, but paused ; a light was breaking around him, soft and white, like the moon's. He waited breathlessly. The light deepened ; things before invisible came to view ; he saw the whole field, and all it sheltered. A chill sharper than that of the frosty air—a chill of fear—smote him. He looked up ; the stars were gone ; the light was dropping as from a window in the sky ; as he looked, it became a splendor ; then, in terror, he cried, "Awake, awake !" Up sprang the dogs, and, howling, ran away. The herds rushed together bewildered. The men clambered to their feet, weapons in hand. "What is it ?" they asked, in one voice. "See !" cried the watchman, " the sky is on fire !" Suddenly

## THE GOLDEN RAY.

J. INGALLS.

1. The gold-en ray of Christmas day Makes to the earth from Heaven away, It greets a Moth-er
2. Now from the stall of Beth-le-hem, Shall rise thy King, Jeru-sa-lem! Oh, not in roy-al
3. The love song of thy grateful life, That sings the strain of heal-ed strife, Thy du-ty, O my

mild, It greets a Mother mild; The Fa-ther's will hath this fulfilled He from e-
guise! Oh, not in roy-al guise! For thee, my soul, in humble stall, Was Je-sus
heart, Thy du-ty, O my heart! With Ma-ry, wise men, shepherds strong, And an-gels

ter-ni-ty hath willed,—She watches o'er her Child, She watch-es o'er her Child.
born, thine "all in all," De-scend-ed from the skies, De-scend-ed from the skies.
with their morning song, With thee no meaner part, With thee no mean-er part.

the light became intolerably bright, and they covered their eyes, and dropped upon their knees ; then, as their souls shrank with fear, they fell upon their faces blind and fainting, and would have died had not a voice said to them, " Fear not !" And they listened. "Fear not : for behold, I bring you good tidings of great joy, which shall be to all people." The voice in sweetness and soothing more than human, and low and clear, penetrated all their being, and filled them with assurance. They rose upon their knees, and, looking worshipfully, beheld in the centre of a great glory the appearance of a man, clad in a robe intensely white ; above its shoulders towered the tops of wings shining and folded ; a star over its forehead glowed with steady lustre, brilliant as Hesperus ; its hands were stretched towards them in blessing ; its face was serene and divinely beautiful. They had often heard, and, in their simple way, talked, of angels ; and they doubted not now, but said, in their hearts, The glory of

God is about us, and this is he who of old came to the prophet by the river of Ulai. Directly the angel continued : "For unto you is born this day, in the city of David, a Saviour, which is Christ the Lord !" Again there was a rest, while the words sank into their minds. "And this shall be a sign unto you," the annunciator said next. "Ye shall find the babe, wrapped in swaddling-clothes, lying in a manger." The herald spoke not again ; his good tidings were told ; yet he stayed awhile. Suddenly the light, of which he seemed the centre, turned roseate and began to tremble ; then up, far as the men could see, there was flashing of white wings, and coming and going of ra-

diant forms, and voices as of a multitude chanting in unison, "Glory to God in the highest, and on earth peace, good-will towards men !" Not once the praise, but many times. Then the herald raised his eyes as seeking approval of one far off ; his wings stirred, and spread slowly and majestically, on their upper side white as snow, in shadow vari-tinted, like mother-of-pearl; when they were expanded many cubits beyond his stature, he arose lightly, and, with out effort, floated out of view, taking the light up with him. Long after he was gone, down from the sky fell the refrain mellowed by distance, "Glory to God in the highest, and on earth peace, good-will towards men."

## CALM WAS THE NIGHT.

A. S. SULLIVAN.
CHARLOTTE ELLIOTT.

1. Calm was the hallowed night ! Dis - cord al - lay'd, Valley and mountain height Slumber'd in shade.
2. Sud - den-ly round them shone, Far thro' the night, Dazzling to look up - on, Splendors of light;

Roofed by Heav'n's azure fair, Making their flocks their care, Shepherds in open air, Tranquilly stayed.
Then drew an angel near, And to al - lay their fear, Poured on their ravished ear Words of de - light.

| | | |
|---|---|---|
| Ne'er since the world began | Well might the tidings told, | Well might the Shepherds haste, |
| Angels of God | Chorus, unseen, | Eager as we, |
| Music so sweet to man | Waken your harps of gold, | Ere yet the night was past, |
| Sounded abroad ; | Wondrous their sheen ! | This sight to see ; |
| On that auspicious morn, | Sweet rang your minstrelsy, | Where light the meteor shed, |
| Changing our state forlorn, | "Glory to God on high !" | Well might the Magi tread, |
| Christ as a babe was born, | "Peace on earth," amnesty, | Joyful, the path that led, |
| Jesus the Lord ! | "Good-will towards men !" | Saviour, to Thee ! |

When the shepherds came fully to their senses, they stared at each other stupidly, until one of them said, "It was Gabriel, the Lord's messenger unto men." None answered. "Christ the Lord is born ; said he not so ?" Then another recovered his voice, and replied, "That is what he said." "And did he not also say, in the city of David, which is our Bethlehem yonder. And that we should find him a babe in swaddling clothes ?" "And lying in a manger." The first speaker gazed into the fire thoughtfully, but at length said, like one possessed of a sudden resolve, "There is but one place in Bethlehem where there are mangers ; but one, and that is in the cave near the

old khan. Brethren, let us go see this thing which has come to pass. The priests and doctors have been a long time looking for the Christ. Now he is born, and the Lord has given us a sign by which to know him. Let us go up and worship him." "But the flocks !" "The Lord will take care of them. Let us make haste." Then they all arose and left the *mârâh.*

Around the mountain and through the town they passed, and came to the gate of the khan, where there was a man on watch. "What would you have ?" he asked. "We have seen and heard great things to-night," they replied. "Well, we too have seen great things, but heard nothing. What

MADONNA DEL GRANDUCA.

did you hear?" "Let us go down to the cave in the enclosure, that we may be sure; then we will tell you all. Come with us, and see for yourself." "It is a fool's errand." "No, the Christ is born." "The Christ! How do you know?" "Let us go and see first." The man laughed scornfully. "The Christ, indeed! How are you to know him?" "He was born this night, and is now lying in a manger, so we were told; and there is but one place in Bethlehem with mangers." "The cave?" "Yes. Come with us." They went through the courtyard without notice, although there were some up even then talking about the wonderful light. The door of the cavern was open. A lantern was burning within, and they entered unceremoniously. "I give you peace," the watchman said to Joseph and the Beth-Dagonite. "Here are people looking for a child born this night, whom they are to know by finding him in swaddling-clothes and lying in a manger." For a moment the face of the stolid Nazarene was moved; turning away, he said, "The child is here." They were led to one of the mangers, and there the child was. The lantern was brought, and the shepherds stood

## SHEPHERDS IN THE FIELD.

G. Verdi.
Cuthbert Bede.

Con espressione.

1. Not to those in soft ap-par-el, Was the Saviour first made known; Not to no-ble or to high-born, Or to court-iers round a throne; Not to kings or mighty monarchs, Was the King of kings re-vealed, But to poor and lonely shepherds In the lone-ly pasture-field.

2. It was towards the dawn of morning, Ere the earliest streak of light, And those lowly men were wak-ing Thro' the watches of the night: Warm and white the flocks were lying, Guarded by the shepherd band; And the night hung like a cur-tain O'er that old Ju-de-an land.

3. Blazing brightly in the darkness, As they lay upon the sward, Golden glo-ry shone a-round them Like the glo-ry of the Lord; And a wing-ed, ra-diant An-gel With a ha-lo round his head, Stood among the startled shepherds Bow'd and awed with holy dread.

by mute. The little one made no sign; it was as others just born. "Where is the mother?" asked the watchman One of the women took the baby, and went to Mary, lying near, and put it in her arms. Then the bystanders collected about the two. "It is the Christ!" said a shepherd, at last. "The Christ!" they all repeated, falling upon their knees in worship. One of them repeated several times over, "It is the Lord, and his glory is above the earth and heaven." And the simple men, never doubting, kissed the hem of the mother's robe, and with joyful faces departed. In the khan, to all the people aroused and pressing about them, they told their story; and through the town, and all the way back to the *mârâh*, they chanted the refrain of the angels, Glory to God in the highest, and on earth peace, good-will towards men! The story went abroad, confirmed by the light so generally seen; and the next day, and for days thereafter, the cave was visited by curious crowds, of whom some believed, though the greater part laughed and mocked.

The eleventh day after the birth of the

child in the cave, about mid-afternoon, the three wise men approached Jerusalem by the road from Shechem. After crossing Brook Cedron, they met many people, of whom none failed to stop and look after them curiously. Judea was of necessity an international thoroughfare; a narrow ridge, raised, apparently, by the pressure of the desert on the east, and the sea on the west, was all she could claim to be; over the ridge, however, nature had stretched the line of trade between the east and the south; and that was her wealth. In other words, the riches of Jerusalem were the tolls she levied on passing commerce. Nowhere else, consequently, unless in Rome, was there such constant assemblage of so many people of so many different nations; in no other city was a stranger less strange to the residents than within her walls and purlieus. And yet these three men excited the wonder of all whom they met on the way to the gates. A child belonging to some women sitting by the roadside opposite the Tombs of the Kings saw the party coming; immediately it clapped its hands, and cried, "Look, look! What pretty bells! What big camels!" The bells were silver;

## CHILDREN'S HOSANNA.

Geo. J. Webb.

1. When His sal-va-tion bring-ing, To Zi-on Je-sus came, The chil-dren all stood sing-ing Ho-san-nas to His name. Nor did their zeal of-fend Him, But as He rode a-long, He let them still at-tend Him, And smiled to hear their song.

2. And since the Lord re-tain-eth His love for children still—Tho' now as King he reign-eth On Zi-on's heav'n-ly hill. We'll flock around His ban-ner, Who sits up-on the throne, And cry a-loud, Ho-san-na! To Dav-id's roy-al Son!

3. For should we fail pro-claim-ing Our great Redeemer's praise, The stones, our si-lence sham-ing Might well Ho-san-nas raise. But shall we on-ly ren-der The trib-ute of our words? No! while our hearts are ten-der, They too shall be the Lord's.

the camels, as we have seen, were of unusual size and whiteness, and moved with singular stateliness; the trappings told of the desert and of long journeys thereon, and also of ample means in possession of the owners, who sat under the little canopies exactly as they appeared at the rendezvous beyond the Jebel. Yet it was not the bells or the camels, or their furniture, or the demeanor of the riders, that were so wonderful; it was the question put by the man who rode foremost of the three. The approach to Jerusalem from the north is across a plain which dips southward, leaving the Damascus Gate in a vale or hollow. The road is narrow, but deeply cut by long use, and in places difficult on account of the cobbles left loose and dry by the washing of the rains. On either side, however, there stretched, in the old time, rich fields and handsome olive-groves, which must, in luxurious growth, have been beautiful, especially to travellers fresh from the wastes of the desert. In this road the three stopped before the party in front of the Tombs. "Good people," said Balthasar, stroking his plaited beard, and bending from his cot, "is not Jerusalem close by?" "Yes," answered the woman into whose arms the child had shrunk. "If the trees on yon swell were a little lower you could see the towers on the market-place." Balthasar gave the Greek and the Hindoo a look, then asked, "Where is he that is born King of the Jews?" The women gazed at each other without reply. "You have not heard of him?" "No." "Well, tell everybody that we have seen his star in the east, and are come to worship him." Thereupon the friends rode on. Of others they asked the same question, with like result. A large company whom they met going to the Grotto of Jeremiah were so astonished by the inquiry and the appearance of the

travellers that they turned about and followed them into the city. * * *

That evening, before sunset, some women were washing clothes on the upper step of the flight that led down into the basin of the Pool of Siloam. They knelt each before a broad bowl of earthenware. A girl at the foot of the steps kept them supplied with water, and sang while she filled the jar. The song was cheerful, and no doubt lightened their labor. Occasionally they would sit upon their heels, and look up the slope of Ophel, and round to the summit of what is now the Mount of Offence, then faintly glorified by the dying sun. While they plied their hands, rubbing and wringing the clothes in the bowls, two other women came to them, each with an empty jar upon

## COME AND WORSHIP.

HENRY SMART.
J. MONTGOMERY, 1819.

1. Angels, from the realms of glory, Wing your flight o'er all the earth; Ye who sang cre-ation's sto-ry,
2. Shepherds, in the field abiding, Watching o'er your flocks by night; God with man is now residing,
3. Sages, leave your contemplations; Brighter visions beam afar; Seek the great De-sire of nations,
4. Saints, before the altar bending, Watching long in hope and fear, Suddenly the Lord, descending,

Now proclaim Messiah's birth! Come and worship, Come and worship, Worship Christ, the new-born King.
Yonder shines the infant-light: Come and worship, Come and worship, Worship Christ, the new-born King.
Ye have seen His na-tal star: Come and worship, Come and worship, Worship Christ, the new-born King.
In His temple shall appear: Come and worship, Come and worship, Worship Christ, the new-born King.

A-men.

her shoulder. "Peace to you," one of the new-comers said. The laborers paused, sat up, wrung the water from their hands, and returned the salutation. "It is nearly night—time to quit." "There is no end to work," was the reply. "But there is a time to rest, and—" "To hear what may be passing," interposed another. "What news have you?" "They say the Christ is born," said the newsmonger, plunging into her story. It was curious to see the faces of the laborers brighten with interest; on the other side down came the jars, which, in a moment, were turned into seats for their owners. "The Christ!" the listeners cried. "So they say." "Who?" "Everybody; it is common talk." "Does anybody

believe it?" "This afternoon three men came across Brook Cedron on the road from Shechem," the speaker replied, circumstantially, intending to smother doubt. "Each one of them rode a camel spotless white, and larger than any ever before seen in Jerusalem." The eyes and mouths of the auditors opened wide. "To prove how great and rich the men were," the narrator continued, "they sat under awnings of silk; the buckles of their saddles were of gold, as was the fringe of their bridles; the bells were of silver, and made real music. Nobody knew them; they looked as if they had come from the ends of the world. Only one of them spoke, and of everybody on the road, even the women and children, he asked this question—'Where is he that is born King of the Jews?' No one gave them answer—no one understood what they meant; so they passed on, leaving behind them this saying: 'For we have seen his star in the east, and are come to worship him.' They put the question to the Roman at the gate; and he, no wiser than the simple people on the road, sent them up to Herod.'' "Where are they now?" "At the khan. Hundreds have been to look at them already, and hundreds more are going." "Who are they?" "Nobody knows. They are said to be Persians—wise men who talk with the stars—prophets, it may be, like Elijah and Jeremiah." "What do they mean by King of the Jews?" "The Christ, and that he is just born." One of the women laughed,

and resumed her work, saying, "Well, when I see him I will believe." Another followed her example: "And I—well, when I see him raise the dead, I will believe." A third said quietly, "He has been a long time promised. It will be enough for me to see him heal one leper." And the party sat talking until the night came, and, with the help of the frosty air, drove them home. * *

Folding his robe about him, Herod left the chamber. Directly the guide came, and led them back to the street, and thence to the khan, at the portal of which the Greek said, impulsively, "Let us to Bethlehem, O brethren, as the king has advised." "Yes," cried the Hindoo. "The Spirit burns within me." "Be it so," said Balthasar, with equal warmth. "The camels

## HARK! THE GLAD SOUND!

N. HERMANN.
PHILIP DODDRIDGE.

1. Hark! the glad sound! the Sav - iour comes, The Sav - iour prom-ised long;
2. He comes the pris - oners to re - lease In Sat - an's bond-age held;
3. He comes from thick - est films of vice To clear the men - tal ray,
4. Our glad ho - san - nas, Prince of Peace, Thy wel - come shall pro - claim;

Let ev - 'ry heart pre - pare a throne, And ev - 'ry voice a song.
The gates of brass be - fore Him burst, The i - ron fet - ters yield.
And on the eyes op - pressed with night To pour ce - les - tial day.
And Heaven's e - ter - nal arch - es ring With Thy be - lov - ed Name.

are ready." They gave gifts to the steward, mounted into their saddles, received directions to the Joppa Gate, and departed. At their approach the great valves were unbarred, and they passed out into the open country, taking the road so lately travelled by Joseph and Mary. As they came up out of Hinnom, on the plain of Rephaim, a light appeared, at first wide-spread and faint. Their pulses fluttered fast. The light intensified rapidly; they closed their eyes against its burning brilliance: when they dared look again, lo! the star, perfect as any in the heavens, but low down and moving slowly before them. And they folded their hands, and shouted, and rejoiced with exceeding great joy. "God is

with us! God is with us!" they repeated, in frequent cheer, all the way, until the star, rising out of the valley beyond Mar Elias, stood still over a house up on the slope of the hill near the town.

It was now the beginning of the third watch, and at Bethlehem the morning was breaking over the mountains in the east, but so feebly that it was yet night in the valley. The watchman on the roof of the old khan, shivering in the chilly air, was listening for the first distinguishable sounds with which life, awakening, greets the dawn, when a light came moving up the hill towards the house. He thought it a torch in some one's hand; next moment he thought it a meteor; the brilliance grew, however, until it became a star. Sore afraid, he cried out, and brought everybody within the walls to the roof. The phenomenon, in eccentric motion, continued to approach; the rocks, trees, and roadway under it shone as in a glare of lightning; directly its brightness became blinding. The more timid of the beholders fell upon their knees, and prayed, with their faces hidden; the boldest, covering their eyes, crouched, and now and then snatched glances fearfully. Afterwhile the khan and everything thereabout lay under the intolerable radiance. Such as dared look beheld the star standing still directly over the house in front of the cave where

## THE STRANGER STAR.

C. F. ALEXANDER.

1. Saw ye nev-er in the twi-light, When the sun had left the skies,
2. Heard ye nev-er of the sto-ry, How they crossed the des-ert wild,
3. Know ye not that low-ly Ba-by Was the bright and Morn-ing Star,

Up in heaven the clear stars shin-ing Thro' the gloom like lov-ing eyes?
Journeyed on by plain and mountain, Till they found the Ho-ly Child?
He who came to light the Gen-tiles, And the darkened isles a-far?

So of old the wise men, watch-ing, Saw a blaz-ing stran-ger star,
How they o-pen'd all their treas-ure, Kneel-ing to that In-fant King,
And we too may seek His cra-dle, There our hearts' best treas-ures bring,

And they knew the King was giv-en, And they fol-lowed it from far.
Gave the gold and fra-grant in-cense, Gave the myrrh in of-fer-ing?
Love and faith and true de-vo-tion, For our Sa-viour, God and King.

the Child had been born. In the height of this scene, the wise men came up, and at the gate dismounted from their camels, and shouted for admission. When the steward so far mastered his terror as to give them heed, he drew the bars and opened to them. The camels looked spectral in the unnatural light, and, besides their outlandishness, there were in the faces and manner of the three visitors an eagerness and exaltation which still further excited the keeper's fears and fancy; he fell back, and for a time could not answer the question they put to him. "Is not this Bethlehem of Judea?" But others came, and by their presence gave him assurance. "No, this is but the khan;

the town lies farther on." "Is there not here a child newly born?" The bystanders turned to each other marvelling, though some of them answered, "Yes, yes." "Show us to him!" said the Greek, impatiently. "Show us to him!" cried Balthasar, breaking through his gravity; "for we have seen his star, even that which ye behold over the house, and are come to worship him." The Hindoo clasped his hands, exclaiming, "God indeed lives! Make haste, make haste! The Saviour is found. Blessed, blessed are we above men!" The people from the roof came down and followed the strangers as they were taken through the court and out into the en-

## WHEN JORDAN HUSHED.

E. C. PHELPS.
THOMAS CAMPBELL.

Andante con moto espress.

1. When Jordan hush'd his waters still, And silence slept on Zion's hill, When Bethlehem's shepherds,
2. "O Zi - on, lift thy raptur'd eye; The long-expected hour is nigh; The joys of na - ture

thro' the night, Watched o'er their flocks by starry light. Hark! from the midnight hills around, A
rise a - gain; The Prince of Sa - lem comes to reign. See, Mer- cy, from her gold - en urn, Pours

voice of more than mor - tal sound In dis- tant hal - le - lu-jahs stole Wild murm'ring o'er the
a rich stream to them that mourn; Behold, she binds, with ten-der care, The bleeding bo - som

raptur'd soul. On wheels of light, on wings of flame, The glorious hosts of Zi - on came; High
of de - spair. He comes to cheer the trembling heart; Bids Satan and his host de - part; A -

heav'n with songs of triumph rang, While thus they struck their harps and sang By Jordan stream the angel song;
gain the day-star gilds the gloom, Again the bowers of Eden bloom, Again the bowers of Eden bloom."

closure; at sight of the star yet above the cave, though less candescent than before, some turned back afraid; the greater part went on. As the strangers neared the house, the orb arose; when they were at the door, it was high up overhead vanishing; when they entered, it went out lost to sight. And to the witnesses of what then took place came a conviction that there was a divine relation between the star and the strangers, which extended also to at least some of the occupants of the cave. When the door was opened, they crowded in. The apartment was lighted by a lantern enough to enable the strangers to find the mother, and the child awake in her lap. "Is the child thine?" asked Balthasar of Mary. And she who had kept all the things in the least affecting the little one, and pondered them in her heart, held it up in the light, saying, "He is my son!" And they fell down and worshipped him. They saw the child was as other children: about its head was neither nimbus nor material crown; its lips opened not in speech; if it heard their expressions of joy, their invocations, their prayers, it made no sign whatever, but, baby-like, looked longer at the flame in the lantern than at them. In a little while they arose, and, returning to

## SOFTLY SLEPT THE HOLY CHILD.

GERMAN.

Andante.

1. Naught of wealth and naught of power Showed itself in that still hour: But the Lord himself was
2. Shepherds by their flocks at night Saw sweet visions with af - fright—Hastened then a - way to

born    In a manger Christmas morn: Soft - ly slept the Ho - ly Child, Watched by
see    If in manger Christ could be: Thus it was in that calm morn, When the

Ma - ry, Mother mild: Wise Men guid - ed by a star Came from dis-tant lands a - far.
Prince of Peace was born, Herald - ed by an - gel choir—Song of Love's celes- tial fire!

the camels, brought gifts of gold, frankincense, and myrrh, and laid them before the child, abating nothing of their worshipful speeches; of which no part is given, for the thoughtful know that the pure worship of the pure heart was then what it is now, and has always been, an inspired song. And this was the Saviour they had come so far to find! Yet they worshipped without a doubt. Why? Their faith rested upon the signs sent them by him whom we have since come to know as the Father; and they were of the kind to whom his promises were so all-sufficient that they asked nothing about his ways. Few there were who had seen the signs and heard the promises—the Mother and Joseph, the shepherds, and the Three—yet they all believed alike: that is to say, in this period of the plan of salvation, God was all and the Child nothing. But look forward, O reader! A time will come when the signs will all proceed from the Son. Happy they who then believe in him! Let us wait that period.—*Lew Wallace.*

## WHEN I VIEW THE MOTHER.

J. BARNBY.
FROM THE LATIN.

1. When I view the Mother holding In her arms the heav'n-ly Boy, Thousand blissful
2. See the Virgin Mother beaming! Je-sus by her arms embraced, Dew on soft-est

thoughts unfolding, Melt my heart with sweetest joy, with sweet-est joy.
ro-ses gleaming, Vi-o-let with li-ly chaste, with li-ly chaste!

With her Babe the hours beguiling, Mary's soul in transport lives:
Each round other fondly twining, Pours the shafts of mutual love,

God her Son upon her smiling,
Thick as flow'rs in meadows shining,

Thousand, thousand kiss-es fond-ly gives, fond-ly gives. As the sun his
Countless as the stars a-bove, as the stars a-bove. Oh, may one such

ra-diance flinging, Shines up-on the bright ex-panse, So the Child to
ar-row glowing, Sweetest Child, which Thou dost dart, Thro' Thy Mother's

Ma-ry cling-ing, Doth her gen-tle heart, her gen-tle heart en-trance.
bo-som go-ing, Bless-ed Je-su, bless-ed Je-su, pierce my heart.

## CHRISTMAS CAROL.

*Moderato.*

A. REICHARDT.

1. The earth is cold and drear to-night, The wind goes moaning through the trees, While summer
2. What care we for the winds without, What care we for the fro-zen earth. For Christmas
3. Oh, may we work for oth-er's good, And ne'er a vile am-bi-tion feed, While there are

birds have winged their flight To greener fields and warmer seas. The dear old
bells will soon ring out To cel-e-brate the Saviour's birth. To cel-e-
those who want for food, And weary, wea-ry hearts that bleed. We may not

year is near-ly gone, Yet as it slow-ly dies a-way, It moves an-oth-er pace a-
brate the birth of Him, "Of wedded man" and virgin born, Who made a-tone-ment for our
be in reach of such As just-ly may our alms demand; But thousands need the balm-y

long, And brings anoth-er festive day; It moves anoth-er pace a-long, And brings an-
sin; Oh, hallowed be the Christmas morn; Who made atonement for our sin; Oh, hallowed
touch Of a warm heart and gen'rous hand; But thousands need the balmy touch Of a warm

oth-er fes-tive day. The hour is near when Christmas bells will chime An
be the Christ-mas morn. May none for-get the one glad Christ-mas day, When
heart and gen-'rous hand. A pleasant smile, or glad-some word of cheer, Will

an-them full of joy and mirth, In mem'ry of that bless-ed time, When Je-sus
God His on-ly Son did give, When he assumed our mor-tal clay, So that a
ev-er out-weigh mines of gold, In ban-ish-ing sore doubt and fear, And mak-ing

Christ was born, was born on earth. Moan on ye night winds if ye will, Yea, moan for
dy - ing, dy - ing world may live. Now we may learn from this great gift Bestowed by
weak - er souls grow strong and bold. And while our hearts with rap - ture swell, For—" Lo! the

the de - part - ing year, But let the troubled heart be still, And Christmas be a day of
God, from Heav'n a - bove, Our selfish hearts and minds to lift To deeds of char - i - ty and
Star of Beth - le - hem!" We hear the bells of Christmas tell Of "Peace on earth, good-will to

cheer; But let the trou - bled heart be still, And Christmas be a day of cheer.
love; Our sel - fish hearts and minds to lift To deeds of char - i - ty and love.
men;" We hear the bells of Christmas tell Of "Peace on earth, good-will to men."

## PAUL AND I.

TAUWITZ.

1. San - ta Claus, last Christ - mas eve, I was hap - py as a King;
2. San - ta Claus, dear San - ta Claus, Could you now bring back to me

We were won - d'ring, Paul and I, What treas - ures prec - ious you would bring;
Lit - tle broth - er Paul a - gain, Oh! how hap - py I should be!

We were won - d'ring, Paul and I, What treas - ures prec - ious you would bring.
Lit - tle broth - er Paul a - gain, Oh! how hap - py I should be!

## SWEET BELLS ARE CHIMING.

E. M. Douglas.
Richard Genee.

*Allegretto non troppo.*

1. Oh, Christmas bells, that, chiming clear, The air with rapture fill! Ye send your message far and near,
2. Oh, loving hearts, how sweet the song That bursts upon the ear, When fancy brings the angel throng

The an-gry storm to   still,   Yule fires are blaz-ing, are blaz-ing, are blaz-ing!
That woke the shepherds' fear!   Sweet bells are chim-ing, are chim-ing, are chim-ing!

*a tempo.*

What joy doth Christmas bring To toiling slave as crown-ed king!   Ah,   fair-er than flush of the
What joy doth Christmas bring To toiling slave as crown-ed king!   Ah,   fair-er than flush of the

*pp*

May-time bloom, The May-time bloom, the May-time bloom; Sweeter than blush of the rose in June, The
May-time bloom, The May-time bloom, the May-time bloom; Sweeter than blush of the rose in June, The

*rall.*      *a tempo.*

rose   in June,   the rose in June, When pine-tree and holly with berries red, With ber-ries red, with
rose   in June,   the rose in June, When pine-tree and holly with berries red, With ber-ries red, with

*f*

ber-ries red,   Laur-el and   mistle-toe* o-ver-head, The Christmas joy pro-long.
ber-ries red,   Laur-el and   mistle-toe o-ver-head, The Christmas joy pro-long.

[* Mis-el-to.]

## ECHOES OF OLDEN TIMES.

T. COMER.
HELEN MARTIN.

1. Lo! the happy morn o'er eastern hills! And the Christmas bells ring cheerily! A - ged hearts are
2. With a silent joy they greet the dawn That comes apace 'mid Christmas chimes! A sweeter calm fills

young a - gain, As they list their chim - ing mer - ri - ly. Like ser-aph tongues do Now stilled are toil - ing
ev - 'ry heart In ten der thoughts of old-en times.

they commune, While thro' the vales the shad - ows lie; The vo - cal air their
hands of care, Re - spon-sive to the bell's sweet voice, That calls a - far thro'

*Small notes to be played.*

hap - py rune Sends far a - broad thro' earth and sky. Ding, dong, ding, dong, ding,
pul - sing air, And makes the wea - ry heart re-joice. Ding, dong, ding, dong, ding,

chim - ing they swing; Of Christmas cheer each glad note tells, While ech - o a - wakes

*8va........*
*Organ*

Fond mem'ries of those dear old Christ-mas bells.

MOTHER AND SON.

# THE LAND AND THE CHILD.

ON the eastern borders of the Mediterranean Sea there lies a country whose moral importance is in striking contrast with its territorial insignificance. This country, in area not so large as Massachusetts, which in shape it somewhat resembles —being in length one hundred and eighty miles and with an average breadth of sixty-five miles—has been the scene of a drama incomparably more influential upon the destinies of mankind than any other in history. The stage is scarcely less remarkable than are the scenes which have been enacted on it. The most extraordinary man of all time had his birth, and passed his life, in the most extraordinary of all lands. A few words, therefore, concerning the geographical features of Palestine, and the character and history of its people, form in some sense a prelude to the life of him who has given it its most ·commonly-accepted title of the Holy Land.

Situated at the junction of three great continents, Europe, Asia, and Africa, Palestine partakes of the characteristic features of the three, and possesses in a diminutive form all their peculiarities. Here, in Southern Judea, is the desert of Africa making its incursion from the peninsula below. Here, bordering the Mediterranean, are plains that rival in fertility those of our own great Western prairies. Here, in the elevated mountain region of Central Palestine, is repeated the hill country which constitutes the characteristic feature of Southern Scotland. Here, in Northern Galilee, are mountains whose rugged steeps remind the traveler of the White Mountains and of the Alps. Here, embosomed in their midst, are lakes unsurpassed for their quiet beauty. Here, in the Jordan, is a mountain stream whose tumultuous torrent finds no equal in any river of its size and length in the world. Here Mount Hermon lifts its head, wrapped in perpetual snow, three thousand feet above our own Mount Washington. Here the waters of the Dead Sea lie in a basin scooped out of the solid rock, nearly, if not quite, as far below the level of the ocean as are the deepest mines of Cornwall. And here, almost in sight of its holy city, beat the waves of the Great Sea upon one hundred and fifty miles of rocky coast; so that in this one province, smaller than Massachusetts or Vermont, are mingled·the ocean, the mountain, the valley, the river, the lake, the desert, and the plain.

Its varieties of climate and production equal those of its physical features, and are in part produced by them. The temperate and the tropic zones overlap each other in Palestine. With a general climate corresponding to that of Northern Florida, it contains mountains whose heads are never free from snow, and valleys that rarely, if ever, witness it, except from afar. Tropical fruits and Northern cereals grow almost side by side. The fig-tree and the grape-vine produce their fruits in perfection on the sunny hill-sides of Judea. The cedars clothe the rocky sides of Lebanon. The apple, the pear, the plum, the quince, grow near neighbors with the date, the pomegranate, the banana, and the almond. The oak, the maple, and the evergreens of our Northern States make here acquaintance with the sycamore, the fig, the olive, residents of Asiatic climes. In a single day you may travel from the climate and productions of the Gulf States to such as characterize New England. In short, in this land, from which issue influences for the redemption of all people, are united in a singular conjunction the characteristic features and productions of all countries.

This land, though contiguous to three continents, and lying in close proximity to the great nationalities of the past—the As-syrian upon the east, the Egyptian on the southwest, and the Greek and Roman on the north and west—was nevertheless, by its singular conformation, shut out from them by barriers which, until after the Christian era, were nearly impassable. The valley of the Jordan on the west, the Mediterranean on the east, the desert on the south, and the mountain range of Lebanon and anti-Lebanon on the north, formed a better protection than the famous wall of the Celestial Empire. Its peculiar location thus fitted it to be the centre, as historically it has been, of the world's civilization, while its peculiar character adapted it to be a home of a peculiar people, kept by the nature of their country, no less than by that of their institutions, separate from the rest of mankind. By its physical features Palestine is divided into three long and narrow sections, parallel to each other, and nearly parallel to the coast—the valley of the Jordan, with the Dead Sea ; the hill country of Central Palestine ; and the rich and fertile lowlands which border the Mediterranean. The Jordan, rising among the mountains of Galilee, flowing in a long and rocky gorge, rapidly descending southward, and issuing in the Dead Sea, one hundred and fifty miles from its source and three thousand feet below the surface of the upper waters, forms a valley which, in its geographical and geological features, is without a parallel in the world. Buried be-

## HARK! THE HERALD ANGELS.

W. MOZART.
CHARLES WESLEY.

1. Hark! the her · ald an · gels sing, "Glo-ry to the new-born King! Peace on earth, and
2. Joy · ful, all ye na-tions, rise; Join the tri · umphs of the skies; With the'an · gel · ic
3. Veiled in flesh the God-head see; Hail th' Incar · nate De · i · ty, Pleased, as man, with
4. Let us then with an · gels sing, "Glo-ry to the new-born King! Peace on earth, and

mer · cy mild, God and sin · ners re · conciled, God and sin · ners re · conciled."
hosts pro-claim, "Christ is born in Beth · le · hem, Christ is born in Beth · le · hem."
men to appear, Je · sus, our Imman · uel, here, Je · sus, our Im-man · uel, here.
mer · cy mild, God and sin · ners re · conciled, God and sin · ners re · conciled!"

tween mountain ranges, effectually shielded from the Mediterranean breezes, this valley possesses a climate whose intolerable heats are without alleviation, a vegetation which, luxuriant in spring, is burnt and withered in summer by a cloudless sun. West of this valley the land rises by an ascent, in the south even precipitous, to an elevated range of hills from fifteen to eighteen hundred in height. In Judea this hill country, heated by breezes from the southern desert, possesses a climate and productions of an almost tropical character. Rounded hills of moderate height, now barren, but once covered with terraced vineyards ; now desolate, but once crowned with villages, are the characteristic features of the scenery. For a few weeks of spring water-torrents fill the ravines, and flowers of the most brilliant hue, daisies, anemones, wild tulips, poppies, clothe the land with dress of scarlet. But the fierce rays of an intolerable sun and the scorching sirocco of the desert soon blight and wither them. "The wind passeth over it and it is gone, and the place thereof shall know it no more." Proceeding northward, the scenery becomes more varied, the mountains more marked, the plains more considerable, the soil better. Wells and springs increase in number, the heat of the desert is escaped or counteracted by breezes from the northern ranges of snow-clad mountains, the shrubs of Southern Judea are supplanted by trees of larger growth and by more enduring vegetation, until at length, in Galilee, we reach a region whose springs and mountain streams, never dry, supply Lakes Merom and Tiberias, the reservoirs of Palestine; whose romantic mountains reach their consummation in the snow-capped peaks of Lebanon and anti-Lebanon, and whose verdure-clad hills and vales strongly contrast with the relatively barren hills of Jewry. Upon the west this plateau descends by a slope, far more gradual than on the east, to the plains of Sharon, Acre, and Esdraelon. These lowlands constitute the most fertile part of Palestine. Their average width is fifteen or sixteen miles. The climate is mild, the soil rich. Orange-trees are laden with fruits and flowers in January, and, when neither oppression nor foreign invasion desolate the land, these plains are covered with the richest and most luxuriant vegetation. It was for the possession of these plains that the ancient Canaanites contended after they were driven from the hill-country, and from which, the Book of Judges naively tells us, "The Lord could not drive them out, because they had chariots of iron." Imagine, then, the State of Vermont, its western shore bounded by the Atlantic Ocean instead of by Lake Champlain; the Connecticut Valley, its eastern boundary, a deep and almost impassable ravine cleft by some great convulsion in the solid rocks; the northern

## THE PRINCE OF PEACE.

W. MOZART.

1. He has come, the Christ of God! Left for us His glad a - bode; Stooping from His
2. He has come, the Prince of peace! Come to bid our sor - rows cease; Come to scat - ter,
3. He, the mighty King, has come! Making this poor earth His home; Come to bear our
4. He has come, whose name of grace Speaks deliver- ance to our race! Left for us His

throne of bliss, To this dark - some wil - der - ness, To this dark - some wil - der - ness!
with His light, All the shad - ows of our night, All the shad - ows of our night.
sin's sad load, Son of Dav - id, Son of God, Son of Dav - id, Son of God!
glad a - bode, Son of Ma - ry, Son of God, Son of Ma - ry, Son of God!

peaks of its Green Mountain range over-topping Mount Washington; its southern hills rounded like those of Western Connecticut; its northern climate and productions not widely different from those of the Middle States; its southern counties akin in both respects to the Gulf States, and the reader will have a tolerably accurate picture of that land which, the birthplace and home of Jesus Christ, is the cradle of Christianity.

In the midst of the civilization which Christianity has brought with it, it is not easy for us to conceive of the condition in which Christ found the world, and the circumstances amidst which he passed his life. Surrounded with all the appliances of modern science and art, we forget that Jesus lived at a time when mankind traveled not only without railroads and steamboats, but without post-roads and carriages; transacted all their business not only without banks, paper currency, or credit, but, for the most part, without internal commerce or any system of domestic trade; acquired such education as was possible not only without adequate schools, but without books, papers, or accessible literature; pursued their various industries not only without the aid of the modern forces of steam and water, but without any considerable labor-saving machinery; and lived not only without the comforts which modern art affords, but without such seeming necessaries of life as chairs and fireplaces. The

6

political condition of Judea under the sceptre of Rome we have already partially described. With the imperial government came its elaborate system of taxation. The Roman provinces were well called tributary, since they did little else than contribute to the already plethoric treasury of its luxurious capital. Every thing in a Roman province was taxed. Every article exported paid for the privilege of going out; every article imported paid for the privilege of coming in ; every article sold paid a tax of one per cent. on the purchase money; every slave twice that amount. To manumit him cost his owner five per cent. additional. Every house paid one tax, every door in it another, every column which adorned it a third. Every man of property paid for its peaceable possession a tax ranging sometimes as high as twelve per cent.; every poor man paid for the privilege of living a poll-tax practically determined by the greed of the gatherer and the poverty of his victim. This system of taxation, oppressive at the best, was made intolerable by the method of its collection, than which a corrupt court never devised one more nefarious. The provinces were farmed out by the Roman government to wealthy individuals, or joint-stock companies, who paid large sums for the privilege of extorting whatever their unscrupulous hands could

## HARK! THOSE HOLY VOICES.

G. J. GEER.
JOHN CAWOOD, 1816.

1. Hark! what mean those ho - ly voi - ces, Sweet-ly sounding thro' the skies?
2. List - en to the won - drous sto - ry, Which they chant in hymns of joy,
3. "Peace on earth, good - will from Heav - en, Reaching far as man is found;

Lo, th'an - gel - ic host re - joic - es, Heav'n'ly al - le - lu - ias rise.
"Glo - ry in the high - est, glo - ry! Glo - ry be to God most high!
Souls redeemed and sins for - giv - en, Loud our golden harps shall sound. A - men.

"Christ is born; the great anointed !
Heaven and earth His praises sing !
O receive whom God appointed
For your prophet, priest, and King.

Hasten, mortals, to adore Him;
Learn His Name to magnify,
Till in Heaven ye sing before Him,
Glory be to God most high!"

wring from a poverty-stricken people. They, in turn, let these provinces in smaller districts to sub-contractors, who employed in the collection of taxes the lowest and worst class of the native population, since no others would assume a task so odious. These are the publicans of the New Testament.

In the days of Christ intercommunication was difficult. To the ancient Jew Palestine was practically almost as great a country as the United States to us. Eighteen centuries have produced but little change, and the modern book of travels depicts with tolerable accuracy the methods in vogue in the first century. There were almost literally no roads. Wild, rocky, and often dangerous paths, barely wide enough for a single mule, leading over the mountains and down the steep ravines, provided the means of transit which are now afforded by our broad wagon roads and swift, smooth railways. The only carriage was a rough, two-wheeled cart, and this was of little service in the hill-country. The men generally traveled on foot ; mules and camels carried the women and children. The insecurity of the country rendered it then, as now, almost indispensable to go in caravans. A staff carried in the hand was the traveler's almost constant companion ; a bag, suspended from the neck or bound upon the back, constituted his usual baggage. Such a thing as an inn, in the modern acceptation of the term, was unknown. In the larger towns were halting-places for travelers, resembling the wagon-yards which are to be found in our Western towns. Here the traveler could procure shelter for his cattle and himself. He could obtain water, and permission to cook, in a court or square, such articles of food as he possessed, in such utensils as he carried with him. Even Jerusalem probably contained no better provision for the traveler than this. Private hospitality helped to provide, however, what public accommodation failed to afford. The Jews were not a commercial people. The commerce which Solomon attempted to establish decayed at his death, and was never revived. But internal trade was greatly developed by the national feasts which called all the people to Jerusalem thrice a year. On these occasions traders opened temporary booths at the public gates, and finally, at the time of Christ, intruding nearer and nearer to the Temple, which was the great centre of attraction, had converted its outer court into a market-place. The money was wholly hard currency—gold, silver, copper. Banks, and notes, and bills, it is hardly necessary to state, were unknown. All business was strictly for cash. The division into whole-sale and retail trade is of later origin. The

## WHILE SHEPHERDS WATCHED.

Jer. Clarke.
Nahum Tate, 1703.

1. While shep-herds watch'd their flocks by night, All seat-ed on the ground,
2. "Fear not," said he, for might-y dread Had seized their trou-bled mind:
3. "To you, in Dav-id's town, this day Is born of Dav-id's line,
4. "The Heaven-ly Babe you there shall find, To hu-man view dis-played,

The an-gel of the Lord came down, And glo-ry shone a-round.
"Glad tid-ings of great joy I bring To you and all man-kind.
The Sav-iour, who is Christ the Lord; And this shall be the sign.
All mean-ly wrapt in swath-ing bands, And in a man-ger laid."

Thus spake the seraph; and forthwith
Appeared a shining throng
Of angels, praising God, who thus
Addressed their joyful song:

"All glory be to God on high,
And to the earth be peace;
Good-will henceforth from Heaven to men
Begin, and never cease."

booths which accompany a modern agricultural fair are a modification of ancient commerce, and afford a fair illustration of its character. Manufactures were of the simplest kind. There was little or no machinery. No busy wheels made the mountain streams of Northern Judea do the work of many men. No priest had yet pronounced the marriage vows between fire and water, and consecrated its giant child to the service of humanity. There were workers in iron, bronze, silver, and gold, who united the labors of the blacksmith with those of the jeweler; but so simple an invention as the bellows had not been thought of, and the workman, with no other means of stimulating the furnace fire than blowing it through a long pipe, had hard work and but poor pay. The carpenter was housebuilder and carver too. But his tools were few; a rude sort of plane, a saw, a chisel, a drill or awl, a mallet in lieu of hammer, an axe and nails, seemingly his chief utensils. Masons worked in brick and stone as early at least as the days of Solomon. Ship-builders constructed the simple vessels which served the fisherman's art on the Sea of Galilee. The women, as in the last century in New England, did all, or nearly all the spinning and weaving, which were known only as household arts; and they added skillful embroidery with the needle, in which later ingenuity has not considerably improved upon them. The chief avocation of the Jew, however, was agriculture. But what modern farmer, with his well-fenced farm, his bursting barns and granaries, his plows, and drills, and reapers, and mowers, and threshers, in the midst of which he stands bewildered by the very multiplicity of the conveniences that are offered to him, would recognize the Jewish agriculturist? An indescribable thing which they called a plow curried the earth for sowing; a second currying covered in the seed, which no wonder the fowls of the air came and devoured. The ripened grain was sometimes gathered by the sickle, more frequently pulled up by the roots. The stalks gave the housewife her fuel; the cattle trampled out the grain to thresh it; the farmer tossed it in the air against the wind to winnow it; and, finally, he buried it in the ground to store it. Wheat was the staple product of the farmer; but the vineyard was a greater favorite than the farm. These vineyards covered the now bare and barren hillsides of Judea, which were terraced to their very summit, and produced every variety of fruit which a climate that commingles the torrid and the temperate zones can easily supply. But wild beasts preyed upon them; wilder men plundered them; and neither the thick walls of stone, nor the almost impenetrable hedges, nor the watchman, who never left them in the ripening season, day or night, were able to afford them adequate protection. In short,

## IN EXCELSIS GLORIA.

THIBAUT, 1254.

1. Christ is born of maid - en fair; Hark! the her - alds in the air!
2. Shep - herds saw those an - gels bright Car - ol - ing in glo - rious light;
3. Christ is come to save man - kind, As in ho - ly page we find,

Thus a - dor - ing hear them there, "In ex - cel - sis glo - ri - a!"
"God, His Son, is born to - night In ex - cel - sis glo - ri - a!"
There - fore sing with rev - 'rent mind, "In ex - cel - sis glo - ri - a!"

agriculture, in the degenerate days of Judaism, was pursued in Palestine under circumstances scarcely more favorable than those which existed in East Tennessee during the late Civil War. Such, briefly etched, was the civil and social condition of the Jews at the time of Christ. A military despotism, that cared nothing for the people except to gather from their hard-earned pittance all that rapacity could extort, subjected them to a most corrupt, oppressive, and nefarious taxation. Courts of justice existed only in name: the military rulers, who occupied every considerable town, were in fact the supreme judges of the land. Robbery and violence were the common curse of the entire country, and compelled the people to dwell in towns and travel in companies for protection. The houses, in the case of the peasants, were wretched one-roomed huts of mud; in the case of the wealthiest, barren of the simplest necessities of modern life, though ornate with luxury. The table was bare of modern delicacies; but the dress outrivaled ours, if not in taste, at least in showy ornaments. An almost roadless country confined the people to their houses, or left them to make their journeys chiefly upon foot; and a territory cut off from other lands, excluding the people from commerce, and all but the simplest domestic manufactures, made them almost of necessity a nation of farmers and gardeners, as a little later their dispersion through the world drove them from the farm to the peddler's pack, and later to the shop. Such, in brief outline, was the condition of the Jewish people when the story of Christ's life opens ; a nation with some forms of luxury, but without the arts and sciences of civilization ; with the ritual of an ancient religion, but without the spirit of a true one ; with the ruins of a once noble republic, but without that life of liberty which alone makes the true state. * *

About five miles south of Jerusalem lies the little village of Bethlehem. It is one of the oldest towns of Palestine, and one of the most noted. Near it is the tomb where Jacob buried his much-loved Rachel. In the valleys which it overlooks was the field of Boaz, where Ruth gleaned for grain and harvested a husband. Within its precincts, David, her great-grandson, was born ; here

he was anointed king ; and in the neighboring fields, where a thousand years later the birth of the Son of David was announced to the watching shepherds, he watched his father's flocks. Here, in his after-history, his three officers broke through the Philistine host to bring their king water from the well of his childhood. And hither, in the fourth century after Christ, Jerome, fleeing from persecution, lived for a quarter of a century, engaged in his great work, the composition of the Latin translation of the Scriptures, the accepted version of the Roman Catholic Church. In this little hamlet, for the village was an inconsiderable one, Jesus was born. The day of his birth is unknown. The Christmas, which by common consent is celebrated throughout

## MORTALS, AWAKE.

GEORGE KINGSLEY.
SAMUEL MEDLEY, 1780.

Con spirito.

1. Mor - tals, a - wake, with an-gels join, And chant the sol - emn lay; Joy, love, and grat - i - tude combine To hail th' aus - pi - cious day, To hail th' aus - pi - cious day.
2. In Heav'n the rapturous song be - gan, And sweet ser - aph - ic fire Thro' all the shin - ing legions ran, And strung and tuned the lyre, And strung and tuned the lyre.
3. Down thro' the por - tals of the sky Th' impetuous tor - rent ran; And an - gels flew, with eager joy, To bear the news to man, To bear the news to man.
4. Hail, Prince of life! for - ev - er hail, Re - deemer, broth - er, friend! Tho' earth, and time, and life should fail, Thy praise shall nev - er end, Thy praise shall nev - er end.

Christendom as his birthday, was fixed upon by Pope Julius I. in the fourth century. Even the year is involved in uncertainty. We know, however, that Cæsar Augustus was emperor of Rome, and that Herod was drawing toward the close of his reign as king of Judea. Of his mother we know but little. She was of the tribe of Judah, belonged to a royal family, traced her genealogy back to David, and was connected by marriage with one of the chief priests. She was a woman of warm heart, ardent impulses, and resolute will. This much the brief sketches of her life and character disclose. At the time of the annunciation, she started, with impetuous haste and unattended, for a journey across the country from Galilee to Judea to visit

her cousin Elizabeth, no slight undertaking in those days. Later, dreading lest in her son's religious zeal he should destroy himself, with the enthusiasm of an invincible love she undertook to pass through the crowd, and, with loving compulsion, bring him home to the rest which her mother-heart saw he so greatly needed. Finally, standing with pierced and broken heart the resolute witness of his sufferings and death upon the cross, she looked on, a patient sufferer with him to the last. She was a devout, God-fearing woman, free from the ceremonial degeneracy of her times, possessed a good religious education, was more familiar with Scripture than with rabbinical lore, was of thoughtful disposition, and possessed in a devout, emotional imagination the characteristics of an ancient prophetess. Her thanksgiving psalm at the time when the angel announced to her the anticipated birth of Jesus, reminds us strongly of the ancient odes which Aaron's sister, Miriam, wrote when Israel had crossed the Red Sea, and Samuel's mother, Hannah, uttered when her child was consecrated to the service of God. Of his reputed father, Joseph, we know even less. He belonged to the poorest of the peasantry. He was a carpenter by trade, an avocation which included house-building and carving. His little shop was in the village of Nazareth. He, too, claimed royal blood, but manifested no such royal characteristics as did his wife. A simple peasant he seems to have been, an upright man, obedient alway to the divine command, but somewhat timid withal, and of no great influence in his little community. He died, apparently, before Jesus became of age, and, as we know but little of him, so with him our history has but little to do. We have called him Christ's reputed father; for Jesus always claimed to be the Son of God, and finally died in attestation of that claim. Its significance is interpreted to us by the annunciation which heralded his advent. For when to the yet Virgin Mary an angelic messenger announced the son to

## SUN OF MY SOUL.
*Reverently.*

W. H. MONK.
REV. J. KEBLE, 1827.

1. Sun of my soul, Thou Sa - viour dear, It is not night if Thou be near;
2. When the soft dews of kind - ly sleep My weary eye - lids gent - ly steep,
3. A - bide with me from morn till eve, For without Thee I can - not live;
4. If some poor wand'ring child of Thine Have spurn'd to-day the voice di - vine,

Oh, may no earth-born cloud a - rise To hide Thee from Thy ser -vant's eyes.
Be my last thought, how sweet to rest For ev - er on my Sa-viour's breast.
A - bide with me when night is nigh, For without Thee I dare not die.
Now, Lord, the gra - cious work be - gin; Let him no more lie down in sin.

Watch by the sick; enrich the poor
With blessings from Thy boundless store;
Be every mourner's sleep to-night,
Like infant slumbers, pure and light.

Come near and bless us when we wake,
Ere through the world our way we take,
Till in the ocean of Thy love
We lose ourselves in heaven above.

whom she should give birth, perplexed, she asked the question, "How shall this be, seeing I know not a man?" and received the answer, "The Holy Ghost shall come upon thee, and the power of the Highest shall overshadow thee; therefore also that holy thing which shall be born of thee shall be called the Son of God." We accept, undoubting, the verity of this narrative, and reverently recognize the mystery of his birth who is the only-begotten Son of the Infinite Father.

He was born, we have said, in Bethlehem, though his parents were Galileans. Cæsar Augustus had ordered a census to be taken, whether of the empire, or only of Palestine, is perhaps uncertain. In compliance with the Jewish custom, each family went up to its own city to be enrolled; for this purpose, Joseph and Mary, of the house and lineage of David, went up to David's city. The little inn was crowded; there was no room for them there; they were compelled to seek refuge in a stable. The limestone hills of Southern Judea abound with caves, which are often used for this purpose. The one in which tradition asserts that Jesus was born is still shown the traveler by the reverential monks. Simple as was the birth of him whose advent was to revolutionize the world, it was attended with some singular and significant events, which have ever since surrounded it with a peculiar romantic interest. The imaginary portraits of the Infant and his mother have been a favorite theme of the artist from the earliest ages of the Church. The account of the shepherds watching their flocks by night, and startled by the angelic announcement of the Messiah's birth; of the devout Simeon and Anna in the Temple, recognizing in the child the promised hope of Israel; of the wise men of the East following the star, and offering to the child Jesus their treasures brought from afar, have become familiarized to every child by many a sermon, song, and story. One of these incidents, however, deserves special mention here, both because of its inherent significance and its influence on the life of Jesus. Not only by the Jews, by the whole world a Messiah was expected. Mankind not only sadly needed, but sorrowfully waited a new revelation. The people believed all religions to be equally true; the philosophers esteemed them all equally false. Humanity confessed itself ignorant of its God and of its future. The poetic fictions of Hades and Elysium no longer satisfied the reason or touched the imagination. "Is there any old woman," cried Cicero, "silly

## THE KING OF LOVE.

Animation.

J. B. DYKES
H. W. BAKER, 1857.

1. The King of Love my Shep-herd is, Whose good - ness fail-eth nev - er; I
2. Where streams of liv - ing wa - ter flow, My ran - som'd soul He lead - eth, And
3. Per - verse and fool - ish, oft I strayed, But yet in love He sought me, And
4. In death's dark vale I fear no ill, With Thee, dear Lord, be - side me; Thy

*After last verse.*

noth - ing lack if I am His, And He is mine for - ev - er.
where the ver-dant pas - tures grow, With food ce - les - tial feed - eth.
on His shoul-der gent - ly laid, And home, re - joic-ing, brought me.
rod and staff my com - fort still, Thy Cross be-fore to guide me. A - men.

Thou spread'st a table in my sight,
Thy blessing grace bestoweth;
And oh, the transport of delight
With which my cup o'erfloweth.

And so, through all the length of days
Thy goodness faileth never;
Good Shepherd, may I sing Thy praise
Within Thy house forever!

enough still to fear the monsters of hell?" In God none longer hoped. For ages in the Egyptain Temple the inscription had been read, "I am she that was, and is, and shall be, and no one has ever drawn aside my veil." For years the Athenians had worshipped at the altar of an unknown god; and no wonder, since the known gods were despicable. They were no longer the subjects of even a superstitious reverence. The oracles were silent. The temples were desecrated by vices which were banished from society. Plato forbade intemperance *except* in the feast of Bacchus. "It is difficult," says Pliny, "to say whether it might not be better for men to have no religion than to have such a one as ours."

Perhaps this universal discontent had begotten a hope of relief. Perhaps the mysterious promise made to Adam in the garden—the seed of the woman shall bruise the serpent's head—had repeated itself vaguely in the expectancy of mankind. Perhaps the echoes of the Jewish prophetic writings had been indistinctly caught up by other nations amongst whom the Jewish people had been dispersed. Certain it is that more or less definitely this expectation had found expression. Socrates in his last hours had commended his disciples to search the world for a Charmer able to redeem from fear of death. Confucius had prophesied the appearance of a sage in the West whose coming should revolutionize the world; and a deputation sent forth from China to learn of him, brought back with them the reformed religion, but heartless philosophy of Buddha. "Among many," writes Tacitus, "there was a persuasion that in the ancient books of the priesthood it was written that at this precise time the East should become mighty, and that the sovereigns of the world should issue from Judea." "In the East," writes Suetonius, "an ancient and consistent opinion prevailed that it was fated there should issue at this time from Judea those who should obtain universal dominion." Among these prophecies of the "coming man," none was so clear and definite as that of Zoroaster, the founder of the Persian religion. He had foretold the coming of a prophet who should be begotten in a supernatural way; should bring a new revelation to a waiting world; should conquer Ahriman, the spirit of evil; should found a kingdom of righteousness and peace. Later

## THE STAR WHOSE SHINING.

Moderato con espress.

JAS. C. SELLERS.

1. The star whose shining led the way Be-fore the wise men's feet, To where the Holy
2. Oh, sym-bol of that greater Light, Once shown in mor-tal guise, Whose glory flashes
3. Lead us across the mountains cold, The plains, the torrents wide, Un-til we too our

In-fant lay In Mary's arms so sweet, Has never ceased its light to shed Adown up-on our
on men's sight From far Judean skies, Shine down on us with hallow'd ray, Pierce thro' dark self and
King behold, Kneel lowly at His side. Lead us across the mountains cold, The plains, the torrents

race, And by its beams they still are led Who yearn to see His face.
sin; En-light-en all this earthly way Our life with-out, with-in.
wide, Un-til we too our King behold, Kneel low-ly at His side.

traditions, borrowed, perhaps, from the Jews during their captivity, led his disciples to expect that he would come of the seed of Abraham. These disciples were careful students of the stars. The heavenly bodies were accepted by them as symbols and manifestations of the deity. Astrology was thus at once the foundation of knowledge and of worship. Science and religion were one. The priests were savants. The stars were the subjects of their studies and their adoration; they were believed to exercise an important influence on the destinies of mankind; a comprehension of their movements was believed to afford valuable information concerning the future. To placate the baneful star, to adore the beneficent one, was in large measure the object of their worship. In their nightly studies, these priests and philosophers of the olden time were surprised by the sudden appearance of a strangely brilliant star. It is historically certain that a remarkable conjunction of Jupiter and Saturn occurred at this time.

Possibly it was this that attracted their attention; possibly a comet or a meteor, specially sent by God as the herald of his Son. Whatever it may have been, they rightly interpreted it as a sign that the long-expected Deliverer had come. A deputation of their number followed it westward. It led them toward the kingdom of Judea; then it seems to have vanished from their sight. Uncertain which way to go, they directed their steps to the capital. Here, in Jerusalem, they thought to find an aroused and enthusiastic people paying their homage to the new-born king. To their surprise, no one had even heard of him. Their anxious inquiries came to the jealous ears of Herod; the Sanhedrim were assembled; all Jerusalem was thrown into ferment. The Scribes, studying their ancient writings, counseled the wise men that Bethlehem was the birthplace of the anticipated Messiah. Directed, first by this prophecy, then by the star—which now re-appeared—they found, at length, the object of their search, and offered to the infant Jesus their treasures of frankincense and

### O COME, EMMANUEL.

J. M. NEALE *fr* FROM 13TH CENTURY.

myrrh. Significant as was this visit of the Magi as a fulfillment of the prophecy, "Gentiles shall come to thy light, and kings to the brightness of thy rising," it was equally important in its effect upon Jesus. Humanly speaking, it nearly cost him his life.

We have said that Herod was the King of the Jews. It is perhaps doubtful whether a worse king ever sat on the throne of a suffering people. He is fairly entitled to the cognomen of Great only by his pre-eminence in wickedness. His whole career exhibits him as a cunning adventurer, an unscrupulous self-seeker, and a relentless despot. He was made governor of Galilee by his father at the early age of fifteen. He demonstrated his energy and courage by his successful campaign against the brigands who infested its northern mountains. But this energy and courage was directed by an ambition wholly selfish. Perceiving the growing power of Rome, he secured its favor by oppressive taxation, at the cost of his own people. So effectually did he alienate their affections, that, on their complaint, he was summoned to trial before the Sanhedrim, and escaped the penalties justly incurred by his oppressions only by flight. Nothing daunted, he courted successfully the favor of the Roman rulers. With the craftiness of a wily politician, studying the complications at Rome which resulted in the establishment of the Roman Empire, he succeeded in securing the favor and patronage, in succession, of Cassius, of Antony, and of Cæsar. Upon the fall of his respective patrons, he transferred his allegiance, with unblushing assurance, to their rivals and successors. Through Antony's influence he was proclaimed King of Judea by the Roman Senate. Upon Antony's fall, Cæsar confirmed him in his position ; and, as he always rendered a good revenue to his Roman masters, the just complaints of his subjects were unavailing against him. A time-server at home as

## CHRISTMAS DAY.

SUSAN COOLIDGE.

1. The Christmas chimes are peal - ing high Beneath the sol - emn Christmas sky, And
2. In low - ly hut and pal - ace hall Peasant and king keep fes - ti - val, And

blow - ing winds their notes pro - long, Like ech - oes from an an - gel's song;
childhood wears a fair - er guise, And tend - 'rer shine all moth - er - eyes;

Good-will and peace, peace and good-will, Ring out the car - ols glad and
The a - ged man for - gets his years, The mirth - ful heart is doub - ly

gay, Telling the heaven - ly mes - sage still, That Christ the Child was born to - day.
gay, The sad are cheat - ed of their tears, For Christ the Lord was born to - day.

well as abroad, all religions were equally accepted by him as a means of securing popular favor. He rebuilt the Temple at Jerusalem for the Jews ; he constructed another on Mount Gerizim for the Samaritans ; he established a heathen worship in Cæsarea for the Romans. He was alike regardless of all considerations of justice, all obligations of religion, and all claims of natural affection. His jealousy of real or fancied rivals increased with his increasing power. He formed a design of establishing on the Jewish throne a permanent Herodian dynasty, and making of the Jewish nation again an independent, though not a free people. Whatever, to his suspicious nature, seemed to stand in the way of this design, no scruple prevented him from removing, at whatever cost. A terrible distemper, which finally brought his wretched life to a yet more wretched end, increased toward its close his unreasonable suspicions, and aggravated the asperities of his temper. Every one seemed, to his jealous disposition, to be conspiring against his throne. In succession, his wife's grandfather, his wife herself, and three of his own sons, were slain by his command, sacrifices to his insane suspicions. Such a monarch could ill brook a rival king of the Jews. The fact that the wise men of his own land agreed in testifying that ancient prophecy foretold the birth of such a prince and deliverer intensified his jealousy, and strengthened his malign purpose. At first, with his customary craft, he bade the Magi seek out the young Messiah, that he too might worship him. That, when he found himself mocked by them, his rage passed all bounds, is consonant with all we know of his character. His cruel order for the massacre of the infant children of Bethlehem is quite in keeping with the cruelties of the age, the absolute authority he possessed, and the other

## THE BIRTH OF CHRIST.

A. REICHARDT.
ALFRED TENNYSON.

Moderato.

1. The time draws near the birth of Christ; The moon is hid— the night is still; The Christmas
2. Each voice four chang-es on the wind, That now di-late and now decrease, Peace and good-

bells from hill to hill Answer each oth - er in the mist. Four voi-ces
will, good-will and peace, Peace and good-will to all mankind. Rise, hap-py

of four hamlets round From far and near, on mead and moor, Swell out and fail, as if a
morn! rise, ho-ly morn! Draw forth the cheerful day from night; O Father! touch the east and

door Were shut be-tween me and the sound; Swell out and fail, as if a door Were shut be-
light The light that shone when hope was born; O Father! touch the east and light The light that

tween me and the sound, Were shut be-tween me and the sound.
shone when hope was born, The light that shone when hope was born.

well-known facts of his career. It fulfilled the prophecy of the Psalmist, "The kings of the earth set themselves, and the rulers take counsel together against the Lord and against his anointed." His measures were as unsuccessful as they were monstrous. Jesus, escaping with his parents from Judea, remained in Egypt till Herod's death, a few months later. Then they returned by a wide detour to Joseph's home, Nazareth in Galilee. Here Joseph resumed his handicraft after his long absence ; and here Jesus spent his childhood and youth, growing up in his parent's home, and subject to their will.

Galilee is the New England of Palestine. The White Mountains of the Holy Land tower up on its northern boundary ten thousand feet above the level of the sea. The snow never leaves their summit. The flowers never leave their verdure-clad vales. "Lebanon carries," says an Arab proverb, "winter on its head, spring on its shoulders, and harvest in its bosom, while summer sleeps at its feet." Cool breezes from these snow-clad peaks fan the country which they overlook. The hills are thickly wooded. Silvery streams water its verdant glades. Wild flowers in abundance fill the air with their fragrance. The walnut, palm, olive, and fig cover its southern slopes. The dwarf oak, intermixed with tangled shrubberies of hawthorn and arbutus, clothes its

## SONGS OF PRAISE.

Sebastian Bach.
J. Montgomery, 1819.

1. Songs of praise the An - gels sang, Heav'n with hal - le - lu - jahs rang,
2. Songs of praise a - woke the morn, When the Prince of Peace was born;
3. Heaven and earth must pass a - way, Songs of praise shall crown that day;
4. And shall man a - lone be dumb, Till that glo - rious king - dom come?

When Je - ho - vah's work be - gun, When He spake, and it was done.
Songs of praise a - rose when He Cap - tive led cap - tiv - i - ty.
God will make new heavens and earth; Songs of praise shall hail their birth.
No; the Church de - lights to raise Psalms and hymns and songs of praise.

5. Saints below, with heart and voice,
Still in songs of praise rejoice;
Learning here, by faith and love,
Songs of praise to sing above.

6. Borne upon the latest breath,
Songs of praise shall conquer death;
Then, amidst eternal joy,
Songs of praise their powers employ.

northern hills. Fertile upland plains, green forest glades, wild, picturesque glens, with the beautiful Lake Tiberias embosomed in the midst of romantic mountain scenery, combine to render Galilee one of the richest and most beautiful sections of Palestine, if not of the Oriental world. Its towns and villages, once busy, though now deserted and in ruins, formerly added the charm of industry and life. Among the most favored spots of this favored region is the village of Nazareth. It reposes in the bosom of a beautiful valley, secluded by surrounding hills, and filled with cornfields, vineyards, and gardens. Sheltered from the bleaker winds of the north, it luxuriates in the fragrant blossoms and ripened fruits of the pomegranate, orange, fig, and olive. The neighboring hill behind the town commands a magnificent view of the surrounding country. From its summit Jesus must often have looked upon Galilee spread out as a map beneath his feet. On the north the snowy peak of Hermon lifts itself up in clear relief against the background of the deep blue sky. On the east, over the intervening hills, a glimpse of the Lake Tiberias reveals itself. Close at hand was the mountain where, later, he preached that ever-memorable discourse known as

FROM MURILLO'S "IMMACULATE CONCEPTION"

the "Sermon on the Mount." Within the range of his vision were Acre, famous in its after-history for its successful resistance to the protracted siege of Napoleon ; Cana, where the water was made wine ; Nain, where the widow's son was raised ; Endor, where the witch appeared to Saul ; Jezreel, the royal residence of the infamous Ahab. Before him nestled his own beautiful village of Nazareth, while beyond it Mount Carmel, the retreat of the ancient prophet Elijah, jutted out into the Mediterranean, the blue of whose waters, sparkling in the sun, was just discernible in the far northwest. Amid these romantic mountains and fertile vales Jesus spent his boyhood. Here he often wandered, picking the wild flowers, gratifying that love of nature which so characterized his after-life and teachings. Into the mountain solitudes with which this rural region abounds he loved to retreat from the distasteful crowd and bustle of the great cities. Here he commenced his ministry. Here he wrought most of his miracles. First in the synagogue, and then in the valleys and on the hill-sides of Galilee, he preached most of the discourses which have been preserved and handed down to us.

## ALL HAIL, THOU BETHLEHEM!

C. E. WRIGHT.

1. The dusky robes of ev - 'ning fell, Where slept the poet in David's well, Shrouding the town of
2. Seraphs, on pin-ions of the dove, With harps of gold and hymns of love, Hung in the star - ry
3. From sacred Jordan's flow - ing tide, Across Judean pastures wide, Pressed on the band with

Is - ra - el, The town of Beth - le - hem. Where pa - tient ox - en eat their corn; Be-
sky a - bove The star of Beth - le - hem. The shepherds saw its dazzling light Gleam
hast - y stride, To greet fair Beth - le - hem. And hark! around that manger low, The

*ritard.*     *ad lib.*

fore the blushing dawn of morn That night a royal babe was born, The babe of Bethlehem.
thro' the chambers of the night, And, guided by its radience bright, Set forth for Bethlehem.
saints a - bove and saints below, Their trumpets of salvation blow! All hail! thou Bethlehem!

From the simple fishermen who lived and labored on the shore of Lake Tiberias he selected most of his companions and apostles. Among these mountains he organized his little Church, and sent his followers forth to preach "the kingdom of heaven is at hand." And at the setting of the sun, in the quiet wooded glades of Galilee, rather than in the synagogue and the Temple, he sought that solitude for which his heart yearned, that he might commune with his Father and His God.

The influences which surrounded Christ in his childhood certainly could have contributed but little to the greatness of his ripened character. The inhabitants of Galilee were a simple humble peasantry, industrious, but plain ; unpretending in their appearance, untutored in their habits. Their pursuits and modes of life were very simple. They caught fish on the lakes ; they reared flocks and herds on the mountain sides ; they cultivated corn and olives in the valleys and on the slopes of the hills. They had little wealth. They had not the culture and refinement which belonged to the richer and more luxurious inhabitants of Judea. Twenty of their chief cities had been given by Solomon to Hiram, King of Tyre, and their inhabitants, intermarried with other races, no longer preserved a pure Jewish blood. Their religion was perhaps as pure, but it was far more simple. The elaborate ceremonialism of the later Pharisees had never taken strong hold among them. Their very speech was provincial. The haughty aristocrats of Southern Palestine despised this peasantry. They scorned their poverty; their simplicity; their corrupted blood; their seeming irreligion. That Jesus was a Galilean was in their eyes a sufficient and conclusive condemnation of his claim to be the Messiah of the nation; while, for some reason unknown, Nazareth possessed throughout the country a particularly evil reputation. "Can any good come out of Nazareth?" was a proverb not only in Judea, but accepted apparently even in Galilee itself. Jesus' education, whether at home or at school, was of the simplest kind. Many years before, Samuel had established the first seats of learning, the schools of the prophets. The ruins of these institutions still remained,

## SLEEP, MY CHILD.

*Stephen Glover.*

*Not too fast.*

*Solo and Chorus.*

1. See the maid-en moth-er-mild, Bend-ing o'er the wondrous child! Is it bless-ed-ness or pain, Joy the heart can scarce con-tain?
2. Could she with the sa-cred seers Pierce the se-crets of the years, Would a mother's yearning pray That the cup might pass a-way!
3. Hear the cra-dle-song she sings To the low-ly King of kings: "Sweetly sleep, O Son of mine, Mys-ter-y of Love di-vine!
4. "Hope of all the a-ges, thou, Ne'er may trou-ble cloud thy brow! Sweet the pain my heart doth thrill, Sleep, my child, nor dream of ill."

*Quartette. pp*

La la la la, La la la la, La la la la, La la la la, La la la la,

La la la la, La la la la, La la la Sleep, my child, nor dream of ill.

*The Chorus should be sung in a subdued and gentle manner.*

in which the degenerate scribes were taught the theological dialectics of the time, and so, in the popular imagination, were prepared for the ministry of the Word. From them proceeded those traditions and ceremonial refinements against which Christ later brought the whole influence of his life and teaching to bear. These schools were mostly at Jerusalem. It is not certain that there were any in Galilee. It is certain Christ never attended them. He never sympathized with the ritualism which they inculcated; and his parents possessed neither the means to give him an elaborate education, nor the learning which they could impart themselves. But, in addition to these higher seminaries, there was a parochial school in every village. Common-school education we have borrowed from Judaism, though we have improved the pattern. A far larger proportion of the people could read and write in Palestine in the days of Christ than in England in the days of Henry the Eighth. The unlearned fishermen by the Sea of Galilee were not absolutely illiterate. Few were the Jews who could not read their own Scriptures. In every synagogue was established an elementary school. Here a Rabbi gathered the children of the village, taught them to read and cipher, instructed them in their own national history and in the requirements of the law, catechized them in the Jewish Scriptures, afforded them some knowledge of the later commentaries which the scribes had founded thereon, and occasionally added some little instruction on such natural history and physical science as the imperfect knowledge of the day afforded. This parish pedagogue gave Christ his only schooling. Of Greek, Roman, and Oriental literature and philosophy he acquired no knowledge by any ordinary method of study. His mother, a devout

## OUR CHRISTMAS FESTAL.

ANATOLIUS, A. D. 450.
JOHN MASON NEALE Jr., 1862.

1. Al - le - lu - ia! Al - le - lu - ia! Al - le - lu - ia! A great and mighty won - der
2. Al - le - lu - ia! Al - le - lu - ia! Al - le - lu - ia! And we with them tri - um-phant,
3. Al - le - lu - ia! Al - le - lu - ia! Al - le - lu - ia! And i - dol forms shall per - ish,

Our Christmas fes - tal brings! On earth, a low - ly in - fant, Be - hold the King of kings!
Re - peat the hymn a - gain, "To God on high be glo - ry, And peace on earth to men!"
And er - ror shall de - cay, And Christ shall wield His sceptre, Our Lord and God for aye!

The word is made in - car - nate, De - scending from on high; And cher - u - bim sing an - thems
Since all He comes to ran - som, By all be He a - dored, The In - fant born in Bethlehem,
And i - dol forms shall per - ish, And er - ror shall de - cay, And Christ shall wield His scep - tre,

To shepherds, from the sky. Al - le - lu - ia! Al - le - lu - ia! Al - le - lu - ia!
The Saviour and the Lord! Al - le - lu - ia! Al - le - lu - ia! Al - le - lu - ia!
Our Lord and God for aye! Al - le - lu - ia! Al - le - lu - ia! Al - le - lu - ia!

and godly woman, taught him the Jewish Scriptures at home. The Jewish law required every parent to teach his children some trade. In compliance with this law, Jesus worked at his father's bench, learning his handicraft. He went with his parents to the village synagogue, where he would hear every Sabbath the law and the prophets read. Perhaps he would hear, too, some scribe expound them, not developing and applying their prophecies and sublime principles but concealing them by puerile discussions concerning idle ceremonies and human traditions. Occasionally he went up with his parents to the Temple at Jerusalem on the Jewish feast-day; but this brief journey of sixty or seventy miles was the utmost extent of his travels. One such visit is the only incident of his youth of which we have any authentic record. In connection with the Temple were rooms which were used by the Rabbis for higher seminaries of learning. Here they were accustomed to gather, and discuss the more difficult problems of their theological science. Jesus, though but twelve years of age, found the chief attractions of the Tem-

ple here. The magnificent courts, the imposing ritual, the solemn sacrificial service, the grand chorals from the trained choirs and accompanying orchestra, had for him no such fascination as these schools, where he might learn more fully the meaning of that law whose true meaning his village Rabbi was utterly unable to unfold to him. Leaving the crowded courts and the solemn

## HARK! A THRILLING SONG.

H. Proch.
T. G. La Moille.

1. Hark! a thrill-ing song from Heaven Wak-ing ju-bi-lee, Where the shining wings come
2. In a man-ger lies the Saviour, Lo! the star o'erhead! And the long-ex-pect-ed

cleaving Thro' yon starry sea. Hear the an-gel chorus telling, "Peace, good-will to men!"
glo-ry Lights His humble bed. Best of Abram's choicest children, Son of man di-vine,

And our hearts with rapture swelling, Ech-o peace a-gain. Hark! they come, re-
We beseech Thy lov-ing fav-or; Make our life like Thine! Hark! the an-gel

joic-ing her-alds, O'er Ju-de-an plain, With good tid-ings of great glad-ness;
band re-peat-ing, O'er ex-pect-ant plain: "Wake, O earth, re-turn glad greet-ing,

"'Tis Mes-si-ah's reign," With good tid-ings of great gladness: "'Tis Mes-si-ah's reign."
For Mes-si-ah's reign, Wake, O earth, re-turn glad greeting For Mes-si-ah's reign!"

7

festal service, he wandered off in search of these Temple schools, and here he was found after the feast was over and the people had dispersed, sitting in the midst of the doctors, listening to their exposition, and eagerly inquiring for some deeper and more spiritual truth than, with all their learning, they were able to afford him. They were astonished at the precocity of his understanding ; and, if we may form any judgment of the catechizing he gave them from his later questioning, were no less puzzled than surprised. This little incident, which impressed itself strongly upon his mother's mind, gives us glimpse enough of his childhood to know that it was no ordinary one. He certainly had an eager appetite for religious truth. He exhibited, though in a vague and shadowy way, some consciousness of his character and his mission. Increasingly he displayed that unconscious and natural grace in heart and in demeanor which in his ministry aided in drawing such crowds to listen to his words. While untaught, save by his Father, God, through the lessons of nature and the inspirations of the Divine Spirit, he grew in stature and knowledge, and in favor with God and with man.

Christ was thirty years of age before he entered upon his public ministry. The universal expectation of a prince who should reëstablish the throne of David and reinstate the ruined kingdom of Israel was then intensified by the appearance of a preacher

## TO THY CRADLE THRONE.

W. B. Bradbury.

1. The wise men to thy cra - dle throne, O In - fant Saviour, brought of old
2. Shine on us too, bright east - ern star, Thine own bap - tiz - ed Gen - tile band,
3. Till we have brought the fine gold rare Of zeal, that giv - eth all for love;
4. Till bit - ter tears our eyes have wept, Be - cause our wil - ful hearts would err;
5. All meet for Thee, our own A - dored! Our suff - 'ring Saviour, God and King!

The incense meet for God a - lone, Sharp myrrh and gifts of shin - ing gold.
Till we have found our Lord from far, And come, an off - 'ring in our hand.
Till we have prayed the heart's true prayer, Earth's fra - grant in - cense borne a - bove.
Worship, and love, and sor - row met, Gold, frankincense, and sa - cred myrrh.
Ac - cept the gold and in - cense, Lord, Ac - cept the myrrh we hum - bly bring.

of singular character and great power, who announced, with seeming authority, " The kingdom of heaven is at hand." To understand the true character and career of Jesus, we must interrogate a little the herald who preceded him and proclaimed his coming. A peculiar characteristic of the ancient Jewish Church was the prophets. Beginning with Moses, and appearing singly in certain epochs of subsequent history, they were first organized as an order under Samuel, during the reigns of Saul and David. Schools for their education were established by him. They became a numerous and influential class. In the darkest days of the church, Obadiah hid a hundred of them in a single cave. In the reign of Jehoshaphat four hundred were gathered by the king for counsel. They were the preachers, the poets, and the political teachers and counselors of Palestine. They were subject to no ecclesiastical superior, and were bound by no rules of discipline, and by no other creed than faith in God and acceptance of his Word. They were set apart to their office by no public ordination. Whoever felt his soul burdened with a message of truth was ordained thereby to proclaim it. They were taken from every tribe and every occupation. Women occasionally, though exceptionally, filled the sacred office. Miriam, Deborah, Huldah, were among the prophets—the latter apparently at the head of the prophetic school in Jerusalem, and recognized by the court as the chief theologian of her time. David and Saul were prophet kings; Amos was a herdsman; Elijah, a Bedouin wanderer; Elisha was called from the plow; Isaiah and Jeremiah were, perhaps, children of prophets. These preachers had neither church, pulpit, or salary; they gathered their congregations wherever they could find them—in the street, the field, the highways. They depended on the hospitality of the pious for their support. They wore a simple dress of sheepskin; lived plainly; abstained from wine; dwelt sometimes in Jerusalem in chambers of the Temple, sometimes in the country in rude huts of their own construction. They generally lived in companies of from twenty to thirty, and traveled through the country, couching their instruction in the form of poems, which they chanted to simple music, accompanying themselves on the rude instruments of their age. A few more leading spirits lived alone, either in the cities, as Isaiah and Jeremiah, or in the wilderness, as Elijah, preaching the truth, still generally in the poetic forms, though not with musical accompaniment. While there were false prophets and time-servers among them, those whose addresses have been preserved were bold, courageous, heroic, patriotic, devout men, fearing God, and therefore not fearing men; denouncing alike the sins of the court, the corruptions of the Church, and

## WHAT STAR IS THIS?

CHAS. COFFIN, 1736.

*mf*

1. What star is this with beams so bright, More beauteous than the noon-day light!
2. See now ful-filled what God decreed, "From Ja-cob shall a star pro-ceed!"
3. The guid-ing star a-bove is bright, With-in them shines a clear-er light,
4. True love can brook no dull de-lay; Nor toil nor dan-gers stop their way;
5. O Je-sus! while the star of grace Al-lures us now to seek Thy face,

It shines to her-ald forth the King, And Gentiles to His cra-dle bring.
And Eastern sa-ges with a-maze Upon the won-drous vis-ion gaze.
Which leads them on with power be-nign To seek the giv-er of the sign,
Home, kindred, fath-erland and all They leave at their Cre-a-tor's call.
Let not our sloth-ful hearts re-fuse The guid-ance of that light to use.

the vices of the people. The most frequent subject of their denunciations was a cold and heartless ceremonialism. The most popular theme of their discourses was the spirituality of true religion. "What doth the Lord require of thee but to do justly, and to love mercy, and to walk humbly with thy God." This was the essence of their teaching.

Such a class could only live in the air of freedom. The destruction of the Jewish independence by the subjugation of the nation under Nebuchadnezzar resulted in the practical destruction of the prophetic order. A few, indeed, surviving that disaster, kept alive the faith and hope of the people during the captivity. The restoration of the state appeared at first to promise the restoration of the Church, with all its functions. But, little by little, the lustre of the ancient prophets dimmed; their voice ceased to echo among the hills of Palestine. Scribes, who united with the priestly party in the endeavor to substitute a religion of ritualism for one of practical godliness, gradually took their place. The manuscripts of some of the more prominent of the prophets were preserved, and read every Sabbath in the public service of the synagogue, but by men who did not appreciate their spirit, and could not, therefore, impart it to others. The reminiscence of this ancient order lingered only as a tradition of the ancient glory of the nation. The sudden reappearance, therefore, of a prophet startled all Palestine. His birth, like that of Jesus, whose second cousin he was, was preceded by singular and supernatural indications of his future character and mission. He was consecrated from his infancy to the life of a Nazarite, the hermit of ancient Judaism. Both his parents belonged to the priestly order, but shared not the priestly vices. He probably received from them an education for the priesthood. In this case he was taught the ancient Hebrew, and was thoroughly instructed in all the details of the Jewish ceremonial law. But he never performed priestly functions. At an early age, disgusted with the political and religious degeneracy of his times, he withdrew from Judea into the wilderness beyond Jordan. Here he lived a solitary life of prayer, of study of the Scripture, and of self-denial. In this he was not alone. Others, like him, had sought refuge from the corruptions of the age in a hermit's life, and had gathered on the banks of the Jordan a few disciples of a misanthropic asceticism. But their efforts at reform had been transitory and inefficacious. From

## GLAD HOPE OF THE AGES.

ELEANOR A. HUNTER.

1. From ev - 'ry spire on Christmas Eve, The Christmas bells ring clearly out Their message of good-
2. A thousand blessed mem'ries throng, The stars are ho - ly signs to them, And from the eyes of
3. To whom that sto - ry, old and sweet, Is but a fa - ble at the best, The Christmas music
4. That they, at last, may see the light Which shines from Bethl'em, and unfold For Christ the treasures

will and peace, With many a call and sil - ver shout. For faithful hearts, the angels' song Still echoes
ev - 'ry child Looks forth the Babe of Bethlehem ; But there are others, not like these, Whose brows are
mocks their ears, And life has naught of joy or rest. Oh! for an angel's voice to pierce The clouds
of their hearts, Richer than spi - cer - y or gold. Hope of the ages, draw Thou near, 'Till all the

in the frost - y air, And by the al - tar low they bow, In ad - o - ra - tion and in prayer.
sad, whose hopes are cross'd, To whom the season brings no cheer, And life's most gracious charm is lost.
grief that o'er them rise, The mists of doubt and un - belief, That veil the blue of Christmas skies.
earth shall own Thy sway, And when Thou reign'st in ev'ry heart It will, indeed, be Christmas day.

this seclusion John at length issued to proclaim to the people the truths which he had made his own by a prayerful study of the ancient prophets, whose successor he was.

His place and time were well chosen. At a ford of the River Jordan, near its mouth, where the highway from the neighboring city of Jerusalem crosses this stream, he commenced his public ministry. The scene around was admirably consonant with the stern and gloomy character of the prophet and his teachings. The limestone hills, unsupplied with springs, lift up their barren and precipitous sides in solemn but sterile grandeur. A thin and unfruitful soil affords few fruits and but scanty pasturage. The Dead Sea, whose briny waters entomb the once fertile plains of Sodom and Gomorrah, afforded a significant type of the moral death of the once fair and prosperous Jewish nation, and of the complete destruction so soon to overwhelm it. It was the Sabbatic year. In accordance with the law of Moses, the land lay fallow. Agriculture was for the time forbidden. Even spontaneous growths were left unreaped. The people, relieved from their customary toils, were easily accessible to religious instruction. The whole law of God was this year read to them in solemn assemblage. Such occasions of rest were the prophet's harvestings. Of such the Baptist availed himself. Doubtless a general discontent and a general expectancy of a coming deliverer prepared them for his message. Yet no ordinary man could have produced the impression he produced. He certainly was no ordinary man. His very appearance compelled attention. He wore a simple dress woven of camel's hair. It was gathered about his loins with a leathern girdle. His food was as simple as his dress, and, like it, marked the ascetic. He neither ate bread nor drank wine. He lived on locusts and wild honey. The former, a kind of grasshopper, cooked in various ways, forms to the present day a staple article of food among the poorer peasantry. The latter is found in such abundance in the trunks of trees and the crevices of the rocks, that, to the

## GOOD-WILL TO MEN.

ALEXANDER LEE.

1. "Good-will to men, and peace!" The Christmas song of old, The shepherds caught the joy-ous strain, But its sweetness nev-er told. They heard the an-gel host, They saw the heav'nly light; As their sheep around them si-lent lay, That wondrous, wondrous night.

2. "Good-will to men, and peace!" Sweet Christmas song of old! As the stars sent back its glad re-frain, More brightly flashed their gold. The light the shepherds saw, On that first Christmas morn, Was a light that shed its ra-diance far To a-ges yet un-born.

3. "Good-will to men, and peace!" Oh, Christmas song of eld! No sweet-er song hath mor-tal heard, Nor a fair-er light be-held: It hal-lows all our joy, It gladdens all our mirth, For the choiring an-gels sang it when They hailed the Saviour's birth.

ancient Israelite, the land was described as one flowing with honey. His hair was uncut, his beard untrimmed, his manners those of one little accustomed to the refinements of society. His preaching was as singular as his dress. He startled the people by the boldness of his denunciations. But, like his dress, it characterized the ascetic rather than the true reformer. He was strong, earnest, practical, but more powerful in a fiery assault on wrong than in tender and winning invitations to right. He aroused the conscience. He never attempted to awaken the affections. Christ closed his indignant denunciations of the Pharisees with the most touching and pathetic of appeals, "O Jerusalem, Jerusalem, thou that killest the prophets, and stonest them which are sent unto thee, how often would I have gathered thy children together, even as a hen gathereth her chickens under her wings, and ye would not!" John the Baptist closed his similar scathing rebuke of the same party with solemn warning—"He will burn up the chaff with un-quenchable fire." Yet whether we test his preaching by its character or its effects, it was certainly remarkable. He scouted the idea that Jewish birth gave favor with God. He denounced with vehemence the cere-monialism of the age. He demanded a pure morality as the evidence of godliness. To the tax-gatherer he preached integrity ; to the soldiers, abstinence from violence ; to all the people, practical benevolence. If he did not mix with the people, he understood their life, and preached to it. Crowds flocked to hear him. All Judea felt the in-fluence of his teaching. The people almost universally accepted him as a prophet. Some thought him the Messiah. Many of the lower classes were effectually reformed.

Both Pharisees and Sadducees endeavored at first to secure the prestige of his name by ranking themselves among his disciples. Even a deputation of priests and Levites

## SUN OF CHRISTMAS-TIDE.

H. WEIDT.
NOCHTENHOFER.

1. This night God's great-est kind-ness Is shown us from a - bove; The Child, whom ho - ly an-gels serve, To earth brings peace and love; A thou - sand suns shine not so bright As shines for us this light! My soul, be thou en-light-en'd, Send not this grace a-way; It shines from low-ly man-ger bed,—To all the world, the world, brings day.

2. Tho' moon and stars on high, And glo-rious sun de - part, This bless - ed Light shall nev - er die In an - y hum-ble heart; The shin - ing of its beams so bright Were Heav'n 'mid darkest night! Sun of fair Christmas - tide, Shine on us by Thy grace, Thy light shall be our Christmas joy Till we be-hold, be-hold Thy face.

was sent out by the Sanhedrim to obtain more accurate information as to his char-acter and mission. But the effect of his preaching, if powerful, was also transient. The people, escaping from the magnetism of his presence, forgot the convictions of conscience he had produced. The Phari-sees, finding they could not use him, denied the authority of his mission, though they dared not deny his prophetic claim. He was not a builder, and, like all negative re-formers, his work lacked permanence. He saw clearly the coming wrath of God, but he knew not how to avert the storm which gathered darkly over his nation. He preached a religion of rigid asceticism and of pure morality. He sought to reform the state by returning to a strict allegiance to the principles of ancient Judaism. Jesus compared him to one who endeavored to mend an old garment by patching it with new cloth. He did not perceive that the Mosaic institutions had fulfilled their purpose, and that the world needed new raiment. He prepared the way for the Gospel by unconsciously demonstrating the inefficacy of the law. Standing aloof from the elaborate ritualism of his day, he employed one single and simple ceremony, which the Christian Church, borrowing from him, has continued to the present time. Those that signified their sorrow for sin and their purpose of reformation, he baptized in the River Jordan. Whether he dipped them in the water, or, descending with them into the stream, poured it upon their head, is a question which to the present day divides the most learned scholars of the Church into two theological parties. Whichever form he used, the signification was the same—purification from the past, and consecration of the life for the future. This symbol was

## HARK! THE HOLY VOICES.

GERARD COBB.
CHR. WORDSWORTH, 1862.

1. Hark! the sound of ho - ly voic - es Chant - ing o'er the crys - tal sea,
2. Pa - tri - arch and ho - ly Proph - et, Who prepar'd the way of Christ,
3. They have come from trib - u - la - tion, And have wash'd their robes in blood,

Al - le - lu - ia, Al - le - lu - ia, Al - le - lu - ia, Lord, to Thee;
King, A - pos - tle, Saint, Con - fes - sor, Mar - tyr and E - van - ge - list,
Wash'd them in the blood of Je - sus; Tried they were, and firm they stood;

Mul - ti - tude, which none can num - ber, Like the stars in glo - ry stands,
Saint - ly maid - en, god - ly ma - tron, Wid - ows who have watch'd to prayer,
Mock'd, im - pris - on'd, stoned, tor - ment - ed, Sawn a - sun - der, slain with sword,

Cloth'd in white ap - par - el, hold - ing Palms of vic - t'ry in their hands.
Join'd in ho - ly con - cert, sing - ing To the Lord of all, are there.
They have conquer'd death and Sa - tan By the might of Christ the Lord.

Marching with Thy Cross their banner,
They have triumph'd, following
Thee the Captain of salvation,
Thee their Saviour and their King;
Gladly, Lord, with Thee they suffer'd,
Gladly, Lord, with Thee they died,
And by death to life immortal
They were born and glorified.

Now they reign in heavenly glory,
Now they walk in golden light,
Now they drink, as from a river,
Holy bliss and infinite:
Love and peace they taste for ever,
And all truth and knowledge see
In the beatific vision
Of the blessed Trinity.

already in universal use in Oriental countries. Ablution was customary not only in Palestine, but in Egypt, Greece, and Rome, as a preparation for prayer, and a token of expiation for sin. But it possessed a peculiar significance in Palestine, where every Gentile who entered the Jewish Church was baptized as a sign that he was washed of his past sins and errors, and entered, cleansed, a new life. John did not, therefore, invent the rite which has given him his name of the Baptist. He only employed it. And Christ, finding it already thus employed, and its significance understood, adopted it as the symbol of separation from the world and consecration unto him. But first he signalized his adoption of the rite by being himself baptized.

It was winter. The early wheat was just beginning to clothe the earth with green when rumors of John's preaching reached the ears of Jesus in Nazareth. He accepted the fact as a sign that the time for his public ministry had come. He joined himself to the people that were already flocking in crowds to the River Jordan. He listened, unnoticed and unknown, to the preaching of his herald. He presented himself, one with the multitude, to be baptized by him. But John recognized at once his cousin. Doubtless they had known each other in their youth; and though he knew not till later Jesus' sacred character and mission, he had already perceived his spiritual superiority. He objected to perform a rite which seemed to imply that he was himself in some way Jesus' superior. Reluctantly,

## O THOU, WHO BY A STAR.

THOS. A. ARNE.

1. O Thou, who by a star didst guide The wise men on their way,
2. Al-though by stars Thou dost not lead Thy servants now be-low,
3. As yet we know Thee but in part, But still we trust Thy word,
4. O Saviour, give us then Thy grace, To make us pure in heart,

Un-til it came and stood be-side The place where Je-sus lay.
The Ho-ly Spir-it when they need, Will show them how to go.
That bless-ed are the pure in heart, For they shall see the Lord.
That we may see Thee face to face, Here-af-ter as Thou art.

and only after persuasion, did he yield. The representative of the Old World, and the type and creator of the New, entered together the water. The people, impressed with a singular solemnity, watched this most sacred baptismal service of all time; while in the dove alighting on the head, and the voice from heaven proclaiming Jesus the divine Messiah, were visible and audible indications of the significance of the service. Why, indeed, one who confessed no sin, and therefore needed no repentance, should receive the baptism of repentance has been a sore perplexity to many. It was to John. Jesus has himself solved the problem. He came to preach, as the summation of all duty, "Follow thou me." Therefore it became him to submit to whatever cere-

monies were proper and significant in the case of sinful humanity, and thus to fulfill all righteousness. But in this significant act we recognize more than an example; we perceive a sublime symbol. In Jesus Christ the human race received its baptism. It laid off old faiths. It was introduced into a new life. In the sacred waters which had cleansed Naaman of his leprosy, humanity buried its dead past, rose a new creature in Christ Jesus. Old things passed then forever away. Henceforth all things were to be new.

The possible effect of John the Baptist's preaching on Jesus has been the subject of some bold surmises. The effect of Jesus on John the Baptist's preaching is far more remarkable, though it has been less remarked. Before the baptism John denounced the vices of the people, and warned them of the judgments of God. "Every tree that bringeth not forth good fruit is hewn down and cast into the fire." This was the spirit of his preaching. But when an alarmed people cried out to him, "What shall we do, then?" he could only reply, "He that hath two coats, let him impart to him that hath none." For the tremendous woe of sin he had no remedy to offer but the recommendation of an external reformation and a practical morality. But after Christ's baptism his preaching underwent a radical change. He no longer denounced the vices of the people; he no longer warned of the wrath to come; he no longer addressed himself chiefly to fear and to conscience. He ceased to be a preacher of the law; he became a prophet of the Gospel. The Messiah, whom he had vaguely foretold, he pointed out in Jesus. The kingdom of grace, which was to be, he contrasted with the kingdom of law that had been. Two of his testimonies concerning Jesus are especially significant. The first is his assertion of Christ's character. "I saw, and bore record, that this is the Son of God." This declaration, which he often repeated, is capable of but one signification. It can bear no other interpretation than that which is afforded by the ancient prophets, who had declared that the Messiah should be "God with us; the Lord our righteousness; the mighty God, the everlasting Father." His declaration concerning Christ's mission is not less significant. "Behold the Lamb of God, which

## THY KING COMETH.

H. G. NAGELI.

1. The Ad-vent of our King   Our prayers must now em-ploy,
2. The ev-er-last-ing Son   In-car-nate deigns to be;
3. Daughter of Zi-on rise   To meet thy low-ly King;
4. As Judge, on clouds of light,   He soon will come a-gain,

And we must hymns of wel-come sing   In strains of ho-ly joy.
Him-self a ser-vant's form puts on,   To set his ser-vants free.
Nor let thy faith-less heart des-pise,   The peace He comes to bring.
And His true mem-bers all u-nite   With Him in Heaven to reign.

taketh away the sin of the world." This was a favorite metaphor with him. To understand it, we must remember that the whole Jewish worship was sacrificial. Every act of adoration, of thanksgiving, of confession, was expressed by a sacrifice. The lamb slain on the altar thus became the type of worship in the Jewish mind, the method of approach to God.

But more than that. There was in the Jewish calendar one great national fast-day. It was called the Day of Atonement. On that day expiation was made for the sins of the nation. Two lambs or goats were selected, as near alike in size, form, and color as possible; they were brought to the temple; the priest chose by lot between them; one of these was sacrificed upon the altar; upon the other was bound a piece of scarlet cloth, typical of the sins of the people. This goat was then led off into the wilderness, where he was set free, and seen no more. The significance of the whole service was unmistakable. By the death of the sacrifice the sins of the people were borne away and lost to sight forever; and since one lamb could not both carry them away and be slain on the altar, two were taken to typify the one truth. It is scarcely possible but that this symbolical service was in the mind both of the preacher and the people when he uttered the sermon whose substance has been condensed into a single significant sentence. It was probably preached in the fall, and about the time of the Day of Atonement. "God," said he, "has provided a Lamb. By the sacrifice of his only-begotten Son God will fulfill the prophecies of the Temple service. Upon him he will lay the iniquities of us all, and they will be borne away and felt no more." John does not seem, however, to have preached these sermons until after Christ's return from the temptation in the wilderness. To the record of this singular, and, in some respects, inexplicable experience, we now turn.

In attempting to form a conception of Christ's experience of temptation in the wilderness, so graphically but dramatically described by the evangelists, we are met at the outset by an almost insuperable difficulty. It is impossible for us to conceive of God as tempted with evil—of the Infinite as struggling with the powers of darkness. We can portray to our own thoughts the temptation of Jesus only as a human experience. But this is only part of the greater mystery of the Incarnation. The whole life of Christ is intensely and characteristically human; and this attests its verity. No imaginary conception of an incarnate Son of God would have presented him as hungering, suffering, weeping, struggling with temptation—finally dying. Yet so the Gospels depict him. The humiliation of Jesus is his glory. Nor do we fully conceive that humiliation until we comprehend that he not only took upon him the external conditions of humanity, but entered into experiences of heart-conflict only to be interpreted to us by our own. In endeavoring, then, to conceive of this mysterious struggle, let us frankly confess our inability to fathom the deeper secrets of Christ's divine

## O ZION, HAIL THY KING.

1. Mes - si - ahl at Thy glad ap - proach The howl - ing winds are still;
2. The in - cense of the spring as - cends Up - on the morn - ing gale;
3. Re - newed the earth a robe of light, A robe of beau - ty wears;
4. Let Is - rael to the Prince of Peace A loud ho - san - na sing;

Thy praises fill the lone - ly waste, And breathe from ev - 'ry hill.
Fresh o'er the hill the ro - ses bloom, The lil - ies in the vale.
And in new skies a bright - er sun Leads on the promised years.
With hal - le - lu - jahs and with hymns, O Zi - on, hail thy King.

nature, and content ourselves with depicting his experience as that of one tempted in all points like as we are, save without sin.

Jesus, then, had long pondered upon the wretched condition, not only of his nation, but of the whole world. Heavier and heavier its woes had pressed upon his heart. The solitudes of Galilee had afforded him time for thought. His occasional visits to Jerusalem had afforded him food for thought. He felt, too, that he was the promised and the long-expected Messiah. When the full consciousness of his divine mission and power possessed him can only be a matter of surmise. Some have thought he was first revealed to himself at his baptism. Others have thought his answer to his mother in the Temple. "Wist ye not that I must be about my Father's business?" indicates that he possessed such a consciousness then. It is certainly difficult to conceive that, as an infant in the cradle, he had a full comprehension of his character and his career. Is it not possible that this comprehension gradually dawned upon him? Power is not always conscious power. Among men, genius sometimes bursts suddenly into full bloom as a primrose at twilight. More often it unfolds gradually and unconsciously, little by little the soul learning what endowments God has given it—what work allotted it. So it may have been with Jesus. His divinity may have dawned upon him as gradually as it has upon the world. He who *grew* in favor with God and man may have grown in his own consciousness of character as well. However this may be, the time had now come when his divine consciousness was to assert itself in action. Jesus felt that the time of his disclosure was at hand. He accepted the voice of one crying in the wilderness as a summons to the battle. From the comparative solitudes of Galilee he emerged for the moment, only to plunge into the absolute solitude of the wilderness; perhaps the wild region of country between Jericho and Jerusalem; perhaps the desolate and inhospitable wild beyond the Jordan. From the baptism by John, in which he had publicly consecrated himself to the service of God and humanity, he retired to this wilderness to perfect himself for his life-battle by a preparatory conflict. Here, in prayer and fasting, he studied the problem of his life.

Others had felt with anguish the degeneracy of their nation. They had taken up the sword to secure its independence. Bravely, but in vain, the Maccabees had sought by revolution to restore the ancient theocracy. Christ's more comprehensive heart felt a heavier woe. He saw, as in a vision, the universal corruption of mankind. He perceived that institutions are the outgrowths of individual life, and that this must be changed if they are to be permanently reformed. He traced all the social and political degeneracy of his times to its source—a heart alienated from God and given up to selfishness. The truths which he later preached orbed themselves before him. He saw that men must be born again. He saw that a world living without God and having no hope must be inspired with

## THOU BETHLEHEM.

J. B. Dykes.

1. Earth has many a no - ble ci - ty; Beth - le'm, thou dost all ex - cel;
2. Fair - er than the sun at morning Was the star that told His birth,
3. East - ern sag - es at his cra - dle Make ob - la - tions rich and rare;
4. Sa - cred gifts of mys - tic meaning: In - cense doth their God dis - close,

Out of Thee the Lord from heav - en Came to rule His Is - ra - el.
To the world its God an - nounc - ing Seen in flesh - ly form on earth.
See them give, in deep de - vo - tion, Gold and frank - in - cense and myrrh.
Gold the King of kings pro - claim - eth, Myrrh His sep - ul - cher fore - shows.

hope by being brought back to God. He saw that humanity waited for a new revelation of Jehovah, not as the king, but as the Father of mankind. He saw that love, and that the love of God, was the only lever which could lift the world out of its slough of despond. He saw that words could never adequately portray that love; that only a life of patience and a death of suffering could do it. He foresaw, keenest anguish of all, that even from such a truth so portrayed many would turn away, deaf, blind, dead. Gradually his life unfolded itself in a solemn indistinctness before him. He perceived—it needed no prophet's eye to do that—the inevitable conflict which he must court with the Pharisaic party. He perceived himself disowned by the Church he

came to redeem. He perceived the people alternating between an ignorant enthusiasm when they understood not his purposes, and an ungovernable rage when they did. He perceived himself left to the companionship of a few uncultured and uncongenial peasants culled from his Galilean home. He perceived that the course of his life must be one of suffering and seeming insignificance, its end an apparently ignominious disaster and defeat. He stood in imagination in Caiaphas's court, the subject of its mock pretense of trial. He stood in Pilate's court, and felt the hot breath of the rabble on his brow, and heard their loud outcries for his death. The Garden of Gethsemane cast its dark shadow on his path. The cross loomed up, sombre and bloody, before him. The exultant Pharisees, the down-cast disciples, his mother, with her pierced and broken heart, all stood before him ; for he perceived that he must needs invite all whom he loved to the banquet of suffering which he was preparing for himself. A deeper sorrow overshadowed him as the darkness of the whole earth closed about him, the sins of the whole world rested on him, and a dim vision of the hour when God would seem to have forsaken, utterly ap-palled him. And was this to be his career ? Must he cast away all bright hopes and brilliant earthly prospects of budding man-hood ? Must he cage and curb his impa-tient spirit ? Must he turn away from all ordinary avenues of usefulness ? Must he content himself with simplest instruction to the simple peasantry ? Must he not only crucify himself, but lay the cross on all who loved and sought to follow him ? From such a prospect, all the native pride, the delicate

## NO MYRRH OF ARABY.

WM. CROSWELL.

1. We come not with a cost-ly store, O Lord, like them of old, The mas-ters
2. But faith and love may bring their best, A spir-it keen-ly tried By fierce af-

of the star-ry lore, From O-phir's shore of gold; No weepings of the incense
flic-tion's fie-ry test, And seven times pu-ri-fied; The fragrant gra-ces of the

tree Are with the gifts we bring; No od'-rous myrrh of Ar-a-by Blends
mind, The vir-tues that de-light To give their per-fume out will find Ac-

with our of-fer-ing, No od'-rous myrrh of Ar-a-by Blends with our of-fer-ing.
cept-ance in thy sight, To give their perfume out will find Ac-cept-ance in thy sight.

sensitiveness, the tender affections of his human nature arose in strong rebellion. He could neither eat nor sleep. For forty days and nights he ate, if not absolutely nothing, at least nothing save an occasional carob plucked from the forest trees, or a mouthful of wild honey gathered from the rocks. Then, wearied and weakened, he entered on that mysterious experience through which all his disciples have ever followed him, and which Bunyan has so graphically depicted in the passage of Christian through the Valley of the Shadow of Death. Evil spirits seemed to surround him, and whispered suggestions of recre-ancy added to the tumultuous experiences of the dark and mystic hour.

Whether Satan really appeared to Jesus in bodily form has always been a matter of serious dispute among Christian men. On the one hand, it is said that nowhere else is he depicted as assuming a visible form; that his power lies in his concealment; that it is because the Christian has to fight, not against flesh and blood, but against the unseen prince of the power of the air, that he is commended to put on the whole armor of God; that a revealed and incarnate devil would, by disclosing himself, defeat his purpose; that it would need no wondrous courage, no remarkable virtue to resist such a tempter; that the language of the Scripture narrative is to be interpreted by the common usages and beliefs of the time; that, in narrating the experience afterward to his disciples, Jesus used that language and confirmed that belief by asserting that an evil spirit instigated the thoughts which tried his soul; and that this really signifies nothing more than that they were presented *to* him by influences from without, not harbored *by* him by the spirit within. On the

## EMMANUEL.

W. CHATTERTON DIX.

1. Joy fills our in - most heart to - day, The Roy - al Child is born; The
2. An - gels are thronging round thy bed, Thine in - fant grace to see; The

an - gel hosts in glad ar - ray His ad - vent keep this morn; For
stars are pal - ing o'er Thy head, The Day-spring dawns with Thee; Thou

us the world must lose its charms Be - fore the man - ger shrine; When
art the ver - y light of light, En - light - en us, sweet Child, That

fold - ed in Thy moth - er's arms, Thou sleep - est, Babe Di - vine.
we may keep Thy birth - day bright With ser - vice un - de - filed.

other hand, it is said that no believer in the Scripture can doubt the existence of evil spirits, who really exert at times an influence on the hearts and lives of men; that belief in such demons is the almost universal belief of the human race; that it is no incredible thing that at certain times and under peculiar circumstances they may assume visible form, as certainly the angels are stated to have done; that the exalted condition of Christ's faculties, and the unnatural condition of his body, may have enabled him to see the invisible world; and that a philosophy which interprets away the plain and simple assertion that "the tempter came to him," and "the devil taketh him," is to be received and regarded with great suspicion. This controversy never has been settled, and probably never will be. It is essential to the proper comprehension of this narrative that we should understand that an evil spirit really assailed Jesus ; that the suggestions of recreancy did not spring spontaneous in his heart from evil desires which lurked unrecognized there, but that they were whispered to him by the tempter only to be instantly and indignantly rejected. But whether this tempter was embodied or unseen it does not seem important for us to know. The substantial significance of the scene is the same, whichever interpretation of its external aspects may be accepted; and it is that spiritual significance alone which we desire to consider. Temptations most frequently present themselves at first in forms seemingly innocent. So it was with Jesus. Exhausted nature re-asserted her long-denied claims. Christ was an hungered. The body, no longer subject to the supremacy of the spirit, demanded food. Jesus was far from human habitations. The few wild fruits of the desolate wilderness were utterly inadequate to supply his needs. But already he felt within himself the mysterious endowment of miraculous power. A word from him,

"HE READS AGAIN THE GLAD OLD STORY."

and the stone beneath his feet would be bread in his hand. Should he speak it, and save himself from perishing from hunger? Why, rather, should he not? He had come to live the life of man among men. He not only took upon himself the form of a servant, he was made in the condition of man. To employ his supernatural power for his own sustenance was to destroy the significance of his mission at the outset. That miraculous power he would not exert for himself. They that taunted him on the cross, "He saved others, himself he can not save." bore an unconscious testimony to the unselfishness of his spirit, and the thoroughness with which he took upon himself the life of common humanity. He that fed five thousand in the wilderness from two small loaves and five little fishes would not supply himself, except by ordinary means, with one. A subtler temptation assailed him. "Go," so the whispered suggestion was uttered to his soul, "go to Jerusalem ; assert your Messiahship ; invite an expectant people to acknowledge you their king ; demonstrate your claim by a miracle wrought in the presence of the multitude ; cast yourself down, unhurt, from the pinnacle of the Temple; so, by one bold master-stroke, assert your right, and secure from a wondering nation their allegiance, while your own doubts of your divine authority and mission shall be thus effectually settled forever." No! Not thus can Jesus' mission be accomplished; not the wonder of the people, but their love, he has come to awaken; not to be enthroned in their palaces, but in their hearts ; not by a miracle that appeals to their senses, but by a miracle of love and mercy, must he conquer his kingdom. Sublime is the work which he has undertaken. Long, slow, weary, is the path which he must traverse in accomplishing it. And if his own mind is sometimes darkened by doubts—if the consciousness of his divinity burns not yet clear in his own bosom—if the whispered skepticism, "If thou be the Son of God," finds momentary lodgment there, this is not the way to banish it. Not by a trial of his

## GREAT JOY WE BRING.

Lewis Edson.

1. Hark! what ce - les - tial sounds, What mu - sic fills the air! Soft warb -ling to the
2. Th' an gel - ic hosts de - scend, With har - mo - ny di - vine; See how from heaven they
3. "He comes, your souls to save, From death's e - ter-nal gloom; To realms of bliss and
4. "Glo - ry to God on high; Ye mor - tals spread the sound, And let your rap - tures

morn, It strikes the rav - ished ear; Now all is still, now wild it floats In
bend, And in full cho - rus join: "Fear not," say they,"great joy we bring : Je -
light He lifts you from the tomb: Your voic - es raise, with sons of light; Your
fly To earth's re - mot - est bound; For peace on earth, from God in heav'n To

tune - ful notes, loud, sweet and shrill. In tune - ful notes, loud, sweet and shrill.
sus, your King, is born to - day. Je - sus, your King, is born to - day.
songs u - nite of end - less praise. Your songs u - nite of. end - less praise.
man is given at Je - sus' birth. To man is given at Je - sus' birth.

supernatural powers, but by the longer, harder trial of his patience and his love, will he attest his Messiahship alike to himself and to mankind. Once more the tempter assails him. "The Devil taketh him up into an exceeding high mountain, and showeth him all the kingdoms of the world and the glory of them ; and saith unto him, 'All these things will I give thee if thou wilt fall down and worship me.' " It is impossible to interpret this literally. It is impossible to suppose that from any moun- tain Jesus could gain a view of all the kingdoms of the world. It is impossible but that Jesus should have known the devil was promising what he could not perform. It is impossible that the suggestion of literal worship to a bodily fiend could offer any temptation—we will not say to Jesus—to any one of ordinary purity of heart and strength of conscience. In the entire narration of the Gospel biographies, we have in graphic form the outlines only of a picture—mere touches, that indicate an experience which can only thus be portrayed. This last temptation was subtlest, and, therefore, most dangerous of all. Let the reader in imagination conceive of Jesus, for the moment unendowed with the divine strength which belonged to the Son of God; let him conceive for a moment the issue as it might have presented itself to a young man full of the buoyant hope, and fire of zeal, and enthusiasm of imagination of ardent youth; thus he may best conceive what the temptation would have been to the humanity in Christ.

In the midst of a ruined world, then, stands Jesus, the mournful spectator of its woes. His pure soul is disgusted by the heartless ritualism of a degenerate religion. His patriotism is wounded and grieved by his nation's present decay and impending

## THE GUARDIAN ANGEL.

OLD CAROL.

1. Last night, as I lay sleeping, When all my prayers were said, My guardian angel keeping His watch above my head, I heard his sweet voice carolling Full softly on mine ear, A song for Christian boys to sing, For Christian men to bear: "The holy Christmas-tide is nigh, The season of Christ's birth; Glory be to God on high, And peace to men on earth!

2. "Thy body is the temple, dear boy, Thy soul be free from sin; I'll shield thee from the world's annoy, And breathe pure thoughts within. Myself and all the heavenly host Were keeping watch of old, And saw the shepherds at their post, And all the sheep in fold. Then told we, with a joyful cry, The tidings of Christ's birth; Glory be to God on high, And peace to men on earth!

3. "He to work his Father's will, And meek he was, as one, And yearly year His tho'ts were still innocent and mild; Like Him be true, like Him be pure, Like Him be full of love; Seek not thine own, and so secure Thine own that is above. And still, when Christmas-tide draws nigh, Sing thou of His dear birth; Glory be to God on high, And peace to men on earth!"

doom. He feels the weight of the Roman yoke. He shudders at the impiety of the Roman polytheism. He loathes and detests the odious oppression which is wearing out the life of his people. He has felt himself irresistibly called to be the ransom, first of his own nation, then of all the oppressed nationalities of the earth. He has purposed within himself to found a kingdom whose law shall be liberty, whose fruit shall be peace. He recognizes that in the Jewish nation and in the Jewish religion are the elements out of which this kingdom is to be constructed. The Jews possess the fundamental principles of the true state. They possess the knowledge of the true God. Salvation is of the Jews. Christianity is to grow out of the ruins of Judaism, as the rose of spring is the resurrection of the faded leaves that lie at its roots and nourish its life. He comes, not to destroy the law and the prophets, but to fulfill. He finds about him the remnants of the ancient church; the descendants of the authorized priesthood; the degenerate scions of the lost prophetic order. He finds a religious party, expectant of a Messiah, anxious for a Messiah, and ready to cast the whole weight of their prestige and influence in with any one who gives promise of restoring to the nation its ancient glory, and will suffer them to be sharers in it. For

## WHAT OF THE NIGHT?

the establishment of such a kingdom Christ had many advantages. He had the grace which attracts men, the eloquence which arouses, the courage which inspirits. If he would but ally himself with the Church party ; if he would but pass by unexposed their veneer of virtue ; if he would put himself at their head ; if he would, in short, study how to maintain and increase his influence among the influential, the kingdom of Judea might be his. He might re-establish the throne of David; reinstate the sceptre of Shiloh ; reform the degenerate worship ; restore the prophetic order ; reordain a holy priesthood. A picture of a nation long enslaved, now disenthralled, redeemed, restored, reformed, purified by his power— this is the picture the wily tempter presents to his imagination. Nor this alone. Alexander, going forth from the little kingdom of Macedon, had vanquished the world. Already Greece had lost its vitality ; already the power of Rome was passing away, though its apparent dominion was at its height. To a devoutly enkindled imagination it would not seem impossible that the conditions of the present might be reversed in the future. The kingdoms of the earth might yet be made subject to a redeemed and ransomed Israel. The Jewish people expected it. The prophets seemed to most of their readers to promise it. The kingdoms of the earth and all their glory were seen as in a vision. And the seductive promise was whispered in the ear of Jesus, "This victory shall be thine. Only yield

## RISE, GLORIOUS CONQUEROR.

"ITALIAN HYMN."
BRIDGES. GIARDINI, 1760.

1. Rise, glorious Conqueror, rise!  In-to Thy na - tive skies,  As-sume Thy right:
2. Vic-tor o'er death and hell!  Cher-u-bic le - gions swell  Thy ra-diant train:
3. Li-on of Ju-dah, hail!  And let Thy name pre-vail  From age to age;

And where in many a fold The clouds are backward rolled, Pass thro' those gates of gold, And reign in light.
Praises all Heav'n inspire, Each angel sweeps his lyre, And waves his wings of fire, Thou Lamb once slain.
Lord of the rolling years, Claim for Thine own the spheres, For Thou hast bought with tears Thy heritage!

something of your religious zeal ; only consent to join hands with the priestly aristocracy of Judea ; only consent to look in silence on their sins ; only compromise a little with conscience ; only employ the arts of policy and the methods of state diplomacy, by which, always and everywhere, men mount to power. Be not righteous overmuch, for why shouldst thou destroy thyself?" Something such was the picture Satan drew. It disclosed the artist; it ended the conflict. The issue was plain. Between a life of self-sacrifice, ending in a shameful death, and a career of self-seeking ambition, there was no alternative. In choosing there was no hesitation. Instantly and indignantly Jesus repels the suggestion. It finds no lodgment in his heart. "Get thee behind me, Satan, for it is written, 'Thou shalt worship the Lord thy God, and him only shalt thou serve,'" is his decisive answer. It is not difficult to conceive with what power of eloquence, inspired by that moment, Christ later preached, "Ye cannot serve God and mammon." The battle was fought. The victory gained by Satan in the Garden of Eden was wrested from him in the wilderness. The cross, with all its shame and suffering, with all its bright but unseen glory too, was chosen. And from the dark valley, where evil spirits hover, and dark suggestions of sin fill the reluctant ear and torment the oppressed spirit, Jesus emerged into an experience of light, while angels came to minister unto him.—*Lyman Abbott.*

## HARK! THE ANGEL SONG.

*Allegro con brio.*

G. A. DAVIS.

1. Be - tween the dark - ness and the morn The Lord of night and day was born, A
2. The song died with the breaking morn; The dark - ness died, for Christ was born, Born
3. Yet still a lit - tle while in rest He lies, a babe up - on her breast, The

lit - tle Child in Beth - le - hem.— Hark! the an - gel song! It thrills the
as a Babe in Beth - le - hem!— And yet they sing! We hear them
Child and King of Beth - le - hem!— Hark! the an - gel song! It thrills us

air and o - ver the plain, While gold - en harps re-ech - o the strain!—The wea - ry
yet, while o - ver the plain The gold - en harps re-ech - o the strain!—There, clear - er
yet, as o - ver the plain Their gold - en harps re - ech - o the strain!—The Child with

world was gray and old, Its creeds were dead, its faiths were cold; And foul the
than the ris - en day, The Day-spring of all glo - ry lay, A Child up -
lov - ing lips and eyes, The Christ of Is - rael's prophe - cies, The Son of

hearts of men had grown, When He looked down and left His throne, For a poor
on her vir - gin breast—The Christ-child and the moth - er blest, The mir - a -
Man, the Lord of Heav'n, The Light un - to a blind world given.—All praise to

stall in Beth - le - hem, For a poor stall in Beth - le - hem.
cle of Beth - le - hem, The mir - a - cle of Beth - le - hem.
God for Beth - le - hem, All praise to God for Beth - le - hem.

## THE MAHOGANY TREE.

W. M. Thackeray.
Fabio Campana.

*Cantabile express e molto accentato.*

1. Christmas is here; Winds whistle shrill, I - cy and chill, Lit - tle care we;
2. Once on the boughs Birds of rare plume Sang, in its bloom: Night-birds are we;
3. Care, like a dun, Lurks at the gate; Let the dog wait; Hap-py we'll be!

Lit - tle we fear Weather with-out, Sheltered a - bout The Ma - ho - ga - ny Tree.
Here we carouse, Sing-ing like them, Perched round the stem Of the jol - ly old Tree.
Pile up the coals; While the song rolls Let us for - get, Round the old Tree.

Eve - nings we know, Hap - py as this; Fa - ces we miss Pleas - ant to
Here let us sport, Boys, as we sit— Laughter and wit Flash - ing so
Sor - rows, be - gone! Life and its ills, Duns and their bills, Bid we to

see. Kind hearts and true, Gen - tle and just, Peace to your dust!
free. Life is but short, When we are gone, Let them sing on,
flee. Come with the dawn, En - vi - ous sprite; Leave us to - night,

We sing round the Tree.
Round the old Tree.
Round the old Tree! } Ah,......... Eve-nings we knew, Hap-py as

Evenings we knew,

*col canto.*

*a tempo.*

this; Fa-ces we miss Pleas-ant to see, Kind hearts and true,

Hap-py as this; Fa-ces we miss Pleasant to see, Kind hearts and

Gen-tle and just, Peace to your dust! We sing round the tree. tree.

true, Gen-tle and just, Peace to your dust!

## 'TWAS CHRISTMAS EVE.

S. Nelson.
F. E. Weatherly.

*Allegro animato.*

'Twas Christmas Eve, at night, The snow deep on the ground, The peas-ant's fire burnt

low, The chil-dren shivered round. Their evening meal, how scant, Lay on the hum-ble

board, But all, with thankful hearts, Arose and blessed the Lord. Hark! some one stands with-

out, The peas-ant opes the door—Who wanders late to-night A-cross the bit-ter

moor? 'Mid win-ter storm so wild, There in the dark He stands. A child, with wistful

*ritard.*

eyes And froz-en, lift-ed hands. He took Him in his arms,—The children wond'ring
*D. S.* But while on beds of straw That night they sleeping

gaze,—He wiped a - way the snows, And warmed Him by the blaze,
lay, The Child a - rose to bless, Then soft - ly went His way.

There on the seat they
Now for each good that

*D.S.*

loved, The dear dead mother's chair, He broke the bread, they gave Each of his scan-ty share.
comes, When life seems doubly drear, They fold their hands and say, "The Christ-Child hath been here."

## BY THY CHRISTMAS CHEER.

*Animato.*

1. Je - sus meek and gen - tle, Son of God Most High, Ten - der, lov - ing Sav - iour,
2. Give us bless-ed free - dom, Fill our hearts with love; Lead us, Child of Prom - ise,

*Treble.*

Hear Thy children's cry; Par - don our of - fen - ces, Loose our cap - tive chains,
To Thy realms a - bove; Lead us on our jour - ney, Be Thy - self the way

*Chorus.*

Break down ev - 'ry i - dol That our soul de - tains. By Thy Christmas guer - don,
Thro' these earth-born sha - dows To ce - les - tial day. By Thy Christmas guer - don,

By Thy Christmas cheer, Help us bear each bur - den In Thy love so dear.

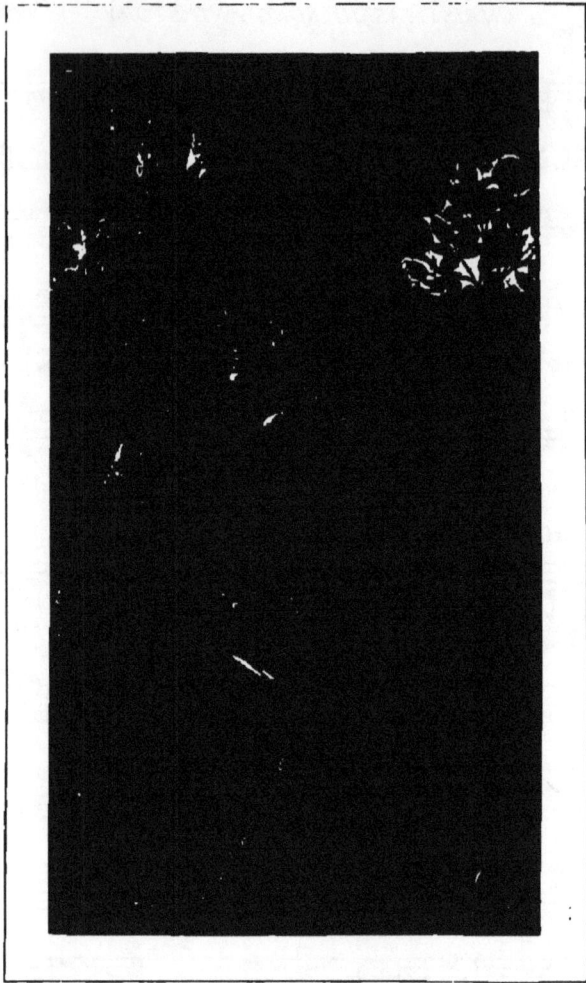

MOTHER AND SON.

# GELLERT'S LAST CHRISTMAS.

THREE o'clock had just struck from the tower of St. Nicholas, Leipzig, on the afternoon of December 22d, 1768, when a man, wrapped in a loose overcoat, came out of the door of the University. His countenance was exceedingly gentle, and on his features cheerfulness still lingered, for he had been gazing upon a hundred cheerful faces; after him thronged a troop of students, who, holding back, allowed him to precede them; the passengers in the streets saluted him, and some students, who pressed forward and hurried past him homewards, saluted him quite reverentially. He returned their salutations with a surprised and almost a deprecatory air, and yet he knew, and could not conceal from himself, that he was one of the best beloved, not only in the good city of Leipzig, but in all lands far and wide.

It was Christian Fürchtegott Gellert, the Poet of Fables, Hymns, and Lays, who was just leaving his college. When we read his Lectures upon Morals, which were not printed until after his death, we obtain but a very incomplete idea of the great power with which they came immediately from Gellert's mouth. Indeed, it was his voice and the touching manner in which he delivered his Lectures, that made so deep an impression upon his hearers; and Rabener was right when once he wrote to a friend, that "the philanthropic voice" of Gellert belonged to his words. Above all, however, it was the amiable and pure personal character of Gellert, which vividly and edifyingly impressed young hearts. Gellert was himself the best example of pure moral teaching; and the best which a teacher can give his pupils is faith in the victorious might, and the stability of the eternal moral laws. His lessons were for the Life, for his life in itself was a lesson. Many a victory over the troubles of life, over temptations of every kind, aye, many an elevation to nobility of thought, and to purity of action, had its origin in that lecture-hall, at the feet of Gellert.

It was as though Gellert felt that it was the last time he would deliver these Lectures, that those words so often and so impressively uttered would be heard no more from his mouth; and there was a peculiar sadness, yet a peculiar strength, in all he said that day. He had this day earnestly recommended Modesty and Humility; and it appeared almost offensive to him, that people as he went should tempt him in regard to these very virtues; for continually he heard men whisper, "That is Gellert!" What is fame, and what is honor? A cloak of many colors, without warmth, without protection; and now, as he walked along, his heart literally froze in his bosom, as he confessed to himself that he had as yet done nothing, nothing which could give him a feeling of real satisfaction. Men honored him and loved him; but what was all that worth? His innermost heart could not be satisfied with that; in his own estimation he deserved no meed of praise; and where, where was there any evidence of that higher and purer life which he fain would bring about! Then, again, the Spirit would comfort him, and say,—"Much seed is lost, much falls in stony places, and much on good ground that brings forth seven-fold." His inmost soul heard not the consolation, for his body was weak and sore burdened from his youth up, and in his latter days yet more than ever; and there are conditions of the body in which the most elevating words, and the cheeriest notes of joy, strike dull and heavy on the soul. It is one of the bitterest experiences of life to discover how little one man can really be to another. How joyous is that youthful freshness which can believe that, by a thought transferred to another's heart, we can induce him to become another being, to live according to what he must acknowl-

edge true, to throw aside his previous de-
lusions and again return to the right path!
The youngsters go on their way! Do your
words follow after? Whither are they going? What are now their thoughts? What
manner of life will be theirs? "My heart
yearns after them, but can not be with them;
oh, how happy were those messengers of the
Spirit, who cried aloud to youth or manhood
the words of the Spirit, that they must leave
their former ways, and thenceforth change
to other beings? Pardon me, O God! that
I would fain be like them; I am weak and
vile, and yet, methinks, there must be words
as yet unheard, unknown—oh! where are
they, those words which at once lay hold
upon the soul?" With such heavy thoughts
went Gellert away from his college gate

to Rosenthal. There was but one small
pathway cleared, but the passers cheerfully
made way for him, and walked in the snow
that they might leave him the pathway un-
impeded; but he felt sad, and "as if each
tree had somewhat to cast at him." Like
all men really pure, and cleaving to the
good with all their might, Gellert was not
only far from contenting himself with work
already done; he also, in his anxiety to be
doing, almost forgot that he had ever done
anything, and thus he was, in the best sense
of the word, modest; he began with each
fresh day his course of action afresh, as if
he now for the first time had anything to
accomplish. And yet he might have been
happy in the reflection how brightly beamed
his teaching forever, though his own life

## THE LIGHT HATH SHONE.

THOMAS HASTINGS.
JOHN MORRISON, 1770.

1. The race that long in dark-ness pined, Hath seen a glo-rious Light The
2. To hail Thy rise, Thou bet-ter Sun, The gath'ring na-tions come, Joy-
3. To us a child of hope is born, To us a Son is given; Him
4. His name shall be the Prince of Peace, For-ev-er-more a-dored; The
5. His power, in-creas-ing, still shall spread; His reign no end shall know; Jus-

peo-ple dwell in day, who dwelt In death's surrounding night, In death's surrounding night.
ous as when the reapers bear The harvest treasures home, The harvest treasures home.
shall the tribes of earth o-bey, Him all the hosts of heaven, Him all the hosts of heaven.
Won-der-ful, the Counsellor, The great and mighty Lord, The great and mighty Lord.
tice shall guard His throne above, And peace a-bound be-low, And peace a-bound be-low.

was often clouded. For as the sun which
glows on summer days, still lives as concentrated warmth in wine, and somewhere
on some winter night warms up a human
heart, so is the sunshine in that man's life
whose vocation it is to impart to others the
conceptions of his own mind. Nay, there
is here far more; for the refreshing draught
here offered is not diminished, though thousands drink thereof.

Twilight had set in when Gellert returned home to his dwelling, which had for
its sign a "Schwarz Brett," or "black-
board." His old servant, Sauer by name,
took off his overcoat: and his amanuensis,
Gödike, asked whether the Professor had
any commands; being answered in the nega-

tive, Gödike retired, and Sauer lighted the
lamp upon the study-table. "Some letters
have arrived," said he, as he pointed to
several upon the table. Gellert inclined
his head and Sauer retired also. Outside,
however, he stood awhile with Gödike, and
both spoke sorrowfully of the fact that the
Professor was evidently again suffering
severely. "There is a melancholy," said
Gödike, "and it is the most usual, in which
the inward depression easily changes to displeasure against every one, and the household of the melancholic suffers thereby intolerably; for the displeasure turns against
them—no one does anything properly, nothing is in its place. How very different is
Gellert's melancholy! Not a soul suffers

from it but himself, against himself alone his gloomy thoughts turn, and towards every other creature he is always kind, amiable, and obliging; he bites his lips; but when he speaks to any one, he is wholly good, forbearing, and self-forgetful." Whilst they were talking together, Gellert was sitting in his room, and had lighted a pipe to dispel the agitation which he would experience in opening his letters; and while smoking he could read them much more comfortably. He reproached himself for smoking, which was said to be injurious to his health, but he could not quite give up the " horrible practice," as he called it. He first examined the addresses and seals of the letters which had arrived, then quietly opened and read them. A fitful smile passed over his features; there were letters from well-known friends, full of love and admiration, but from strangers also, who, in all kinds of heart-distress, took counsel of him. He read the letters full of friendly applause, first hastily, that he might have the right of reading them again, and that he might not know all at once; and when he had read a friend's letter for the second time, he sprang from his seat and cried, "Thank God! thank God! that I am so fortunate as to have such friends!" To his inwardly diffident nature, these helps were a real requirement; they served to cheer him, and only those who did not know him called his joy at the reception of praise—conceit; it was, on the contrary, the truest modesty. How often did he sit there, and all that he had taught and writ-

## BLEST BE THE TIE.

JOHN FAWCETT.
H. G. NAGELI. "DENNIS."

```
1. Blest be the tie that binds   Our hearts in Chris-tian love;
2. Be-fore our Fa-ther's throne,  We pour our ar-dent prayers;
3. We share our mu-tual woes,    Our mu-tual bur-dens bear;
4. When we a-sun-der part,       It gives us in-ward pain;

The fel-low-ship of kin-dred minds  Is like to that a-bove.
Our fears, our hopes, our aims are one,  Our com-forts and our cares.
And oft-en for each oth-er flows   The sym-pa-thiz-ing tear.
But we shall still be joined in heart,  And hope to meet a-gain.
```

ten, all that he had ever been to men in word and deed, faded, vanished, and died away, and he appeared to himself but a useless servant of the world. His friends he answered immediately; and as his inward melancholy vanished, and the philanthropy, nay, the sprightliness of his soul beamed forth, when he was among men and looked in a living face, so was it also with his letters. When he bethought him of the friends to whom he was writing, he not only acquired tranquillity, that virtue for which his whole life long he strove; but his loving nature received new life, and only by slight intimations did he betray the heaviness and dejection which weighed upon his soul. He was, in the full sense of the word, "philanthropic," in the sight of good men; and in thoughts for their welfare, there was for him a real happiness, and a joyous animation. When, however, he had done writing, and felt lonely again, the gloomy spirits came back; he had seated himself, wishing to raise his thoughts for composing a sacred song; but he was ill at ease, and had no power to express that inward, firm, and self-rejoicing might of faith which lived in him. Again and again the scoffers and free-thinkers rose up before his thoughts: he must refute their objections, and not until that was done did he become himself.

It is a hard position, when a creative spirit can not forget the adversaries which on all sides oppose him in the world; they come unsummoned to the room, and will not be expelled; they peer over the shoulder, and tug at the hand which fain would write; they turn images upside down, and distort the thoughts; and here and there, from ceiling and wall, they grin, and scoff, and oppose; and what is just gushing as an aspiration from the soul, is converted to a confused absurdity. At such a time, the spirit, courageous and self-dependent, must take refuge in itself, and show a firm front to a world of foes. A strong nature, like Luther, boldly hurls his inkstand at the devil's head; goes to battle with his opponents with words both written and spoken; and keeps his own individuality free from the perplexities with which opponents disturb all that has been previously done, and make the soul unsteadfast and unnerved for what is to come. Gellert's was no battling, defiant nature, which relies upon itself; he did not hurl his opponent down, and go his way; he would convince them, and so they were always ready to encounter him. And as the applause of

## GLORIOUS SONG OF OLD.

E. H. Sears, 1860.
Old English Melody.

1. It came up-on the midnight clear, That glorious song of old, From an-gels bending
2. Still thro' the cloven skies they come, With peaceful wings unfurled; And still ce-les-tial
3. O ye, beneath life's crushing load, Whose forms are bending low, Who toil a-long the
4. For lo, the days are hastening on, By proph-et-bards fore-told, When with the ev-er-

near the earth To touch their harps of gold: "Peace to the earth, good-will to man, From
mu-sic floats O'er all the wea-ry world; A-bove its sad and low-ly plains They
climbing way, With pain-ful steps and slow, Look up! for glad and gold-en hours Come
cir-cling years Comes round the age of gold! When peace shall o-ver all the earth Its

Heaven's all-gracious King:" The earth in solemn still-ness lay, To hear the an-gels sing.
bend on heavenly wing, And ev-er o'er its Babel sounds, The bless-ed an-gels sing!
swift-ly on the wing: Oh, rest be-side the wea-ry road, And hear the an-gels sing!
fin-al splendors fling, And the whole world send back the song Which now the an-gels sing!

his friends rejoiced him, so the opposition of his enemies could sink him in deep dejection. Besides, he had always been weakly; he had, as he himself complained, in addition to frequent coughs, and a pain in his loins, a continual gnawing and pressure in the centre of his chest, which accompanied him from his first rising in the morning until he slept at night. Thus he sat for awhile, in deep dejection; and, as often before, his only wish was, that God would give him grace whereby when his hour was come, he might die piously and tranquilly. It was past midnight when he sought his bed and extinguished his light. * * *

And the buckets at the well go up and go down. About the same hour, in Duben Forest, the rustic Christopher was rising from his bed. As with steel and flint he scattered sparks upon the tinder, in kindling himself a light, his wife, awakening, cried: "Why that heavy sigh?" "Ah! life is a burden: I'm the most harassed mortal in the world. The pettiest office-clerk may now be abed in peace, and needn't break off his sleep; while I must go out and brave wind and weather." "Be content," replied his wife: "why, I dreamt you had actually been made magistrate, and wore something on your head like a king's crown." "Oh, you women! As though what you see isn't enough, you like to chatter about what you dream!" "Light the lamp too," said his wife, "and I'll get up and make you a nice porridge." The peas-

ant, putting a candle in his lantern, went to the stable; and after giving some fodder to the horses, he seated himself upon the manger. With his hands squeezed between his knees and his head bent down, he reflected over and over again what a wretched existence he had of it. "Why," thought he, "are so many men so well-off, so comfortable, whilst you must be always toiling? What care I if envy be not a virtue?—and yet I'm not envious; I don't grudge others being well-off, only I should like to be well-

## JOYFUL TIDINGS.

G. VERDI.
CUTHBERT BEDE.

*Con espressione.*

1. Spake the Angel, "Lo! to all men joyful tidings now I bring: For to you, in Dav-id's
2. On a sudden, with the Angel There were shining spirit throngs, Who a-woke the sleeping
3. Rose the shepherds eager, trembling, And to David's ci-ty sped, Where they found their infant
4. Oh! that we too, like the shepherds, Trusting in the angel's word, Saw in that low cra-dled

ci - ty, Born this day a might-y King, Comes the Christ, the Lord, the Saviour! And this
ech - oes With their joy-ous car - ol-songs: "Glo-ry in the highest! glory! Peace, good-
Sav - iour, Ly - ing as the An-gel said, Lo, His pal-ace was a sta-ble, And a
In - fant, Promised Sav-iour and the Lord! Then should we, too, like the shepherds, List the

sign shall meet your eyes, Babe, enwrapped in swaddling raiment, Low within a manger lies."
will to men on earth!" And in awe the shepherds listened To the angels' sacred mirth.
manger was his throne; There to lowly shepherd courtiers Was the King of Heav'n made known.
song the An-gel sings, And in His thorn-crown-ed manhood, See the longed-for King of kings.

off too; oh, for a quiet, easy life! Am I not worse off than a horse? He gets his fodder at the proper time, and takes no care about it. Why did my father make my brother a minister? He gets his salary without any trouble, sits in a warm room, has no care in the world; and I must slave, and torment myself." Strange to say, his very next thought, that he would like to be made local magistrate, he would in no wise confess to himself. He sat still a long while; then he went back again to the sitting-room,

past the kitchen, where the fire was burning cheerily. He seated himself at the table and waited for his morning porridge. On the table lay an open book; his children had been reading it the previous evening; involuntarily taking it up, he began to read. Suddenly he started, rubbed his eyes, and then read again. How comes this verse here just at this moment? He kept his hand upon the book, and so easily had he caught the words, that he repeated them to himself softly with his lips, and nodded several times, as much as to say: "That's true!" And he said aloud: "It's all there together; short and sweet!" and he was still staring at it when his wife brought in the smoking porridge. Taking off his cap, he folded his hands and said aloud:

Accept God's gifts with resignation,
　Content to lack what thou hast not;
In every lot there's consolation;
　There's trouble, too, in every lot!

The wife looked at her husband with amazement. What a strange expression was upon his face! And as he sat down and began to eat, she said: "What is the mean-ing of that grace? What has come to you? Where did you find it?" "It's the best of all graces, the very best,—real God's word. Yes, and all your life you've never made such nice porridge before. You must have put something special in it!" "I don't know what you mean. Stop! There's the book lying there—ah! that's it—and it's by Gellert, of Leipzig." "What! Gellert, of Leipzig! Men with ideas like that don't live now; there may have been such a thousand years ago, in holy lands, not among us; those are the words of a saint of old." "And I tell you they are by Gellert, of Leipzig,

## WITH GLOWING HEART.

FRANCIS S. KEY. "AUTUMN."
SPANISH MELODY fr. MARECHIO.

1. Lord, with glowing heart I'd praise Thee, For the bliss Thy love bestows; For the pardoning grace that
2. Praise, my soul, the God that sought thee, Wretched wanderer, far astray; Found thee lost and kindly
3. Lord, this bosom's ar-dent feel-ing, Vainly would my lips ex-press; Low be-fore Thy footstool

saves me, And the peace that from it flows; Help, O God, my weak en-deav-or; This dull
brought thee From the paths of death a-way; Praise, with love's devout-est feel-ing, Him who
kneeling, Deign Thy suppliant's prayer to bless; Let Thy grace, my soul's chief treasure, Love's pure

soul to rapture raise, Thou must light the flame, or nev-er Can my love be warmed to praise.
saw thy guilt-born fear, And, the light of hope revealing, Bade the blood-stained Cross appear.
flame within me raise; And, since worlds can never measure, Let my life show forth Thy praise.

of whom your brother has told us; in fact, he was his tutor, and haven't you heard how pious and good he is?" "I wouldn't have believed that such men still lived, and so near us, too, as Leipzig." "Well, but those who lived a thousand years ago were also once living creatures; and over Leipzig is just the same heaven, and the same sun shines, and the same God rules, as over all other cities." "Oh! yes, my brother has an apt pupil in you!" "Well, and why not? I've treasured up all he has told us of Professor Gellert." "Professor!" "Yes, Professor!" "A man with such a proud, new-fangled title couldn't write anything like that." "He didn't give himself the title, and he is poor enough withal! and how hard it has fared with him! Even from childhood he has been well acquainted with poverty; his father was a poor minister in Haynichen, with thirteen children; and Gellert, when quite a little fellow, was obliged to be a copying office-clerk; who can tell whether he didn't then contract that physical weakness of his? And now that he's an old man, things will never go better with him; he has often no wood, and must be pinched with cold. It is with him, perhaps, as with that student of whom your brother has told us, who is as poor as a rat, and yet must read; and so in winter he lies in bed with an empty stomach, until day is far advanced, and he has his book before him, and first he takes out one hand to hold his book, and then, when that is numb with cold, the other. Ah! tongue can not tell how poorly the man must live; and yet your brother has told me if he has but a few pounds, he doesn't think at all of himself; he always looks out for one still poorer than he is, and then he gives all away; and he's always engaged in aiding and assisting others. Oh! dear, and yet he is so poor! Maybe at this moment he is hungry and cold; and he is said to be in ill health, besides." "Wife, I would willingly do the man a good turn if I could. If, now, he had some land, I would plough, and sow, and reap, and carry, and thresh by the week together for him. I should like to pay him attention in such a way that he might know there was at least one who cared for him. But his profession is one in which I can't be of any use to him." "Well, just seek him out and speak with him once; you are going to-day,

## MY JESUS, AS THOU WILT.

C. M. VON WEBER. "JEWETT."

BENJ. SCHMOLKE.

1. My Je - sus, as thou wilt: O may thy will be mine; In - to thy hand of love I would my all re - sign. Through sor - row or through joy, Con - duct me as thine own, And help me still to say, "My Lord, thy will be done."

2. My Je - sus, as thou wilt; Though seen through many a tear, Let not my star of hope Grow dim or dis - ap - pear. Since thou on earth hast wept, And sor - rowed oft a - lone, If I must weep with thee, "My Lord, thy will be done."

3. My Je - sus, as thou wilt; All shall be well for me; Each changing fu - ture scene I glad - ly trust with thee. Straight to my home a - bove, I trav - el calm - ly on, And sing in life or death, "My Lord, thy will be done."

you know, with your wood to Leipzig. Seek him out and thank him; that sort of thing does such a man's heart good. Anybody can see him." "Yes, yes; I should like much to see him, and hold out to him my hand—but not empty; I wish I had something!" "Speak to your brother, and get him to give you a note to him." "No, no; say nothing to my brother; but it might be possible for me to meet him in the street. Give me my Sunday coat; it will come to no harm under my cloak." When his wife brought him the coat, she said:— "If, now, Gellert had a wife, or a household of his own, one might send him something; but your brother says he is a bachelor, and also that he lives quite alone."

Christopher had never before so cheerily harnessed his horses and put them to his wood-laden wagon; for a long while he had not given his hand so gayly to his wife at parting as to-day. Now he started with his heavily-laden vehicle through the village; the wheels creaked and crackled in the snow. At the parsonage he stopped, and looked away yonder where his brother was still sleeping; he thought he would wake him and tell him his intention; but suddenly be whipped up his horses, and continued his route. He wouldn't yet bind himself to his intention—perchance it was but a passing thought; he doesn't own that to himself, but he says to himself that he will surprise his brother with the news of what he has done; and then his thoughts wandered away to the good man still sleeping yonder in the city; and he hummed the verse to himself in an old familiar tune. Wonderfully in life do effects manifest themselves, of which we have no trace. Gellert, too, heard, in his dreams, a singing; he knew not what it was, but it rang so consolingly, so joyously ! . . . . Christopher

drove on, and he felt as though a bandage had been taken from his eyes; he reflected what a nice house, what a bonny wife and rosy children he had, and how warm the cloak which he had thrown over him was, and how well off were both man and beast; and through the still night he drove along, and beside him sat a spirit; but not an illusion of the brain, such as in olden time men conjured up to their terror; a good spirit sat beside him—beside the woodman who, his whole life long, had never believed that anything could have power over him but what had hands and feet. It is said, that on troublous nights, evil spirits settle upon

## NO WAR NOR BATTLE SOUND.

JOHN ZUNDEL.
JOHN MILTON. (Adapted.)

1. No war nor battle's sound Was heard the world around; No hostile chiefs to furious combat ran; But
2. The shepherds on the lawn, Before the point of dawn, In social cir - cle sat; while all around, The
3. When, lo! with ravished ears, Each swain delighted hears, Sweet music, offspring of no mortal hand; Di-
4. They saw a glorious light Burst on their wond'ring sight; Harping in solemn choir, in robes arrayed, The

peaceful was the night, In which the Prince of light His reign of peace upon the earth be - gan.
gen - tle, fleecy brood, Or cropped the flowery food, Or slept, or sported on the ver - dant ground.
vine-ly-warbled voice, Answ'ring the stringed noise, With blissful rapture charmed the list'ning hand.
helm - ed cheru - bim And sworded sera - phim Are seen in glittering ranks, with wings displayed.

Sounds of so sweet a tone,
Before were never known,
But when of old the sons of morning sung,
While God disposed in air,
Each constellation fair,
And the well-balanced world on hinges hung.

" Hail, hail, auspicious morn !
The Saviour Christ is born!"
Such was th' immortal seraph's song sublime;
" Glory to God in Heaven!
To man sweet peace be given,
Sweet peace and friendship to the end of time."

the necks of men, and belabor them so that they gasp and sweat for very terror; quite another sort it was which to-day sat by the woodman; and his heart was warm, and its beating quick. In ancient times, men also carried loads of wood through the night, that heretics might be burned thereon; these men thought they were doing a good deed in helping to execute justice, and who can say how painful it was to their hearts when they were forced to think: To-morrow, on this wood which now you carry, will shriek and crackle, and gasp, a human being like yourself? Who can tell what black

spirits settled on the necks of those who bore the wood to make the funeral-pile? How very different was it to-day with our woodman Christopher! And earlier still, in ancient times, men brought wood to the temple, whereon they offered victims in the honor of God; and, according to their notions, they did a good deed; for when words can no longer suffice to express the fervency of the heart, it gladly offers what it prizes, what it dearly loves, as a proof of its devotion, of the earnestness of its intent. How differently went Christopher from the Duben Forest upon his way! He knew not whether he were intending to bring a purer offering than men had brought in by-gone ages; but his heart grew warm within him.

It was day as he arrived before the gates of Leipzig. Here there met him a funeral-procession; behind the bier the scholars of St. Thomas, in long black cloaks, were chanting. Christopher stopped, and raised his hat. Whom were they burying? Supposing it were Gellert! Yes, surely he thought, it is he; and how gladly, said he to himself, would you now have done him a kindness,—aye, even given him your wood! Yes, indeed you would, and now he is dead, and you can not give him any help! As soon as the train had passed, Christopher asked who was being buried. It was a simple burgher, it was not Gellert; and in the deep breath which Christopher drew lay a double signification; on the one hand, was joy that Gellert was not dead; on the other, a still small voice whispered to him that he had now really promised to give him the wood; ah! but whom had he promised!—himself; and it is easy to argue with one's own conscience. Superstition babbles of conjuring-spells, by which, without the co-operation of the patient, the evil spirit can be summarily ejected. It would be convenient if one had that power, but, in truth, it

## BEHOLD THY KING.

Isaac Watts.

1. How beauteous are their feet, Who stand on Zi-on's hill; Who bring sal-va-tion on their tongues, And words of peace re-veal! How charming is their voice, How sweet their tidings are! "Zi-on, be-hold thy Saviour-King, He reigns and triumphs here."

2. How happy are our ears That hear this joy-ful sound, Which kings and prophets wait-ed for, And sought, but nev-er found! How bless-ed are our eyes That see this heavenly light! Prophets and kings de-sired it long, But died without the sight.

3. The watchmen join their voice, And tune-ful notes em-ploy; Je-ru-salem breaks forth in songs, And des-erts learn the joy. The Lord makes bare his arm Thro' all the earth a-broad; Let ev'-ry na-tion now be-hold Their Saviour and their God.

is not so; it is long ere the evil desire and the evil habit are removed from the soul into which they have nestled; and the will, for a long while in bondage, must co-operate, if a releasing spell from without is to set the prisoner free. One can only be guided, but himself must move his feet. As Christopher now looked about him, he found that he had stopped close by an inn; he drove his load a little aside, went into the parlor, and drank a glass of warmed beer. There was already a goodly company, and not far from Christopher sat a husbandman with his son, a student here, who was telling him how there had been lately quite a stir. Professor Gellert had been ill, and riding a well-trained horse had been recommended for his health. Now Prince Henry of Prussia, during the Seven Years' War, at the occupation of Leipzig, had sent him a piebald, that had died a short time ago; and the Elector, hearing of it, had sent Gellert from Dresden another—a chestnut—with golden bridle, blue velvet saddle, and gold-embroidered housings. Half the city had assembled when the groom, a man with iron-gray hair, brought the horse; and for several days it was to be seen at the stable; but Gellert

9

dared not mount it, it was so young and high-spirited. The rustic now asked his son whether the professor did not make money enough to procure a horse of his own, to which the son answered,—"Certainly not. His salary is but $125, and his further gains are inconsiderable. His Lectures on Morals he gives publicly, *i. e.*, gratis, and he has hundreds of hearers; and, therefore, at his other lectures, which must be paid for, he has so many the fewer. To be sure, he has now and then presents from grand patrons; but no one gives him, once and for all, enough to live upon, and to have all over with a single acknowledgment."

Our friend Christopher started as he heard this; he had quite made up his mind to take Gellert the wood, but he had yet to do it. How easy were virtue, if will and deed were the same thing! if performance could immediately succeed to the moment of burning enthusiasm! But one must make way over obstacles; over those that outwardly lie in one's path, and over those that are hidden deep in the heart; and negligence has a thousand very cunning advocates. How many go forth, prompted by good intentions, but let little hindrances turn them from their way—entirely from their way of life! In front of the house Christopher met other woodmen whom he knew, and—"You are stirring betimes!" "Prices are good to-day!" "But little comes to the market now!" was the cry from all sides. Christo-

## SONS OF MEN, BEHOLD.

THIBAUT, 1854.
CHARLES WESLEY, 1739.

1. Sons of men, be - hold from far, Hail the long ex - pect ed Star;
2. Mild it shines on all be - neath, Pierc - ing thro' the shades of death,
3. Na - tions all, re - mote and near, Haste to see your God ap - pear;

Ja - cob's Star that gilds the night Guides be - wil - dered na - ture right.
Scat - t'ring er - ror's wide - spread night, Kind - ling dark - ness in - to light.
Haste, for Him your hearts pre - pare, Meet Him man - i - fest - ed there.

4. There behold the Day-Spring rise,
   Pouring light upon your eyes;
   See it chase the shades away,
   Shining to the perfect day.

5. Sing, ye morning stars, again,
   God descends on earth to reign,
   Deigns for man His life t'employ;
   Shout, ye sons of God, for joy.

pher wanted to say that all that didn't concern him, but he was ashamed to confess what his design was, and an inward voice told him he must not lie. Without answering, he joined the rest and wended his way to the market; and on the road he thought, "There are Peter, and Godfrey, and John, who have seven times your means, and not one of them, I'm sure, would think of doing anything of this kind; why will you be the kind-hearted fool? Stay! What matters it what others do or leave undone? Every man shall answer for himself. Yes, but go to market—it is better it should be so; yes, certainly, much better; sell your wood—who knows? perhaps he doesn't want it—and take him the proceeds, or at least the greater portion. But is the wood still yours? You have, properly speaking, already given it away; it has only not been taken from your keeping." There are people who can not give; they can only let a thing be taken either by the hand of chance, or by urgency and entreaty. Christopher had such fast hold of possession, that it was only after sore wrestling that he let go; and yet his heart was kind, at least to-day it was so disposed, but the tempter whispered,—"It is not easy to find so good-natured a fellow as you. How readily would you have given, had the man been in want, and your good intention must go for the deed." Still,

THE HOLY FAMILY.

on the other hand, there was something in him which made opposition—an echo from those hours when, in the still night, he was driving hither, and it burned in him like sacred fire, and it said, " You must now accomplish what you intended. Certainly no one knows of it and you are responsible to no one; but you know of it yourself, and One above you knows, and how shall you be justified?" And he said to himself, "I'll stand by this: Look, it is just nine; if no one ask the price of your wood until ten o'clock, until the stroke of ten,—until it has done striking, I mean; if no one ask, then the wood belongs to Professor Gellert; but if a buyer come, then it is a sign that you need not—should not give it away. There that's all settled. But how? what means this? Can you make your good dependent on such a chance as this? No, no; I don't mean it. But yet—yet—only for a joke, I'll try it." Temptation kept him turning as it were in a circle, and still he stood with an apparently quiet heart by his wagon in the market. The people who heard him muttering in this way to himself, looked at him with wonder, and passed by him to another wagon as though he had not been there. It struck nine. Can you wait patiently another hour? Christopher lighted his pipe, and looked calmly on, while this and that load was driven off. It struck the quarter, half-hour, three-quarters. Christopher now put his pipe in his pocket; it had

## HAIL THE BLEST MORN.

LOWELL MASON.
REGINALD HEBER, 1811.

1. Hail the blest morn! see the great Mediator    Down from the re - gions of glo-ry descend;
2. Bright in the East, lo! the Son of the morning    Dawns on our darkness, and lends us His aid;
3. Cold on His cradle the dew-drops are shining,    Low lies His head with the beasts of the stall,
4. Say, shall we yield Him, in costly de - vo - tion,    O - dors of E - dom, and off 'rings divine?
5. Vain-ly we of - fer each ample ob - la - tion;    Vain - ly with gifts would His favor se - cure:

Shepherds, go worship the Babe in the manger,    Lo! for His guard the bright angels at - tend.
While His pure light, the horizon a - dorn - ing,    Guides where our infant Redeemer is laid.
An - gels adore Him in slumber reclin - ing,    Ma - ker, and Monarch, and Saviour of    all,
Gems of the mountain, and pearls of the ocean,    Myrrh from the forest, or gold from the mine?
Rich - er by far is the heart's ad - o - ration;    Dear - er to God are the prayers of the poor.

long been cold, and his hands were almost frozen; all his blood had rushed to his heart. Now it struck the full hour, stroke after stroke. At first he counted; then he fancied he had lost a stroke and miscalculated. Either voluntarily or involuntarily he said to himself, when it had finished striking, "You're wrong; it is nine, not ten." He turned round that he might not see the dial, and thus he stood for some time, with his hands upon the wagon-rack, gazing at the wood. He knew not how long he had been thus standing, when some one tapped him on the shoulder, and said, "How much for the load of wood?" Christopher turned round; there was an odd look of irresolution in his eyes as he said: "Eh? eh? What time is it?" "Half-past ten." "Then the wood is now no longer mine —at least to sell;" and, collecting himself, he became suddenly warm, and with firm hand turned his horses round, and begged the woodman who accompanied him to point him out the way to the house with the "Schwarz Brett," Dr. Junius's. There he delivered a full load; at each log he took out of the wagon, he smiled oddly. The wood-measurer measured the wood carefully, turning each log and placing it exactly, that there might not be a crevice anywhere. "Why are you so over-particular to-day, pray?" asked Christopher, and he received for answer: "Professor Gellert must have a fair load; every shaving kept back from him were a sin." Christopher laughed aloud, and the wood-measurer looked at him with amazement, for such particularity generally provoked a quarrel. Christopher had still some logs over; these he kept by him on the wagon. At this moment the servant Sauer came up, and asked to whom the wood belonged. "To Professor Gellert," answered Christopher. "The man's mad! it isn't true. Professor Gellert has not bought any wood; it is my business to look after that." "He has not bought it, and yet it is his!" cried Christopher.

Sauer was on the point of giving the mad peasant a hearty scolding, raising his voice so much the louder, as it was striking eleven by St. Nicholas. At this moment, however, he became suddenly mute, for yonder from the University there came, with tired gait, a man of a noble countenance; at every step he made, on this side and on that, off came the hats and the caps of the passers-by, and Sauer simply called out, "There comes the Professor himself." What a peculiar expression passed over Christopher's face! He looked at the newcomer, and so earnest was his gaze that Gellert, who always walked with his head bowed, suddenly looked up. Christopher said: "Mr. Gellert, I am glad to see you still alive." "I thank you," said Gellert, and made as though he would pass on, but Christopher stepped up closer to him, and, stretching out his hand to him, said: "I have taken

## KYRIE ELEISON.

MARTIN LUTHER, 1524.

1. In - carnate Je - sus Christ be praised, Born of vir - gin pure and chaste, That as a
2. As God the Father's on - ly Son Guest in - to this world has come, To lead us
3. To earth He came so meek and poor, Making our sal - va - tion sure, That in the
4. Our Je - sus Christ this work has done, Love for us to be made known, Rejoice, then

man thou cam'st to earth. Rejoice, all an - gels in His birth! Ky - rie E - leis!
from this tearful vale, That we thro' tri - al might pre - vail, Ky - rie E - leis!
heaven our notes should vie With angel's songs that swell on high. Ky - rie E - leis!
all in Christendom, And thank Him thro' all time to come. Ky - rie E - leis!

The music of this hymn is from Spiritual Volksong of the 15th century. *Kyrie A-leise,* "O Lord, have mercy."

the liberty—I should like—will you give me your hand, Mr. Gellert." Gellert drew his long, thin hand out of his muff and placed it in the hard, oaken-like hand of the peasant; and at this moment, when the peasant's hand lay in the scholar's palm, as one felt the other's pressure in actual living grasp, there took place, though the mortal actors in the scene were all unconscious of it, a renewal of that healthy life which alone can make a people one. How long had the learned world, wrapped up in itself separated from the fellow-men around, thought in Latin, felt as foreigners, and lived buried in contemplation of by-gone worlds! From the time of Gellert commences the ever-increasing unity of good-fellowship throughout all classes of life, kept up by mutual giving and receiving. As the scholar—as the solitary poet endeavors to work upon others by lays that quicken, and songs that incite, so he in his turn is a debtor to his age; and the lonely thinking and writing become the property of all; but the effects are not seen in a moment; for higher than the most highly gifted spirit of any single man is the spirit of a nation. With the pressure which Gellert and the peasant exchanged commenced a mighty change in universal life, which never more can cease to act. "Permit me to enter your room?" said Christopher and Gellert nodded assent. He was so courteous that he motioned to the peasant to enter first;

however, Sauer went close after him; he thought it must be a madman; he must protect his master; the man looked just as if he were drunk. Gellert, with his amanuensis, Gödike, followed them.

Gellert, however, felt that the man must be actuated by pure motives; he bade the others retire, and took Christopher alone into his study; and as he clasped his left with his own right hand, he asked: "Well, my good friend what is your business?" "Eh? oh! nothing—I've only brought you a load of wood there—a fair, full load; however, I'll give you the few logs which I have in my wagon, as well." "My good man, my servant Sauer looks after buying my wood." "It is no question of buying. No, my dear sir, I give it to you." "Give

it to me? Why me particularly" "Oh! sir, you do not know at all what good you do, what good you have done me; and my wife was right; why should there not be really pious men in our day too? Surely the sun still shines as he shone thousands of years ago; all is now the same as then; and the God of old is still living." "Certainly, certainly; I am glad to see you so pious." "Ah! believe me, dear sir, I am not always so pious; and that I am so disposed to-day is owing to you. We have no more confessionals now, but I can confess to you; and you have taken a heavier load from my heart than a wagon-load of wood. Oh! sir, I am not what I was. In my early days I was a high-spirited, merry lad, and out in the field, and indoors in the inn and

## FROM HEAVEN'S SPHERE.

Martin Luther, 1558.

1. From Heaven's sphere I come down here To bring you news of right good
2. To-day a babe was born to all; A true, pure vir-gin had the
3. Now this is Je-sus Christ, our God, From all dis-tress, He'll lead your
4. Now praise your God on His high throne, Who sent us e'en His on-ly

cheer; Of this good cheer so much I bring, That thereof I can speak and sing.
call To be its mother, and so fair The child is, 'tis a joy for-e'er.
road; Him-self will your true Sav-iour be, And from all sins will make you free.
Son, His sight the an-gels praise and cheer, And wish to us a glad new year.

the spinning-room, there was none who could sing against me; but that is long past. What has a man on whose head the grave-blossoms are growing," and he pointed to his gray head, "to do with all that trash? And besides, the Seven Years' War has put a stop to all our singing. But last night, in the midst of the fearful cold, I sang a lay set expressly for me—all old tunes go to it; and it seemed to me as though I saw a sign-post which pointed I know not whither—or, nay, I do know whither." And now the peasant related how discontented and unhappy in mind he had been, and how the words in the lay had all at once raised his spirits and accompanied him upon the journey, like a good fellow who

talks to one cheerfully. At this part of the peasant's tale, Gellert folded his hands in silence, and the peasant concluded: "How I always envied others, I can not now think why; but you I do envy, sir; I should like to be as you." And Gellert answered: "I thank God, and rejoice greatly that my writings have been of service to you. Think not so well of me. Would God I were really the good man I appear in your eyes! I am far from being such as I should, such as I would fain be. I write my books for my own improvement also, to show myself as well as others what manner of men we should be." Laughing, the peasant replied: "You put me in mind of the story my poor mother used to tell of the old minister; he stood up once in the pulpit and said: 'My dear friends: I speak not only for you, but for myself also; I, too, have need of it.'" Christopher laughed outrageously when he had finished, and Gellert smiled and said: "Yes, whoever in the darkness lighteth another with a lamp, lighteth himself also; and the light is not part of ourselves,— it is put into our hands by Him who hath appointed the suns their courses." The peasant stood speechless, and looked upon the ground; there was something within him which took away the power of looking up; he was only conscious that it ill became him to laugh so loudly just now, when he told the story of the old minister.

A longer pause ensued, and Gellert seemed to be lost in reflection upon this ref-erence to a minister's work, for he said half to himself: "Oh! how would it fulfill my dearest wish to be a village pastor! To move about among my people, and really be one with them; the friend of their souls my whole life long, never to lose them out of my sight! Yonder goes one whom I have led into the right way; there another, with whom I still wrestle, but whom I shall as-suredly save; and in them all the teaching lives which God proclaims by me. Did I not think that I should be acting against my duty, I would this moment choose a country life for the remnant of my days. When I look from my window over the country, I have before me the broad sky, of which we citizens know but little, a scene entirely new; there I stand and lose

## BRIGHT WAS THE STAR.

H. Auber.
W. B. Bradsbury.

1. Bright was the guiding star that led, With mild, be - nig - nant ray,
2. But lo! a brighter, clear - er light, Now points to His a - bode;
3. Oh, haste to fol - low where it leads; The gra - cious call o - bey,
4. Oh, glad - ly tread the nar - row path, While light and grace are given:

The Gen - tiles to the low - ly shed Where the Redeem - er lay.
It shines thro' sin and sorrow's night, To guide us to our God.
Be rug - ged wilds or flow - ry meads The Christian's destined way.
Who meek - ly fol - low Christ on earth Shall reign with Him in Heaven.

myself for half-an-hour in gazing and in thinking. Yes, good friend, envy no man in the rank of scholars. Look at me; I am almost always ill; and what a burden is a sickly body! How strong, on the contrary, are you! I am never happier than when, without being remarked, I can watch a din-ner-table thronged by hungry men and maids. Even if these folks be not generally so happy as their superiors, at table they are certainly happier." "Yes, sir; we relish our eating and drinking. And, lately, when felling and sorting that wood below, I was more then usually lively; it seems as though I had a notion I was to do some good with it." "And must I permit you to make me a present?" asked Gellert, resting his chin upon his left hand. The peasant answered, "It is not worth talking about." "Nay; it might be well worth talking about; but I accept your present. It is pride not to be ready to accept a gift. Is not all we have a gift from God? and what one man gives another, he gives, as is most appro-priately said, for God's sake. Now, were I your minister, I should be pleased to accept a present from you. You see, good friend, we men have no occasion to thank each other. You have given me nothing of yours, and I have given you nothing of mine. That the trees grow in the forest is none of your doing; it is the work of the Creator and Preserver of the world; and the soil is not yours; and the sun and the rain are not yours; they are all the works of His hand; and if, perchance, I have some healthy thoughts rising up in my soul, which benefit my fellow-men, it is none of mine, it is His doing. The word is not mine, and the spirit is not mine; and I am but an instrument in His hand. Therefore one man needs not to utter words of thanks to his fellow, if every one would but acknowledge who it really is that gives." The peasant looked up in astonishment. Gellert re-

marked it, and said: "Understand me aright. I thank you from my heart; you have done a kind action. But that the trees grow is none of yours, and it is none of mine that thoughts arise in me; every one simply tills his field, and tends his woodland, and the honest, assiduous toil he gives thereto is his virtue. That you felled, loaded, and brought the wood, and wish no recompense for your labor, is very thankworthy. My wood was more easily felled;

## HARK! THE ANGEL CHOIR.

PHŒBE CARY.

1. Oh, blind eyes, be no more tearful, Drooping spir-it, rise, be glad! Heavy soul, why art thou fearful?
2. Tho' thy treasure Death hath taken, They that "sleep" are never lost; They shall hear the trump and waken,

Why so wea-ry, why so sad? Oh, the weakness and the mad-ness Of a heart that holdeth grief,
Christmas tri-umph o'er the dust. Rise, sad soul, from thy de-jec-tion, His promise ne'er give o'er;

When all else is light and gladness In a joy beyond be-lief. }
Birth and death and resur-rec-tion— Rise, wonder and adore.   } Hark! the Christmas bells are ringing,

And their chiming fills the air; Hark, the an-gel choir is singing PEACE! to souls forspent with care.

but those still nights which I and all of my calling pass in heavy thought—who can tell what toil there is in them? There is in the world an adjustment which no one sees, and which but seldom discovers itself; and this and that shift thither and hither, and the scales of the balance become even, and then ceases all distinction between 'mine' and 'thine,' and in the still forest rings an axe for me, and in the silent night my spirit thinks and my pen writes for you."

The peasant passed both his hands over his temples, and his look was as though he said to himself, "Where are you? Are you still in the world? Is it a mortal man who speaks to you? Are you in Leipzig, in that populous city where men jostle one another for gain and bare existence?"

Below might be heard the creaking of the saw as the wood was being sundered; and now the near-horse neighs, and Christopher is in the world again. "It may injure the horse to stand so long in the cold; and no money for the wood! but perhaps a sick horse to take home into the bargain; that would be too much," he thought. "Yes, yes, Mr. Professor," said he—he had his hat under his arm, and was rubbing his hands —"yes, I am delighted with what I have done; and I value the lesson, believe me, more than ten loads of wood; and never shall I forget you to my dying day. And though I see you are not so poor as I had

imagined, still I don't regret it. Oh! no, certainly not at all." "Eh! did you think me so very poor, then?" "Yes, miserably poor." "I have always been poor, but God has never suffered me to be a single day without necessaries. I have in the world much happiness which I have not deserved, and much unhappiness I have not, which perchance I have deserved. I have found much favor with both high and low, for which I can not sufficiently thank God.

## WHEN LOVE WAS BORN.

Milton Wellings.

1. Sweet Christmas month, the month that Love was born, That ev-er was an a-lien un-til now, What tho' the blos-soms hang not on the bough, What tho' the earth of beauty's grace be shorn! Lo! in the woods be-neath the frost-kissed hill, The hol-ly lights the path, December's rose, And un-derneath the scar-let ber-ry grows, To tell us Love is liv-ing still, As if to tell us love is liv-ing still.

2. Liv-ing, it may be, un-der rud-er skies, Though the glad glo-ry of the year be past, With frost and death Love lingers to the last, And in Love's breast her blossom never dies. 'Tis nursed with thoughts that come with Christmas chimes, That gracious time when Love and Peace are crown'd, When the world's woes by one great joy are drowned, Glad summer of the Christmas time! The sum-mer of the soul is Christ-mas time.

And now tell me, can not I give you something, or obtain something for you? You are a local magistrate, I presume?" "Why so?" "You look like it; you might be." Christopher had taken his hat into his hands, and was crumpling it up now; he half closed his eyes, and with a sly inquiring glance, he peered at Gellert. Suddenly, however, the expression of his face changed, and the muscles quivered, as he said: "Sir, what a man are you! How can you dive into the recesses of one's heart! I have really pined night and day, and been cross with the whole world, because I could not be magistrate, and you, sir, you have actually helped to overcome that in me. Oh! sir, as soon as I read that verse in your book, I had an idea, and now I see still more plainly, that you must be a man of God, who can pluck the heart from one's bosom, and turn it round and round. I had thought I could never have another moment's happiness, if my neighbor, Hans Gottlieb, should be magistrate; and with that verse of yours, it has been with me as when one calms the blood with a magic spell."

## GOOD CHRISTIAN MEN, REJOICE.

GERMAN.

1. Good Christian men, re - joice   With heart and soul and voice,   Give ye heed to
2. Good Christian men, re - joice   With heart and soul and voice;   Now ye hear of
3. Good Christian men, re - joice   With heart and soul and voice;   Now ye need not

what we say: News! news! Je - sus Christ is born to - day!   Ox and ass before Him bow, And
endless bliss: Joy! joy! Je - sus Christ was born for this!   He hath ope'd the heav'nly door, And
fear the grave: Peace! peace! Jesus Christ was born to save!   Calls you one and calls you all, To

He is in the man - ger now. Christ is born to - day!   Christ is born to - day!
man is bless - ed ev - er - more. Christ was born for this!   Christ was born for this!
gain His ev - er - last - ing hall: Christ was born to save!   Christ was born to save!

"Well, my good friend, I am rejoiced to hear it; believe me, every one has in himself alone a whole host to govern. What can so strongly urge men to wish to govern others? What can it profit you to be local magistrate; when to accomplish your object you must perhaps do something wrong? What were the fame, not only of a village, but even of the whole world, if you could have no self-respect? Let it suffice for you to perform your daily duties with uprightness; let your joys be centred in your wife and children, and you will be happy. What need you more? Think not that honor and station would make you happy. Rejoice, and again I say, rejoice; 'a contented spirit is a continual feast.' I often whisper this to myself when I feel disposed to give way to dejection; and although misery be not our fault, yet lack of endurance and of patience in misery is undoubtedly our fault." "I would my wife were here too, that she also might hear this; I grudge myself the hearing of it all alone; I can not remember it all properly, and yet I should like to tell it to her, word for word. Who would have thought, that, by standing upon a load of wood, one could get a peep into Heaven!''

Gellert in silence bowed his head; and afterwards he said: ''Yes, rejoice in your deed, as I do in your gift. Your wood is sacrificial wood. In olden time—and it was right in principle, because man could not yet offer prayer and thanks in spirit—it was a custom and ordinance to bring something from one's possessions, as a proof of devotion; this was a sacrifice. And the more important the gift to be given, or the request to be granted, the more costly was the sacrifice. Our God will have no victims; but whatsoever you do unto one of the least of His, you do unto Him. Such are our sacrifices. My dear friend, from my heart I thank you; for you have done me a kindness in that you have given me a real, undeniable proof that my words have penetrated your heart, and that I do not live on for nothing; and treasure it up in your heart, that you have caused real joy to one who is often, very often, weighed down with heaviness and sorrow. You have not only kindled bright tapers upon my Christ-

## NEW PRINCE, NEW POMP.

SCOTCH AIR.
ROBT. SOUTHWELL. 1585.

*Andante moderato.*

1. Be - hold a lit - tle, tender Babe, In freezing win - ter night, In homely man - ger
2. Weigh not his crib, his wooden dish, Nor beasts that by him feed; Weigh not his mother's
3. The persons in that poor at - tire His roy - al liv - 'ries wear; The Prince himself is

trembling lies; A - las! a pit - eous sight. The inns are full; no man will yield This
poor at - tire, Nor Joseph's sim - ple weed. This sta - ble is a Prince's court, The
come from Heav'n; This pomp is prais-ed there. With joy approach, O Christian wight! Do

lit - tle Pil - grim bed; But forced he is with sil - ly beasts In crib to shroud his head.
crib his chair of state; The beasts are par - cel of his pomp, The wooden dish his plate.
homage to thy King; And highly praise this humble pomp, Which he from Heav'n doth bring.

mas tree, but the tree itself burns, gives light, and warms; the bush burns, and is not consumed, which is an image of the presence of the Holy Spirit, and its admonition to trust in the Most High in this wilderness of life, in mourning and in woe. Oh! my dear friend, I have been nigh unto death. What a solemn, quaking stride is the stride into eternity! What a difference between ideas of death in the days of health, and on the brink of the grave! And how shall I show myself worthy of longer life? By learning better to die. And, mark, when I sit here, in solitude pursuing my thoughts, keeping some and driving away others, then I can think, that in distant valleys, upon distant mountains, even beyond the mighty seas, there are living men who carry my thoughts within their hearts; and for them I live, and they are near and dear to me, till one day we shall meet where there is no more parting, no more separation. Peasant and scholar, let us abide as we are. Give me your hand—farewell!''

And once again, the soft and the hard hand were clasped together; and Christopher really trembled as Gellert laid his hand upon his shoulder. They shook hands, and therewith something touched the heart of each more impressively, more completely, than ever words could touch it. Christopher got down-stairs without knowing how; below, he threw down the extra logs of wood, which he had kept back, with a clatter from the wagon, and then drove briskly from the city. Not till he arrived at Lindenthal, did he allow himself and his horses rest or food. He had driven away empty; he had nothing on his wagon, nothing in his purse; and yet who can tell what treasures he took home; and who can tell what inextinguishable fire he left behind him yonder, by that lonely scholar! Gellert, who usually dined at his brother's, to-day had dinner brought into his own room, remained quite alone, and did not go out again; he had experienced quite enough excitement, and society he had in his own thoughts. Oh! to find that there are open, susceptible hearts, is a blessing to him that writes in solitude, and is as wondrous to him as though he dipped his pen in streams of sunshine, and as if all he wrote were light. The rain-drop which falls from the cloud can not tell upon what plant it drops; there is a quickening power in it, but for what? And a thought which finds expression from a human heart; an action, nay, a whole life is like the rain-drop falling from the cloud; the whole period of a life endures no longer than the rain-drop needs for its falling. And as for

## NOW, OH, PREPARE.

MARTIN FRITZSCH, 1589.
CH. FURCHTEGOTT GELLERT, 1765.

1. Now, oh, pre - pare with zeal and care, The Saviour's day with thanks and praise re - mem -
2. Speak, grateful strain, a - gain, a - gain! Our Lord the world in His own Son has lov -
3. Ex - alt the Lord with one accord! Oh, seek Him, all, His gracious fav - or win -

ber; Love is the thanks that He receives, Ex-tol the Lord, come, soul, arise from slum - ber!
ed. Oh, who am I, Lord, that Thou me With grace divine, in Thine own Son, hast lov - ed?
ning. Al - le - lu - ia, Al - le - lu - ia! In God rejoice, saved and redeemed from sin - ning.

knowing where your life is continued, how your work proceeds, you can not attain to that. And in the night all was still around, nothing was astir; the whole earth was simple rest, as Gellert sat in his room by his lonely lamp; his hand lay upon an open book, and his eyes were fixed upon the empty air; and on a sudden came once more upon him that melancholy gloom, which so easily resumes its place after more than usual excitement. It is as though the soul, suddenly elevated above all, must still remember the heaviness it but now experienced though that expresses itself as tears of joy in the eye. In Gellert, however, this melancholy had a more peculiar phase; a sort of timidity had rooted itself in him, connected with his weak chest, and that secret gnawing pain in his head; it was a fearfulness which his manner of life only tended to increase. Surrounded though he was by nothing but love and admiration in the world, he could not divest himself of the fear that all which is most horrible and terrible would burst suddenly upon him; and so he gazed fixedly before him. He passed his hand over his face, and with an effort concentrated his looks and thoughts upon surrounding objects, saying to himself almost aloud: "How comforting is light! Were there no light from without to illumine objects for us, we should perish in gloom, in the shadows of night. And night is a gentle friend that watches by us, and, when we are sunk in sorrow, points out to us that the world is still here, that it calls and beckons us, and requires of us duty and cheerfulness. 'You must not be lost in self,' it says; 'See! the world is still here;' and a friend beside us is as a light which illumines surrounding objects; we can not forget them, we must see them and mingle with them. How hard is life, and how little I accomplish! I would fain awaken the whole world to goodness and to love; but my voice is weak, my strength is insufficient: how insignificant is all I do!" And he now rose up and strode across the room; then he stood at the hearth where the fire was burning, made of wood given to him that very day, and his thoughts reverted to the man who had given it. Why had he not asked his name; and where he came from? Perchance he might have been able in thought to follow him all the way, as he drove home; and now . . . but yet 'tis more—'tis better as it is: it is not an individual, it is not So-and-so, who has shown his gratitude, but all the world by the mouth of one. "The kindnesses I receive," he thought, "are indeed trials; yet I ought to accept them with thanks. I will try henceforth to be a benefactor to others, as others are to me, without display, and with grateful thanks to God, our highest Benefactor: this will I do, and search no further for the why and for the wherefore." And again a voice spoke within him; he stood erect. "Who knows," he thought, "whether at this moment I have not been in this or that place, to this or that man, a brother, a friend, a comforter, a saviour;

## SING GOD PRAISES.

Ambrosius.
Heinrich Weld, 1643.

1. Sing God prais-es loud and deep, Ev-'ry promise He doth keep;
2. What to our fore-fa-thers' race Greatest wish and long-ings trace,
3. Oh, be welcome, grace di-vine! Oh, ho-san-nah, Sa-viour mine!
4. That when Thou, Heav'n's glorious King, Thy new reign at last shall bring,

He the sinner's Guardian, Friend, To us sin-ners once did send.
And what they have proph-e-sied, Glo-ri-ous-ly is veri-fied.
God, so gracious and so kind, In my heart Thy dwell-ing find.
I may go to meet Thee, Lord, Be with Thee in full ac-cord.

and from house to house, may be, my spirit travels, awakening, enlivening, refreshing —yonder in the attic, where burns a solitary light; and afar in some village a mother is sitting by her child, and hearing him repeat the thoughts I have arranged in verse; and peradventure some solitary old man, who is waiting for death, is now sitting by his fireside, and his lips are uttering my words. And yonder in the church, the choir is chanting a hymn; could I have written this hymn without its vigor in my heart? Oh! no, it must be there." And with trembling he thought: "There is nothing so small as to have no place in the government of God: should you not, then, believe that He suffered this day's incident to happen for your joy? Oh! were it so, what great happiness were yours! A heart renewed." He moved to the window, looked up to Heaven, and prayed inwardly: "My soul is with my brothers and sisters: nay, it is with thee, my God, and in humility I acknowledge how richly thou hast blessed me. And if, in the kingdom of the world to come, a soul should cry to me: 'Thou didst guide and cheer me on to happiness eternal!' All hail! my friend, my benefactor, my glory in the presence of God. . . In these thoughts let me die, and pardon me my weakness and my sins!" * *

"And the evening and the morning were the first day." At early morning, Gellert was sitting at his table, and reading according to his invariable custom, first of all in the Bible. He never left the Bible open—

he always shut it with a peaceful, devotional air, after he had read therein ; there was something grateful as well as reverential in his manner of closing the volume ; the holy words should not lie uncovered. To-day, however, the Bible was lying open when he rose. His eye fell upon the History of the Creation, and at the words, " And the evening and the morning were the first day," he leaned his head back against the arm-chair, and kept his hand upon the book, as though he would grasp with his hand also the lofty thought, how Night and Day were divided. For a long while he sat thus, and he was wondrously bright in spirit, and a soft reminiscence dawned upon

## NOW, COURAGE TAKE.

JOHANN RIST, 1641.
JOHANN SCHOPP, 1641.

1. Now, cour - age take, my trembling soul, And show thine in - most long - ing
2. Oh, joy - ous time! oh, wondrous night! More wondrous man saw nev - er.
3. Praise be to Thee, Lord Je - sus Christ, And thanks by us be chant - ed.

To hail the Son, Sav - iour of all, With joy and praise be - long - ing
The Fa - ther sent Him by His might, His heir, our Friend and Sav - iour.
That Thou, my broth - er high - ly prized, Thy cross for us hast plant - ed.

This is the night in which He came And took on Him a hu - man
In Him Thou send'st the trust - y man That fire and clouds, too, con - quer
Help that Thy conquering grace sub - lime I val - ue in Thy glo - rious

frame; The world, by pa - tient su - ing, His bride, He still is woo - ing.
can; Thro' Him the heavens trem - ble: Ye an - gels, now as - sem - ble.
time, And there, in end - less spac - es, May sing Thee end - less prais - es.

him; of a glad, bright day in his childhood, when he had been so happy, having gone out with his father for a walk. An inward warmth roused his heart to quicker pulsation ; and suddenly he started and looked about him ; he had been humming a tune.

Up from the street came the busy sound of day ; at other times how insufferable he had found it! and now how joyous it seemed that men should bestir themselves, and turn to all sorts of occupations. There was a sound of crumbling snow ; and how nice to have a house and a blaze upon the hearth ! "And the evening and the morning were the first day !" And man getteth himself a light in the darkness ; but how long, O man! could you make it endure? What could you do with your artificial light, if God did not cause his sun to shine? Without it grows no grass, no corn. On the hand lying upon the book there fell a bright sunbeam. How soon, at other times, would Gellert have drawn the defensive curtain! Now he watches the little motes that play about in the sunbeam. The servant brought in the cup of coffee, and the faithful amanuensis, Gödike, asked if there were anything to do. Generally, Gellert scarce lifted his head from his books, hastily acknowledging the attention, and reading on in silence; to-day he motioned to Gödike to stay, and said to Sauer. "Another cup;

## CHRISTMAS TREASURES.

V. BELLINI.
EUGENE FIELD.

*Moderato, con espress.*

1. I count my treasures o'er with care— A lit-tle toy that ba-by knew, A lit-tle sock of fad-ed hue, A lit-tle lock of gold-en hair. Long years a-go this Christ-mas time, My lit-tle one— my all to me— Sat, robed in white, up-on my knee, And heard the Mer-ry Christmas chime.

2. "Tell me, my lit-tle gold-en-head, If San-ta Claus should come to-night, What shall he bring my ba-by bright, What treasure for my boy?" I said. And then he named the lit-tle toy, While in his round and truth-ful eyes There came a look of glad sur-prise That spoke his trust-ful, child-ish joy.

3. And, as he lisped his ev-'ning prayer, He asked the boon with ba-by grace, And, tod-dling to the chim-ney place, He hung his lit-tle stock-ing there. That night, as lengthening shadows crept, I saw the white-winged an-gels come With mu-sic to our hum-ble home, And kiss my dar-ling as he slept.

He must have heard that baby prayer,
  For in the morn, with glowing face,
  He toddled to the chimney place
And found the little treasure there.
They came again one Christmas-tide,
  That angel host, so fair and white,
  And, singing all the Christmas night,
They lured my darling from my side.

A little sock, a little toy,
  A little lock of golden hair,
  The Christmas music on the air,
A watching for my baby boy.
But if again that angel train
  And golden-head come back for me,
  To bear me to eternity,
My watching will not be in vain.

Mr. Gödike will take coffee with me. God has given me a day of rejoicing." Sauer brought the cup, and Gellert said, "Yes, God has given me a day of rejoicing, and what I am most thankful for is, that he has granted me strength to thank him with all my heart; not so entirely, however, as I should like." "Thank God, Mr. Professor, that you are once more in health, and cheerful; and permit me, Mr. Professor, to tell you that I was myself also ill a short time ago, and I then learnt a lesson which I shall never forget. Who is most grateful? The convalescent. He learns to love God and his beautiful world anew; he is grateful for everything, and delighted with everything. What a flavor has his first cup of coffee! How he enjoys his first walk outside the house, outside the gate! The houses, the trees, all give us greeting; all is again in us full of health and joy!" So said Gödike, and Gellert rejoined: "You are a good creature, and have just spoken good words. Certainly, the convalescent is the most grateful. We are, however, for the most part, sick in spirit, and have not strength to recover; and a sickly, stricken spirit is the heaviest pain." Long time the two sat quietly together; it struck eight. Gellert started up, and cried irritably: "There, now, you have allowed me to forget that I must be on my way to the University." "The vacation has begun; Mr. Professor has no lecture to-day." "No lec-

## JESUS LIVES.

F. E. Cox *tr.* "St. Albinus."
Ch. Furchtegott Gellert, 1757.

1. Jesus lives! no lon-ger now Can thy terrors, Death, ap-pall us; Je-sus lives! by this we know Thou, O Grave, canst not enthrall us. Al-le-lu-ia!
2. Jesus lives! henceforth is death But the gate of life im-mor-tal; This shall calm our trembling breath, When we pass its gloomy por-tal. Al-le-lu-ia!
3. Jesus lives! for us He died; Then, alone to Je-sus liv-ing, Pure in heart may we a-bide, Glo-ry to our Saviour giv-ing. Al-le-lu-ia!
4. Jesus lives! to Him the throne O-ver all the world is giv-en: May we go where He is gone, Rest and reign with Him in Heav-en. Al-le-lu-ia! A-men.

ture to-day? Ah! and I believe to-day is just the time when I could have told my young friends something that would have benefited them for their whole lives." There was a shuffling of many feet outside the door; the door opened, and several boys from St. Thomas' School choir advanced and sang to Gellert some of his own hymns; and as they chanted the verse—

And haply there—oh! grant it, Heaven!
Some blessed saints will greet me too;
All hail! all hail! to you was given
To save my life and soul, to you!
Oh God! my God! what joy to be
The winner of a soul to Thee!

Gellert wept aloud, folded his hands, and raised his eyes to Heaven. A happier Christ-mas than that of 1768 had Gellert never seen; and it was his last. Scarcely a year after, on the 13th of December, 1769, Gellert died a pious, tranquil death, such as he had ever coveted. As the long train which followed his bier moved to the churchyard of St. John's, Leipzig, a peasant with his wife and children in holiday clothes entered among the last. It was Christopher with his family. The whole way he had been silent; whilst his wife wept passionately at the pastor's touching address, it was only by the working of his features that Christopher showed how deeply moved he was. But on the way home he said: "I am glad I did him a kindness in his lifetime; it would now be too late."—*Berthold Auerbach.*

## CHRISTMAS HYMN.

Henry Dielman.
Rev. John McCaffrey.

*Maestoso con spirito.*

1. With glo - ry lit the mid - night air Re - vealed bright an - gels
2. Then sweet - ly spoke th' an - gel - ic voice: "Fear not; let Heaven and
3. The choirs of Heaven still bless the morn, When God through love for

hover - ing there, In fear beheld the raptured swains When rose the Heaven-inspired strains.
earth re - joice; The Child, in Bethlehem's crib that lies, Is God, descended from the skies."
man was born, That God we humbly bow be - fore, And praise with angels and a - dore.

*dolce.*

Glo - ry, glo - ry, glo - ry to God, and peace to earth, and peace to

*mf*

earth, Made glo - ri-ous by the Sav - iour's birth, by the Sav - iour's birth.

*Chorus.*

And peace to earth,

Glo - ry to God, glo - ry to God, And peace to earth, and peace to

Made glorious by the Sav-iour's birth.

earth, Made glo - rious by the Sav - iour's birth, by the Sav - iour's birth.

10

## RING OUT, WILD BELLS.

F. Paolo Tosti.
Alfred Tennyson.

1. Ring out, wild bells, to the wild sky, The flying cloud, the frosty light, The year is dy - ing in the
2. Ring out false pride in place and blood, The civic slander and the spite, Ring in the love of truth and

night Forev - er    and for - ev - er; Ring out the old, ring in the new, Ring, happy bells, across the
right Forev - er    and for - ev - er; Ring out old shapes of foul disease, Ring out the harrowing lust of

snow, The year is  go - ing, let him go    For-ev - er  and for - ev - er;    Ring
gold, Ring out the  thou - sand wars of old  For-ev - er  and for - ev - er;    Ring

out    the grief that saps the mind For those that here we see no more, Ring out  the feud of rich and
out    the want, the care, the sin, The faithless coldness of the times, Ring out,  ring out my mournful

poor  For - ev - er and for - ev - er; Ring out a  slow - ly dy - ing  cause  And  ancient
rhymes  For - ev - er and for - ev - er; Ring out the  dark - ness of the  land,  Ring  in the

forms of par-ty strife, Ring in the no - bler modes of life Forev-er and for - ev   .   .  er.
valiant man and free, Ring in the Christ that is to  be  Forev-er and for - ev   .   .  er.

## ON CHRISTMAS MORNING.

PONIATOWSKI.
*Air—"Yeoman's Wedding Song."*

*Allegretto giojoso.*

1. Ding dong, ding dong, ding dong, peal out the bells, For it is the Christmas morn - ing;
2. Ding dong, ding dong, ding dong, peal out the bells, For it is the Christmas morn - ing;

Peal on, peal on your glad re - frain The Christmas glow is now the sky a -
Peal on, peal on your glad re - frain The Christmas glow is now the sky a -

dorn - - - ing. An an - them blest is the song ye sing, Is the
dorn - - - ing. Ye tell of rest from the world's hard toil, When the

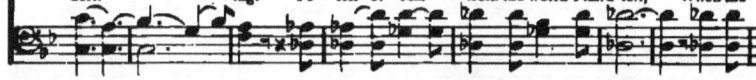

old tale of won - der ye tell As thro' the land, o'er hill and o'er
lau - rel and hol - ly en - twine, When Mer - riment, with its best of good

plain Goes the message of joy on your swell, Ding dong, ding dong, all merrily ring The
cheer, Bids old Care his dull sceptre resign, Ding dong, ding dong, all merrily ring The

bells on Christmas morning, Ding dong, all merrily ring The bells on Christmas morn - ing.

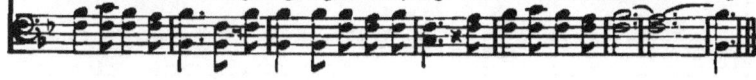

## SWEET VILLAGE BELLS.

DONIZETTI.
ELLEN DOUGLAS.

1. Sweet vil-lage bells are peal - ing Far thro' the frosty air; Tender as love's re - veal - ing,
2. Bright to the old man's dreaming Come scenes of long ago, Joyous to youth's fair seem - ing,

Telling release from care. Snow o'er the hills is fall-ing, Dimming the light of day;
Swing the bells to and fro; Far o'er the qui - et riv - er, Tune-ful the sto - ry goes, With

Sto - ry of hope re - call-ing, Ring on the bells al - way: Bethlehem's child of prom - ise,
thoughts of the gracious Giver, And love that o - ver - flows: Bethlehem's child of prom - ise,

Wise Men that knew His star, Beth-le-hem's child of prom - ise, Wise Men that knew His star,

Melchoir with gift all gold - en, Gaspard and Bal - tha - zar; Angels that sang for shepherds,

Choiring a glad re - frain, "Peace and good-will to mortals, Gladness for all their pain."

## FIRST CHRISTMAS GIFTS.

JOHN SELWYN.
MRS. CHAS. BARNARD.

*Moderato.*

1. Long had their watch been and drear - y, Wise men who looked for the dawn;
2. Mountain and des - ert they tra - verse, Cit - y and tem - ple they see,

Prophet and King had grown wea - ry, In - to death's mys - ter - y gone.
Nor yet the Star of their guid - ance Pauses o'er up - land or lea.

End - ed the long night of wait - ing, See the morn promised ap - pears;
Crowded the inn and the dwell - ing, A Child in a manger is born;

Glo - ry their wearied eyes sa - ting, Lo! the bright dream of their years!
An - gels the shepherds are tell - ing, Dawning the first Christmas morn.

Yonder is blazing the Day - Star, Promised from a - ges un - told!
Low bows the swarthy Bal - tha - zar, Myrrh is his gift to the King;

Fol - low it, a - ged Bal - tha - zar, Melchoir, and Gaspard the bold.
Frankincense bears the fair Gas - pard, Gol - den gifts Melchoir doth bring.

THE SNOW ANGEL.

# A CHRISTMAS CAROL.

MARLEY was dead, to begin with. There is no doubt whatever about that. The register of his burial was signed by the clergyman, the clerk, the undertaker, and the chief mourner. Scrooge signed it. And Scrooge's name was good upon 'Change for anything he chose to put his hand to. Old Marley was as dead as a door-nail. Mind! I don't mean to say that I know, of my own knowledge, what there is particularly dead about a door-nail. I might have been inclined, myself, to regard a coffin-nail as the deadest piece of ironmongery in the trade. But the wisdom of our ancestors is in the simile; and my unhallowed hands shall not disturb it, or the Country's done for. You will therefore permit me to repeat, emphatically, that Marley was as dead as a door-nail.

Scrooge knew he was dead? Of course he did. How could it be otherwise? Scrooge and he were partners for I don't know how many years. Scrooge was his sole executor, his sole administrator, his sole assignee, his sole residuary legatee, his sole friend, and sole mourner. And even Scrooge was not so dreadfully cut up by the sad event but that he was an excellent man of business on the very day of the funeral, and solemnized it with an undoubted bargain. The mention of Marley's funeral brings me back to the point I started from. There is no doubt that Marley was dead. This must be distinctly understood, or nothing wonderful can come of the story I am going to relate.

If we were not perfectly convinced that Hamlet's Father died before the play began, there would be nothing more remarkable in his taking a stroll at night, in an easterly wind, on his own ramparts, than there would be in any other middle-aged gentleman rashly turning out after dark in a breezy spot—Saint Paul's Churchyard, for instance —literally to astonish his son's weak mind.

Scrooge never painted out old Marley's name. There it stood, years afterwards, above the warehouse door : Scrooge & Marley. The firm was known as Scrooge & Marley. Sometimes people new to the business called Scrooge Scrooge, and sometimes Marley, but he answered to both names. It was all the same to him. Oh ! But he was a tight-fisted hand at the grindstone, Scrooge ! a squeezing, wrenching, grasping, scraping, clutching, covetous, old sinner ! Hard and sharp as flint, from which no steel had ever struck out generous fire ; secret and self-contained, and solitary as an oyster. The cold within him froze his old features, nipped his pointed nose, shrivelled his cheek, stiffened his gait; made his eyes red, his thin lips blue ; and spoke out shrewdly in his grating voice.

A frosty rime was on his head, on his eyebrows, and his wiry chin. He carried his own low temperature always about with him ; he iced his office in the dog days ; and didn't thaw it one degree on Christmas. External heat and cold had little influence on Scrooge. No warmth could warm, no wintry weather chill him. No wind that blew was bitterer than he, no falling snow was more intent upon its purpose, no pelting rain less open to entreaty. Foul weather didn't know where to have him. The heaviest rain, and snow, and hail, and sleet, could boast of the advantage over him in only one respect. They often "came down" handsomely, and Scrooge never did. Nobody ever stopped him in the street to say, with gladsome looks, "My dear Scrooge, how are you? When will you come to see me?" No beggars implored him to bestow a trifle, no children asked him what it was o'clock, no man or woman ever once in all his life inquired the way to such and such a place of Scrooge. Even the blind men's dogs appeared to know him ;

151

and when they saw him coming on, would tug their owners into doorways and up courts ; and then would wag their tails as though they said, "No eye at all is better than an evil eye, dark master!" But what did Scrooge care ! It was the very thing he liked. To edge his way along the crowded paths of life, warning all human sympathy to keep its distance, was what the knowing ones call "nuts" to Scrooge.

Once upon a time—of all the good days in the year, on Christmas Eve—old Scrooge sat busy in his counting house. It was cold, bleak, biting weather : foggy withal :

and he could hear the people in the court outside, go wheezing up and down, beating their hands upon their breasts, and stamping their feet upon the pavement stones to warm them. The city clocks had only just gone three, but it was quite dark already —it had not been light all day—and candles were flaring in the windows of the neighboring offices, like ruddy smears upon the palpable brown air. The fog came pouring in at every chink and keyhole, and was so dense without, that, although the court was of the narrowest, the houses opposite were mere phantoms. To see the dingy cloud

## CHRISTMAS LULLABY.

A. F. HARRISON.
SHIRLEY TALFORD.

*Andante.*

1. Twi-light fall-ing ba - by wea-ry, Ceased its laughter and its play, Nes-tled to the
2. An - gels guarding ba - by's slumber, Here from high-est Heaven a-bove, Once ye came, a
3. Hark! your Song ce - les - tial ringing, "Peace on earth, to men good-will!" Through the ages

*rall.*     *agitato.*

heart most lov - ing, That doth o'er it ev - er pray: "Ba - by dar-ling, an - gels guard thee,
countless num - ber, Round a babe in heavenly love; As ye gath - er by this cra-dle,
still guessing - ing, Echoes through the heavens still! And the Star still sheds its splendor,

*con anima.*

Treasure of our heart and home, May they hold thee in their keeping, Ne'er in devious paths to roam !"
Are your thoughts of long a - go, When on far Ju - de - a's hillside Shepherds whispered soft and low ?
As it gleam'd before you then, While, their gifts of Christmas bringing, Countless Wise Men throng your ken.

come drooping down, obscuring everything, one might have thought that Nature lived hard by, and was brewing on a large scale. The door of Scrooge's counting house was open, that he might keep his eye upon his clerk, who in a dismal little cell beyond, a sort of tank, was copying letters. Scrooge had a very small fire, but the clerk's fire was so very much smaller that it looked like one coal. But he couldn't replenish it, for Scrooge kept the coal-box in his own room ; and so surely as the clerk came in with the shovel, the master predicted that it would be necessary for them to part.

Wherefore the clerk put on his white comforter, and tried to warm himself at the candle ; in which effort, not being a man of strong imagination, he failed.

"A merry Christmas, uncle ! God save you !" cried a cheerful voice. It was the voice of Scrooge's nephew, who came upon him so quickly that this was the first intimation he had had of his approach. "Bah!" said Scrooge. "Humbug !" He had so heated himself with rapid walking in the fog and frost, this nephew of Scrooge's, that he was all in a glow ; his face was ruddy and handsome; his eyes sparkled, and his breath smoked again. "Christmas a humbug, uncle!" said Scrooge's nephew. "You don't mean that, I am sure." "I do," said Scrooge. "Merry Christmas! What right have you to be merry? What reason have you to be merry? You're poor enough." "Come, then," returned the nephew, gaily, "What right have you to be dismal? What reason have you to be morose? You're rich enough." Scrooge having no better answer ready on the spur of the moment, said, "Bah!" again; and followed it up with "Humbug!" "Don't be cross, uncle!" said the nephew. "What else can I be," returned the uncle, "when I live in such a world of fools as this? Merry Christmas! Out upon merry Christmas! What's Christmas time to you but a time for paying bills without money; a time for finding yourself a year older, and not an hour richer; a time for balancing your books and having every item in 'em, through a round dozen of months, presented dead against you? If I could work my will," said Scrooge indignantly, "every idiot who goes about with 'Merry Christmas' on his lips, should be boiled with his own pudding, and buried with a stake of holly through his heart. He

## THEIR SWEETEST SONG.

N. N. PENDLETON.

1. Lis - ten, chil - dren! Bells are ring - ing, Loud they peal their mer - ry chime,
2. Oh! the ring - ers ring with spir - it, And the bells, too, seem to know
3. Clear the stars a - bove are shin - ing, And they seem to shine more bright,

As they with their sweet - est mu - sic Ush - er in the Christmas time.
All a - bout the Christ-child com - ing Down to earth so long a - go.
Do - ing hon - or to the Christ-child Who was born to be our light.

Hark! they sound o'er plain and mountain, Bring - ing peace and hope sub - lime,
Can the heart know scorn and an - ger, Joy bells swing - ing to and fro?
And I think the hap - py an - gels Sing their sweet - est song to - night.

should!" "Uncle!" pleaded the nephew. "Nephew!" returned the uncle, sternly, "keep Christmas in your own way, and let me keep it in mine." "Keep it!" repeated Scrooge's nephew. "But you don't keep it." "Let me leave it alone, then," said Scrooge; "much good may it do you! much good it has ever done you!" "There are many things from which I might have derived good, by which I have not profited, I dare say," returned the nephew, "Christmas among the rest. But I am sure I have always thought of Christmas time, when it has come round—apart from the veneration due to its sacred name and origin, if anything belonging to it can be apart from that—as a good time; a kind, forgiving, charitable, pleasant time; the only time I know of in the long calendar of the year, when men and women seem by one consent to open their shut-up hearts freely, and to think of people below them as if they really were fellow-passengers to the grave, and not another race of creatures bound on other journeys. And, therefore, uncle, though it has never put a scrap of gold or silver in my pocket, I believe that it *has* done me good, and *will* do me good; and I say God bless it."

The clerk in the tank involuntarily applauded. Becoming immediately sensible of the impropriety, he poked the fire, and extinguished the last frail spark forever. "Let me hear another sound from *you*," said Scrooge, "and you'll keep your Christmas by losing your situation. You're quite a powerful speaker, sir," he added, turning to his nephew. "I wonder you don't go into Parliament." "Don't be angry, uncle.

Come! Dine with us to-morrow." Scrooge said that he would see him—yes, indeed he did. He went the whole length of the expression, and said that he would see him in that extremity first. "But why?" cried Scrooge's nephew; "why?" "Why did you get married?" said Scrooge. "Because I fell in love." "Because you fell in love!" growled Scrooge, as if that were the only one thing in the world more ridiculous than a

## BRIGHTEST OF GOLDEN DAYS.

M. W. Balfe.
Clara Wallace.

*Allegro.*

1. Once more we meet thee, all sad-ness a-part, Sing-ing the old-en lays;
2. Once more we meet thee, all sad-ness a-part, Sing ing the old-en lays;

Joy-ous we greet thee, in gladness of heart, Brightest of gold-en days. End-less thy reign
Joy-ous we greet thee, in gladness of heart, Brightest of gold-en days. Car-ol the song,

o'er land and main, 'Neath the Star whose pure light Scat-ters dark-ness and night.
sound it a-long, Nor in pal-ace or cot, Be it ev-er for-got!

Once more we meet thee, all sad-ness a-part, Sing-ing the old-en lays.
Joy-ous we greet thee in glad-ness of heart, Bright-est of gold-en days.

merry Christmas; "Good-afternoon!" "Nay, uncle, but you never came to see me before that happened. Why give it as a reason for not coming now?" "Good-afternoon," said Scrooge. "I want nothing from you; I ask nothing of you; why cannot we be friends?" "Good-afternoon," said Scrooge. "I am sorry, with all my heart, to find you so resolute. We have never had any quarrel to

which I have been a party. But I have made the trial in homage to Christmas, and I'll keep my Christmas humor to the last. So, a Merry Christmas, uncle!" "Good-afternoon!" said Scrooge. "And a Happy New Year!" "Good-afternoon!" said Scrooge.

His nephew left the room without an angry word, notwithstanding. He stopped at the outer door to bestow the greetings of the season on the clerk, who, cold as he was, was warmer than Scrooge; for he returned them cordially. "There's another fellow," muttered Scrooge, who overheard him; "my clerk, with fifteen shillings a week, and a wife and family, talking about a merry Christmas. I'll retire to Bedlam." This lunatic, in letting Scrooge's nephew out, had let two other people in. They were portly gentlemen, pleasant to behold, and now stood with their hats off, in Scrooge's office. They had books and papers in their hands, and bowed to him. "Scrooge & Marley's, I believe," said one of the gentlemen, referring to his list. "Have I the pleasure of addressing Mr. Scrooge, or Mr. Marley?" "Mr. Marley has been dead these seven years," Scrooge replied. "He died seven years ago, this very night." "We have no doubt his liberality is well repre-

## THE BIRTHDAY OF A KING.

GUGLIELMO.
HELEN MARTIN.

*Andante mosso.*

1. The flow'rs so fair have faded, The birds of summer flown; Thro' branches swaying leafless The
2. The holly's bright leaves glisten, The pine bough lends its grace; The mistletoe and lau - rel Add

winds of win-ter moan; Tho' far those dear delightful friends, The year for loss makes glad amends:
cheer to Winter's face; The Christmas tree glows in the light Of yule-tide fires all gleaming bright:

A - gain the mer - ry Christmas chimes, Their mes - sage bring, their message bring,

*con anima.*

And tell the birthday of a King, And tell the birthday of a King, the birthday of a King!

sented by his surviving partner," said the gentleman, presenting his credentials. It certainly was; for they had been two kindred spirits. At the ominous word, "liberality," Scrooge frowned, and shook his head, and handed the credentials back. "At this festive season of the year, Mr. Scrooge," said the gentleman, taking up a pen, "it is more than usually desirable that we should make some slight provision for the poor and destitute, who suffer greatly at the present time. Many thousands are in want of common necessaries; hundreds of thousands are in want of common comforts, sir." "Are there no prisons?" asked Scrooge. "Plenty of prisons," said the gentleman, laying down the pen again. "And the Union workhouses?" demanded Scrooge;

"are they still in operation?" "They are. Still," returned the gentleman, "I wish I could say they were not." "The treadmill and the Poor Law are in full vigor then?" said Scrooge. "Both very busy, sir.". "Oh! I was afraid from what you said at first, that something had occurred to stop them in their useful course," said Scrooge; "I am very glad to hear it." "Under the impression that they scarcely furnish Christian cheer of mind or body to the multitude," returned the gentleman, "a few of us are endeavoring to raise a fund to buy the Poor some meat and drink, and means of warmth. We choose this time, because it is a time, of all others, when Want is keenly felt, and Abundance rejoices. What shall I put you down for?" "Nothing!"

Scrooge replied. "You wish to be anonymous?" "I wish to be left alone," said Scrooge. "Since you ask me what I wish, gentlemen, that is my answer. I don't make merry myself at Christmas, and I can't afford to make idle people merry. I help to support the establishments I have mentioned; they cost enough: and those who are badly off must go there." "Many can't go there; and many would rather die." "If they would rather die," said Scrooge, "they had better do it, and decrease the surplus population; besides, excuse me, I don't know that." "But you might know it," observed the gentleman. "It's not my business," Scrooge returned. "It's enough for a man to understand his own business, and not to interfere with other people's. Mine occupies

## THE CHRISTMAS TREE.

German Air.

1. Let In-dia boast her spi-cy trees Whose fruitage rare and gor-geous bloom,
2. Let Flo-ri-da and haughty Spain Boast of their beau-teous or-ange groves,
3. The wide world knows a tree full strong, And fair-er yet than each or all;
4. The Christmas tree whose thought of love To men up-on these shores of Time;

Give to each faint and languid breeze Its pass-ing rich and rare per-fume.
And France ex-ult her vines to train A-round her trim and bright al-coves.
More wor-thy of the minstrel's song In cot-tage low or princely hall.
Still bears glad tid-ings from a-bove, And news to all of truth sub-lime.

me constantly. Good-afternoon, gentlemen!" Seeing clearly that it would be useless to pursue their point, the gentlemen withdrew. Scrooge resumed his labors with an improved opinion of himself, and in a more facetious temper than was usual with him.

Meanwhile the fog and darkness thickened so, that people ran about with flaring links, proffering their services to go before horses in carriages, and conduct them on their way. The ancient tower of a church, whose gruff old bell was always peeping slyly down at Scrooge out of a gothic window in the wall, became invisible, and struck the hours and quarters in the clouds, with tremulous vibrations afterwards, as if its teeth were chattering in its frozen head

up there. The cold became intense. In the main street, at the corner of the court, some laborers were repairing the gas-pipes, and had lighted a great fire in a brazier, round which a party of ragged men and boys were gathered: warming their hands and winking their eyes before the blaze in rapture. The water-plug being left in solitude, its overflowings suddenly congealed, and turned to misanthropic ice. The brightness of the shops where holly sprigs and berries crackled in the lamp heat of the windows, made pale faces ruddy as they passed. Poulterers' and grocers' trades became a splendid joke: a glorious pageant, with which it was next to impossible to believe that such dull principles as bargain and sale had anything to do. The Lord Mayor, in the stronghold of the mighty Mansion House, gave orders to his fifty cooks and butlers to keep Christmas as a Lord Mayor's household should; and even the little tailor, whom he had fined five shillings on the previous Monday for being drunk and bloodthirsty in the streets, stirred up to-morrow's pudding in his garret, while his lean wife and the baby sallied out to buy the beef. Foggier yet, and colder! Piercing, searching, biting cold. If the good St. Dunstan had but nipped the Evil Spirit's nose with a touch of such weather as that, instead of using his familiar weapons, then indeed he would have roared to lusty purpose. The owner of one scant young nose, gnawed and mumbled by the hungry cold, as bones are gnawed by dogs, stooped down at Scrooge's keyhole to regale him with a Christmas carol; but at the first sound of

God bless you, merry gentlemen,
May nothing you dismay!

Scrooge seized the ruler with such energy of action, that the singer fled in terror, leaving the keyhole to the fog, and even more congenial frost.

At length the hour of shutting up the counting house arrived. With an ill-will Scrooge dismounted from his stool, and tacitly admitted the fact to the expectant clerk in the tank, who instantly snuffed his candle out, and put on his hat. "You'll want all day to-morrow, I suppose?" said Scrooge. "If quite convenient, sir." "It's not convenient," said Scrooge, "and it's

## FOREVERMORE.

M. WELLINGS.
HELEN MATHER.

*Moderato.*

1. All hail! gone is our night! All hail! ye glad angels bright! Ring, ring, from shore to shore,
2. Chime, bells, freedom from care! Ring out thro' the ambient air! Tell, tell it o'er and o'er
3. Peace! sweet message di-vine, Brood gen-tly o'er thine and mine! Good-will thou dost out-pour,

Song of joy, song of joy, Song of joy, For-ev - er-more!
His great gift, His great gift, His great gift, For-ev - er-more!
Love of love, Love of love, Love of love, For-ev - er-more!

not fair. If I was to stop half-a-crown for it, you'd think yourself ill-used, I'll be bound?" The clerk smiled faintly. "And yet," said Scrooge, "you don't think *me* ill-used when I pay a day's wages for no work." The clerk observed that it was only once a year. "A poor excuse for picking a man's pocket every twenty-fifth of December!" said Scrooge, buttoning his great-coat to the chin. "But I suppose you must have the whole day. Be here all the earlier next morning." The clerk promised that he would; and Scrooge walked out with a growl. The office was closed in a twinkling, and the clerk, with the long ends of his white comforter dangling below his waist (for he boasted no great-coat), went down a slide on Cornhill, at the end of a lane of boys, twenty times, in honor of its being Christmas Eve, and then ran home to Camden Town as hard as he could pelt, to play at blindman's buff.

Scrooge took his melancholy dinner in his usual melancholy tavern; and having read all the newspapers, and beguiled the rest of the evening with his banker's book, went home to bed. He lived in chambers which had once belonged to his deceased partner. They were a gloomy suite of rooms, in a lowering pile of building up a yard, where it had so little business to be, that one could scarcely help fancying it must have run there when it was a young house, playing at hide-and-seek with other houses, and have forgotten the way out again. It was old enough now, and dreary enough; for nobody lived in it but Scrooge, the other rooms being all let out as offices. The yard was so dark that even Scrooge, who knew its every stone, was fain to grope with his hands. The fog and frost so hung about the black old gateway of the house, that it seemed as if the Genius of the Weather sat in mournful meditation on the threshold. Now it is a fact that there was nothing at all particular about the knocker on the door, except that it was very large. It is also a fact that Scrooge had seen it, night and morning, during his whole residence in that place; also that Scrooge had as little of what is called fancy about him as any man in the City of London, even including—which is a bold word—the corporation, aldermen, and livery. Let it also be borne in mind that Scrooge had not bestowed one thought on Marley since his last mention of his seven-years'-dead partner that afternoon. And then let any man explain to me, if he can, how it happened that Scrooge, having his key in the lock of the door, saw in the knocker, without its undergoing any inter-

## O EVERGREEN.

*Andante.*

PINE-TREE CAROL.

1. O ev-er-green, O ev-er-green! How are thy leaves so ver-dant! O ev-er-green, O ev-er-green! How are thy leaves so ver-dant! Not on-ly in the sum-mer time, But e'en in win-ter is thy prime. O ev-er-green, O ev-er-green! How are thy leaves so ver-dant?

2. O ev-er-green, O ev-er-green! We sing in hap-py meas-ure, O ev-er-green, O ev-er-green! We sing in hap-py meas-ure, Thy praise who dost our Christmas greet, With verdure fair and mem'ries sweet. O ev-er-green, O ev-er-green! Tree of un-fail-ing treas-ure!

3. O ev-er-green, O ev-er-green! Thy garb un-fail-ing show-eth, O ev-er-green, O ev-er-green! Thy garb un-fail-ing show-eth, The flower of joy a-bout my door, Good cheer that faileth nev-ermore! O ev-er-green, O ev-er-green! My heart thy lesson know-eth!

mediate process of change—not a knocker, but Marley's face. Marley's face! It was not in impenetrable shadow, as the other objects in the yard were, but had a dismal light about it, like a bad lobster in a dark cellar. It was not angry or ferocious, but looked at Scrooge as Marley used to look: with ghostly spectacles turned up on its ghostly forehead. The hair was curiously stirred, as if by breath or hot air; and, though the eyes were wide open, they were perfectly motionless. That, and its livid color, made it horrible; but its horror seemed to be in spite of the face, and be- yond its control, rather than a part of its own expression. As Scrooge looked fixedly at this phenomenon, it was a knocker again. To say that he was not startled, or that his blood was not conscious of a terrible sensation to which it had been a stranger from infancy, would be untrue. But he put his hand upon the key he had relinquished, turned it sturdily, walked in, and lighted his candle. He *did* pause, with a moment's irresolution, before he shut the door; and he *did* look cautiously behind it first, as if he half-expected to be terrified with the sight of Marley's pig-tail sticking out into the hall. But there was nothing on the back of the door, except the screws and nuts that held the knocker on, so he said, "Pooh, pooh!" and closed it with a bang. The sound resounded through the house like thunder. Every room above, and every cask in the wine merchant's cellars below, appeared to have a separate peal of echoes of its own. Scrooge was not a man to be frightened by echoes. He fastened the door, and walked across the hall, and up the stairs; slowly, too: trimming his candle as he went. You may talk vaguely about driving a coach-and-six up a good old flight of stairs, or through a bad young Act of Parliament; but I mean to say you might have got a hearse up that staircase, and taken it broadwise, with the splinter-bar towards the wall and the door towards the balustrades: and done it easy. There was plenty of width for that, and room to spare; which is perhaps the reason why Scrooge thought he saw a locomotive hearse going on before him in the gloom. Half-a-dozen gas lamps out of the street wouldn't have lighted the entry too well, so you may suppose that it was pretty dark with Scrooge's dip. Up Scrooge went, not car-

## O TANNENBAUM.

*Andante.*

GERMAN FOLKSONG.

1. O Tan-nenbaum, O Tannenbaum! Wie grün sind deine Blät-ter. O Tannenbaum, O
2. O Tan-nenbaum, O Tannenbaum! Du kannst mir sehr ge-fal-len. O Tannenbaum, O
3. O Tan-nenbaum, O Tannenbaum! Dein Kleid will mich was lehren: O Tannenbaum, O

Tannenbaum! Wie grün sind deine Blät-ter. Du grünst nicht nur zur Sommer-zeit, Nein
Tannenbaum! Du kannst mir sehr ge-fal-len. Wie oft hat nicht zur Weihnachtszeit, Ein
Tannenbaum! Dein Kleid will mich was leh-ren: Die Hoffnung und Be-stän-dig-keit Gibt

auch im Winter, wenn es schneit. O Tannenbaum, O Tannenbaum, Wie grün sind deine Blät-ter!
Baum von dir mich hoch erfreut! O Tannenbaum, O Tannenbaum, Du kannst mir sehr gefal-len!
Trost und Kraft zu je-der Zeit. O Tannenbaum, O Tannenbaum! Das soll dein Kleid mich lehren.

ing a button for that. Darkness is cheap, and Scrooge liked it. But, before he shut his heavy door, he walked through his rooms to see that all was right. He had just enough recollection of the face to desire to do that. Sitting-room, bedroom, lumber-room. All as they should be. Nobody under the table, nobody under the sofa; a small fire in the grate; spoon and basin ready; and the little saucepan of gruel (Scrooge had a cold in his head) upon the hob. Nobody under the bed; nobody in the closet; nobody in his dressing-gown, which was hanging up in a suspicious atti-tude against the wall. Lumber-room as usual. Old fire-guard, old shoes, two fish-baskets, washing-stand on three legs, and a poker. Quite satisfied, he closed his door, and locked himself in; double-locked himself in, which was not his custom. Thus secured against surprise, he took off his cravat; put on his dressing-gown and slippers, and his night-cap; and sat down before the fire to take his gruel.

It was a very low fire, indeed; nothing on such a bitter night. He was obliged to sit close to it, and brood over it, before he could extract the least sensation of warmth from such a handful of fuel. The fireplace was an old one, built by some Dutch merchant long ago, and paved all round with quaint Dutch tiles, designed to illustrate the Scriptures. There were Cains and Abels, Pharaoh's daughters, Queens of Sheba, Angelic messengers descending through the air on clouds like feather beds, Abrahams, Belshazzars, Apostles putting off to sea in butter boats, hundreds of figures to attract his thoughts; and yet that face of Marley, seven years dead, came like the ancient Prophet's rod, and swallowed up the whole. If each smooth tile had been a blank at first, with power to shape some picture on its surface from the disjointed fragments of his thoughts, there would have been a copy of old Marley's head on every one. "Humbug!" said Scrooge, and walked across the room. After several turns, he sat down again. As he threw his head back in the chair, his glance happened to rest upon a bell, a disused bell, that hung in the room, and communicated for some purpose now forgotten with a chamber in the highest story of the building. It was with great astonishment, and with a strange, inexplicable dread, that, as he looked, he saw this bell begin to swing. It swung so softly in the outset that it scarcely made a sound; but soon it rang out loudly, and so did every bell in the house. This might have lasted half a minute, or a minute, but it seemed an hour. The bells ceased as they had begun, together. They were succeeded by a clanking noise, deep down below, as if some persons were dragging a heavy chain over the casks in the wine mer-

## GOD REST YE.

*Moderato.*     TRADITIONAL.

1. God rest ye, mer-ry gen-tle-men, Let nothing you dis-may, For Je-sus Christ, our
2. God rest ye, lit-tle children. all, Let nothing you af-fright, For Je-sus Christ, our
3. God rest ye, all good Christian men, Up-on this blessed morn, The Lord of all sweet,

Sa-viour dear, Was born on Christmas day, Was born on Christmas day.
Sa-viour dear, Was born this hap-py night, Was born this hap-py night.
earn-est souls, Was of a Vir-gin born, Was of a Vir-gin born.

chant's cellar. Scrooge then remembered to have heard that ghosts in haunted houses were described as dragging chains. The cellar door flew open with a booming sound, and then he heard the noise much louder, on the floors below; then coming up the stairs; then coming straight towards his door. "It's a humbug still!" said Scrooge. "I won't believe it." His color changed though, when, without a pause, it came on through the heavy door, and passed into the room before his eyes. Upon its coming in, the dying flame leaped up, as though it cried, "I know him! Marley's ghost!" and then fell again.

The same face; the very same. Marley in his pig-tail, usual waistcoat, tights, and boots; the tassels on the latter bristling like his pig-tail, and his coat-skirts, and the hair upon his head. The chain he drew was clasped about his middle. It was long and wound about him like a tail; and it was made (for Scrooge observed it closely) of cash-boxes, keys, padlocks, ledgers, deeds, and heavy purses wrought in steel. His body was transparent; so that Scrooge, observing him, and looking through his waistcoat, could see the two buttons on his coat behind. Scrooge had often heard it said that Marley had no bowels, but he had never believed it until now. No, nor did he believe it even now. Though he looked the phantom through and through, and saw it standing before him; though he felt the chilling influence of its death-cold eyes; and marked the very texture of the folded

CHRISTMAS WAITS SINGING CAROLS.

kerchief bound about the head and chin, which wrapper he had not observed before; he was still incredulous, and fought against his senses. "How now!" said Scrooge, caustic and cold as ever; "what do you want with me?" "Much!"—Marley's voice, no doubt about it. "Who are you?" "Ask me who I was." "Who *were* you, then?" raising his voice; "you're particular, for a shade." "He

was going to say "to a shade," but substituted this, as more appropriate. "In life I was your partner, Jacob Marley." "Can you—can you sit down?" asked Scrooge, looking doubtfully at him. "I can." "Do it, then." Scrooge asked the question, because he didn't know whether a ghost so transparent might find himself in a condition to take a chair; and felt that in the event of its

## UNDER THE HOLLY BOUGH.

Chas. Mackay.
Mrs. Chas. Barnard.

*Not too fast.*

1. Ye who have scorned each other  In this fast-fad-ing year,  Or wronged a friend or broth-er, Come gath-er hum-bly here:  Let sinned a-gainst and sin-ning For-get their strife's be-gin-ning, Be links no long-er brok-en  Be-neath the hol-ly bough, Be sweet for-give-ness spok-en  Be-neath the hol-ly bough.

2. Ye who have loved each oth-er  In this fast-fad-ing year,  Sis-ter, or friend or broth-er, Come gath-er hap-py here:  And let your hearts grow fond-er As mem-'ry glad shall pon-der Old loves and lat-er woo-ing  Be-neath the hol-ly bough, So sweet in their re-new-ing  Be-neath the hol-ly bough.

3. Ye who have nourished sadness  In this fast-fad-ing year,  Estranged from joy and glad-ness, Come gath-er hope-ful here:  No more let use-less sor-row Pur-sue you night and mor-row; Come join in our em-bra-ces  Be-neath the hol-ly bough, Take heart, un-cloud your fa-ces  Be-neath the hol-ly bough.

being impossible, it might involve the necessity of an embarrassing explanation. But the ghost sat down on the opposite side of the fireplace, as if he were quite used to it. "You don't believe in me," observed the Ghost. "I don't," said Scrooge. "What evidence would you have of my reality beyond that of your own senses?" "I don't

know," said Scrooge." "Why, then, do you doubt your senses?" "Because," said Scrooge, "a little thing affects them. A slight disorder of the stomach makes them cheats. You may be an undigested bit of beef, a blot of mustard, a crumb of cheese, a fragment of an underdone potato. There's more of gravy than of grave about you, whatever you are !'' Scrooge was not much in the habit of cracking jokes, nor did he feel in his heart by any means waggish then. The truth is, he tried to be smart, as a means of distracting his own attention, and keeping down his terror ; for the spectre's voice disturbed the very marrow in his bones.

To sit, staring at those fixed, glazed eyes, in silence for a moment, would play,

Scrooge felt, the very deuce with him. There was something very awful, too, in the spectre's being provided with an infernal atmosphere of his own. Scrooge could not feel it himself, but this was clearly the case ; for though the Ghost sat perfectly motionless, its hair, and skirts, and tassels, were still agitated as by the hot vapor from an oven. '' You see this toothpick ?''

## WITH EVERY GOLDEN STRING.

D. F. E. AUBER.

1. Hark! to the harps of gold! What an-them do they sing? The ra-diant clouds have backward rolled, And an-gels smite the string. Glo-rious bright their wings Spread glis-t'ning and a - far, And on the hal-lowed rap-ture rings From circ-ling star to star. Tri-um-phant is their hymn; Earth greets it and the sea; And ev - 'ry wind and bil-low fleet Bears on the ju-bi-lee.

2. Soft swells the music now A - long that shin-ing choir, And ev-'ry ser-aph bends his brow And breathes up-on his lyre. What words of heav'nly birth Thrill deep our hearts a-gain, And fall like dew-drops to the earth?'' "Peace and good-will to men!" Sound, harps, and hail the morn With ev-'ry gold-en string; For un-to us this day is born A Sav-iour and a King!

said Scrooge, returning quickly to the charge, for the reason just assigned; and wishing, though it were only for a second, to divert the vision's stony gaze from himself. "I do," replied the Ghost. "You are not looking at it," said Scrooge. "But I see it," said the Ghost, "notwithstanding." "Well!" returned Scrooge, "I have but to swallow this, and be for the rest of my days persecuted by a legion of goblins, all of my own creation. Humbug, I tell you; humbug!" At this the spirit raised a frightful cry and shook its chain with such a dismal and appalling noise that Scrooge held on tight to his chair, to save himself from falling in a swoon. But how much greater was his horror, when the phantom taking off the bandage round its head, as if it were too warm to wear in-doors, its lower jaw dropped down upon its breast! Scrooge fell on his knees, and clasped his hands before his face. "Mercy!" he said. "Dreadful apparition, why do you trouble me?" "Man of the worldly mind!" replied the Ghost, "do you believe in me or not?" "I do," said Scrooge; "I must. But why do spirits walk the earth, and why do they come to me?" "It is required of every man," the Ghost returned, "that the spirit

## WHAT OF CHRISTMAS DAY?

JOHN SELWYN.

1. "And what of Christmas day? Can you tell, can you tell? Oh, what of Christmas day? Can you tell me?" "There's the beau-ty of a star, That was fol-lowed from a - far By the Wise Men, hope-ful and be - liev - ing."

day? Can you tell me?" "There's the won-der of a song, That has ech-oed all a - long Thro' the a - ges dark with wrong and griev-ing."

day? Can you tell me?" "There's the sto - ry of a Child, And a saint-ed moth-er mild, And a man-ger in ox-en stall so low - ly."

day? Can you tell me?" "There's a prom-ise of a love To be giv-en from a-bove That shall fill our wait-ing hearts ah, nev-er!"

within him should walk abroad among his fellow-men, and travel far and wide; and if that spirit goes not forth in life, it is condemned to do so after death. It is doomed to wander through the world—oh, woe is me!—and witness what it cannot share, but might have shared on earth, and turned to happiness!" Again the spectre raised a cry, and shook its chain and wrung its shadowy hands. "You are fettered," said Scrooge, trembling. "Tell me why?" "I wear the chain I forged in life," replied the Ghost, "I made it link by link, and yard by yard; I girded it on of my own free will, and of my own free will I wore it. Is its pattern strange to *you?*" Scrooge trembled more and more. "Or would you know," pursued the Ghost, "the weight and length of the strong coil you bear yourself? It was full as heavy and as long as this, seven Christmas Eves ago. You have labored on it since. It is a ponderous chain!" Scrooge glanced about him on the floor, in the expectation of finding himself surrounded by some fifty or sixty fathoms of iron cable; but he could see nothing. "Jacob," he said imploringly. "Old Jacob Marley, tell me more. Speak comfort to me, Jacob!" "I have none to give," the Ghost replied. "It comes from other regions, Ebenezer Scrooge, and is conveyed by other ministers, to other kinds of men. Nor can I tell you what I would. A very little more is all that is permitted to me. I cannot rest, I cannot stay, I cannot linger anywhere. My spirit never walked beyond our counting-house—mark me!—in life my spirit never roved beyond the narrow limits of our money-changing hole; and weary journeys lie before me!" It was a habit with Scrooge, whenever he became thoughtful, to put his hands in his breeches' pockets. Pondering on what the Ghost had said, he did so now, but without lifting up his eyes, or getting off his knees. "You must have been very slow about it, Jacob," Scrooge observed, in a business-like manner, though with humility and deference. "Slow!" the Ghost repeated. "Seven years dead," mused Scrooge. "And travelling all the time?" "The whole time," said the Ghost. "No rest, no peace! Incessant torture of remorse." "You travel fast?" said Scrooge. "On the wings of the wind," replied the Ghost.

## OLD CHRISTMAS CHEER.

George Wither

1. The cli - ent now his suit forbears, The pris'ner's heart is eas - ed; The debtor rids him
2. Hark! how the wags abroad do call Each other forth to ramb - ling; Anon you'll see them
3. Then wherefore, in these mer - ry days, Should we, I pray, be dull - er? Shall we not sing our

of his cares And for the time is pleas-ed; Tho' oth - er purs - es be more fat, Why
in the hall For nuts and ap - ples scrambling. Hark! how the roofs with laughter sound! A -
roundelays, To make our mirth the full - er? And while we thus in - spired do sing, Let

should we pine or grieve at that? Hang sorrow! Care will kill a cat, And therefore let's be mer - ry.
non they'll think the house goes round, For they the cellar's depths have found, And they will e'en be merry.
all the streets with echoes ring, The woods and hills and everything Bear witness we are mer - ry.

"You might have got over a great quantity of ground in seven years," said Scrooge. The Ghost on hearing this, set up another cry, and clanked its chain so hideously in the dead silence of the night, that the Ward would have been justified in indicting it for a nuisance. "Oh! captive, bound, and double-ironed," cried the phantom, "not to know that ages of incessant labor, by immortal creatures, for this earth must pass into eternity before the good of which it is susceptible is all developed. Not to know that any Christian spirit working kindly in its little sphere, whatever it may be, will find its mortal life too short for its vast means of usefulness. Not to know that no space of regret can make amends for one life's opportunities misused! Yet such was I! Oh! such was I!" "But you were always a good man of business, Jacob," faltered Scrooge, who now began to apply this to himself. "Business!" cried the Ghost, wringing his hands again. "Mankind was my business. The common welfare was my business; charity, mercy, forbearance, and benevolence, were all my business. The dealings of my trade were but a drop of water in the comprehensive ocean of my business!" It held up its chain at arm's length, as if that were the cause of all its unavailing grief, and flung it heavily upon the ground again. "At this time of the rolling year," the spectre said, "I suffer most. Why did I walk through crowds of fellow-beings with my eyes turned down, and never raise them to that blessed Star which led the Wise Men to a poor abode! Were there no poor homes to which its light would have conducted *me!*"

Scrooge was very much dismayed to hear the spectre going on at this rate, and began to quake exceedingly. "Hear me!" cried the Ghost. "My time is nearly gone."

"I will," said Scrooge. "But don't be hard upon me! Don't be flowery, Jacob!" "How it is that I appear before you in a shape that you can see, I may not tell. I have sat invisible beside you many and many a day." It was not an agreeable idea. Scrooge shivered, and wiped the perspiration from his brow. "That is no light part of my penance," pursued the Ghost. "I am here to-night to warn you that you have yet a chance and hope of escaping my fate. A chance and hope of my procuring, Ebenezer." "You were always a good friend to me," said Scrooge; "Thank 'ee!" "You will be haunted," resumed the Ghost, "by Three Spirits." Scrooge's countenance fell almost as low as the Ghost's had done. "Is

## WAKING OR SLEEPING.

J. V. BLAKE.

1. Wake, hap-py children, On the Christmas morn, Wake when the bells ring For the bless-ed
2. Play, hap-py children, In the gold-en noon, Soon day is end-ed And the night comes
3. Sleep, hap-py children, In the ho-ly night, Gone is the day-beam, But the stars are
4. Morn, noon and night-time, God your soul shall keep, Wak-ing or play-ing, Or in qui-et

dawn. Wake at dawn, wake at dawn, Oh,............ wake in the blessed dawn, Starry night is gone.
soon. Play at noon, play at noon, Oh,............ play in the golden noon. It will pass too soon.
bright. Sleep at night, sleep at night, Oh,............ sleep in the holy night, When the stars are bright.
sleep. Safe shall keep, safe shall keep, Oh,............ waking or sleeping, He our souls shall keep.

that the chance and hope you mentioned, Jacob?" he demanded, in a faltering voice. "It is." "I—I think I'd rather not," said Scrooge. "Without their visits," said the Ghost, "you cannot hope to shun the path I tread. Expect the first to-morrow, when the bell tolls One." "Couldn't I take 'em all at once, and have it over, Jacob?" hinted Scrooge. "Expect the second on the next night at the same hour. The third, upon the next night when the last stroke of Twelve has ceased to vibrate. Look to see me no more; and look that, for your own sake, you remember what has passed between us!" When it had said these words, the spectre took its wrapper from the table and bound it round its head, as

before. Scrooge knew this by the smart sound its teeth made, when the jaws were brought together by the bandage. He ventured to raise his eyes again, and found his supernatural visitor confronting him in an erect attitude, with its chain wound over and about its arm.

The apparition walked backward from him; and at every step it took, the window raised itself a little, so that when the spectre reached it, it was wide open. It beckoned Scrooge to approach, which he did. When they were within two paces of each other, Marley's Ghost held up its hand, warning him to come no nearer. Scrooge stopped. Not so much in obedience, as in surprise and fear; for on the raising of the hand, he became sensible of confused noises in the air ; incoherent sounds of lamentation and regret ; wailings inexpressibly sorrowful and self-accusatory. The spectre, after listening for a moment, joined in the mournful dirge ; and floated out upon the bleak, dark night. Scrooge followed to the window: desperate in his curiosity.

He looked out. The air was filled with phantoms, wandering hither and thither in restless haste, and moaning as they went. Every one of them wore chains like Marley's Ghost ; some few (they might be guilty governments) were linked together ; none were free. Many had been personally known to Scrooge in their lives. He had been quite familiar with one old ghost, in a white waistcoat, with a monstrous iron safe attached to its ankle, who cried piteously at being unable to assist a wretched woman with an infant, whom it saw below upon a doorstep. The misery with them all was, clearly, that they sought to interfere, for good, in human matters, and had lost the power forever. Whether these creatures faded into mist, or mist enshrouded them, he could not tell. But they and their spirit voices faded together ; and the night became as it had been when he walked home. Scrooge closed the window, and examined the door by which the Ghost had entered. It was double-locked, as he had locked it with his own hands, and the bolts were undisturbed. He tried to say "Humbug!" but stopped at the first syllable. And being, from the emotion he had undergone, or the fatigues of the day, or his glimpse of the Invisible World, or the dull conversation of the Ghost, or the lateness of the hour, much in need of repose, went straight to bed, without undressing, and fell asleep upon the instant.

---

## STAVE II.

### THE FIRST OF THE THREE SPIRITS.

WHEN Scrooge awoke, it was so dark that, looking out of bed, he could scarcely distinguish the transparent window from the opaque walls of his chamber. He was endeavoring to pierce the darkness with his ferret eyes, when the chimes of a neighboring church struck the four quarters. So he listened for the hour. To his great astonishment, the heavy bell went on from six to seven, and from seven to eight, and regularly up to twelve ; then stopped. Twelve! It was past two when he went to bed. The clock was wrong. An icicle must have got into the works. Twelve ! He touched the spring of his repeater, to correct this most preposterous clock. Its rapid little pulse beat twelve, and stopped.

"Why, it isn't possible," said he, "that I can have slept thro' a whole day and far into another night. It isn't possible that anything has happened to the sun, and this is twelve at noon !" The idea being an alarming one, he scrambled out of bed, and groped his way to the window. He was obliged to rub the frost off with the sleeve of his dressing-gown before he could see anything; and could see very little then. All he could make out was, that it was still very foggy and extremely cold, and that there was no noise of people running to and fro, and making a great stir, as there unquestionably would have been if night had beaten off bright day, and taken possession of the world. This was a great relief, because "Three days after sight of this First of Exchange pay to Mr. Ebenezer Scrooge or his order," and so forth, would have become a mere United States security if there were no days to count by. Scrooge went to bed again, and thought, and thought, and thought it over and over, and could make nothing of it. The more he thought, the more perplexed he was ; and the more he endeavored not to think, the more he thought. Marley's Ghost bothered him exceedingly. Every time he resolved within himself, after mature inquiry, that it was all a dream, his mind flew back again, like a strong spring released, to its first position, and presented the same problem to be worked all through, "Was it a dream or not ?" Scrooge lay in this state until the chime had gone three-quarters more, when he remembered, on a sudden, that the Ghost had warned him of a visitation when the bell tolled one. He resolved to lie awake until the hour was passed ; and, considering that he could no more go to sleep than go to Heaven, this was perhaps the wisest resolution in his power.

The quarter was so long, that he was more than once convinced he must have sunk into a doze unconsciously, and missed the clock. At length it broke upon his listening ear. "Ding, dong !" "A quarter past," said Scrooge, counting. "Ding, dong !" "Half-past!" said Scrooge. "Ding, dong!" "A quarter to it," said Scrooge. "Ding, dong!" "The hour itself," said Scrooge, triumphantly, "and nothing else!" He spoke before the hour bell sounded, which it now did with a deep, dull, hollow, melancholy *one*. Light flashed up in the room upon the instant, and the curtains were drawn.

The curtains of his bed were drawn aside, I tell you, by a hand. Not the curtains at his feet, nor the curtains at his back, but those to which his face was addressed. The curtains of his bed were drawn aside; and

Scrooge, starting up into a half-recumbent attitude, found himself face to face with the unearthly visitor who drew them: as close to it as I am now to you, and I am standing in the spirit at your elbow. It was a strange figure—like a child: yet not so like a child as like an old man, viewed through some supernatural medium, which gave him the appearance of having receded from the view, and being diminished to a child's proportions. Its hair, which hung about its neck and down its back, was white as if with age; and yet the face had not a wrinkle

## ONLY A BABY FAIR.

G. KINGSLEY.
HELEN MARTIN.

*Moderato.*

1. On - ly a ba - by fair Come from a - bove; On - ly a moth - er heart,
2. On - ly a sin - gle star, Shin - ing so bright, Cast - ing its stead - y beam
3. Hark! now the ser - aph song Rings thro' the skies, "Good-will and peace to men"—

Rich in its love, Ma - ny a soul in pain Hath lived to hope a -
Far thro' the night; Yet 'twas the star that led On to thy man - ger
Earth's dis - cord dies; Souls joy to bless thy name, Crown it with death - less

gain, Ba - by, for thee, Ba - by, for thee, Ba - by, so dear.
bed, Ba - by, to thee, Ba - by, to thee, Ba - by, so dear.
fame, Ba - by, so dear, Ba - by, so dear, Ba - by, so dear.

in it and the tenderest bloom was on the skin. The arms were very long and muscular; the hands the same, as if its hold were of uncommon strength. Its legs and feet, most delicately formed, were, like those upper members, bare. It wore a tunic of the purest white; and round its waist was bound a lustrous belt, the sheen of which was beautiful. It held a branch of fresh green holly in its hand; and, in singular contradiction of that wintry emblem, had its dress trimmed with summer flowers.

But the strangest thing about it was, that from the crown of its head there sprung a bright clear jet of light, by which all this was visible; and which was doubtless the occasion of its using, in its duller moments, a great extinguisher for a cap, which it now held under its arm. Even this, though, when Scrooge looked at it with increasing steadiness, was *not* its strangest quality. For as its belt sparkled and glittered, now in one part and now in another, and what was light one instant, at another time was dark, so the figure itself fluctuated in its distinctness : being now a thing with one arm, now with one leg, now with twenty legs, now a pair of legs without a head, now a head without a body : of which dissolving parts, no outline would be visible in the dense gloom wherein they melted away. And in the very wonder of this, it would be itself again ; distinct and clear as ever. "Are you the Spirit, sir, whose coming was foretold to me?" asked Scrooge. "I am!" The voice was soft and gentle. Singularly low, as if instead of being so close beside him, it were at a distance. "Who, and what are you?" Scrooge demanded. "I am the Ghost of Christmas Past." "Long Past?" inquired Scrooge, observant of its dwarfish stature. "No ; your past." Perhaps Scrooge could not have told anybody why, if anybody could have asked him ; but he had a special desire to see the Spirit in his cap ; and begged him to be covered. "What!" exclaimed the Ghost, "would you so soon put out, with worldly hands, the light I give? Is it not enough that you are one of those whose passions made this cap, and force me

## THE BEST OF HOLIDAYS.

1. "A mer-ry, mer-ry Christmas! a mer-ry Christmas, oh!" So sang a lit-tle
2. "I sometimes think my birth-day the dear-est hol-i-day, Be-cause I have such
3. "And then, that day in sum-mer—that dreadful hol-i-day—The Fourth, when wild con-
4. "The hap-py days are man-y, but that's the hol-i-day That's better than all

maid-en whose face was all a-glow; "I am so ver-y hap-py this
pres-ents as make life glad and gay; But it would seem too sel-fish and
fus-ion holds ev'-ry-where its sway— Where fun is tame and sil-ly, un-
oth-ers, what-ev-er you may say; My pleasures all are sweet-er, and

bright and joy-ous morn, The dear-est and the gay-est I've seen since I was born,
make life all con-ceit, To set-tle on one's birthday as best of all to greet,
less it's on-ly noise; For me it wouldn't answer, al-tho' it might for boys.
bright-er all my plays Up-on dear mer-ry Christmas, the best of hol-i-days."

through whole trains of years to wear it low upon my brow!" Scrooge reverently disclaimed all intention to offend or any knowledge of having wilfully "bonneted" the Spirit at any period of his life. He then made bold to inquire what business brought him there. "Your welfare!" said the Ghost. Scrooge expressed himself much obliged, but could not help thinking that a night of unbroken rest would have been more conducive to that end. The Spirit must have heard him thinking, for it said immediately: "Your reclamation then. Take heed!" It put out its strong hand as it spoke, and clasped him gently by the arm. "Rise, and walk with me!"

It would have been in vain for Scrooge to plead that the weather and the hour were not adapted to pedestrian purposes ; that bed was warm, and the thermometer a long way below freezing ; that he was clad but lightly in his slippers, dressing-gown, and night-cap ; and that he had a cold upon him at that time. The grasp, though gentle as a woman's hand, was not to be resisted. He rose: but finding that the Spirit made towards the window, clasped its robe in supplication. "I am a mortal," Scrooge remonstrated, "and liable to fall." "Bear but a touch of my hand *there*," said the Spirit, laying it upon his heart, "and you shall be upheld in more than this!" As the words were spoken, they passed through the wall and stood upon an open country road, with fields on either hand. The city had entirely vanished. Not a vestige of it was to be seen. The darkness and the mist had vanished with it, for it was a clear, cold, winter day, with snow upon the ground. "Good Heaven!" said Scrooge, clasping his hands together, as he looked about him. "I was bred in this place. I was a boy here!" The Spirit gazed upon him mildly. Its gentle touch, though it had been light and instantaneous, appeared still present to the old man's sense of feeling. He was conscious of a thousand odors floating in the air, each one connected with a thousand thoughts, and hopes, and joys, and cares, long, long, forgotten. "Your lip is tremb-

## BID THE DAY BE BORN.

A. Randegger.
A. C. Swinburne.

1. Thou whose birth on earth an-gels sang to men, While the stars made
2. From the height of night was not Thine the star That led forth with

mirth, this day born a-gain; As this night was bright
might— wise men from a-far. Yet the Wise Men's eyes

With thy cra-dle ray, Ver-y Light of light, oh, turn our night to day!
Saw Thee not more clear Than, in Shepherd guise, who drew as poor men near.

Thou whose ways we praise, clear alike and dark,
Keep our works and ways safe inside Thine ark.
Who shall keep Thy sheep, Lord, and lose not one?
Who, save One, shall keep, oh, who beside the Son?

From the grave-deep wave, from the sword and flame,
Thou, e'en Thou, shalt save only by Thy Name.
Bid our peace increase, Thou that madest morn;
Bid oppression cease, oh, bid the day be born!

ling," said the Ghost. "And what is that upon your cheek?" Scrooge muttered, with an unusual catching in his voice, that it was a pimple; and begged the Ghost to lead him where he would. "You recollect the way?" inquired the Spirit. "Remember it!" cried Scrooge, with fervor; "I could walk it blindfold." "Strange to have forgotten it for so many years!" observed the Ghost. "Let us go on." They walked along the road. Scrooge recognizing every gate, and post, and tree; until a little market-town appeared in the distance, with its bridge, its church, and winding river. Some shaggy ponies now were seen trotting towards them with boys upon their backs, who called to other boys in country gigs and carts, driven by farmers. All these boys were in great spirits, and shouted to each other, until the broad fields were so full of merry music, that the crisp air laughed to hear it. "These are but shadows of the things that have been," said the Ghost. "They have no consciousness of us." The

" BOTH HEARING THEM AND ASKING THEM QUESTIONS."

jocund travellers came on; and as they came, Scrooge knew and named them every one. Why was he rejoiced beyond all bounds to see them! Why did his cold eye glisten, and his heart leap up as they went past! Why was he filled with gladness when he heard them give each other Merry Christmas, as they parted at cross-roads and by-ways, for their several homes! What was merry Christmas to Scrooge? Out upon merry Christmas! What good had it ever done to him? "The school is not quite deserted," said the Ghost. "A solitary child, neglected by his friends, is left there still." Scrooge said he knew it; and he sobbed.

They left the high-road, by a well-remembered lane, and soon approached a mansion of dull red brick, with a little weathercock-surmounted cupola, on the roof, and a bell hanging in it. It was a large house, but

## THE VOICES IN THE SKY.

Ellen Douglas.

1. Oh, sweet were the voices once heard in the sky, As in chorus they hymned his glad birth! Are ye sing-ing that pæ-an of joy still on high, Ye that sang "Peace and good-will on earth?" To us yet speak the strains that were heard o'er those plains In a night of the a-ges gone by; 'Mid the clear shining light of the shepherds' blest sight Came the voices that rang through the sky.

2. Oh, Star that leads onward to him whom we love, Who hath brought us glad ransom so free, Dost thou yet beam in splendor 'mid bright hosts above? Can a mor-tal still gaze up-on thee? And the har-mo-ny sweet of an-gel-ic-choirs meet, Doth it yet sing of Hope free from care? Ah, the Star still shines on, and the Light is not gone, And the Voi-ces still ring in the air!

one of broken fortunes; for the spacious offices were little used, their walls were damp and mossy, their windows broken, and their gates decayed. Fowls clucked and strutted in the stables, and the coach-houses and sheds were overrun with grass. Nor was it more retentive of its ancient state within; for entering the dreary hall, and glancing through the open doors of many rooms, they found them poorly furnished, cold, and vast. There was an earthy savour in the air, a chilly bareness in the place, which associated itself somehow with too much getting up by candle-light, and not too much to eat. They went, the Ghost and Scrooge, across the hall, to a door at the back of the house. It opened before them, and disclosed a long, bare, melancholy room, made barer still by lines of plain deal forms and desks. At one of these a lonely boy was reading near a feeble fire; and Scrooge sat down upon a form, and wept to see his poor forgotten self as he had used to be. Not a latent echo in the house, not a squeak and scuffle from the mice behind the panelling, not a drip from the half-thawed water-spout in the dull yard behind, not a sigh among the leafless boughs of one despondent poplar, not the idle swinging of an empty-store-house door, no, not a clicking in the fire, but fell upon the heart of Scrooge with softening influence, and gave a freer passage to his tears. The spirit touched him on the arm, and pointed to his younger self, intent upon his reading. Suddenly a man in foreign garments: wonderfully real and distinct to look at: stood outside the win-

## FAIR CHRISTMAS COMES.

LABITZKY.
HELEN MARTIN.

1. Fair Christ - mas comes with all his train, His man - tle white of er-mine down; Glad
2. No bud - ding spray, nor smiling bloom! No leaf - y bow'r, nor flow-'ry dell! Ah,

D.C. Fair Christ - mas comes with all his train, His man - tle white of er-mine down; Glad

wel - come his from hill to plain, And from the bu - sy town.
Win - ter spake his word of doom, And Na - ture heard it well.

wel - come his from hill to plain, And from the bu - sy town.

Him choir - ing voi - ces greet With songs of sa - cred cheer, In
But hearts of love are rife With thoughts of man - ger birth, Of

words of love most meet, That an - gels bend to hear.
hope, and joy, and life, That Christ - mas gave to earth.

dow, with an axe stuck in his belt, and leading by the bridle an ass laden with wood. "Why, it's Ali Baba!" Scrooge exclaimed in ecstasy. "It's dear old honest Ali Baba! Yes, yes, I know. One Christmas time, when yonder solitary child was left here all alone, he did come, for the first time, just like that. Poor boy! And Valentine," said Scrooge, "and his wild brother, Orson; there they go! And what's his name, who was put down in his drawers, asleep at the gate of Damascus; don't you see him! And the Sultan's groom turned upside down by the Genii: there he is upon his head. Serve him right. I'm glad of it. What business had he to be married to the princess!" To hear Scrooge expending all the earnestness of his nature on such subjects, in a most extraordinary voice between laughing and crying ; and to see his heightened and excited face ; would have been a surprise to his business friends in the city, indeed. "There's the parrot!" cried Scrooge. "Green body and yellow tail, with a thing like lettuce growing out of the top of his head ; there he is ! Poor Robin Crusoe, he called him, when he came home again after sailing round the island. " Poor Robin Crusoe, where have you been. Robin Crusoe?" The man thought he was dreaming, but he wasn't. It was the parrot, you know. There goes Friday, running for his life to the little creek ! Halloa ! Hoop ! Halloo !" Then, with a rapidity of transition very foreign to his usual character, he said, in pity for his former self, " Poor boy !" and cried again. " I wish," Scrooge muttered, putting his hand in his pocket, and looking about him, after drying his eyes with his cuff : " but it's too late now." "What is the matter?" asked the Spirit. "Nothing," said Scrooge. " Nothing. There was a boy

## THE GLAD NEW DAY.

THOMAS MOORE.

1. And why should not that land re-joice, And darkness flee a - way, When on its dim, be -
2. Re - joice, ye nations blest with peace, Let all the earth be glad; The Prince of Peace comes
3. Oh! for the time when men shall spend This day as all men should, When an - gels shall with

night - ed hills, Has dawned the glad new day? For now be - hold the shepherds go, The
down to - day, In robes of pit - y clad. Yea, thus should all man - kind rejoice, On
joy at - tend, And dwell a - mong the good. Then will this earth an E - den be, A

wondrous babe to see; Ah, then methinks that all around Was one grand ju - bi - lee!
this glad day of love; But yet, a - las! how far we are From those blest heights above!
Par - a - dise of love; And all shall know the per-fect bliss Of those bright realms a-bove.

singing a Christmas Carol at my door last night. I should like to have given him something ; that's all."

The Ghost smiled thoughtfully, and waved its hand : saying as it did so, " Let us see another Christmas !" Scrooge's former self grew large at the words, and the room became a little darker and more dirty. The panels shrunk, the windows cracked ; fragments of plaster fell out of the ceiling, and the naked laths were shown instead ; but how all this was brought about, Scrooge knew no more than you do. He only knew that it was quite correct : that everything had happened so; that there he was, alone again, when all the other boys had gone home for the jolly holidays. He was not reading now, but walking up and down despairingly. Scrooge looked at the Ghost, and, with a mournful shaking of his head, glanced anxiously towards the door. It opened; and a little girl, much younger than the boy, came darting in, and putting her arms about his neck, and often kissing him, addressed him as her "Dear, dear brother." "I have come to bring you home, dear brother!" said the child, clapping her tiny hands, and bending down to laugh. "To bring you home, home, home!" "Home, little Fan?" returned the boy. "Yes!" said the child, brimful of glee. "Home, for good and all. Home, forever and ever. Father is so much kinder than he used to be, that home's like Heaven. He spoke so gently to me one dear night when I was going to bed, that I was not afraid to ask him once more if you might come home; and he said Yes, you should; and sent me in a coach to bring you. And you're to be a man!" said the child, opening her eyes; "and are never to come back here; but first we're to be together all the Christmas long, and have the merriest time in all the world." "You are quite a woman, little Fan!" exclaimed the boy. She clapped her hands and laughed, and tried to touch his head; but being too little, laughed again, and stood on tiptoe to em-

## ROBINSON CRUSOE.

*Spirited.*      *Air:* ROGUES' MARCH.

1. When I was a lad, I had cause to be sad, A ver-y good friend I did
2. But he saved from a-board an old gun and a sword, And another odd mat-ter or
3. His hut was a match for um-brel-la of thatch, And his clothes were too old to be

lose, O! I warrant you, Dan, you have heard of this man, His name it was Rob-in-son
two, so That by dint of his thrift he just managed to shift, And keep a-live Rob-in-son
new, so That his parrot at last would cry out as he passed, "Hurrah for old Rob-in-son

*Chorus.*

Cru-soe.   Oh, Rob-in-son Cru-soe!   Oh, poor Robin-son Cru-soe!   He
Cru-soe.   Oh, Rob-in-son Cru-soe!   Oh, poor Robin-son Cru-soe!   Whether
Cru-soe!"   Oh, Rob-in-son Cru-soe!   Oh, poor Robin-son Cru-soe!   His

went off to sea and be-tween you and me, Old Neptune wreck'd Robinson Cru-soe.
tempest or Turk, or wild man or work, No mat-ter to Rob-in-son Cru-soe.
par-rot is dead, and his goats have all-fled The home of old Rob-in-son Cru-soe.

The cannibals came to his island one day,
   To feast, for all cannibals do so,
But Friday, their man, jumped out of their pan,
   And ran off to Robinson Crusoe.
Oh, Robinson Crusoe! Oh, poor Robinson Crusoe!
He fired off his gun, and then there was fun
   For lonely old Robinson Crusoe.

But he never lost hope, and he never would mope,
   And he always had faith, as should you, so
That come as it might, it always was right
   With honest old Robinson Crusoe.
Oh, Robinson Crusoe! Good old Robinson Crusoe!
Where can school-boy be found to stop at a round
   "Hurrah for old Robinson Crusoe!"

brace him. Then she began to drag him, in her childish eagerness, towards the door ; and he nothing loth to go accompanied her. A terrible voice in the hall cried, "Bring down Master Scrooge's box, there !" and in the hall appeared the schoolmaster himself, who glared on Master Scrooge with a ferocious condescension, and threw him into a dreadful state of mind by shaking hands with him. He then conveyed him and his sister into the veriest old well of a shivering best-parlor that ever was seen, where the maps upon the wall, and the celestial and terrestrial globes in the windows, were waxy with cold. Here he produced a decanter of curiously light wine, and a block of curiously heavy cake, and administered instalments of those dainties to the young people : at the same time sending out a meager servant to offer a glass of "something" to the postboy, who answered that he thanked the gentleman, but if it was the same tap as he

## HAPPY CHRISTMAS TO ALL.

CHILDHOOD SONG.

*Allegretto.*

1. Come, children, and join in our fes-ti-val song, And hail the sweet joys Christmas
2. Thou Child of the Man-ger, we lift up to Thee, Our voice of thanks-giv-ing, our
3. And grant, as this glad day shall draw to its close, Mid fragrance of pine bough and

day brings a-long; We'll join our glad voi-ces to-geth-er in praise, To
glad ju-bi-lee; Oh, bless us, and guide us, dear Sav-iour, we pray, That
per-fume of rose, No sor-row may reach us, nor an-y grief come, To

*Chorus.*

Him who has blessed us, and brightened our days. Mer-ry Christmas to
from Thy blest pre-cepts we nev-er may stray. Hap-py Christmas to
shad-ow the joy in our hav-en of home. Mer-ry Christmas to

1. all! merry Christmas to all! Mer-ry Christmas, merry Christmas, merry Christmas to all !
2. 3. all! happy Christmas to all! Mer-ry Christmas, happy Christmas, merry Christmas to all !

had tasted before, he had rather not. Master Scrooge's trunk being by this time tied on to the top of the chaise, the children bade the schoolmaster good-bye right willingly ; and getting into it, drove gaily down the garden-sweep : the quick wheels dashing the hoar-frost and snow from off the dark leaves of the evergreens like spray. "Always a delicate creature, whom a breath might have withered," said the Ghost ; "but she had a large heart !" "So she had," cried Scrooge ; "you're right. I will not gainsay it, Spirit. God forbid !" "She died a woman," said the Ghost, "and had, as I think, children." "One child," Scrooge returned. "True," said the Ghost ; "your nephew !" Scrooge seemed uneasy in his mind ; and answered briefly, "Yes."

Although they had but that moment left the school behind them, they were now in the busy thoroughfares of a city, where shadowy passengers passed and repassed; where shadowy carts and coaches battled for the way, and all the strife and tumult of a real city were. It was made plain enough, by the dressing of the shops, that here too it was Christmas time again; but it was evening, and the streets were lighted up. The Ghost stopped at a certain warehouse door, and asked Scrooge if he knew it. "Know it!" said Scrooge. "Was I apprenticed here!" They went in. At sight of an old gentleman in a Welsh wig, sitting behind such a high desk, that if he had been two inches taller he must have knocked his head against the ceiling, Scrooge cried in great excitement: "Why, it's old Fezziwig! Bless his heart; it's Fezziwig alive again!" Old Fezziwig laid down his pen, and looked up at the clock, which pointed to the hour of seven. He rubbed his hands; adjusted his capacious waistcoat; laughed

## ONCE TOO OFTEN.

GAYLORD GROWLER.

1. My head is sole-ly fore-head now I'm threatened with con-ges-tion, Mince
2. And John, my man, and Jill, my maid, The sly coin-scent-ing fox-es, Ex-

pie, plum pud-ding, raise a row That troubles my di-ges-tion. This
pect not on-ly to be paid, But to get Christ-mas box-es. It's

dread-ful mood of sen-ti-ment Too long it now has tar-ried, And
mon-ey there and mon-ey here, My heart, how can it soft-en! It

I to raise funds for my rent Dis-tress-ing-ly am har-ried.
comes, I know, "but once a year,"—Ex-act-ly once too oft-en!

[ of-ten.]

all over himself, from his shoes to his organ of benevolence; and called out in a comfortable, oily, rich, fat, jovial voice: "Yo ho, there! Ebenezer! Dick!" Scrooge's former self, now grown a young man, came briskly in, accompanied by his fellow-'prentice. "Dick Wilkins, to be sure!" said Scrooge to the Ghost. "Bless me, yes. There he is. He was very much attached to me, was Dick. Poor Dick! Dear, dear!"

"Yo ho, my boys!" said Fezziwig. "No more work to-night. Christmas Eve, Dick. Christmas, Ebenezer! Let's have the shutters up," cried old Fezziwig, with a sharp clap of his hands, "before a man can say Jack Robinson!" You wouldn't believe how those two fellows went at it! They charged into the street with the shutters—one, two, three—had 'em up in their places—four, five, six—barred 'em and

12

pinned 'em—seven, eight, nine—and came back before you could have got to twelve, panting like race-horses. "Hilli-ho!" cried old Fezziwig, skipping down from the high desk, with wonderful agility. "Clear away, my lads, and let's have lots of room here! Hilli-ho, Dick! Chirrup, Ebenezer!" Clear away! There was nothing they wouldn't have cleared away, or couldn't have cleared away, with old Fezziwig looking on. It was done in a minute. Every movable was packed off, as if it were dismissed from public life for evermore; the floor was swept and watered, the lamps were trimmed, fuel was heaped upon the fire; and the warehouse was as snug, and warm, and dry, and bright a ball-room as you would desire to see upon a winter's night. In came a fiddler with a music-book, and went up to the lofty desk and made an orchestra of it, and tuned like fifty stomach-aches. In came Mrs. Fezziwig, one vast, substantial smile. In came the three Miss Fezziwigs, beaming and lovable. In came the six young followers whose hearts they broke. In came all the young men and women employed in the business. In came the housemaid, with her cousin, the baker. In came the

## WAKE, WAKE, CHILDREN.

CLARA WALLACE.

1. "Wake, wake, chil · dren!" for San · ta Claus has come! Doll and trum · pet
2. "Wake, wake, chil · dren!" the won · drous Christ · mas tree San · ta Claus has
3. "Wake, wake, chil · dren!" With · out a thought of care Eyes all bright and

he has left and nois · y lit · tle drum; Stock · ings all are heav · y with
decked so fair—it's just a sight to see! Pic · ture books and can · dies, and
footsteps light come troop · ing down the stair; Sounds of mer · ry laugh · ter, and

Christ · mas treas · ures gay; Here's a sled for lit · tle Tom—and not a cent to pay."
su · gar-plums and toys, Eve · ry · thing he's brought us— he knows what each en · joys."
hap · py in their glee—San · ta Claus a bless · ing both to them and me.

cook, with her brother's particular friend, the milkman. In came the boy from over the way, who was suspected of not having board enough from his master; trying to hide himself behind the girl from next door but one, who was proved to have had her ears pulled by her mistress. In they all came, one after another; some shyly, some boldly, some gracefully, some awkwardly, some pushing, some pulling; in they all came, anyhow and everyhow. Away they all went, twenty couple at once; hands half round and back again the other way; down the middle and up again; round and round in various stages of affectionate grouping; old top couple always turning up in the wrong place; new top couple starting off again, as soon as they got there; all top couples at last, and not a bottom one to help them! When this result was brought about, old Fezziwig, clapping his hands to stop the dance, cried out, "Well done!" and the fiddler plunged his hot face into a pot of porter especially provided for that purpose. But, scorning rest, upon his re-appearance he instantly began again, though there were no dancers yet, as if the other fiddler had been carried home, exhausted, on a shutter, and he were a brand-new man resolved to beat him out of sight, or perish. There were more dances, and there were forfeits, and more dances, and there was cake, and there was negus, and there was a great piece of Cold Roast, and there was a great piece of Cold Boiled, and there were mince pies, and plenty of beer. But the great effect of the evening came after the Roast and Boiled, when the fiddler (an artful dog, mind! The sort of man who knew his business better than you or I could have told it him!) struck up "Sir Roger de Coverley." Then old Fezziwig stood out to dance with Mrs. Fezziwig. Top couple, too; with a good stiff piece of work cut out for them; three or four and twenty pairs of partners; people who were not to be trifled with; people who *would* dance, and had no notion of walking. But if they had been twice as many—ah, four times—old Fezziwig would have been a match for them, and so would Mrs. Fezziwig. As to *her*, she was worthy to be his partner in every sense of the term. If that's not high praise, tell me higher, and I'll use it. A positive light

## LITTLE EMPTY STOCKING.

Spanish Air.

*Sadly.*

1. Oh! lit-tle emp-ty stock-ing, Left of the dain-ty pair We hung be-side the chim-ney When ba-by was our care! The tears that fell like rain; Have we no smile or greet-ing For Christmas come a-gain?

2. One lit-tle emp-ty stock-ing To 'mind us of our joys, The glee of hap-py childhood At find-ing pret-ty toys. For lit-tle feet are still, There's but an emp-ty stock-ing We nev-er-more shall fill.

3. For all that God hath tak-en A re-com-pense he brings, And from the gloomy shad-ows Are lift-ed an-gel wings; Our hearts within the sun-shine Of Christmas love and grace, Must glad the hearts of ma-ny Where late but one held place.

appeared to issue from Fezziwig's calves. They shone in every part of the dance like moons. You couldn't have predicted, at any given time, what would become of them next. And when old Fezziwig and Mrs. Fezziwig had gone all through the dance—advance and retire, both hands to your partner, bow and curtsey, corkscrew, thread-the-needle, and back again to your place—Fezziwig "cut"—cut so deftly that he appeared to wink with his legs, and came upon his feet again without a stagger. When the clock struck eleven this domestic ball broke up. Mr. and Mrs. Fezziwig took their stations, one on either side the door, and shaking hands with every person individually as he or she went out, wished him or her a Merry Christmas. When everybody had retired but the two 'prentices, they did the same to them; and thus the cheerful voices died away, and the lads were left to their beds, which were under a counter in the back-shop. During the whole of this time Scrooge had acted like a man out of his wits. His heart and soul were in the scene, and with his former self. He corroborated everything, remembered everything, enjoyed everything, and underwent the strangest agitation. It was not until now, when the bright faces of his former self and Dick were turned from them, that he remembered the Ghost, and became conscious that it was looking full upon him, while the light upon its head burned very clear. "A small matter," said the Ghost, "to make these silly folks so full of gratitude." "Small!" echoed Scrooge. The Spirit signed to him to listen to the two apprentices, who were pouring out their hearts in praise of Fezziwig; and when he had done so, said: "Why! Is it not? He has spent but a few pounds of your mortal money: three or four, perhaps. Is that so much that he deserves this praise?" "It isn't that," said Scrooge, heated by the remark, and speaking unconsciously like his former, not his latter self. "It isn't that, Spirit. He has the power to render us happy or unhappy; to make our service light or burdensome; a pleasure or a toil. Say that his power lies in words and looks; in things so slight and insignificant that it is impossible to add and count 'em up; what then? The happiness he gives is quite as great as if it cost a fortune." He felt the Spirit's glance, and stopped. "What is the matter?" asked the Ghost. "Nothing partic-

## THE JOY OF THE MORROW.

ELLEN DOUGLAS.

1. The joy bells once a-gain we hear, As peal-ing forth in mer-ry chime, For-
2. A-cross the plain and far and near, Is borne up-on the mist-y air The
3. Thrice-welcome bells, ye Christ-mas bells We hear a-gain your mu-sic sweet, The

ev-er new, for-ev-er dear, They tell the hap-py Christmas time. Ring! for the joy of the
message sweet in tones so clear, Its ech-oes bid re-lief from care. Ring! for the joy of the
heart with grateful pulses swells As Star and Babe a-gain we greet. Ring! for the joy of the

mor-row! Ring! for the hope that we bor-row! Ring! for our surcease from sor-row!

ular," said Scrooge. "Something, I think?" the Ghost insisted. "No," said Scrooge. "No. I should like to be able to say a word or two to my clerk just now. That's all." His former self turned down the lamps as he gave utterance to the wish; and Scrooge and the Ghost again stood side by side in the open air. "My time grows short," observed the Spirit. "Quick!" This was not addressed to Scrooge, or to any one whom he could see, but it produced an immediate effect. For again Scrooge saw himself. He was older now; a man in the prime of life. His face had not the harsh and rigid lines of later years; but it had begun to wear the signs of care and avarice. There was an eager, greedy, restless motion in the eye, which showed the passion that had taken root, and where the shadow of the growing tree would fall. He was not alone, but sat by the side of a fair young girl in a mourning-dress: in whose eyes there were tears, which sparkled in the light that shone out of the Ghost of Christmas Past. "It matters little," she said, softly. "To you, very little. Another idol has displaced me; and if it can cheer and comfort you in time to come, as I would have tried to do, I have no just cause to grieve." "What Idol has displaced you!" he rejoined. "A golden one," was her reply. "This is the even-handed dealing of the world!" he said; "there is nothing on which it is so hard as poverty; and there is nothing it professes to condemn with such severity as the pursuit of wealth!" "You fear the world too much," she answered, gently; "all your other hopes have merged into the hope of being beyond the chance of its sordid reproach. I have seen your nobler aspirations fall off one by one, until the master-passion, Gain, engrosses you. Have I not?" "What then!" he retorted; "even if I

have grown so much wiser, what then! I am not changed towards you." She shook her head. "Am I?" he asked. "Our contract is an old one," she replied. "It was made when we were both poor and content to be so, until, in good season, we could improve our worldly fortune by our patient industry. You *are* changed. When it was made, you were another man." "I was a boy," he said impatiently. "Your own feeling tells you that you were not what you are," she returned; "I am. That which promised happiness when we were one in heart, is fraught with misery now that we are two. How often and how keenly I

## LIST THE CHIMING!

HELEN MARTIN.

1. List the chim-ing! oh, list the chim-ing! As it swells thro' all the frosty evening air,
2. Lone and wea-ry, sad and for-sak-en, Hear the message glad of peace, good-will to men.

Sweet bells, your music, sinking and swell-ing, Wafts the old sto-ry, of rap-ture tell-ing. List the
Welcome the tid-ings! new hopes a-wak-en, Hearts hopeless, grieving, captive are tak-en! List the

chim-ing! oh, list the chim-ing! Bells whose music thrills thro' all our Christmas joy.

have thought of this, I will not say. It is enough that I *have* thought of it, and can release you." "Have I ever sought release?" "In words. No. Never." "In what, then?" "In a changed nature; in an altered spirit; in another atmosphere of life; another Hope as its great end. In everything that made my love of any worth or value in your sight. If this had never been between us," said the girl, looking mildly, but with steadiness, upon him, "tell me, would you seek me out and try to win me now? Ah, no!" He seemed to yield to the justice of this supposition, in spite of him-

self. But he said, with a struggle, "You think not." "I would gladly think otherwise if I could," she answered, "Heaven knows! When *I* have learned a truth like this, I know how strong and irresistible it must be. But if you were free to-day, to-morrow, yesterday, can even I believe that you would choose a dowerless girl—you who, in your very confidence with her, weigh everything by Gain: or, choosing her, if for a moment you were false enough to your one guiding principle to do so, do I not know that your repentance and regret would surely follow? I do; and I release you. With a full heart, for the love of him you once were." He was about to speak ; but, with her head turned from him, she resumed. "You may—the memory of what is past half makes me hope you will—have pain in this. A very, very brief time, and you will dismiss the recollection of it, gladly, as an unprofitable dream, from which it happened well that you awoke. May you be happy in the life you have chosen !" She left him, and they parted.

"Spirit !" said Scrooge, "show me no more ! Conduct me home. Why do you delight to torture me?" "One shadow more !" exclaimed the Ghost. "No more !" cried Scrooge. "No more. I don't wish to see it. Show me no more !" But the relentless Ghost pinioned him in both his arms, and forced him to observe what happened next. They were in another scene and place ; a room, not very large or handsome, but full of comfort. Near to the winter fire sat a beautiful young girl, so like that last that Scrooge believed it was the same, until he saw *her*, now a comely matron, sitting opposite her daughter. The

## SANTA CLAUS IS COME TO TOWN.

JOHN DRAKE.

1. { When low the sun his lat - est ray A - cross the hills is send - ing, Old
   { The lau - rel green and hol - ly bright Bid wel - come to his com - ing; He
2. { That night he vis - its ev - 'ry land With team of rein - deer po - nies, And
   { And dream - ing chil - dren, boys and girls, Their stockings hung up du - ly, See

San - ta Claus starts on his way, The world's good - will at - tend - ing.
greets them all on left and right, A Christ - mas dit - ty hum - ming.
scat - ters gifts with o - pen hand To all his lit - tle cro - nies.
balls and skates and dolls with curls, And all they long for tru - ly.

**Chorus.**

"San - ta Claus is come to town," The bells ring as he pass - es, "In rein - deer sleigh and furs so brown, With gifts for lads and lass - es."

3. He notes the merry dancers' feet,
   He sees the lights burn brightly,
   He pauses for the music sweet,
   Then onward speeds so lightly.
   Afar he goes from cot to town,
   From town to cot unending,
   And everywhere the weary frown
   From faces grim is sending.—*Cho.*

4. Down chimney way, thro' open door,—
   And everybody knows it—
   For forty thousand leagues or more
   The old man gaily goes it.
   Full four-and-twenty hours he drives
   As only he is able,
   Until his reindeer team arrives
   Again at their own stable.—*Cho.*

noise in this room was perfectly tumultuous, for there were more children there than Scrooge in his agitated state of mind could count ; and, unlike the celebrated herd in the poem, they were not forty children conducting themselves like one, but every child was conducting itself like forty. The consequences were uproarious beyond belief, but no one seemed to care ; on the contrary, the mother and daughter laughed heartily, and enjoyed it very much ; and the latter, soon beginning to mingle in the sports, got pillaged by the young brigands most ruthlessly. What would I not have given to be one of them ! Though I never could have been so rude, no, no ! I wouldn't for the wealth of all the world have crushed that braided hair, and torn it down ; and for the precious little shoe, I wouldn't have plucked it off, God bless my soul ! to save my life. As to measuring her waist in sport, as they did, bold young brood, I couldn't have done it ; I should have expected my arm to have grown round it for a punishment, and never come straight again. And yet I should have dearly liked, I own, to

## CHRISTMAS COME AGAIN.

C. Pinsuti.
Ellen Douglas.

1. 'Tis the Christmastide, With its joy and mirth ; Hearts are open wide, Love has here its birth!
Manger far a-way," Thus the chorus clear, " Once a Ba - by lay,—This our Christmas cheer ;

Fair it is to see, Round the fir-tree bright, Children merri - ly Gather in de - light.
May thy gift so rare, Oh, thou best of days, Gift beyond compare. Wake the world to praise !"

Sweet their voices ring, " Christmas come a - gain !" Glad the song they sing, " Christmas come a-

gain !" Snow is in the dells, Snow is on the plain, But a sweet song tells

" Christmas come a - gain !" But a sweet song tells " Christ-mas come a-gain !" 2. " In

have touched her lips ; to have questioned her, that she might have opened them ; to have looked upon the lashes of her downcast eyes, and never raised a blush ; to have let loose waves of her hair, an inch of which would be a keepsake beyond price ; in short, I should have liked, I do confess, to have had the lightest license of a child, and yet to have been man enough to know its value. But now a knocking at the door was heard, and such a rush immediately ensued that she with laughing face and plundered dress was borne towards it in the centre of a flushed and boisterous group, just in time to greet the father, who came home attended by a man laden with Christmas toys and presents. Then the shouting and the struggling, and the onslaught that was made on the defenceless porter! The scaling him, with chairs for ladders, to dive into his pockets, despoil him of brown-paper parcels, hold on tight by his cravat, hug him round the neck, pommel his back, and kick his legs in irrepressible affection! The shouts of wonder and delight with which the development of every package was re-

## SWEET HARPS, RESOUND AGAIN.

Mary Ryan.
A. S. Sullivan.

1. Time  by prophets told, Time waited  long of old! Thrice-blessed hour when Christ was born,
2. With thee we greet the Child, Thou mother, meek and mild, E - lect of Heav'n, forev - er blest,
3. With all-abounding grace, His gift in  ev - 'ry place, Think of the  silent child who stands

Earth's one fair na - tal  morn! When an - gels, all  a - flame, Bring-ing glad  tid - ings,
Of  all earth's maidens  best! Wise men in awe pro - found Spread near thee,  on  the
To - day with emp - ty  hands! Then brighten long-ing eyes With grate - ful  glad  sur -

came  To  shepherds on far  Ju - de - a's plain! Sweet harps! re - sound  a - gain.
ground, Rich spi - cer - y  and cost - ly  gem, To  Christ in Beth - le - hem!
prise, And serve with the an - gels of  the Lord In  joy - ful, sweet ac - cord.

ceived ! The terrible announcement that the baby had been taken in the act of putting a doll's frying-pan into his mouth, and was more than suspected of having swallowed a fictitious turkey, glued on a wooden platter ! The immense relief of finding this a false alarm ! The joy, and gratitude, and ecstasy ! They are all indescribable alike. It is enough that, by degrees, the children and their emotions got out of the parlor, and, by one stair at a time, to the top of the house, where they went to bed, and so subsided.

And now Scrooge looked on more attentively than ever, when the master of the house, having his daughter leaning fondly on him, sat down with her and her mother at his own fireside ; and when he thought that such another creature, quite as graceful and as full of promise, might have called him father, and been a spring-time in the haggard winter of his life, his sight grew very dim indeed. "Belle," said the husband, turning to his wife with a smile, "I saw an old friend of yours this afternoon."

"Who was it?" "Guess!" "How can I? Tut, don't I know?" she added, in the same breath, laughing as he laughed. "Mr. Scrooge." "Mr. Scrooge it was. I passed his office window; and as it was not shut up, and he had a candle inside, I could scarcely help seeing him. His partner lies upon the point of death, I hear; and there he sat alone. Quite alone in the world, I do believe." "Spirit!" said Scrooge, in a broken voice, "remove me from this place." "I told you these were shadows of the things that have been," said the Ghost; "that they are what they are, do not blame me!" "Remove me!" Scrooge exclaimed; "I cannot bear it" He turned upon the Ghost, and seeing that it looked upon him with a face in which, in some strange way, there were fragments of all the faces it had shown him, wrestled with it. "Leave me! Take me back. Haunt me no longer!"

In the struggle—if that can be called a struggle in which the Ghost, with no visible resistance on its own part was undisturbed by any effort of its adversary—Scrooge observed that its light was burning high and bright; and dimly connecting that with its influence over him, he seized the extinguisher-cap, and by a sudden action pressed it down upon its head. The Spirit dropped beneath it, so that the extinguisher covered its whole form; but though Scrooge pressed it down with all his force, he could not hide the light, which streamed from under it, in an unbroken flood upon the ground.

He was conscious of being exhausted, and overcome by an irresistible drowsiness; and, further, of being in his own bedroom. He gave the cap a parting squeeze, in which his hand relaxed; and had barely time to reel to bed, before he sank into a heavy sleep.

---

## STAVE III.

### THE SECOND OF THE THREE SPIRITS.

A WAKING in the middle of a prodigiously tough snore, and sitting up in bed to get his thoughts together, Scrooge had no occasion to be told that the bell was again upon the stroke of One. He felt that he was restored to consciousness in the right nick of time, for the especial purpose of holding a conference with the second messenger despatched to him through Jacob Marley's intervention. But, finding that he turned uncomfortably cold when he began to wonder which of his curtains this new spectre would draw back, he put them every one aside with his own hands, and lying down again, established a sharp look-out all round the bed. For he wished to challenge the Spirit on the moment of its appearance, and did not wish to be taken by surprise and made nervous.

Gentlemen of the free and easy sort, who plume themselves on being acquainted with a move or two, and being usually equal to the time-of-day, express the wide range of their capacity for adventure by observing that they are good for anything from pitch-and-toss to manslaughter; between which opposite extremes, no doubt, there lies a tolerably wide and comprehensive range of subjects. Without venturing for Scrooge quite as hardily as this, I don't mind calling on you to believe that he was ready for a good broad field of strange appearances, and that nothing between a baby and a rhinoce-

ros would have astonished him very much. Now, being prepared for almost anything, he was not by any means prepared for nothing; and, consequently, when the Bell struck One, and no shape appeared, he was taken with a violent fit of trembling. Five minutes, ten minutes, a quarter of an hour went by, yet nothing came. All this time, he lay upon his bed, the very core and centre of a blaze of ruddy light, which streamed upon it when the clock proclaimed the hour; and which, being only light, was more alarming than a dozen ghosts, as he was powerless to make out what it meant, or would be at; and was sometimes apprehensive that he might be at that very moment an interesting case of spontaneous combustion, without having the consolation of knowing it. At last, however, he began to think—as you or I would have thought at first; for it is always the person not in the predicament who knows what ought to have been done in it, and would unquestionably have done it too—at last, I say, he began to think that the source and secret of this ghostly light might be in the adjoining room, from whence, on further tracing it, it seemed to shine. This idea taking full possession of his mind, he got up softly and shuffled in his slippers to the door.

The moment Scrooge's hand was on the lock, a strange voice called him by his name, and bade him enter. He obeyed. It was his own room. There was no doubt about that. But it had undergone a surprising transformation. The walls and ceiling were so hung with living green, that it looked a perfect grove; from every part of which bright gleaming berries glistened. The crisp leaves of holly, mistletoe, and ivy reflected back the light, as if so many little mirrors had been scattered there; and such a mighty blaze went roaring up the chimney, as that dull petrification of a hearth had never known in Scrooge's time, or Marley's, or for many and many a winter season gone. Heaped up on the floor, to form a kind of throne, were turkeys, geese, game, poultry, brawn, great joints of meats, sucking-pigs, long wreaths of sausages, mince pies, plum puddings, barrels of oysters, red-hot chestnuts, cherry-cheeked apples, juicy oranges, luscious pears, immense twelfth-cakes, and seething bowls of punch, that made the chamber dim with their delicious steam. In easy state upon this couch there sat a jolly Giant, glorious to see: who bore a glowing torch, in shape not unlike Plenty's horn, and held it up, high up, to shed its light on Scrooge, as he came peeping round the door. "Come in!" exclaimed the Ghost. "Come in! and know me better, man!" Scrooge entered timidly, and hung his head

## THE STAR OF HIS BIRTH.

SHIRLEY DAVIS

1. Come cheer-ful and gay as the glad sun in May, Let us car-ol al-
2. A man - ger his bed but the star shone o'er-head! Oh, what fa - ces were
3. Our griefs we will fling to the winds as we sing, And our voi - ces shall

way for the bright Christ-mas day, 'Tis the star of his birth shin-ing
turned to its light as it burned! Still the star of his birth shin-eth
ring with the praise of our King, For the star of his birth shin-eth

white o'er the earth, Then in trans-ports henceforth we will car-ol his worth.

before this Spirit. He was not the dogged Scrooge that he had been; and though the Spirit's eyes were clear and kind, he did not like to meet them. "I am the Ghost of Christmas Present," said the Spirit. "Look upon me!" Scrooge reverently did so. It was clothed in one simple deep-green robe, or mantle, bordered with white fur. This garment hung so loosely on the figure that its capacious breast was bare, as if disdaining to be warded or concealed by any artifice. Its feet, observable beneath the ample folds of the garment, were also bare; and on its head it wore no other covering than a holly wreath. set here and there with shining icicles. Its dark brown curls were long and free; free as its genial face, its sparkling eye, its open hand, its cheery voice, its unconstrained demeanor, and its joyful air. Girded round its middle was an antique scabbard; but no sword was in it; and the ancient sheath was eaten up with rust. "You have never seen the like of me before?" exclaimed the Spirit. "Never," Scrooge made answer to it. "Have never walked forth with the younger members of my family; meaning (for I am very young) my elder brothers born in these later years?"

pursued the Phantom. "I don't think I have," said Scrooge. "I am afraid I have not. Have you had many brothers, Spirit?" "More than eighteen hundred," said the Ghost. "A tremendous family to provide for," muttered Scrooge. The Ghost of Christmas Present rose. "Spirit," said Scrooge, submissively, "conduct me where you will. I went forth last night on compulsion, and I learned a lesson which is working now. To-night, if you have aught to teach me, let me profit by it." "Touch my robe!" Scrooge did as he was told, and held it fast. Holly, mistletoe, red berries, ivy, turkeys, geese, game, poultry, brawn,

meat, pigs, sausages, oysters, pies, puddings, fruit, and punch, all vanished instantly. So did the room, the fire, the ruddy glow, the hour of night, and they stood in the city streets on Christmas morning, where (for the weather was severe) the people made a rough, but brisk and not unpleasant, kind of music, in scraping the snow from the pavement in front of their dwellings, and from the tops of their houses, whence it was mad delight to the boys to see it come plumping down into the road below, and splitting into artificial little snow-storms. The house fronts looked black enough, and the windows blacker, contrasting with the

## LOUD STRIKE THE STRINGS.

BEETHOVEN.
JOHN DRAKE

*Andante semplice.*

1. Loud strike the sounding strings, in joy-ous measure, Loud strike the sounding strings!
2. Gray fell thine aged locks, thou harp-er hoar-y, Gray fell thine a-ged locks.
3. A-new thy song re-told the old-en sto-ry, A-new the Christ-child story;

And thy harp went pul-sing sweet To the dance of will-ing feet.
But thine eye it flashed a-gain, To the an-cient mu-sic strain.
And thy harp went pul-sing sweet Through the songs they loved to greet

*rall.*

Gleamed the lights o'er all, Of Christmas bon-nie, Gleamed the lights o'er all.
Wel-come guest wert thou On Christmas bon-nie, Wel-come guest wert thou.
In the hut and hall, On Christmas bon-nie, In the hut and hall.

smooth white sheet of snow upon the roofs, and with the dirtier snow upon the ground; which last deposit had been ploughed up in deep furrows by the heavy wheels of carts and wagons; furrows that crossed and recrossed each other hundreds of times where the great streets branched off; and made intricate channels, hard to trace, in the thick yellow mud and icy water. The sky was gloomy, and the shortest streets were choked up with a dingy mist, half thawed, half frozen, whose heavier particles descended in a shower of sooty atoms, as if all the chimneys in Great Britain had, by one con-

sent, caught fire, and were blazing away to their dear hearts' content. There was nothing very cheerful in the climate or the town and yet was there an air of cheerfulness abroad that the clearest summer air and brightest summer sun might have endeavored to diffuse in vain. For the people who were shovelling away on the house-tops were jovial and full of glee; calling out to one another from the parapets, and now and then exchanging a facetious snowball—better-natured missile far than many a wordy jest—laughing heartily if it went right, and not less heartily if it went wrong.

The poulterers' shops were still half open, and the fruiterers' were radiant in their glory. There were great, round, pot-bellied baskets of chestnuts, shaped like the waistcoats of jolly old gentlemen, lolling at the doors, and tumbling out into the street in their apoplectic opulence. There were ruddy, brown-faced, broad-girthed Spanish onions, shining in the fatness of their growth like Spanish Friars, and winking from their shelves in wantom shyness at the girls as they went by, and glanced demurely at the hung-up mistletoe. There were pears and apples, clustered high in blooming pyramids; there were bunches of grapes, made, in the shopkeepers' benevolence, to dangle from conspicuous hooks, that people's mouths might water gratis as they passed ; there were piles of filberts, mossy and brown, recalling, in their fragrance, ancient walks amongst the woods, and pleasant shufflings ankle deep through withered leaves ; there were Norfolk Biffins, squab and swarthy, setting off the yellow of the oranges and lemons, and, in the great compactness of their juicy persons, urgently entreating and beseeching to be carried home in paper bags and eaten after dinner. The very gold and silver fish, set forth among these choice fruits in a bowl, though members of

## IN MERRY CHORUS.

J. OFFENBACH.

*Lively.*

1. Come, let us join in merry chorus, Our hearts and voices light and gay; The sun of
2. Oh, there is music on the mountain, When winds are whistling wild and free; Tho' frozen
3. Now let our hearts, with pleasure beating, Join in our grateful, joyous lays; We ever

joy shines brightly o'er us, For 'tis the happy Christmas day: Tra la, la, Tra, la, la,
be each stream and fountain, Wide rolls the song from sea to sea. Tra la, la, Tra, la, la,
look for kind-ly greet-ing These glad-return-ing, hap-py days. Tra la, la, Tra, la, la,

*Chorus.*

La, la, la, la, la, la, la, la, la, la, la, la, la, la, la, la, la, la, la, la, la.

a dull and stagnant-blooded race, appeared to know that there was something going on ; and, to a fish, went gasping round and round their little world in slow and passionless excitement. The Grocers ! oh, the Grocers ! nearly closed, with perhaps two shutters down, or one ; but through those gaps such glimpses ! It was not alone that the scales, descending on the counter, made a merry sound, or that the twine and roller parted company so briskly, or that the canisters were rattled up and down like juggling tricks, or even that the blended scents of tea and coffee were so grateful to the nose, or even that the raisins were so plentiful and rare, the almonds so extremely white, the sticks of cinnamon so long and straight, the other spices so delicious, the candied fruits so caked and spotted with molten sugar, as to make the coldest lookers-on feel faint and subsequently bilious. Nor was it that the figs were moist and pulpy, or that the French plums blushed in modest tartness from their highly-decorated boxes, or that everything was good to eat and in its Christmas dress ; but the customers were all so hurried and so eager in the hopeful promise of the day, that they tumbled up against each other at the door, crashing their wicker baskets wildly, and left their

THE VERY THING ELSIE WANTED.

*She found it on Christmas Eve in Grandpa's Overcoat Pocket.*

purchases upon the counter, and came running back to fetch them, and committed hundreds of the like mistakes, in the best humor possible ; while the Grocer and his people were so frank and fresh that the polished hearts with which they fastened their aprons behind might have been their own, worn outside for general inspection, and for Christmas daws to peck at if they chose.

But soon the steeples called good people all to church and chapel, and away they came, flocking through the streets in their best clothes, and with their gayest faces. And at the same time there emerged from scores of by-streets, lanes, and nameless turnings, innumerable people, carrying their dinners to the bakers' shops. The sight of these poor revellers appeared to in-

## STAR OF BETHLEHEM.

Henry Kirke White.

1. When, marshalled on the night - ly plain, The glitt'ring host be - stud the sky,
2. Once on the rag - ing seas I rode; The storm was loud the night was dark;
3. It was my guide, my light, my all; It bade my dark fore - bod - ings cease;

One star a - lone of all the train, Can fix the sin - ner's wand'ring eye.
The Ocean yawned, and rude - ly blew The wind that tossed my found'ring bark.
And through the storm and danger's thrall, It led me to the port of peace.

Hark! hark! to God the cho - rus breaks, From ev - 'ry host, from ev - 'ry gem.
Deep hor - ror then my vi - tals froze; Death - struck, I ceased the tide to stem,
Now safe - ly moored, my per - ils o'er, I'll sing first in night's di - a - dem,

But one a - lone the Sa - viour speaks,— It is the Star of Beth - le - hem!
When sud - den - ly a Star a - rose,— It was the Star of Beth - le - hem!
For - ev - er, and for - ev - er - more,— The Star, the Star of Beth - le - hem!

terest the Spirit very much, for he stood with Scrooge beside him in a baker's doorway, and taking off the covers as their bearers passed, sprinkled incense on their dinners from his torch. And it was a very uncommon kind of torch, for once or twice when there were angry words between some dinner-carriers who had jostled each other,

he shed a few drops of water on them from it, and their good-humor was restored directly. For they said it was a shame to quarrel upon Christmas Day. And so it was ! God love it, so it was ! In time the bells ceased, and the bakers were shut up ; and yet there was a genial shadowing forth of all these dinners and the progress of their cooking, in the thawed blotch of wet above each baker's oven; where the pavement smoked as if its stones were cooking too. "Is there a peculiar flavor in what you sprinkle from your torch?" asked Scrooge. "There is. My own." "Would it apply to any kind of dinner on this day?" asked Scrooge. "To any kindly given. To a poor one most." "Why to a poor one most?" asked Scrooge. "Because it needs it most." "Spirit," said Scrooge, after a moment's thought, "I wonder you, of all the beings in the many worlds about us, should desire to cramp these people's opportunities of innocent enjoyment." "I!" cried the Spirit. "You would deprive them of their means of dining every seventh day, often the only day on which they can be said to dine at

## CHRISTMAS JOY FOREVER.

THOMAS. MILLER.
CHARLES C. CONVERSE.

1. Those Christmas bells as sweetly chime As once when first they rang So joy-ous in the old-en time, When conscious Na-ture sang; They shake the tall, great-i-vied tow-er, Pro-claiming to each ear, With all their deep melodious power, The glad-ness of the year. And thus they ring while an-gels sing The song that fail-eth nev-er, "The Child be-hold, so long fore-told, Our Christ-mas joy for-ev-er!"

2. The bells that ush-er in the morn Oft draw my mind a-way To Bethlehem, where Christ was born, The sta-ble where he lay, In which the large-eyed ox-en fed, No dread of dan-ger near, To Ma-ry bowing low her head, In rev-'rent love sin-cere. I hear a voice that bids re-joice, Whose prom-ise dies— ah, nev-er! "The

all," said Scrooge; "wouldn't you?" "I!" cried the Spirit. "You seek to close these places on the Seventh Day?" said Scrooge; "and it comes to the same thing." "I seek!" exclaimed the Spirit. "Forgive me if I am wrong. It has been done in your name, or at least in that of your family," said Scrooge. "There are some upon this earth of yours," returned the Spirit, "who lay claim to know us, and who do their deeds of passion, pride, ill-will, hatred, envy, bigotry, and selfishness in our name, who are as strange to us, and all our kith and kin, as if they had never lived. Remember that, and charge their doings on themselves, not us." Scrooge promised that he would; and they went on, invisible, as they had been before, into the suburbs of the town. It was a remarkable quality of the Ghost (which Scrooge had observed at the baker's), that, notwithstanding his gigantic size, he could accommodate him-

## HOME, SWEET HOME.

John Howard Payne.

1. 'Mid pleas-ures and pal - a-ces though we may roam, Be it ev - er so humble, there's no place like home; A charm from the skies seems to hal - low us there, Which, seek thro' the world, is ne'er met with elsewhere. Home, home,

2. I gaze on the moon as I tread the drear wild, And feel that my mother now thinks of her child; As she looks on that moon from our own cottage door, Thro' the woodbine whose fragrance shall cheer me no more. Home, home,

3. An ex - ile from home, splendor daz - zles in vain, Oh, give me my low - ly thatch'd cot-tage again; The birds singing gai-ly, that came at my call; Give me them, and that peace of mind dear - er than all. Home, home,

sweet, sweet home, There's no place like home, Oh, there's no place like home.

self to any place with ease; and that he stood beneath a low roof quite as gracefully and like a supernatural creature as it was possible he could have done in any lofty hall. And perhaps it was the pleasure the good Spirit had in showing off this power of his, or else it was his own kind, generous, hearty nature, and his sympathy with all poor men, that led him straight to Scrooge's clerk's; for there he went, and took Scrooge with him, holding to his robe; and on the threshold of the door the Spirit smiled, and stopped to bless Bob Cratchit's dwelling with the sprinklings of his torch. Think of that! Bob had but fifteen "Bob" a week himself; he pocketed on Saturdays but fifteen copies of his Christian name ; and yet the ghost of Christmas Present blessed his four-roomed house ! Then up rose Mrs. Cratchit, Cratchit's wife, dressed out but poorly in a twice-turned gown, but brave in ribbons, which are cheap and make a goodly show for sixpence ; and she laid the cloth, assisted by Belinda Cratchit, second of her daughters, also brave in ribbons ; while Master Peter Cratchit plunged a fork into the saucepan of potatoes, and getting the corners of his monstrous shirt collar (Bob's private property, conferred upon his son and heir in honour of the day) into his mouth, rejoiced to find himself so gallantly attired, and yearned to show his linen in the fashionable Parks. And now two smaller Cratchits, boy and girl, came tearing in, screaming that outside the baker's they had smelled the goose, and known it for their own ; and basking in luxurious thoughts of sage and onion, these young Cratchits

## HOME IS DEAR!

JOHN SELWYN.

1. Swing, bells ! Christmas is near ! Ring, bells ! gladness is here, Voi-ces air - i - ly call, Home is
2. Fond eyes long for the sight, Yule-fire blaz-ing so bright, Old friends glad in its light, Home is

dear! Joy bells, welcome are ye ! While from for-est and sea Voi-ces mer-ri-ly call,
dear! Lone hearts pine for its joys, Gone Earth's glitter-ing toys, Once more girls and boys,

"Home is dear!" List! In ac-cents so clear, "Home is dear!" O - ver mountain and mere,

"Home is dear!" Back joy-ous we come, joy-ous we come, joy-ous we come. Swing, bells!

Christmas is near! Ring, bells ! gladness is here. Voi-ces mer-ri-ly call, "Home is dear!"

13

danced about the table, and exalted Master Peter Cratchit to the skies, while he (not proud, although his collar nearly choked him) blew the fire, until the slow potatoes, bubbling up, knocked loudly at the saucepan lid to be let out and peeled. "What has ever got your precious father, then?" said Mrs. Cratchit. "And your brother, Tiny Tim! And Martha warn't as late last Christmas Day by half an hour!" "Here's Martha, mother," said a girl appearing as she spoke. "Here's Martha, mother!" cried the two young Cratchits. "Hurrah! There's *such* a goose, Martha!" "Why, bless your heart alive, my dear, how late you are!" said Mrs. Cratchit, kissing her a dozen times, and taking off her shawl and bonnet for her with officious zeal. "We'd a deal of work to finish up last night," replied the girl, "and had to clear away this morning, mother!" "Well! never mind, so long as you are come," said Mrs. Cratchit. "Sit ye down before the fire, my dear, and have a warm, Lord bless ye!" "No, no!

## THE WIND MAY SHOUT.

J. L. MOLLOY.
ALBERT SMITH.

1. The wind may shout as it likes with-out; It may rage, but can-not
2. All the froz-en ground is in fet-ters bound; Ho! the yule-log we will

harm us; For a mer-ri-er din shall re-sound with-in, And our Christmas cheer will
burn it; For Christmas is come and in ev-'ry home To Summer our hearts will

warm us. There is gladness to all at its an-cient call, While its rud-dy fires are
turn it. There is gladness to all at its an-cient call, While its rud-dy fires are

gleam-ing; And from far and near, o'er the landscape drear, The Christmas light is streaming.

There's father coming," cried the two young Cratchits, who were everywhere at once; "hide, Martha, hide!" So Martha hid herself, and in came little Bob, the father, with at least three foot of comforter exclusive of the fringe hanging down before him; and his threadbare clothes darned up and brushed, to look seasonable; and Tiny Tim upon his shoulder. Alas for Tiny Tim, he bore a little crutch, and had his limbs supported by an iron frame! "Why, where's our Martha?" cried Bob Cratchit, looking round. "Not coming," said Mrs. Cratchit. "Not coming!" said Bob, with a sudden declension in his high spirits; for he had been Tim's blood horse all the way from church, and had come home rampant. "Not coming upon Christmas Day!" Martha didn't like to see him disappointed, if it were only in joke, so she came out prematurely from behind the closet door, and ran into his arms, while the two young Cratchits hustled Tiny Tim, and bore him off into the wash-house, that he might hear the pudding singing in the copper. "And how did little Tim behave?" asked Mrs. Cratchit, when she had rallied Bob on his credulity, and Bob had hugged his daughter to his heart's content. "As good as gold," said Bob, "and better. Somehow he gets thoughtful, sitting by himself so much, and thinks the strangest things you ever heard.

He told me, coming home, that he hoped the people saw him in the church, because he was a cripple, and it might be pleasant to them to remember upon Christmas Day who made lame beggars walk, and blind men see." Bob's voice was tremulous when he told them this, and trembled more when he said that Tiny Tim was growing strong and hearty. His active little crutch was heard upon the floor, and back came Tiny Tim before another word was spoken, escorted by his brother and sister to his stool

## CHRISTMAS VIOLETS.

ANDREW LANG.
STEPHEN GLOVER.

*Andante con espressione.*

1. Last night I found the  vi-o-lets You sent me once a-cross the sea; From
2. But  you have reached a wondrous age, The ha-ven of a  hap-py clime; You

gar-dens that the win-ter frets, In summer lands they come to me.  Still fragrant of the
do not dread the winter's rage, Although we missed the summer-time; And like the flow'r's breath

English earth, Still hu-mid of the fro-zen dew; To me they spoke of Christmas mirth, They
o-ver sea, A-cross the gulf of time and pain, To-night re-turns the mem-o-ry Of

spoke of love, they spoke of you. Oh, flow'rs now scentless, black and sere, The perfume long has
love that lived not all in vain. Oh, like the flower's breath o-ver sea, A-cross the gulf of

passed a-way; The sea whose tides are year by year, Is set between us chill and gray!
time and pain, To-night re-turns the mem-o-ry Of love that lived not all in vain!

beside the fire ; and while Bob, turning up his cuffs—as if, poor fellow, they were capable of being made more shabby—compounded some hot mixture in a jug with gin and lemons, and stirred it round and round and put it on the hob to simmer, Master Peter and the two ubiquitous young Cratchits went to fetch the goose, with which they soon returned in high procession.

Such a bustle ensued that you might have thought a goose the rarest of all birds ; a feathered phenomenon, to which a black swan was a matter of course—and in truth it was something very like it in that house.

Mrs. Cratchit made the gravy (ready beforehand in a little saucepan) hissing hot ; Master Peter mashed the potatoes with incredible vigor ; Miss Belinda sweetened up the apple sauce ; Martha dusted the hot plates ; Bob took Tiny Tim beside him in a tiny corner at the table ; the two young Cratchits set chairs for everybody, not forgetting themselves, and mounting guard upon their posts, crammed spoons into their mouths, lest they should shriek for goose before their turn came to be helped. At last the dishes were set on, and grace was said. It was succeeded by a breathless

## AN ODD OLD MAN.

JOHN DRAKE.
ARTHUR SULLIVAN.

1. Con-ceive me, if you can,    An  odd,   de-lightful man; That  no one on earth, wher-
2. With-laugh-of-cheer old man,    To - chil - dren-dear old man, Eyes twinkling so merry, cheeks
3. A  go - as-you-please old man,    With a-weakness-for-trees old man, And he covers them over, this

ev - er his birth, Has  had   the luck to scan; A matter-of-fact old man, Never-caught-in-the-act old
brown as a berry, And-never - a-tear old man; A marvel-of-sense old man, Where-icebergs-are-dense old
happy old rover, With gifts that please, old man! Fond-of-sleet-and-of-snow old man, With-a-team-that-
[can-go-old

man, But he comes and he goes, as all his-to-ry shows, With sleigh well packed, old man !
man, But  once a year coming, his merry song humming, Then quick speeding hence, old man !
man, Then away like the wind, a gay welcome to  find  In homes high and low,  old man !

pause, as Mrs. Cratchit, looking slowly all along the carving-knife, prepared to plunge it in the breast ; but when she did, and when the long-expected gush of stuffing issued forth, one murmur of delight arose all round the board, and even Tiny Tim, excited by the two young Cratchits, beat on the table with the handle of his knife, and feebly cried "Hurrah !" There never was such a goose. Bob said he didn't believe there ever was such a goose cooked. Its tenderness and flavor, size and cheapness, were the themes of universal admira-

tion. Eked out by apple sauce and mashed potatoes, it was a sufficient dinner for the whole family ; indeed, as Mrs. Cratchit said with great delight (surveying one small atom of a bone upon the dish), they hadn't ate it all at last ! Yet every one had had enough, and the youngest Cratchits, in particular, were steeped in sage and onion to the eyebrows ! But now the plates being changed by Miss Belinda, Mrs. Cratchit left the room —too nervous to bear witnesses—to take the pudding up and bring it in. Suppose it should not be done enough ! Suppose it should break in turning out! Suppose somebody should have got over the wall of the back-yard, and stolen it, while they were merry with the goose—a supposition at which the two young Cratchits became livid! All sorts of horrors were supposed. Hallo! A great deal of steam! The pudding was out of the copper. A smell like a washing-day! That was the cloth. A smell like an eating-house and a pastrycook's next door to each other, with a laundress's next to that! That was the pudding! In half a minute Mrs. Cratchit entered--flushed, but smiling proudly—

with the pudding, like a speckled cannon ball, so hard and firm, blazing in half of half-a-quartern of ignited brandy, and bedight with Christmas holly stuck into the top. Oh, a wonderful pudding! Bob Cratchit said, and calmly too, that he regarded it as the greatest success achieved by Mrs. Cratchit since their marriage. Mrs. Cratchit said that, now the weight was off her mind, she would confess she had her doubts about the quantity of flour. Everybody had something to say about it, but nobody said or thought it was at all a small pudding for a large family. It would have

## "GOD BLESS US, EVERY ONE."

1. O bless the hap-py Christmas morn On which the Child was born! Its songs so glad; its
2. O bless the hallowed joy it brings; The hope from which it springs; The goodness trooping

words of cheer, To heart and mem-'ry dear! Its gifts to young, and old as well; Its
in its train From yon far dis-tant plain. And so, with Ti-ny Tim, we pray, Up-

mer-ry chimes, which sweetly tell The sto-ry of his humble birth, The King of all the earth!
on this peaceful Christmas day, "God bless us!—bless us ev'ry one," With deeds of kindness done.

been flat heresy to do so. And Cratchit would have blushed to hint at such a thing. At last the dinner was all done, the cloth was cleared, the hearth swept, and the fire made up. The compound in the jug being tasted, and considered perfect, apples and oranges were put upon the table, and a shovel full of chestnuts on the fire. Then all the Cratchit family drew round the hearth, in what Bob Cratchit called a circle, meaning half a one; and at Bob Cratchit's elbow stood the family display of glass. Two tumblers and a custard-cup

without a handle. These held the hot stuff from the jug, however, as well as golden goblets would have done; and Bob served it out with beaming looks, while the chestnuts on the fire sputtered and cracked noisily. Then Bob proposed: "A Merry Christmas to us all, my dears. God bless us!" Which all the family re-echoed. "God bless us every one!" said Tiny Tim, the last of all. He sat very close to his father's side, upon his little stool. Bob held his withered little hand in his, as if he loved the child, and wished to keep him by his side, and dreaded that he might be taken from him. "Spirit," said Scrooge, with an interest he had never felt before, "tell me if Tiny Tim will live." "I see a vacant seat," replied the Ghost, "in the poor chimney-corner, and a crutch without an owner, carefully preserved. If these shadows remain unaltered by the Future the child will die." "No, no," said Scrooge. "Oh. no, kind Spirit ! say he will be spared." "If these shadows remain unaltered by the Future, none other of my race," returned the Ghost, "will find him here. What then ? If he be like to die, he had better do it, and decrease the surplus population." Scrooge hung his head to hear his own words quoted by the Spirit, and was overcome with penitence and grief. "Man," said the Ghost, "if man you be in heart, not adamant, forbear that wicked cant until you have discovered What the surplus is, and Where it is. Will you decide what men shall live, what men shall die ? It may be that, in the sight of Heaven, you are more worthless and less fit to live than millions like this poor man's child. Oh, God ! to hear the Insect on the leaf pronouncing on the too much life among his hungry brothers in the dust !" Scrooge

## DECK THE HALL.

FROM THE WELSH.

1. Deck the hall with boughs of hol - ly,
2. See the blaz - ing yule be - fore us,
3. Fast away the old year passes,
Fa la la la la la la la la.

'Tis the season to be jol - ly,
Strike the harp and join the chorus,
Hail the new, ye lads and lasses!
Fa la la la la la la la la.
Don we now our
Follow me in
Sing we joyous

gay apparel, Troll the ancient Christmas carol,
merry measure, While I tell of Christmas treasure,
all together, Heedless of the wind and weather.
Fa la la la la la la la la.

bent before the Ghost's rebuke, and trembling cast his eyes upon the ground. But he raised them speedily on hearing his own name. "Mr. Scrooge !" said Bob ; "I'll give you Mr. Scrooge, the founder of the feast!" "The founder of the feast, indeed!" cried Mrs. Cratchit, reddening. "I wish I had him here. I'd give him a piece of my mind to feast upon, and I hope he'd have a good appetite for it." "My dear," said Bob, "the children ! Christmas Day." "It should be Christmas Day, I am sure," said she, "on which one drinks the health of such an odious, stingy, hard, unfeeling man as Mr. Scrooge. You know he is, Robert ! Nobody knows it better than you do, poor fellow ?" "My dear," was Bob's mild answer ; "Christmas Day." "I'll drink his health for your sake and the Day's," said Mrs. Cratchit, "not for his. Long life to him ! A merry Christmas and a happy New Year ! He'll be very merry and very happy, I have no doubt !" The children drank the toast after her. It was the first of their proceedings which had no heartiness in it. Tiny Tim drank it last of all, but he didn't care twopence for it. Scrooge was the Ogre of the family. The mention of his name cast a dark shadow on the party, which was not dispelled for full five minutes. After it had passed away, they were ten times merrier than before, from the mere relief of Scrooge the Baleful being done with. Bob Cratchit told them how he had a situation in his eye for Master Peter, which would bring in, if obtained, full five-and-sixpence weekly. The two young Cratchits laughed tremendously at the idea of Peter's being a man of business; and Peter himself looked thoughtfully at the fire from between his collar, as if he were deliberating what particular investments he should favor when he came into the receipt of that bewildering income. Martha, who was a poor apprentice at a milliner's, then told them what kind of work she had to do, and how many hours she worked at a stretch, and how she meant to lie a-bed to-morrow morning for a good long rest; to-morrow being a holiday she passed at home. Also how she had seen a countess and a lord some days before, and how the lord "was much about as tall as Peter;" at which Peter pulled up his collar so high that you couldn't have seen his head if you had been there. All this time the chestnuts and the jug went round

## CHRISTMAS BELLS.

*Allegretto.*

1. Christ-mas bells are sounding clear, O-ver church and dwelling, Call-ing ev-'ry
2. Ma-ny hun-dred years a-go, Thus to save the dy-ing, Christ be-came a
3. Christ-mas bells, ring on, ring on, Ev-'ry pas-sion still-ing, All our souls with

soul to hear, What they're sweet-ly tell-ing. Ah! how sil-very are their tones,
lit-tle child, In a man-ger ly-ing. No sweet bells to wel-come Him,
peace-ful tho'ts, Hopes of heav-en fill-ing; And, as roll the long years by,

As they tell the sto-ry, How to earth the Lord came down, Leaving heaven's glo-ry.
O'er the hill-tops sounded, But the an-gels' ho-ly song Through the night resounded.
May our tones grow clear-er; May we feel, with ev-'ry year, Heaven is com-ing near-er.

and round; and by-the-bye they had a song, about a lost child traveling in the snow, from Tiny Tim, who had a plaintive little voice, and sang it very well indeed. There was nothing of high mark in this. They were not a handsome family; they were not well dressed; their shoes were far from being water-proof; their clothes were scanty; and Peter might have known, and very likely did, the inside of a pawnbroker's. But they were happy, grateful, pleased with one another, and contented with the time; and when they faded, and looked happier yet in the bright sprinklings of the Spirit's torch at parting, Scrooge had his eye upon them, and especially on Tiny Tim, until the last.

By this time it was getting dark and snowing pretty heavily; and, as Scrooge and the Spirit went along the streets, the brightness of the roaring fires in kitchens, parlors, and all sorts of rooms, was wonderful. Here the flickering of the blaze showed preparations for a cosy dinner, with hot plates baking through and through before the fire, and deep red curtains, ready to be drawn to shut out cold and darkness. There, all the children of the house were running out into the snow to meet their married sisters, brothers, cousins, uncles, aunts, and be the first to greet them. Here, again, were shadows on the window-blinds of guests assembling ; and there a group of handsome girls, all hooded and fur-booted, and all chattering at once, tripped lightly off to some near neighbor's house ; where, woe upon the single man who saw them enter—artful witches, well they knew it—

in a glow. But, if you had judged from the numbers of people on their way to friendly gatherings, you might have thought that no one was at home to give them welcome when they got there, instead of every house expecting company, and piling up its fires half-chimney high. Blessings on it, how the Ghost exulted ! How it bared its breadth of breast, and opened its capa-

## ONCE MORE ACROSS THE LAND.

CLEMENT SCOTT.

1. Once more a - cross the leaf - less land, We hear the joy - ous Christmas chimes,
2. Ring on, ring on, ye bells of peace; Ring on of love that nev - er dies;
3. Ring out the mu - sic of the chimes, That crush - es hate and blind de - spair;

The young, the old, now hand in hand, Sing o'er their mer - ry Christmas rhymes.
The love that glad - dens life may cease, But Christ - mas joy is of the skies.
The gos - pel of the good old times, That fills with love the am - bient air.

There is a sto - ry in the bells, That comes in mu - sic through the air ; Of
"Good will and peace !" in leaf - y scroll We see a - bove the chancel dim ; We
Though hope lie bur - ied it will rise ; Though sor - row tri - umph 'twill de - part ; Love

love to some their chim - ing tells, To some they sigh of sad de - spair.
hear the full - toned or - gan roll The mu - sic of the Christ - mas hymn.
will re - light grief - was - ted eyes And fill with joy the emp - ty heart.

cious palm, and floated on, outpouring, with a generous hand, its bright and harmless mirth on everything within its reach ! The very lamplighter, who ran on before, dotting the dusky street with specks of light, and who was dressed to spend the evening somewhere, laughed out loudly as the Spirit passed, though little kenned the lamplighter that he had any company but

Christmas ! And now, without a word of warning from the Ghost, they stood upon a bleak and desert moor, where monstrous masses of rude stone were cast about, as though it were the burial-place of giants ; and water spread itself wheresoever it listed ; or would have done so, but for the frost that held it prisoner ; and nothing grew but moss and furze, and coarse, rank grass. Down in the west the setting sun had left a streak of fiery red, which glared upon the desolation for an instant, like a sullen eye, and frowning lower, lower, lower yet, was lost in the thick gloom of darkest night. "What place is this?" asked Scrooge. "A place where miners live, who labor in the bowels of the earth," returned the Spirit. "But they know me. See!"

A light shone from the window of a hut, and swiftly they advanced towards it. Passing through the wall of mud and stone, they found a cheerful company assembled round a glowing fire. An old, old man and woman, with their children, and their children's children, and another generation beyond that, all decked out gaily in their holiday attire. The old man, in a voice

## THE CHRIST-CHILD.

W. V. WALLACE.

*Dolce.*

1. What time in strife and woe the world had travailed long, There thrilled a-cross the skies a strain of lof-ty song, And flamed a glo-ry on the night, and Kings from reg-ions far, Came with the pa-tient pil-grim staff where led the Star, Where led the blaz-ing Star, Where led the blaz-ing Star.

2. Since then far o'er the earth hath been the Christ-Child's reign! The dove His shoulder bore hath nev-er gathered stain; Still peace and love and kind-li-ness His pen-non bears un-furled, Till ev'-ry land and sea a-round the roll-ing world Be-holds the sa-cred Star, Be-holds the sa-cred Star.

3. And still the an-gel song is ring-ing down the years, And list'-ning men for-get their wea-ri-ness, their tears, The lit-tle Child upholds the globe, whose rad-iant life ex-pands In bloom and fragrance, at the clasp-ing of His hands, And knows its Ris-en Star, And knows its Ris-en Star.

*molto espress.*

that seldom rose above the howling of the wind upon the barren waste, was singing them a Christmas song; it had been a very old song when he was a boy; and from time to time they all joined in the chorus. So surely as they raised their voices, the old man got quite blithe and loud; and so surely as they stopped, his vigor sank again. The Spirit did not tarry here, but he bade

Scrooge hold his robe, and passing on above the moor, sped whither? Not to sea? To Sea. To Scrooge's horror, looking back, he saw the last of the land, a frightful range of rocks, behind them; and his ears were deafened by the thundering of water, as it rolled, and roared, and raged among the dreadful caverns it had worn, and fiercely tried to undermine the earth. Built upon a dismal reef of sunken rocks, some leagues or so from shore, on which the waters chafed and dashed the wild year through, there stood a solitary lighthouse. Great heaps of sea-weed clung to its base, and storm-birds—born of the wind one might suppose, as sea-weed of the water—rose and fell about it, like the waves they skimmed. But even here, two men who watched the light had made a fire, that through the loophole in the thick stone wall shed out a ray of brightness on the awful sea. Joining their horny hands over the rough table at which they sat, they wished each other Merry Christmas in their can of grog; and one of them—the elder too, with his face all damaged and scarred with hard weather, as the figure-head of an old ship might be—

## COME, SHOW ME THE WAY.

*Andante allegro.*                                                    EDITH THOMAS.

1. Grandma, please tell me the way, You've been there quite often they say;— I'm anxious to
2. Tom needs a trumpet and drum, He's waiting for Santa to come; And our Bob he must

know it be - cause I'm go-ing to see San-ta Claus There is something I want him to
have a new sled, For there's nothing but ice in his head; As for John, it's a foot-ball he

know When he starts on his ride thro' the snow, My sister's May's Dolly is old And the
says, And dear Santa don't know that he plays. I'll think of all these things and more When

skates that he gave Dick are sold, I promised I'd tell him to-day, So, grandma, come show me the way.
I'd ly I knock at his door, I promised I'd see him to-day, So, grandma, come show me the way.

struck up a sturdy song that was like a gale in itself. Again the Ghost sped on, above the black and heaving sea—on, on—until, being far away, as he told Scrooge, from any shore, they lighted on a ship. They stood beside the helmsman at the wheel, the look-out in the bow, the officers who had the watch; dark, ghostly figures in their several stations; but every man among them hummed a Christmas tune, or had a Christmas thought, or spoke below his breath to his companion of some by-gone Christmas Day, with homeward hopes belonging to it. And every man on board, waking or sleeping, good or bad, had had a kinder word for one another on that day than on any day in the year; and had shared to some extent in its festivities; and had remembered those he cared for at a distance, and had known that they delighted to remember him.

It was a great surprise to Scrooge, while listening to the moaning of the wind, and thinking what a solemn thing it was to move on through the lonely darkness over an unknown abyss, whose depths were secrets as profound as death: it was a great surprise to Scrooge, while thus engaged, to hear a hearty laugh. It was a much greater surprise to Scrooge to recognize it as his nephew's, and to find himself in a bright, dry, gleaming room, with the Spirit standing smiling by his side, and looking at that same nephew with approving affability!

## KRISS KINGLE'S DRIVE.

Animato.                                                                          ALPINE MELODY.

1. Who dashes on in sleet and snow, Tra, la la la la la, With ears and cheeks a rud-dy glow? Tra
2. He cracks his whip, now left, now right, Tra la la la la la, The reindeers speed with all their might, Tra
3. "Now we'll go thro' this narrow street, Tra la la la la la, And give the children here a treat, Tra
4. "Look out, now, there's a sled broke loose! Tra la la la la, And there's a doll caught in a noose! Tra

la la la la la, His cap he raises with a shout, His beard and hair blow all about—Kriss
la la la la la, A mil-lion stockings must be filled, And not a single toy be spilled. Kriss
la la la la la, For once a year at least I'll see The poorest child shall happy be. Kriss
la la la la la, Now dash away o'er hill and dale, For stars and moon begin to pale. Kriss

Kingle's on his round, O'er all the wide earth bound! Hurrah! hurrah! tra la la la la, hurrah! Hur-

rah! tra la la la la, Tra la, Tra la, Tra la la la la la la.

"Ha! ha!" laughed Scrooge's nephew. "Ha, ha, ha!" If you should happen, by any unlikely chance, to know a man more blessed in a laugh than Scrooge's nephew, all I can say is, I should like to know him too. Introduce him to me, and I'll cultivate his acquaintance. It is a fair, even-handed, noble adjustment of things, that while there is infection in disease and sorrow, there is nothing in the world so irresistibly contagious as laughter and good-humor. When Scrooge's nephew laughed in this way: holding his sides, rolling his head, and twisting his face into the most extravagant contortions: Scrooge's niece, by marriage, laughed as heartily as he.

And their assembled friends being not a bit behindhand, roared out lustily. "Ha, ha! Ha, ha, ha, ha!" "He said that Christmas was a humbug, as I live!" cried Scrooge's nephew. "He believed it, too!" "More shame for him, Fred!" said Scrooge's niece, indignantly. Bless those women! they never do anything by halves. They are always in earnest. She was very pretty; exceedingly pretty. With a dimpled, surprised-looking, capital face; a ripe little mouth, that seemed made to be kissed—as no doubt it was; all kinds of good little dots about her chin, that melted into one another when she laughed; and the sunniest pair of eyes you ever saw in any little creature's head. Altogether she was what you would have called provoking, you know; but satisfactory, too. Oh, perfectly satisfactory. "He's a comical old fellow," said Scrooge's nephew, "that's the truth; and not so pleasant as he might be. However, his offences carry their own punishment, and I have nothing to say against him." "I'm sure he is very rich, Fred," hinted Scrooge's niece. "At least you always tell *me* so." "What of that, my dear!" said Scrooge's nephew. "His wealth is of no use to him. He don't do any good with it. He don't make himself comfortable with it. He hasn't the satisfaction of thinking—ha, ha, ha!—that he is ever going to benefit Us with it." "I have no patience with him," observed Scrooge's

## BABY'S NIGHT.

Heavenly music I can hear
Falling on my raptured ear,
When my baby's cooing voice,
Makes the mother's heart rejoice.

Since the Lord of Glory shares
Such a form as baby wears,
Every little child should be
Vested with new sanctity.

Twinkle brightly, stars of light,
Christmas Eve is Baby's night;
Sweet my darling, God is good
Thus to honor babyhood.

niece. Scrooge's niece's sisters, and all the other ladies, expressed the same opinion. "Oh, I have!" said Scrooge's nephew. "I am sorry for him; I couldn't be angry with him if I tried. Who suffers by his ill whims! Himself, always. Here, he takes it into his head to dislike us, and he won't come and dine with us. What's the consequence? He don't lose much of a dinner." "Indeed, I think he loses a very good dinner," interrupted Scrooge's niece. Everybody else said the same, and they must be allowed to have been competent judges, because they had just had dinner; and with the dessert upon the table, were clustered round the fire, by lamplight. "Well! I am very glad to hear it," said Scrooge's nephew, "because I haven't any great faith in these young housekeepers. What do *you* say, Topper?" Topper had clearly got his eye upon one of Scrooge's niece's sisters, for he answered that a bachelor was a wretched outcast, who had no right to express an opinion on the subject. Whereat Scrooge's niece's sister—the plump one with the lace tucker: not the one with the roses—blushed. "Do go on, Fred," said Scrooge's niece, clapping her hands. "He never finishes what he begins to say! He is such a ridiculous fellow!" Scrooge's nephew revelled in another laugh, and as it was impossible to keep the infection off; though

CHRISTMAS KNITTING.

the plump sister tried hard to do it with aromatic vinegar; his example was unanimously followed. "I was only going to say," said Scrooge's nephew, "that the consequence of his taking a dislike to us, and not making merry with us, is, as I think, that he loses some pleasant moments, which could do him no harm. I am sure he loses pleasanter companions than he can find in his own thoughts, either in his mouldy old office, or his dusty chambers. I mean to give him the same chance every year, whether he likes it or not, for I pity him. He may rail at Christmas till he dies, but he can't help thinking better of it—I defy him—if he finds me going there, in good temper, year after year, and saying, 'Uncle Scrooge, how are you?' If it only puts him in the vein to leave his poor clerk fifty pounds, *that's* something; and I think

## WE GREET THEE, OLD FRIEND.

Scotch Air.
Ellen M. Douglas.

*Allegretto con spirito.*

1. We greet thee old friend in our merriest rhyme, Tho' cold the wind blows at the glad Christmas time, The
2. His fur cap is wreath'd with the holly's green leaves, His pack it is filled as on all Christmas eves, And
3. Oh, Santa Claus, Santa Claus, how do you know The way to each home thro' the fast-falling snow? We

fields they are hid-den but why should we grieve? For San-ta Claus knows it is fair Christmas eve.
with him come thronging the friends that we love, While mem'ry brings back all the dear ones that rove.
know you will be there, we know you will come! But how can you find out each little one's home?

Tra la la la la la la la la la la la la la la la la la la la la, Tra

la la la la la la la la, Tra la la la la la la la la la la la.

I shook him yesterday." It was their turn to laugh now, at the notion of his shaking Scrooge. But being thoroughly good-natured, and not much caring what they laughed at, so that they laughed at any rate, he encouraged them in their merriment, and passed the bottle, joyously.

After tea, they had some music. For they were a musical family, and knew what they were about, when they sung a glee or catch, I can assure you: especially Topper, who could growl away in the bass like a good one, and never swell the large veins in his forehead, or get red in the face over it. Scrooge's niece played well upon the harp; and played among other tunes a simple little air (a mere nothing: you might learn to whistle it in two minutes), which had been familiar to the child who fetched Scrooge from the boarding-school, as he had been reminded by the Ghost of Christmas Past. When this strain of music sounded all the things that the Ghost had shown him came upon his mind; he softened more and more; and thought that if he could have listened to it often, years ago, he might have cultivated the kindness of life for his own happiness with his own hands, without resorting to the sexton's spade that buried Jacob Marley. But they didn't devote the whole evening to music. After a while they played at forfeits; for it is good to be children sometimes, and never better than at Christmas, when its mighty Founder was a child himself. Stop! There was first a game at blind-man's buff. Of course there was. And I no more believe Topper was really blind than I believe he had eyes in his boots. My opinion is, that it was a done thing between him and

## SING THE HOLLY.

BELLINI.

1. Sing the hol-ly! oh, twine it with bay, Come give to the hol-ly a
2. Sing the hol-ly! the fair Christmas bough That hangs o-ver peas-ant and

song, For it drives the stern Win-ter a-way With his garment so som-bre and
king, While we laugh in our joy neath it now, To the rare Christmas hol-ly we'll

long; When the flow'rs and the fruits all are dead, And not even the dai-sy is
sing, For the gale and the frost they may come, To fet-ter the mu-si-cal

seen, It comes with its berries of red, And its leaves in their glos-si-est green.
rill; In the woods all its warblers be dumb, But the hol-ly is beau-ti-ful still.

Scrooge's nephew; and that the Ghost of Christmas Present knew it. The way he went after that plump sister in the lace tucker, was an outrage on the credulity of human nature. Knocking down the fire-irons, tumbling over the chairs, bumping up against the piano, smothering himself among the curtains, wherever she went, there went he! He always knew where the plump sister was. He wouldn't catch anybody else. If you had fallen up against him (as some of them did) on purpose, he would have made a feint of endeavoring to seize you, which would have been an affront to your understanding, and would instantly have sidled off in the direction of the plump sister. She often cried out that it wasn't fair; and it really was not. But when at last he caught her; when, in spite of all her silken rustlings, and her rapid flutterings past him, he got her into a corner whence there was no escape; then his conduct was the most execrable. For his pretending not to know her; his pretending that it was necessary to touch her head-dress, and further to assure himself of her identity by pressing a certain ring upon her finger, and a certain chain about her neck; was vile, monstrous! No doubt she told him her opinion of it, when, another blind-man being in office, they were so very confidential together, behind the curtains. Scrooge's niece was not one of the blind-man's-buff party, but was made comfortable with a large chair and a footstool, in a snug corner where the Ghost and Scrooge were close behind her. But she joined in the forfeits, and loved her love to admiration with all the letters of the alphabet. Likewise at the game of How, When, and Where, she was very great, and, to the secret joy of Scrooge's nephew, beat her sisters hollow: though they were sharp girls too, as Topper could have told you. There might have been twenty people there, young and old, but they all played, and so

## SANTA CLAUS IS COMING.

did Scrooge; for, wholly forgetting in the interest he had in what was going on that his voice made no sound in their ears, he sometimes came out with his guess quite loud, and very often guessed right, too; for the sharpest needle, best Whitechapel, warranted not to cut in the eye, was not sharper than Scrooge; blunt as he took it in his head to be. The Ghost was greatly pleased to find him in this mood, and looked upon him with such favor, that he begged like a boy to be allowed to stay until the guests departed. But this the spirit said could not be done.

"Here is a new game," said Scrooge. "One half hour, Spirit, only one!" It was a Game called Yes and No, where Scrooge's nephew had to think of something, and the rest must find out what; he only answering to their questions yes or no, as the case was. The brisk fire of questioning to which he was exposed, elicited from him that he was thinking of an animal, a live animal, rather a disagreeable animal, a savage animal, an animal that growled and grunted sometimes, and talked sometimes, and lived in London, and walked about the streets, and wasn't made a show of, and wasn't led by anybody, and didn't live in a menagerie, and was never killed in a market, and was not a horse, or an ass, or a cow, or a bull, or a tiger, or a dog, or a pig, or a cat, or a bear. At every fresh question that was put to him, this nephew burst into a fresh roar of laughter; and was so inexpressibly tickled, that he was obliged to get up off the sofa and stamp. At last the plump sister, falling into a similar state, cried out: "I have found it out! I know what it is, Fred! I know what it is!" "What is it?" cried Fred. "It's your uncle Scro-o-o-oge?" Which it certainly was. Admiration was the universal sentiment, though some objected that the reply to "Is it a bear?" ought to have been "Yes;" inasmuch as an answer in the negative was sufficient to have diverted their thoughts from Mr. Scrooge, supposing they had ever had any tendency that way. "He has given us plenty of merriment, I am sure," said Fred, "and it would be ungrateful not to drink his health. Here is a glass of mulled wine ready to our hand at the moment; and I

## MERRY JOY BELLS RING.

J. L. MOLLOY.
RUWENA SELDEN.

1. Christmas time is near, Skies more blue and clear; Sunshine beams so bright For our hearts are light.
2. In the evening glow Fan - cies come and go, While on airy wing Joy doth soar and sing:
3. Joy bells ring thy praise, Best of hol - i - days, Care and wasting grief Know thy sweet re - lief.

In our gladsome cheer Seem our friends more dear; All the earth a - bout is fair,
"Up! and play thy part, Hap - py hu - man heart; Up! and play thy wel - come part,
Heaven is more sure, Earth, we know, more pure, For the helpful, kind - ly deed

Glad - ness ev - 'ry - where, All the earth a - bout is fair, Gladness ev - 'ry - where.
Hap - py hu - man heart! Up! and play thy welcome part, Hap - py hu - man heart!"
That doth an - swer need. Joy - bells merry ring thy praise, Best of ho - li - days!

say, 'Uncle Scrooge!'" "Well! Uncle Scrooge!" they cried. "A Merry Christmas and a Happy New Year to the old man, whatever he is!" said Scrooge's nephew. "He wouldn't take it from me, but may he have it, nevertheless. Uncle Scrooge!" Uncle Scrooge had imperceptibly become so gay and light of heart, that he would have pledged the unconscious company in return, and thanked them in an inaudible speech if the Ghost had given him time. But the whole scene passed off in the breath of the last word spoken by his nephew; and he and the Spirit were again upon their travels. Much they saw, and far they went, and many homes they visited, but always with a happy end. The Spirit stood beside sick beds, and they were cheerful; on foreign lands, and they were close at home; by struggling men, and they were patient in their greater hope; by poverty, and it was rich. In almshouse, hospital and jail, in misery's every refuge, where vain man in his little brief authority had not made fast the door, and barred the Spirit out, he left his blessing, and taught Scrooge his precepts.

14

It was a long night, if it were only a night; but Scrooge had his doubts of this, because the Christmas Holidays appeared to be condensed into the space of time they passed together. It was strange, too, that while Scrooge remained unaltered in his outward form, the Ghost grew older, clearly older. Scrooge had observed this change, but never spoke of it, until they left a children's Twelfth Night party, when, looking at the Spirit as they stood together in an open place, he noticed that his hair was grey. "Are spirits' lives so short?" asked Scrooge. "My life upon this globe is very brief," replied the Ghost. "It ends to-night," "To-night!" cried Scrooge "To-night at midnight. Hark! The time is drawing near." The chimes were ringing

## GLAD TIDINGS.

JOHN IMLAH.
MARTIN LUTHER, 1535.

Good news, good news the an - gels bring, Glad tid - ings to the
Earth they sing, To crown us with the joy of Heav'n, A Child to us is given!

1. This is the Christ, our God and Lord, Who in all need shall aid af - ford; From
2. All hail, Thou no - ble guest, this morn, Whose love did not the sin - ner scorn; In
3. Were earth a thou - sand times as fair, Be - set with gold and jew - els rare, She
4. Ah, dear - est Je - sus, Ho - ly Child! Make Thee a bed soft, un - de - filed, With -
5. Praise God up - on His heavenly throne, Who gave to us His on - ly Son; For

sin and sor - row set us free, He will our Sav - iour be! Good
my dis - tress Thou cam'st to me; What thanks owe I to Thee! Good
yet were far too poor to be A cra - dle, Lord, for Thee. Good
in my heart, that it may be A cham - ber kept for Thee. Good
this His hosts on joy - ful wing New Year of Mer - cy sing. Good

the three-quarters past eleven at that moment. "Forgive me if I am not justified in what I ask," said Scrooge, looking intently at the Spirit's robe, "but I see something strange, and not belonging to yourself, protruding from your skirts. Is it a foot or a claw?" "It might be a claw, for the flesh there is upon it," was the Spirit's sorrowful reply. "Look here." From the foldings of its robe, it brought two children; wretched, abject, frightful, hideous, miserable. They knelt down at its feet, and clung upon the outside of its garment. "Oh, Man! look here. Look, look, down here!" exclaimed the Ghost.

They were a boy and a girl. Yellow, meagre, ragged, scowling, wolfish; but prostrate, too, in their humility. Where graceful youth should have filled their features out, and touched them with its freshest tints, a stale and shrivelled hand, like that of age, had pinched, and twisted them, and pulled them into shreds. Where angels might have sat enthroned, devils lurked, and glared out menacing. No change, no degradation, no perversion of humanity, in any grade, through all the mysteries of wonderful creation, has monsters half so horrible and dread.

Scrooge started back, appalled. Having them shown to him in this way, he tried to say they were fine children, but the words choked themselves, rather than be parties to a lie of such enormous magnitude. "Spirit! are they yours?" Scrooge could say no more. "They are Man's," said the Spirit, looking down upon them. "And they cling to me, appealing from their fathers. This boy is Ignorance. This girl is Want. Beware of them both, and all of their degree, but most of all beware this boy, for on his brow I see that written which is Doom, unless the writing be erased. Deny it!" cried the Spirit, stretching out its hand towards the city. "Slander those who tell it ye! Admit it for your factious purposes, and make it worse! And bide the end!" "Have they no refuge or resource?" cried Scrooge. "Are there no prisons!" said the Spirit, turning on him for the last time with his own words. "Are there no work-houses?"

The bell struck twelve. Scrooge looked about him for the Ghost, and saw it not. As the last stroke ceased to vibrate, he remembered the prediction of old Jacob Marley, and lifting up his eyes, beheld a solemn Phantom, draped and hooded, coming like a mist along the ground towards him.

## STAVE IV.

### THE LAST OF THE SPIRITS.

THE Phantom slowly, gravely, silently approached. When it came near him, Scrooge bent down upon his knee; for in the very air thro' which this Spirit moved it seemed to scatter gloom and mystery. It was shrouded in a deep black garment, which concealed its head, its face, its form, and left nothing of it visible, save one outstretched hand. But for this it would have been difficult to detach its figure from the night, and separate it from the darkness by which it was surrounded. He felt that it was tall and stately when it came beside him, and that its mysterious presence filled him with a solemn dread. He knew no more, for the Spirit neither spoke nor moved.

"I am in the presence of the Ghost of Christmas Yet To Come?" said Scrooge. The Spirit answered not, but pointed onward with its hand. "You are about to show me shadows of the things that have not happened, but will happen in the time before us," Scrooge pursued. "Is that so, Spirit?" The upper portion of the garment was contracted for an instant in its folds, as if the Spirit had inclined its head. That was the only answer he received.

Although well used to ghostly company by this time, Scrooge feared the silent shape so much that his legs trembled beneath him, and he found that he could hardly stand when he prepared to follow it. The Spirit paused a moment, as observing his condition, and giving him time to recover. But Scrooge was all the worse for this. It thrilled him with a vague uncertain horror, to know that behind the dusky shroud, there were ghostly eyes intently fixed upon him, while he, though he stretched his own to the utmost, could see nothing but a spectral hand and one great heap of black.

"Ghost of the Future!" he exclaimed, "I fear you more than any spectre I have seen. But as I know your purpose is to do me good, and as I hope to live to be another man from what I was, I am prepared to bear your company, and do it with a thankful heart. Will you not speak to me?" It gave him no reply. The hand was pointed straight before them.

"Lead on!" said Scrooge. "Lead on! The night is waning fast, and it is precious time to me, I know. Lead on, Spirit!" The phantom moved away as it had come towards him. Scrooge followed in the shadow of its dress, which bore him up, he thought, and carried him along. They scarcely seemed to enter the city; for the city rather seemed to spring up about them, and compass them of its own act. But there they were in the heart of it; on 'Change amongst the merchants; who hurried up and down, and chinked the money in their pockets, and conversed in groups, and looked at their watches, and trifled thoughtfully with their great gold seals; and so forth, as Scrooge had seen them often.

The Spirit stopped beside one little knot

of business men. Observing that the hand was pointed to them, Scrooge advanced to listen to their talk. "No," said a great fat man with a monstrous chin, "I don't know much about it either way. I only know he's dead." "When did he die?" inquired another. "Last night, I believe." "Why, what was the matter with him?" asked a third, taking a vast quantity of snuff out of a very large snuff box. "I thought he'd never die." "God knows," said the first, with a yawn. "What has he done with his money?" asked a red-faced gentleman with a pendulous excrescence on the end of his nose, that shook like the gills of a turkey-cock. "I haven't heard," said the man with the large chin, yawning again. "Left it to his company, perhaps.

## HOW GLORIOUS THE DAY.

1. How glorious was the blessed day when Christ appeared on earth! And bless-ed was the
2. He suffered shame for sin-ful men, scorn, hatred, pain and woe; And cru-el death up-
3. Hosanna to His peerless Name, who came to earth from Heaven; For fall-en man's re-

chosen land that gave the Saviour birth; And gold-en bright the gleaming star, That
on the Cross, His wondrous love to show; And sighed, His race so near-ly run, Thy
demption sent, for our sal-va-tion given; Oh! let that Name the world a-dore Till

Wise Men followed far, To greet the Child, the heavenly Babe that an-gel hosts a-
will not mine, be done!" And then He died, our Sav-iour King, our El-der Brother
death shall be no more. Oh! let it sound from shore to shore, from Earth to highest

dore, To greet the Child, the heavenly Babe, that an-gel hosts a-dore.
born, And then He died, our Sav-iour King, our El-der Brother born.
Heaven, Oh! let it sound from shore to shore, from Earth to highest Heaven.

He hasn't left it to *me*. That's all I know." This pleasantry was received with a general laugh. "Its likely to be a very cheap funeral," said the same speaker; "for upon my life I don't know of anybody to go to it. Suppose we make up a party and volunteer?" "I don't mind going if a lunch is provided," observed the gentleman with the excrescence on his nose. "But I must be fed if I make one." Another laugh. "Well, I am the most disinterested among you, after all," said the first speaker, "for I never wear black gloves, and I never eat lunch. But I'll offer to go, if anybody else will. When I come to think of it, I'm not at all sure that I wasn't his most particular friend; for we used to stop and speak whenever we met. Bye, bye!" Speakers and listeners strolled away, and mixed with other groups. Scrooge knew the men, and looked towards the Spirit for an explanation. The Phantom glided on into a street. Its finger pointed to two persons meeting. Scrooge listened again, thinking that the explanation might lie here. He knew these men, also, perfectly. They were men of business; very wealthy, and of great importance. He had made a point always of standing well in their esteem: in a business point of view, that is; strictly in a business point of view. "How are you?" said one. "How are you?" returned the other. "Well!" said the first, "Old Scratch has got his own at last, hey?" "So I am told," returned the second. "Cold, isn't it!" "Seasonable for Christmas time. You are

## CHRISTMAS CAROL.

*With expression.*

MARY V. LOCKE.

1. When Christ was born in Beth-le-hem 'Twas night but seemed the day; The stars, their light full pure and bright, Shone with un-fail-ing ray; But one, in glo-ry o'er them all, The Bright and Morn-ing Star Fore-told — and to Ju-de-a's plains Led Wise Men from a-far.

2. Mild Peace then ruled o'er all the land; The li-on with the lamb, And near the kid the leop-ard fierce Broke not the bliss-ful calm; To-geth-er lay the ox and bear, All cru-el dread for-got,— With kite and gen-tle dove at rest; For fear and hate were not.

3. And patient shepherds watch'd their flocks That qui-et won-der-night, While sud-den came the shin-ing host, Dis-played in heav'n-ly light, They sang of peace, good-will to men! Fear not, but lift your eyes; Lo, Earth be-comes, shall be a-gain, A smil-ing Par-a-dise.

not a skater, I suppose?" "No. No. Something else to think of. Good-morning!" Not another word. That was their meeting, their conversation, and their parting. Scrooge was at first inclined to be surprised that the Spirit should attach importance to conversations apparently so trivial; but feeling assured that they must have some hidden purpose, he set himself to consider what it was likely to be. They could scarcely be supposed to have any bearing on the death of Jacob, his old partner, for that was Past, and this Ghost's province was the Future. Nor could he think of any one immediately connected with himself, to whom he could apply them. But nothing doubting that to whomsoever they applied they had some latent moral for his own improvement, he resolved to treasure up every word he heard, and everything he saw ; and especially to observe the shadow of himself when it appeared.   For he had an expectation that the conduct of his future self would give him the clue he missed, and would render the solution of these riddles easy.   He looked about in that very place for his own image :  but another man stood in his accustomed corner, and though the clock pointed to his usual time of day for being there, he saw no likeness of himself among the multitudes that poured in through the porch.   It gave him little surprise, however ;  for he had been revolving in his mind a change of life, and thought and hoped he saw his new-born resolutions carried out in this.   Quiet and dark, beside him stood the Phantom, with its outstretched hand.   When he roused himself from his thoughtful quest, he fancied from the turn of the hand, and its situation in reference to himself, that the Unseen Eyes were looking at him keenly.   It made him shudder, and feel very cold.

They left the busy scene, and went into an obscure part of the town, where Scrooge had never penetrated before, although he recognised its situation, and its bad repute. The ways were foul and narrow ; the shops and houses wretched ; the people half-naked, drunken. slip-shod, ugly.  Alleys and archways, like so many cesspools, disgorged their offences of smell, and dirt, and

## CHANT OF BRETON PEASANTS.

NAUMANN.
LAURA C. REDDEN.

1. "What is new up - on the earth? What fresh won - der go - eth forth,
2. Sounds of glad - ness on the air! Hap - py fa - ces ev - 'ry where!
3. "Lo the sa - cred hour is near! What was dark-ness now is clear.
4. Lo, the Prince of Peace is born! Lo, on high the star of morn!

That its ways are full of pil - grims, And its dwell - ings full of mirth ?
Tell us, O ye si - lent vir - gins, Where - fore is the night so fair ?"
Christ is com - ing! raise your voi - ces, Say fare - well to doubt and fear.
And it shall not fade for - ev - er, Nor its brill - ian - cy be shorn."

First two verses may be sung by Semi-Chorus, last two by Full Chorus.

life, upon the straggling streets ; and the whole quarter reeked with crime, with filth and misery.  Far in this den of infamous resort, there was a low-browed. beetling shop, below a pent-house roof, where iron, old rags, bottles, bones, and greasy offal, were bought.   Upon the floor within, were piled up heaps of rusty keys, nails, chains, hinges, files, scales, weights, and refuse iron of all kinds.   Secrets that few would like to scrutinize were bred and hidden in mountains of unseemly rags, masses of corrupted fat, and sepulchres of bones.   Sitting in among the wares he dealt in, by a charcoal stove, made of old bricks, was a grey-haired rascal, nearly seventy years of age ;  who had screened himself from the cold air without, by a frousy curtaining of miscellaneous tatters hung upon a line ; and smoked his pipe in all the luxury of calm retirement.  Scrooge and the Phantom came into the presence of this man, just as a woman with a heavy bundle slunk into the shop. But she had scarcely entered, when another woman, similarly laden, came in too ; and she was closely followed by a man in faded black, who was no less startled by the sight of them, than they had been upon the recognition of each other.   After a short period of blank astonishment, in which the old man with the pipe had joined them, they all three burst into a laugh.   "Let the charwoman alone to be the first!" cried she who had entered first.   "Let the laundress alone to be the second: and let the undertaker's man alone to be the third. Look here, old Joe, here's a chance! If we haven't all three met here without meaning it!" "You couldn't have met in a better place," said old Joe, removing his pipe from his mouth. "Come into the parlor. You were made free of it long ago, you know; and the other two ain't strangers. Stop till I shut the door of the shop. Ah! How it skreeks! There ain't such a rusty bit of metal in the place as its own hinges, I believe; and I'm sure there's no such old bones here, as mine. Ha, ha! We're all suitable to our calling, we're well matched. Come into the parlor. Come into the parlor." The parlor was the space behind the screen of rags. The old man raked the fire together with an old stair-rod, and having trimmed his smoky lamp (for it was night) with the stem of his pipe, put it into his mouth again. While he did this, the woman who had already spoken threw her bundle on the floor and sat down in a flaunting manner on a stool; crossing her elbows on her knees, and looking with a bold defiance at the other two. "What odds then! What odds, Mrs. Dilber?" said the woman. "Every person has a right to take care of themselves. *He* always did!" "That's true, indeed!" said the laundress. "No man more so," "Why, then, don't stand staring as if you were afraid, woman; who's the wiser? We're not going to pick holes

## THE CHRIST-CHILD.

*Moderato.*  GERMAN.

1. At yule-tide, so the sto-ry tells, There comes an An-gel-child From
2. It pass-es thro' the sleeping street, All night with noiseless tread, All
3. It bends above the sleeping forms Of no-bles, slaves and kings, Sweet
4. Oh, nev-er may that an-gel face, In sor-row pass us by, Dear

far-off lands where no man dwells, Far o-ver, far o-ver, the waste of waters wild,
clothed in white to fair white feet, Gold ha-lo, gold ha-lo gleams round the golden head.
thoughts and sinless slumber sheds, And hap-py, and hap-py their dreams of heav'nly things!
Christ-child, look on us in grace, And bless us, and bless us all where we sleeping lie!

in each other's coats, I suppose?" "No, indeed!" said Mrs. Dilber and the man together. "We should hope not." "Very well, then!" cried the woman. "That's enough. Who's the worse for the loss of a few things like these? Not a dead man, I suppose." "No, indeed," said Mrs. Dilber, laughing. "If he wanted to keep 'em after he was dead, a wicked, old screw," pursued the woman, "why wasn't he natural in his lifetime? If he had been, he'd have had somebody to look after him when he was struck with Death, instead of lying gasping out his last there, alone by himself." "It's the truest word that ever was spoke," said Mrs. Dilber; "it's a judgment on him." "I wish it was a little heavier judgment," replied the woman; " and it should have been, you may depend upon it, if I could have laid my hands on anything else. Open that bundle, old Joe, and let me know the value of it. Speak out plain. I'm not afraid to be the first, nor afraid for them to see it. We knew pretty well that we were helping ourselves, before we met here, I believe. It's no sin. Open the bundle, Joe." But the gallantry of her friends would not allow of this; and the man in faded black, mounting the breach first, produced *his* plunder. It was not extensive. A seal or two, a pencil-case, a pair of sleeve buttons, and a brooch of no great value, were all. They were severally examined and appraised by old Joe, who chalked the sums he was disposed to give for each upon the wall, and added them up into a total when he found that there was nothing more to come. "That's your account," said Joe, "and I wouldn't give another sixpence, if I was to be boiled for not doing it. Who's next?" Mrs. Dilber was next. Sheets and towels, a little wearing apparel, two old-fashioned silver teaspoons, a pair of sugar tongs, and a few boots. Her account was stated on the wall in the same manner." "I always give too much to ladies. It's been a weakness o' mine, and that's the way I ruin myself," said old Joe.

"That's your account. If you ask me for another penny, and made it an open question, I'd repent of being so liberal, and knock off half-a-crown." "And now undo *my* bundle, Joe," said the first woman. Joe went down on his knees for the greater convenience of opening it, and having unfastened a great many knots, dragged out a large heavy roll of some dark stuff. "What do you call this?" said Joe. "Bed-curtains!" "Ah!" returned the woman, laughing and leaning forward on her crossed arms. "Bed-curtains!" "You don't mean to say you took 'em down rings and

## AROUND OUR BLAZING FIRES.

S. Nelson.

Moderato.

1. When we around our blaz-ing fires These fes-tive moments spend, En - joy the sweets our
2. We soar on fan - cy's ea - ger wings To Ju-dah's sa - cred hills, Be - hold the star whose
3. "Fear not," the shin-ing an - gel says, "For joy-ful news I bring; In Beth - le - hem is

Maker gives, 'Midst childhood, home, and friends; When glad our hearts are made with these, Tho'
silv - 'ry light With joy the Wise Men fills; There all a - round the shepherds' flocks, The
born this day, A Sa - viour, Christ your King. And soon a host of an - gels sing In

sometimes mixed with tears, We think on scenes of oth - er lands, And joys of oth - er years.
Heav - en - ly light appears, And when 'midst this the angel comes, The tim - id shepherd fears.
all their bright ar - ray, That God to man is re - conciled, With "Peace on earth" alway.

all, with him lyin' there?" said Joe. "Yes, I do," replied the woman. "Why not?" "You were born to make your fortune," said Joe, "and you'll certainly do it." "I certainly shan't hold my hand, when I can get anything in it by reaching it out, for the sake of such a man as He was, I promise you, Joe," returned the woman, coolly. "Don't drop that oil upon the blankets, now." "His blankets?" asked old Joe. "Whose else's do you think?" replied the woman. "He isn't likely to take cold without 'em, I dare say." "I hope he

didn't die of anything catching? Eh?" said Joe, stopping in his work, and looking up. "Don't you be afraid of that," returned the woman. "I ain't so fond of his company that I'd loiter about him for such things, if he did. Ah! You may look through that shirt till your eyes ache; but you won't find a hole in it, nor a threadbare place. It's the best he had, and a fine one, too. They'd have wasted it, if it hadn't been for me." "What do you call wasting of it?" asked old Joe. "Putting it on him to be buried in, to be sure," replied the woman with a laugh. "Somebody was fool enough to do it, but I took it off again. If calico ain't good enough for such a purpose, it isn't good enough for anything. It's quite as becoming to the body. He can't look uglier than he did in that one." Scrooge listened to this dialogue in horror. As they sat grouped about their spoil, in the scanty light afforded by the old man's lamp, he viewed them with a detestation and disgust which could hardly have been greater, though they had been obscene demons, marketing the corpse itself. "Ha, ha!" laughed the same woman, when old Joe, producing a flannel bag with money in it, told out their several gains upon the ground. "This is the end of it, you see? He frightened every one away from him when he was alive, to profit us when he was dead! Ha, ha, ha!"

"Spirit!" said Scrooge, shuddering from head to foot. "I see, I see. The case of this unhappy man might be my own. My life tends that way, now. Merciful Heaven, what is this!" He recoiled in terror, for the scene had changed, and now he almost touched a bed: a bare, uncurtained bed: on which, beneath a ragged sheet, there lay a some-

## WHEN SNOW LIES DEEP.

Rossini.

1. When snow lies deep upon the ground, And winter winds are blow-ing, And on the hearth with crackling blaze, The win-ter fires are glow-ing; Then thro' the land a mag-ic voice A pleasant song is humming, Friends parted long shall meet again, For Christmas day is com - ing.

2. The school-boy hears it at his task, His heart is light-er beat-ing; The plodding stu-dent lifts his head, And thinks of home and greet-ing; To old and young, to rich and poor, The gen - tle voice is humming, Friends parted long shall meet again, For Christmas day is com - ing.

3. The dreaming po - et hears the voice, It seems that bells are ringing, And an - gel choirs a Christmas song To all mankind are sing-ing; He ech - oes forth the notes of peace, The voice to him is humming, God bless each friend, forgive each foe, For Christmas day is com-ing.

thing covered up, which, though it was dumb, announced itself in awful language. The room was very dark, too dark to be observed with any accuracy, though Scrooge glanced round it in obedience to a secret impulse, anxious to know what kind of room it was. A pale light rising in the outer air, fell straight upon the bed: and on it, plundered and bereft, unwatched, unwept, uncared for, was the body of this man. Scrooge glanced towards the Phantom. Its steady hand was pointed to the head. The cover was so carelessly adjusted that the slightest raising of it, the motion of a finger upon Scrooge's part, would have disclosed the face. He thought of it, felt how easy it would be to do, and longed to do it: but had no more power to withdraw the veil than to dismiss the spectre at his side. Oh, cold, cold, rigid, dreadful Death, set up thine altar here, and dress it with such terrors as thou hast at thy command: for this is thy dominion! But of the loved, revered and honored head, thou canst not turn one hair to thy dread purposes, or make one feature odious. It is not that the hand is heavy and will fall down when released; it is not that the heart and pulse are still; but that the hand *was* open, generous, and true; the heart brave, warm, and tender; and the pulse a man's. Strike, Shadow, strike! And see his good deeds springing from the wound, to sow the world with life immortal.

No voice pronounced these words in Scrooge's ears, and yet he heard them when he looked upon the bed. He thought, if this man could be raised up now, what would be his foremost thoughts? Avarice, hard dealing, griping cares? They have brought him to a rich end truly! He lay, in the dark, empty house, with not a man, a woman, or a child to say he was kind to me in this or that, and for the memory of one kind word I will be kind to him. A cat was tearing at

"I'VE FOUND YOU OUT, MY DEAR OLD SANTA CLAUS."

the door, and there was a sound of gnawing rats beneath the hearth-stone. What *they* wanted in the room of death, and why they were so restless and disturbed, Scrooge did not dare to think. "Spirit!" he said "this is a fearful place. In leaving it I shall not leave its lesson, trust me. Let us go!" Still the Ghost pointed with an unmoved finger to the head. "I understand you," Scrooge returned, "and I would do it if I could. But I have not the power, Spirit. I have not the power." Again it seemed to look upon him. "If there is any person in the town who feels emotion caused by this man's death," said Scrooge, quite agonized, "show that person to me, Spirit, I beseech you!" The phantom spread its dark robe before him for a moment, like a wing; and withdrawing it, revealed a room by daylight, where a mother and her children were. She was expecting some one, and with anxious eagerness; for she walked up and down the room, started at every sound, looked out from the window, glanced at the clock; tried, but in vain, to work with her needle; and could hardly bear the voices of her children in their play. At length the long-expected knock was heard.

She hurried to the door and met her husband; a man whose face was careworn and depressed, though he was young. There was a remarkable expression in it now; a kind of serious delight of which he felt ashamed, and which he struggled to repress. He sat down to the dinner that had been hoarding for him by the fire, and when she asked him faintly what news (which was not

## WELCOME TO CHRISTMAS.

JOHN DRAKE.

1. Mer-ry all! mer-ry all! and with hol-ly deck the hall, hol-ly deck the hall, To wel-come Christmas in; Sing the song, spread the feast, let the viol sound, vi-ol sound, Thro' all the mer-ry din! What day the yearly sea-sons round Doth with like mirth abound? Merry all! merry all! and with holly deck the hall, holly deck the hall, Be green our Christmas all!

2. Tuneful bells, tuneful bells, how your mer-ry mu-sic swells, mer-ry music swells, Thro' all the am-bient air! Starry tree, starry tree, with your fruitage ever free, fruitage ever free, Still gleams your light so fair! The chimes of choiring seraphs tell; The star shines, "All is well!" Tuneful bells, tuneful bells, how your merry music swells, merry music swells, As Christmas joy it tells.

3. Once a-gain, once a-gain, 'tis the old-en hap-py lay, old-en hap-py lay, We sing in chorus glad, "Love shall reign!" "Love shall reign!" sweetest carol of the day, carol of the day, To hearts that elsewhere sad "Good-will increase, and all strife cease, Each heart be filled with peace!" Once a-gain, once again, 'tis the olden happy lay, olden hap-py lay, The an-gel song al-way!

until after a long silence), he appeared embarrassed how to answer. "Is it good news," she said, "or bad?"—to help him. "Bad," he answered. "We are quite ruined?" "No; there is hope yet, Caroline." "If *he* relents," she said, amazed, "there is! Nothing is past hope, if such a miracle has happened." "He is past relenting," said her husband; "he is dead." She was a mild and patient

creature, if her face spoke truth; but she was thankful in her soul to hear it, and she said só, with clasped hands. She prayed forgiveness the next moment, and was sorry; but the first was the emotion of her heart. "What the half-drunken woman, whom I told you of last night, said to me, when I tried to see him and obtain a week's delay, and what I thought was a mere excuse to avoid me, turns out to have been quite true; he was not only very ill, but dying, then." "To whom will our debt be transferred?" "I don't know. But before that time we shall be ready with the money; and even though we were not, it would be bad fortune indeed to find so merciless a creditor in his successor. We may sleep to-night with light hearts, Caroline!" Yes. Soften it as they would, their hearts were lighter. The children's faces, hushed and clustered round to hear what they so little understood, were brighter; and it was a happier house for this man's death! The only emotion that the Ghost could show him, caused by the event, was one of pleasure.

"Let me see some tenderness connected with a death," said Scrooge; "or that dark chamber, Spirit, which we left just now, will be forever present to me." The Ghost conducted him through several streets familiar to his feet; and as they went along, Scrooge looked here and there to find himself, but nowhere was he to be seen. They entered poor Bob Cratchit's house; the dwelling he had visited before; and found the mother and the children seated round the fire. Quiet. Very quiet.

## OVER THE HAPPY TOWN.

D. P. F. Auber.

1. All hail! the bells are ring - ing, The merry, merry Christmas bells, Sweet re - sounding
2. Hark! the tale they're tell - ing, The olden tale of Man - ger born—Gen - tle maid - en,
3. "Good news!" the song is ring - ing, The song divine the an - gels sang To rude shepherds

thro' the vale, Never that joy can fail! We greet their chime with gladness, The merry, merry
mother mild, And the Heav'nly Child; Of light the Wise Men guiding O'er mountain, moor, and
when that night Shone the Heav'nly light. Good news of God's great kindness, His gift of love to

Christmas chime, While stars are shin - ing bright - ly down O - ver the hap - py town.
des - ert plain, Bring - ing gifts of love from far, Under the wondrous star.
man for - lorn, Where - in peace and joy doth blend, Love that hath no end.

The noisy little Cratchits were as still as statues in one corner, and sat looking up at Peter, who had a book before him. The mother and her daughters were engaged in sewing. But surely they were very quiet! "'And he took a child, and set him in the midst of them.'" Where had Scrooge heard those words? He had not dreamed them. The boy must have read them out, as he and the Spirit crossed the threshold. Why did he not go on? The mother laid her work upon the table, and put her hand up to her face. "The color hurts my eyes," she said. The color? Ah, poor Tiny Tim!

"They're better now again," said Cratchit's wife. "It makes them weak by candle-light; and I wouldn't show weak eyes to your father when he comes home, for the world. It must be near his time." "Past it rather," Peter answered, shutting up his book. "But I think he has walked a little slower than he used, these few last evenings, mother." They were very quiet again. At last she said, and in a steady, cheerful voice, that faltered only once, "I have known him walk with—I have known him walk with Tiny Tim upon his shoulder, very fast, indeed." "And so have I," cried

Peter—"often." "And so have I," exclaimed another. So had all. "But he was very light to carry," she resumed, intent upon her work, "and his father loved him so, that it was no trouble, no trouble. And there is your father at the door!" She hurried out to meet him; and little Bob in his comforter—he had need of it, poor fellow—came in. His tea was ready for him on the hob, and they all tried who should help him to it most. Then the two young Cratchits got upon his knees and laid, each child, a little cheek against his face, as if they said, "Don't mind it, father. Don't be grieved!" Bob was very cheerful with them, and spoke pleasantly to all the family. He looked at the work upon the table, and praised the industry and speed of Mrs. Cratchit and the girls. They would be done long before Sunday, he said. "Sunday! You went to-day, then, Robert?" said his wife. "Yes, my dear," returned Bob. "I wish you could have gone. It would have done you good to see how green a place it is. But you'll see it often. I promised him that I would walk there on a Sunday. My little, little child!" cried Bob. "My little child!" He broke down

## THE CHILDREN'S VOICES.

Alpine Melody.
Richard E. Burton.

1. Hear the chil-dren's voi-ces   Ris-ing clear and strong!   All the world re-
2. For they tell of old-en   Days and men a-far,   Who be-held a
3. Of the Wise Men far-ing   From the East by night,   Gems and jew-els
4. Of the shepherds, fold-ing   Qui-et flocks be-low,   In the skies be-

joic-es   With them in the song.   With the Christ-mas bells vy-ing, In
gold-en   Night-dis-pell-ing Star.   With the Christ-mas bells vy-ing, In
bear-ing   Guid-ed by its light.   With the Christ-mas bells vy-ing, In
hold-ing   An-gels come and go.   With the Christ-mas bells vy-ing, In

"Good-will to men!"   Sa-lute them, re-ply-ing, a-gain and a-gain.

all at once. He couldn't help it. If he could have helped it, he and his child would have been farther apart perhaps than they were. He left the room, and went upstairs into the room above, which was lighted cheerfully, and hung with Christmas. There was a chair set close beside the child, and there were signs of some one having been there, lately. Poor Bob sat down in it, and when he had thought a little and composed himself, he kissed the little face. He was reconciled to what had happened, and went down again quite happy.

They drew about the fire, and talked, the girls and mother working still. Bob told them of the extraordinary kindness of Mr. Scrooge's nephew, whom he had scarcely seen but once, and who, meeting him in the street that day, and seeing that he looked a little—"just a little down, you know," said Bob, inquired what had happened to distress him. "On which," said Bob, "for he is the pleasantest-spoken gentleman you ever heard, I told him. 'I am heartily sorry for it, Mr. Cratchit,' he said, 'and heartily sorry for your good wife.' By-the-by, how he ever knew that I don't know." "Knew what, my dear?" "Why, that you were a good wife," replied Bob. "Everybody knows that!" said Peter. "Very well observed, my boy!" cried Bob; "I hope they do. 'Heartily sorry,' he said, 'for your good wife. If I can be of service to you in any way,' he said, giving me his card, 'that's where I live. Pray come to me.' Now it wasn't," cried Bob, "for the sake of anything he might be able to do for us, so much as for his kind way, that this was quite delightful. It really seemed as if he had known our Tiny Tim, and felt with us." "I'm sure he's a good soul!" said Mrs. Cratchit. "You would be sure of it, my dear," returned Bob, "if you saw and spoke to him. I shouldn't be at all

## THEY COME WITH BLISSFUL SONG.

W. T. WRIGHTON.

1. 'Tis Christ-mas eve once more, and mer-ri-ly the bells Their Ju-bi-la-te
2. God's an-gels have not yet for-sak-en err-ing men, They come with blissful
3. All glo-ry then to Him— for-ev-er, ev-er-more! Our souls repeat the

peal, in rich and joy-ous swells; Glad hearts beat quickly now for this, Time's festal
song a-gain and yet a-gain; They're with us ere the morn has come with radiant
strain in cho-rus o'er and o'er; To Him who now on high in ma-jes-ty doth

hour, Comes to our Christmas mirth with all its soft'ning power—A power which breathes o'er
light, And a star-ry glo-ry shed that scat-ters all our night; His min-is-ters they
reign Be hon-or ev-er-more throughout Earth's wide domain! High Heaven bends down to

joy its breath of life di-vine To make the restless heart a calm and ho-ly shrine.
are to pu-ri-fy from wrong, To glad His wea-ry ones with burst of sweetest song.
men, and 'neath that arch of light Earth hears their song of songs, "Goodwill and peace," to-night!

surprised—mark what I say!—if he got Peter a better situation." "Only hear that, Peter," said Mrs. Cratchit. "And then," cried one of the girls, "Peter will be keeping company with some one, and setting up for himself." "Get along with you!" retorted Peter, grinning. "It's just as likely as not," said Bob, "one of these days; though there's plenty of time for that, my dear. But however and whenever we part from one another, I am sure we shall none of us forget poor Tiny Tim—shall we—or this first parting that there was among us?" "Never, father!" cried they all. "And I know," said Bob, "I know, my dears, that when we recollect how patient and how mild he was; although he was a little, little child, we shall not quarrel easily among ourselves, and forget poor Tiny Tim in doing it." "No, never, father!" they all cried again. "I am very happy," said little Bob; "I am very happy!" Mrs. Cratchit kissed him, his daughters kissed him, the two young Cratchits kissed him, and Peter and himself shook hands. Spirit of Tiny Tim, thy childish essence was from God. "Spectre," said Scrooge, "something informs me that our parting moment is at hand. I know it, but I know not how. Tell me what man that was whom we saw

## THREE CHRISTMAS EVES.

CHAS. OSGOOD.

*Moderato.*

1. He gave her a ring and a hol-ly wreath That eve as the sun went
2. 'Twas Christ-mas Eve and a maid-en's heart Grieved as the sun went
3. Hearts were hap-py and eyes were bright, One eve as the sun went

down; "Ah, nev-er was lov-er more true than I!" Lo! the moon o'er the fro-zen
down; A ship that had sailed on a sum-mer day, Would nev-er come back to the
down; For the sea had giv-en up its dead, And joy come a-gain to the

town! A great star shone in the dark-'ning west, The red fox sought his
town. The wind sang a dirge in the chim-ney old For the lov-er, his heart now
town. There was on-ly mirth in the night-wind's call, Wierd phantoms had fled the

nest. But the fire was bright, and their hearts were light, And glad-ness filled the
cold, And sad were the eyes that watched the stars Till dawn at the win-dow-
hall; And mu-sic and rev-el-ry filled the night Till east-ern skies were

night, Till loud rang the bells, the mer-ry bells For joy on that Christmas morn.
bars, And loud rang the bells, the cru-el bells On a cheer-less Christmas morn.
bright, And loud rang the bells, the hap-py bells For joy on that Christmas morn!

Second verse more slow and sad, third quick and joyous.

lying dead?" The Ghost of Christmas Yet To Come conveyed him, as before—though at a different time, he thought: indeed, there seemed no order in these latter visions, save that they were in the Future—into the resorts of business men, but showed him not himself. Indeed, the Spirit did not stay for anything, but went straight on, as to the end just now desired, until besought by Scrooge to tarry for a moment.

"This court," said Scrooge, "through which we hurry now, is where my place of occupation is, and has been for a length of time. I see the house. Let me behold what I shall be in the days to come." The Spirit stopped; the hand was pointed elsewhere. "The house is yonder," Scrooge exclaimed. "Why do you point away?" The inexorable finger underwent no change. Scrooge hastened to the window of his

## OUR CHRISTMAS ROSE.

Thomas Cooke.

1. Out in the snow storm, what does she care,— Lit - tle maid Nell, with
2. Clad in her coat and furs all so warm Brave lit - tle Nell fears
3. Poor Mis - tress Brown and her lit - tle ones three, Hap - py to - night that

bright gold - en hair? White flakes are fall - ing soft o - ver her head,
nev - er the storm; Stored in her bas - ket of boun - ti - ful size,
bas - ket to see, Greet their good an - gel with wel - come so true,

Laugh - ing her blue eyes, her cheeks bon - ny red; Dar - ling maid Nel - lie,
Dain - ties for Christmas to glad - den your eyes; Dar - ling maid Nel - lie,
Nell thinks it worth a snow storm or two; Dar - ling maid Nel - lie,

on - ward she goes, Love ev - er shield her, our own Christ - mas rose!
fear - less she goes, Love ev - er shield her, our own Christ - mas rose!
hap - py she goes, Love ev - er shield her, our own Christ - mas rose!

office, and looked in. It was an office still, but not his. The furniture was not the same, and the figure in the chair was not himself. The Phantom pointed as before. He joined it once again, and wondering why and whither he had gone, accompanied it until they reached an iron gate. He paused to look around before entering. A churchyard. Here, then, the wretched man whose name he had now to learn, lay underneath the ground. It was a worthy place. Walled in by houses; overrun by grass and weeds, the growth of vegetation's death, not life; choked up with too much burying, fat with repleted appetite. A worthy place!

The Spirit stood among the graves, and pointed down to One. He advanced toward it trembling. The Phantom was exactly as it had been, but he dreaded that he saw new meaning in its solemn shape. "Before I draw nearer to that stone to which you point," said Scrooge, "answer me one question. Are these the shadows of the things that Will be, or are they shadows of the things that May be, only?" Still the Ghost pointed downward to the grave by which it stood. "Men's courses will foreshadow certain ends, to which, if persevered in, they must lead," said Scrooge. "But if the courses be departed from, the ends will change. Say it is thus with what you show me!" The Spirit was immovable as ever.

Scrooge crept towards it, trembling as he went; and following the finger, read upon the stone of the neglected grave his own name, "Ebenezer Scrooge." "Am *I* that man who lay upon the bed?" he cried, upon his knees. The finger pointed from the grave to him, and back again. " No, Spirit! Oh, no, no!" The finger still was there.

"Spirit!" he cried, tight clutching at his robe, "hear me! I am not the man I was. I will not be the man I must have been but for this intercourse. Why show me this, if I am past all hope!" For the first time the hand appeared to shake. "Good Spirit," he pursued, as down upon the ground he fell before it: "Your nature intercedes for me, and pities me. Assure me that I yet may change these shadows you have shown me by an altered life?" The kind hand trembled. "I will honor Christmas in my heart, and try to keep it all the year. I will live in the Past, the Present, and the Future. The Spirits of all three shall strive within me. I will not shut out the lessons that they teach. Oh, tell me I may sponge away the writing on this stone!"

In his agony he caught the spectral hand. It sought to free itself, but he was strong in his entreaty, and detained it. The Spirit, stronger yet, repulsed him. Holding up his hands in a last prayer to have his fate reversed, he saw an alteration in the Phantom's hood and dress. It shrunk, collapsed, and dwindled down into a bedpost.

---

## STAVE V.

### THE END OF IT.

YES! and the bedpost was his own. The bed was his own, the room was his own. Best and happiest of all, the Time before him was his own, to make amends in! "I will live in the Past, the Present, and the Future!" Scrooge repeated, as he scrambled out of bed. "The Spirits of all three shall strive within me. Oh, Jacob Marley! Heaven, and the Christmas time be praised for this! I say it on my knees, old Jacob; on my knees!"

He was so fluttered and so glowing with his good intentions, that his broken voice would scarcely answer to his call. He had been sobbing violently in his conflict with the Spirit, and his face was wet with tears. "They are not torn down," cried Scrooge, folding one of his bed curtains in his arms; "they are not torn down, rings and all. They are here—I am here—the shadows of the things that would have been, may be dispelled. They will be. I know they will!"

His hands were busy with his garments all this time; turning them inside out, putting them on upside down, tearing them, mislaying them, making them parties to every kind of extravagance. "I don't know what to do!" cried Scrooge, laughing and crying in the same breath; and making a perfect Laocoön of himself with his stockings. "I am as light as a feather, I am as happy as an angel, I am as merry as a school-boy, I am as giddy as a drunken man. A merry Christmas to everybody! A happy New Year to all the world! Hallo here! whoop! hallo!"

He had frisked into the sitting-room, and was now standing there, perfectly winded. "There's the saucepan that the gruel was in!" cried Scrooge, starting off again, and going round the fire-place. "There's the door by which the Ghost of Jacob Marley entered! There's the corner where the Ghost of Christmas Present sat! There's the window where I saw the wandering spirits! It's all right, it's all true, it all happened. Ha, ha, ha!"

Really, for a man who had been out of practice for so many years, it was a splendid laugh, a most illustrious laugh. The father of a long, long line of brilliant laughs! "I don't know what day of the month it is," said Scrooge. "I don't know how long I have been among the spirits. I don't know anything. I'm quite a baby. Never mind. I don't care. I'd rather be a baby. Hallo! Whoop! Hallo here!"

He was checked in his transports by the churches ringing out the lustiest peals he had ever heard. Clash, clash, hammer; ding, dong, bell. Bell, dong, ding; hammer, clang, clash! Oh, glorious, glorious! Running to the window, he opened it, and put out his head. No fog, no mist ; clear,

15

bright, jovial, stirring, cold; cold, piping for the blood to dance to; golden sunlight; heavenly sky; sweet fresh air; merry bells. Oh, glorious! Glorious!

"What's to-day?" cried Scrooge, calling downward to a boy in Sunday clothes, who perhaps had loitered in to look about him. "*Eh?*" returned the boy, with all his might of wonder. "What's to-day, my fine fellow?" said Scrooge. "To-day!" replied the boy. "Why, *Christmas Day.*" "It's Christmas Day!" said Scrooge to himself. "I haven't missed it. The spirits have done it all in one night. They can do anything they like. Of course they can. Of course they can. Hallo, my fine fellow!" "Hallo!" returned the boy. "Do you know the poulterer's in the next

## SANTA CLAUS TO-NIGHT.

J. L. HATTON.

1. Go to sleep, my lit - tle dar - ling, Close your eyes, my pret - ty flow'er, For the
2. On the tops of all the hous - es He will drive his deer and sleigh, And a -
3. In the morn - ing, bright and ear - ly, When you leave your lit - tle bed, You can

clock is striking sev - en, And you've been awake an hour; Lis - ten how the wind is
down the lof - ty chimneys He will sure - ly find the way; In the morn your scar - let
see if he has brought you An - y - thing your Pa - pa said. Now, my dar - ling, sweetly

sigh - ing, As it takes its rap - id flight, And re - mem - ber, lit - tle an - gel, San - ta
stocking Will be filled with presents bright, For a lit - tle bir - die told me San - ta
slumber, Close your eyes so sweet and bright, For I'm sure, my precious jew - el, San - ta

*ad lib.*

Claus will come to-night; And re - mem-ber, lit - tle an - gel, San - ta Claus will come to-night.
Claus will come to-night; For a lit - tle bir - die told me, San - ta Claus will come to-night.
Claus will come to-night; For I'm sure, my precious jew - el, San - ta Claus will come to-night.

street but one, at the corner?" Scrooge inquired. "I should hope I did," replied the lad. "An intelligent boy!" said Scrooge. "A remarkable boy! Do you know whether they sold the prize turkey that was hanging up there? Not the little prize turkey; the big one?" "What, the one as big as me?" returned the boy. "What a delightful boy!" said Scrooge. "It's a pleasure to talk to him. Yes, my buck!" "It's hanging there now," replied the boy. "Is it?" said Scrooge. "Go and buy it." "Walk-*er!*" exclaimed the boy. "No, no," said Scrooge, "I am in earnest. Go and buy it, and tell 'em to bring it here, that I may give them the directions where to take it. Come back with the man, and I'll give you a shilling. Come in less than five minutes, and I'll give you half-a-crown!"

The boy was off like a shot. He must have had a steady hand at a trigger who could have got a shot off half so fast. "I'll send it to Bob Cratchit's," whispered Scrooge, rubbing his hands, and splitting with a laugh. "He shan't know who sends it. It's twice the size of Tiny Tim. Joe Miller never made such a joke as sending it to Bob's will be!" The hand in which he wrote the address was not a steady one; but write it he did, somehow, and went down-stairs to open the street door, ready for the coming of the poulterer's man. As he stood there, waiting his arrival, the knocker caught his eye. "I shall love it

## RING FOREVER.

CHARLES GOUNOD.

1. When at nightfall so sweetly their chime breaks on mine ear, And re-calls the fond mem'ries of old, than aught more dear,
   I but live o'er the days of my childhood now thronging so near. Ring, then ring, ah! ring for-ev-er, then ring, ah! ring to me, Then ring, ah! ring for-ever, ring still to me. Ah! ring for-ev-er, still ring to me!

2. While their mel-o-dy lingers up-on the frosty air, Golden hours! ye come back, all your ro-ses pass-ing fair,
   And I breathe once again your sweet perfume, in freedom from care.

3. From far hill-top and valley a-gain the angel song Is re-ech-oed in chorus of good-will, sweet and strong,
   Till the round world is chiming, as gladly it rolls far a-long,

as long as I live!" cried Scrooge, patting it with his hand. "I scarcely ever looked at it before. What an honest expression it has in its face! It's a wonderful knocker! Here's the Turkey. Hallo! Whoop! How are you! Merry Christmas!" It *was* a Turkey! He never could have stood upon his legs, that bird. He would have snapped 'em short off in a minute, like sticks of sealing-wax. "Why, it's impossible to carry that to Camden Town," said Scrooge. "You must have a cab." The chuckle with which he said this, and the chuckle with which he paid for the Turkey, and the chuckle with which he paid for the cab, and the chuckle with which he recompensed the boy, were only to be exceeded by the chuckle with which he sat down breathless in his chair again, and chuckled till he cried. Shaving was not an easy task, for his hand continued to shake very much ; and shaving requires attention, even when you don't dance while you are at it. But if he had cut the end of his nose off, he would have put a piece of sticking-plaster over it, and been quite satisfied. He dressed himself "all in his best," and at last he got out into the streets. The people were by this time pouring forth, as he had seen them with the Ghost of Christmas Present; and walking with his hands behind him, Scrooge regarded every one with a delighted smile. He looked so irresistibly pleasant, in a word, that three or four good-humored fellows said "Good-morning. sir! A merry Christmas to you!" And Scrooge said

## THE HEAVENLY GUEST.

Margaret Sidney.

1. The chimes rang on till all the air, Its mu-sic passing sweet, Breathing one
2. And voice of heaven-ly sweetness came From out the deep'ning gloom, Of win-try
3. Ah! then we knew the Christ-child dear, In ver-y, ver-y deed, Had paused at

thought, full clear and strong, In rhythmic swell com-plete, Lo! from a-mid the whirling
chill and lurk-ing shade, In that quaint si-lent room: "Who loveth me and trusteth
our poor, lone-ly door, Our Christ-mas song to heed! A sud-den ra-diance filled the

sleet And blind-ing win-ter storm, A radiant pres-ence seemed to stand, In
when He can-not plain-ly see Shall ev-er have the Christmas joy In
room, Our hearts were filled with rest At lov-ing ben-e-dic-tion given By

child-like gen-tle form. A radiant pres-ence seemed to stand, In child-like gen-tle form.
deep-est ver-i-ty. Shall ev-er have the Christmas joy, In deep-est ver-i-ty."
our dear Heavenly Guest. At lov-ing ben-e-dic-tion given By our dear Heavenly Guest.

often afterwards, that, of all the blithe sounds he had ever heard, those were the blithest in his ears.

He had not gone far, when coming on toward him he beheld the portly gentleman, who had walked into his counting-house the day before, and said "Scrooge and Marley's, I believe?" It sent a pang across his heart to think how this old gentleman would look upon him when they met; but he knew what path lay straight before him. and he took it. "My dear sir," said Scrooge, quickening his pace, and taking the old gentleman by both hands. "How do you do? I hope you succeeded yesterday. It was very kind of you. A merry

Christmas to you, sir!" "Mr. Scrooge?" "Yes," said Scrooge. "That is my name, and I fear it may not be pleasant to you. Allow me to ask your pardon. And will you have the goodness—" here Scrooge whispered in his ear. "Lord bless me!" cried the gentleman, as if his breath were taken away. "My dear Mr. Scrooge, are you serious?" "If you please," said Scrooge. "Not a farthing less. A great many back payments are included in it, I assure you. Will you do me that favor?" "My dear sir," said the other, shaking hands with him. "I don't know what to say to such munifi—" "Don't say anything, please," retorted Scrooge. "Come and see me. Will you come and see me?" "I will!" cried the old gentleman. And it was clear he meant to do it. "Thank'ee," said Scrooge; "I am much obliged to you.

## HARK! WHAT MERRY VOICES.

J. HECKER.

1. Hark! what merry voi-ces thro' the air are sing-ing, While the the joyful bells gladsome peal are ringing! 'Tis the birthday of our Lord, We will all adore Him, Let us here on earth below Bow the knee before Him. Gladly then our car-ol raise, Sing with heart and voice, Glad on earth this day Let us all re-joice; And now with hearts u-ni-ted, Loud our songs we'll sing, Peace on earth, good-will to men, Glo-ry to our King.

2. O-ver hill and val-ley, let the mu-sic steal-ing, Fill our hearts with love and joy, The bells, joy-ful bells glorious tale re-vealing. Christ is born to us this day, From His throne in Heaven, He became a lit-tle child, That we might be forgiven! Gladly then our car-ol raise, Hark! the angels say, "Un-to all mankind 'Tis a ho-ly day," So now with hearts u-ni-ted, Loud our prais-es sing, Peace on earth, good-will to men, Glo-ry to our King.

I thank you fifty times. Bless you!" He went to church, and walked about the streets, and watched the people hurrying to and fro, and patted the children on the head, and questioned beggars, and looked down into the kitchens of houses, and up to the windows; and found that everything could yield him pleasure. He had never dreamed that any walk—that anything—could give him so much happiness. In the afternoon he turned his steps towards his nephew's house. He passed the door a dozen times, before he had the courage to go up and knock. But he made a dash, and did it. "Is your master at home, my dear?" said Scrooge to the girl. "Nice girl! Very." "Yes, sir." "Where is he, my love?" said Scrooge. "He's in the dining-room, sir, along with mistress. I'll show you up stairs, if you please." "Thank'ee. He knows me," said Scrooge, with his hand already on the dining-room lock. "I'll go in here, my dear." He turned it gently, and sidled his face in round the door. They were looking at the table (which was spread out in great array); for these young housekeepers are always nervous on such points, and like to see that

## MERRY CHRISTMAS.

Mary Ryan.
Stephen Glover.

1. Mer-ry is De-cem-ber, mer-ry as the May, Mer-ry all the peo-ple for the mer-ry day, Hear the mer-ry bells peal out their mer-ry chimes, And the mer-ry chil-dren sing their mer-ry rhymes, And the mer-ry chil-dren sing their mer-ry rhymes.
2. Mer-ry is the peas-ant, mer-ry is the king, Mer-ry are the waits whose mer-ry voi-ces bring Mer-ry thoughts of Christmas, mer-ry hearts to cheer With their merry mu-sic all the mer-ry year, With their merry mu-sic all the mer-ry year.
3. Mer-ry lights are gleam-ing from the mer-ry tree, Mer-ry eyes are glad the mer-ry sight to see; Mer-ry girls and boys all mer-ry in their play, Mer-ry voi-ces vo-cal all the mer-ry day, Mer-ry voi-ces vo-cal all the mer-ry day.

everything is right. "Fred!" said Scrooge. Dear heart alive, how his niece by marriage started! Scrooge had forgotten, for the moment, about her sitting in the corner with the footstool, or he wouldn't have done it, on any account. "Why, bless my soul!" cried Fred, "who's that?" "It's I. Your uncle Scrooge. I have come to din-ner. Will you let me in, Fred?" Let him in! It is a mercy he didn't shake his arm off. He was at home in five minutes. Noth-ing could be heartier. His niece looked just the same. So did Topper when he came. So did the plump sister when she came. So did everyone when they came. Wonderful party, wonderful games, won-derful unanimity. won-der-ful happiness!

But he was early at the office next morn-ing. Oh;he was early there. If he could only be there first, and catch Bob Cratchit coming late! That was the thing he had set his heart upon. And he did it; yes, he did! The clock struck nine. No Bob. A quarter-past. No Bob. He was full eigh-teen minutes and a half behind his time. Scrooge sat with his door wide open, that he might see him come into the tank. His hat was off, before he opened the door; his comforter too. He was on his stool in a jiffy; driving away with his pen, as if he were trying to overtake nine o'clock. "Hallo!" growled Scrooge, in his accustomed voice as near as he could feign it, "what do you mean by coming here at this time of day?" "I am very sorry, sir," said Bob, "I *am* behind my time." "You are!" repeated Scrooge. "Yes. I think you are. Step this way, sir, if you please." "It's only once a year, sir," pleaded Bob, appearing from the tank. "It shall not be repeated. I was making rather merry yesterday, sir." "Now I'll tell you what, my friend," said Scrooge. "I am not going to stand this sort of thing any longer. And therefore," he continued, leaping from his stool, and giving Bob such a dig in the waistcoat that he staggered back into the tank again, "and therefore I am about to raise your salary!" Bob trembled, and got a little nearer to the ruler. He had a momentary idea of knocking Scrooge down with it, holding him, and calling to the people in the court for help and a straitwaistcoat. "A merry Christmas, Bob!"

## JOY MUST REIGN TO-NIGHT.

F. CAMPANA.
W. W. CAMPBELL.

Cantabile espressivo.

1. Glad with sound of children's laugh-ter; Glad with fires and fa - ces bright,
2. Put a - side all hate and mal - ice; Ev - ery thought of sor - row shun;
3. Let us half the past re-deem - ing In the bless - ed pres - ent here,

Let our homes from wall to raf - ter Ring and glow this sa - cred night.
Joy must reign from hut to pal - ace, Thank-ing God for tri - umph won.
Send our fires of Christ-mas gleaming Far in - to the com - ing year.

a tempo.　p con express.

Oh! let the ho - ly Christ-Child find us, Not with ash - es cold and gloom,
Oh! ne'er can chill and bleak De - cem-ber Blow a - cross our hearth-stone bright,
Oh! gen - ial flame of love and blessing Guide us on to bet - ter things;

rall.

But with sa - cred ties that bind us— Ties of love and hope and home.
If our spir - its but re - mem - ber Christ our Lord was born to - night.
Hate and scorn and strife re-dress-ing,— Light all blest that Christmas brings.

said Scrooge, with an earnestness that could not be mistaken, as he clapped him on the back. "A merrier Christmas, Bob, my good fellow, than I have given you for many a year! I'll raise your salary, and endeavor to assist your struggling family, and we will discuss your affairs this very afternoon, over a Christmas bowl of smoking bishop, Bob! Make up the fires, and buy another coal-scuttle before you dot another i, Bob Cratchit!" Scrooge was better than his word. He did it all, and infinitely more; and to Tiny Tim, who did not die, he was a second father. He became as good a friend, as good a master, and as good a man, as the good old city knew, or any other good old city, town, or borough, in the good old world. Some people laughed to see the alteration in him, but he let them laugh, and little heeded

## FAR AWAY.

M. LINDSAY.

1. Where is now the mer-ry par-ty, I remem-ber long a-go; Laughing round the Christmas fire-side, Brighten'd by its rud-dy glow: Or in summer's balm-y eve-nings, In the field up-on the hay? They have all dispers'd, and wander'd Far a-way, . . far a-way, They have all dispers'd, and wander'd Far a-way, far a-way.

2. Some have gone to lands far dis-tant, And with strangers made their home; Some up-on the world of wa-ters All their lives are forced to roam; Longer here they might not stay,—They have reached a fair-er re-gion Far a-way, . . far a-way, They have reached a fairer re-gion Far a-way, far a-way.

3. There are still some few re-main-ing, Who remind us of the past, But they change as all things change here, Nothing in this world can last; What is coming, who can say? Ere this clos-es ma-ny may be Far a-way, . . far a-way, Ere this clos-es ma-ny may be Far a-way, far a-way.

them; for he was wise enough to know that nothing ever happened on this globe, for good, at which some people did not have their fill of laughter in the outset; and knowing that such as these would be blind anyway, he thought it quite as well that they should wrinkle up their eyes in grins, as have the malady in less attractive forms. His own heart laughed: and that was quite enough for him. He had no further intercourse with Spirits, but lived upon the Total Abstinence principle ever afterwards; and it was always said of him, that he knew how to keep Christmas well, if any man alive possessed the knowledge. May that be truly said of us, and all of us! and so, as Tiny Tim observed, God bless Us, Every One!—*Charles Dickens.*

## CAROL, CAROL, CHRISTIANS.

ARTHUR CLEVELAND COXE.

Carol, carol, Christians! Carol joy-ful-ly; Carol for the coming of Christ's nativity. And

*Chorus (Forte) Animated.*   *Unison.*

Carol, carol, Christians! Carol joy-ful-ly; Carol for the coming of Christ's nativity. And

*Fine.*

pray a gladsome Christmas For all good Christian men. Carol, carol, Christians, For Christmas come again

*Semi-Chorus.*

| | | | |
|---|---|---|---|
| 1. Go ye to the for - est | Where the myr - tles | grow; | Where the pine and |
| 2. Wreathe your Christmas gar - land | Where to Christ we | pray; | It shall smell like |
| 3. Ca - rol ca - rol, Christians! | Like the Ma - gi | now; | Ye must lade your |
| 4. Give us grace, O Sav - iour, | To put off in | might | Deeds and dreams of |

| | | | |
|---|---|---|---|
| lau - rel bend be - neath the snow, | Gath - er them | for Je - sus; |
| Car - mel on our fes - tal day; | Lib - an - us | and Sha - ron |
| cask - ets with a grate - ful vow; | Ye must have | sweet in - cense, |
| dark - ness, For the robes of light! | And to live | so low - ly |

*D.C. Chorus.*

Wreathe them for His shrine; Make His tem - ple glorious With the box and pine.
Shall not greener be Than our ho - ly chan - cel On Christ's na - tiv - i - ty.
Myrrh and finest gold, At our Christ - mas al - tar Humbly to un - fold.
As Thy - self with men; So to rise in glo - ry When Thou com'st again.

## GLORIOUS, BEAUTEOUS.

Maria Tiddeman.
Anna M. Nichols.

1. Glorious, beauteous, golden bright, Shedding softest, purest light, Shone the
2. But the stars' sweet golden gleam Faded quickly as a dream 'Mid the

stars that Christmas night, When the Jewish shepherds kept Watch beside their flocks that slept.
wondrous glo-ry stream, That il-lumined all the earth, When Christ's Angels sang His birth.

3. Soft and pure and ho-ly glo-ry, Kings and seers and prophets hoary, Shed throughout the sacred
4. But that light no more a-vail-ed, All its splendor straightway paled In His light whom Angels
5. Now no more on Christmas night, Is the sky with Angels bright, But for-ev-er shines the

story: While the priests, like shepherds true, Watched beside God's chos-en few.
hailed; Even as the stars of old 'Mid the brightness lost their gold.
Light; Even He whose birth they told To the shepherds by the fold.

6. Since that Light then darkens never, Let us all, with glad endeavor, Sing the song that echoes

*rall.*    *ff*    *pp*    *rall.*

ev-er: Glo-ry in the highest Heaven! Peace on earth to us for-giv-en.

### AVE MARIA.

CHARLES GOUNOD.
Transcription from Bach.

Moderato.

A - ve, Ma - ri - a, gra - ti - a ple - na, Do - mi - nus
A - ve, Ma - ri - a, Thou happy moth - er, God is

te - cum! Be - ne - dic - ta tu in mu - li - e - ri - bus!
with thee, Bless - ed, bless - ed art thou a - bove .... all moth - ers,

et be - ne - dic - tus fruc - tus ven - tris tu - i, Je - sus.
Since . . . in Bethlehem came . . . to thee . . . the an - gel of the Lord.

cres. molto.

Sanc - ta Ma - ri - a, sanc - ta Ma - ri - a, Ma - ri - a, O - ra pro
Honored and bless - ed, hon - ored and bless - ed Ma - ri - a, moth - er of

no - bis, no - bis pec - ca - to - ri - bus, nunc et in ho - ra, in
Je - sus, In - fant Re - deem - er, Born . . . to save us from our

ho - - ra mor - tis no - stræ! A - ve! A - ve!
sins . . . and all our heav - y woes! A - men!

## SILVER CHIMES.

CLARIBEL.

They are chiming gai - ly now, as they chimed so long a - go, Sil - ver tones that we loved so

well; And what is it that they say To our in - ner thoughts to - day? And

what is the tale that they tell?
{ 1. They whisper first of all, In that qui - et e - ven
{ 2. Of a waking up to life, Of a long and bit - ter
{ 3. Of a peaceful life at last, Of a sense of per - il

fall, Of the hap - py days of childhood that we passed; When each
strife, Of a rest - less spir - it fret - ting in its pain; Of a
past, Of a fu - ture left in saf - er hands than ours; Of a

gar - land that we made, Seem'd too beau - ti - ful to fade; And each but - ter - fly more
sea - son when the bells On - ly racked us with their spells, On - ly mocked us with old
sweet, re - fresh - ing dew, Fall - ing on our lives a - new, As the rain - drops fall and

D.S. *After last stanza.*

ra - diant than the last, the last.
mem - o - ries a - gain, a - gain.
sat - is - fy the flowers, the flowers.
} They are chiming gai - ly now, As they

chimed so long a - go, Sil - ver tones that we loved so well. Like a

*rit.* *dim.* *pp*

sto - ry that is told, Seem those memories of old, Haunting still with a mag-ic spell, magic spell.

## CHRISTMAS GREEN.

GEORGE COLES.

1. A - gain the trail-ing for-est-moss, the lau - rel, ce - dar, fir and pine, In
2. Not as a day of thoughtless mirth, for rev - el meaning - less and wild, We
3. Then mer-ry Christmas let it be, a day when love hath most to give, But
4. Let Christmas bloom be thine and mine, with Love's fair banner all un-furled, In

green festoons,—with wreath and cross, a - round our walls and windows twine; With-
hail its dawn, but for the birth of Him who was Earth's dear-est child, We
first best gift of all is He who came to Earth that we might live. And
mem-'ry of that Flower Di - vine whose heav'nly fra - grance fills the world! Let

in the pleas-ant light-ed hall are hol - ly boughs and ber - ries seen, Sweet
keep this glad home fes - ti - val, and with a child-like Christ-mas cheer His
all things beau-ti - ful are His, and what is His he mak - eth ours; So
all men Christmas glad-ness know, let Christmas cheer be ev - er seen; Bring

sum - mer mem-'ries to re - call, and keep our an - cient Christ-mas green.
an - gel-ush-ered birth-day call the day most glad of all the year.
bring each bud that burst-ing is, all Christ-mas - bloom-ing beauteous flowers.
cross and gar-land from the snow, and keep your mer - ry Christ-mas green.

THE LITTLE FROST QUEEN.

*Out in the snow storm what does she care,*
*Little Maid Nell with bright golden hair!*

# CHRISTMASSE OF OLDE.

GREGORY the Great, in the oft-quoted letter to Mellitus, a British abbot, afterward a successor of Augustine in the see of Canterbury, says: "Whereas the people were accustomed to sacrifice many oxen in honor of demons, let them celebrate a religious and solemn festival, and not slay the animals, *diabolo*—to the devil, but to be eaten by themselves *ad laudem Dei*—to the praise of God."

This idea seems to have been suggested to this Patron of the Anglo-Saxon Church by the success of a very similar experiment or transformation, which in an earlier age had resulted in the conversion to Christianity of the populous district of Neo-Cæsarea in Pontus. For it is said that Gregory, Bishop of that Diocese, changed the observance of the Pagan festivals to those of the Christian saints and martyrs, retaining such of their ancient festivities and ceremonies as were in themselves harmless and to which the people were greatly attached. Objections to compliances such as these have been made by the precise and scrupulous both in ancient and modern times. Thus we read that Gregory Nazianzen and other Fathers of the Church warned their flocks against the secularizing tendency of their age, and the dangers of excess in feasting, dancing, crowning the doors, and like practices. They feared that these things would carry their people back into Paganism or Judaism, not perceiving that Paganism had died a natural death, and that Judaism had been superseded by Christianity —the Law being indeed the shadow of good things to come. However this may be, Gregory the Great, undeterred by these serious apprehensions expressed by the early Fathers, and considering the wants of human nature, and especially those of his spiritual children, recommended, as we have seen, to the Anglo-Saxon missionaries,

commissioned by him, a more liberal course in regard to these festivities, which appears to have greatly promoted the social well-being of the Anglo-Saxon race. St. Augustine and the other Roman missionaries derived no inconsiderable assistance from the Calendar they found already in existence among their heathen converts. For the great pagan festivals of the ancient world were regulated by the sun, their feast of Yule, or "Juul," being about the winter solstice, or Christmas; the festival of Eoster, or Easter, about the vernal equinox; and that of midsummer, or St. John Baptist's Day, at the summer solstice. These most ancient of the world's festivals, under changed names and with new objects, are still kept in our own times. We are not, however, warranted in concluding from the above, as many archæologists have affirmed, that the social festivities of the Christian holidays are altogether of heathen origin, but, on the contrary, it will appear that they claim for themselves a much higher authority. In answer to certain puritanical objections, of the kind just alluded to, we quote from a rare tract of 1648, entitled "The Vindication of the Solemnity of the Nativity of Christ": "If it doth appeare that the time of this festival doth comply with the time of the Heathen's *Saturnalia*, this leaves no charge of impiety upon it, for since things are best cured by their contraries, it was both wisdom and piety in the ancient Christians, whose work it was to convert the Heathens from such, as well as other superstitions and miscarriages, to vindicate such times from the service of the Devil, by appoynting them to the more solemne and especiall service of God."

Moreover, it appears that our Christmas, Easter, and Whitsuntide festivals, have taken the place of those three great feasts of the Jewish Church,—the feasts of Passover, of Weeks, and of Tabernacles, instituted by divine appointment. In the social festivities of the most joyous of these festivals, the Feast of Tabernacles, there is a striking resemblance to those of our Christmas holidays. The requirements of The Law, with respect to the Feast of Tabernacles, as found in Deuteronomy, were : "And thou shalt rejoice in thy feast, thou, and thy son, and thy daughter, and thy man-servant, and thy maid-servant, and the Levite, the stranger, and the fatherless, and the widow, that are within thy gates. Seven days shalt thou keep a solemn feast unto the Lord thy God in the place which the Lord shall choose : because the Lord thy God shall bless thee in all thine increase, and in all the works of thine hands, therefore thou shalt surely rejoice." Smith, in his " Dictionary of the Bible," gives an interesting account of the manner in which this injunction of Moses was observed in aftertimes by the Jews in Jerusalem. He says : "Though all the Hebrew annual festivals were seasons of rejoicing, the Feast of Tabernacles was in this respect distinguished

## WHY, ALAS! IN LOWLY STALL?

From the Latin.
Jean Mauburne, 1500.

1. Why, alas! in lowly stall, For a cradle cry ing, Should the Lord who made us all,
2. "Hither now the love of man Drew Me to re store him, Since for hurtful sin Death's ban
3. Ah! with thousand notes of praise I will aye a dore Thee; For Thy wondrous grace I'll raise
4. Pen - u - ry a - lone be here, Pen - u - ry Thy glo - ry; Palace marked by want severe,

Healer blest, be ly - ing? Where the pur - ple robe of King? Subjects hom - age
Hung in judgment o'er him, Thro' my need y state, and low, Streams of grace for
Songs of joy be - fore Thee! Glo - ry to our Sav - iour be, Praise in lov - ing
Strange and new the sto - ry! To His love then tes - ti - fy, Ye who strike your

mur - mur - ing? Home of re - gal glo - ry? Home of re - gal glo - ry?
thee shall flow, Streams of wealth and glad - ness, Streams of wealth and glad - ness."
mem - o - ry, Glo - ry high, un - end - ing! Glo - ry high, un - end - ing!
harps on high, Heav'nly mu - sic blend - ing! Heav'nly mu - sic blend - ing!

above them all. The huts and the *lûlâbs* must have made a gay and striking spectacle over the city by day ; and the lamps, the flambeaux, the music, and the joyous gatherings in the court of the Temple, must have given a still more festive character to the night. . . At the Temple in the evening, after the day with which the festivals had commenced had ended, both men and women assembled in the court of the women, expressly to hold a rejoicing for the drawing of the water of Siloam. On this occasion a degree of unrestrained hilarity was permitted, such as would have been unbecoming while the ceremony itself was going on, in the presence of the Altar, and in connection with the offering of the morning sacrifice. . . At the same time there were set up in the court two lofty stands, each supporting four great lamps. These were lighted on each night of the festival ; and, as it is said, they cast their light over nearly the whole compass of the city. Many in the assembly carried flambeaux ; a body of

Levites stationed on the fifteen steps leading up to the women's court, played instruments of music and chanted the fifteen psalms (120 to 134), which are called 'songs of degrees.' Singing and dancing were afterwards continued for some time; the same ceremonies in the day, and the same joyous meetings in the evening, were renewed on each of the seven days." The austerity and intolerance of the seventeenth century in regard to social festivities have, in a great measure, given place in modern times to more rational ideas. The learned, it appears, to the confusion of Judaizing zealots of the old puritanical school, have clearly established the fact that the Jewish festivals were, even in the time of our Saviour and his apostles, seasons of general social enjoyment. In conformity with the positive injunctions of the Mosaic law, the new moons, the Passover, the feast of Pentecost and of Tabernacles, were observed with a degree of hilarity altogether inconsistent with the modern puritanical notions of propriety. Indeed, they applied very literally the words of the psalmist "Serve

## CHRISTMASSE OF OLDE.

EUGENE FIELD.

1. God rest you, Chrysten gentil men, Wher-ev-er you may be, wher-ev-er you may be, God rest you all in fielde or hall, Or on ye stormy sea; For on this morn, this morn, our Chryst is born, That saveth you and me, that saveth, saveth, you and me, For on this morn our Chryst was born, That saveth you and me.

2. Last night ye shepherds in ye east Saw many a wondrous thing, saw many a wondrous thing; Ye sky last night flamed passing bright Whiles that ye stars did sing, And angels came to bless, to bless ye name Of Jesus Chryst, our Kyng, Our Kyng, For on this morn our Chryst was born, That saveth you and me.

3. God rest you, Chrysten gentil men, Far-ing where'er you may, far-ing wher-e'er you may; In noblesse court do thou no sport, In tournament no playe, In Paynim land hyld thou thy hand, thy hand, From bloudy works this daye, this daye, From bloudy works this daye, For on this morn our Chryst was born, That saveth you and me.

4. But thinking on ye gentil Lord That died up-on ye tree, that died up-on ye tree, Let troublings cease and deeds of peace A-bound in Chrystan-tie— For on this morn, this morn, ye Chryst is born, That saveth you and me, that saveth, saveth, you and me, For on this morn our Chryst was born, That saveth you and me.

16

the Lord with gladness and come before His presence with a song.'' It seems, therefore, reasonable to conclude that, as our Saviour went up regularly to these feasts at Jerusalem, and as the apostles also continued, even after His ascension and the outpouring of the spirit on the day of Pentecost, to take part in these national festivals, there was nothing in these holiday festivities inconsistent with the profession of the principles of Christianity; for ''they continuing daily with one accord in the Temple, and breaking bread from house to house, did eat their meat with gladness and singleness of heart.'' The severity of our puritanical forefathers in imagining the social festivities of their times to be merely heathenish vanities, is equaled only by their misconception in regard to the character of the Jewish holidays. This mistake of theirs, however, is not more remarkable than that made by the Roman historian Tacitus, who erroneously supposed that the Jewish Feast of Tabernacles, held at the time of the vintage, in the month of October, was celebrated in honor of Bacchus.

Brady, in his ''Clavis Calendaria,'' says: ''The first Christians, who, it is proper to remark, were all converts from the Hebrews, solemnized the Nativity on the first

## GLORIA IN EXCELSIS.

German Carol.
Tune, 16th Century.

1. When Christ was born of Ma - ry free In Beth - le - hem that fair ci - ty, An - gels sang with mirth and glee ''In ex - cel - sis Glo - ri - a.'' An - gels sang with mirth and glee, In ex - cel - sis glo - ri - a, In ex - cel - sis glo - ri - a, glo - ri - a.''

2. The shepherds saw the angels bright, They shone with such a heav'nly light, ''God's dear Son is born to-night, In ex - cel - sis Glo - ri - a. God's dear Son is born to - night,

of January, conforming in this computation to the Roman year, though it is to be particularly noticed, that on the day of the Feast of Tabernacles they ornamented their churches with green boughs, as a memorial that Christ was actually born at that time, in like manner as the ancient Jews erected booths or tents which they inhabited at this season, to keep up by an express command from God the remembrance of their deliverance from Egyptian bondage, and of their having dwelt in tents or tabernacles in the wilderness.'' The word ''Christmas'' is derived from *Christ* and the Saxon *maisse*, signifying the Mass, and a feast. The religious observance of the day dates from a period as early, at least, as the second century. Haydn says it was first observed A. D. 98. Clement, a co-worker of St. Paul, mentioned by him in his Epistle to the Philippians (iv. 3), says: ''Brethren, keep diligently feast days; and truly in the first place the day of Christ's birth.'' It was ordered to be kept as a solemn feast, and with the performance of divine services, on the 25th December, by Telesphorus, bishop of Rome, about A. D. 137. His injunctions are, '' that in the holy night of the Nativity of our Lord and Saviour, they do celebrate public church services, and in them solemnly sing the Angel's Hymn, because also the same night he was declared unto the shepherds by an angel, as the truth itself doth witnesse." In the same age Theophilus, bishop of Cæsarea, recommends "the celebration of the birth-day of our Lord, on what day soever the 25th of December shall happen." In the following century, Cyprian begins his treatise on the Nativity, thus: "The much wished-for and long expected Nativity of Christ is come, the famous solemnity is come." Gregory Nazianzen and St. Basil both have sermons on this day. St. Chrysostom also says: "This day was of great antiquity, and of long continuance, being famous and renowned in the Church from the beginning, far and wide, from Thrace as far as Gades in Spain." And he styles it, "the most venerable and tremendous of all festivals, and the Metropolis or Mother of all Festivals." Blunt, also, in his annotated Book of Common Prayer, observes: "Most of the Fathers have left sermons which were preached on Christmas day, or during the continuance of the festival. And secular decrees of the Christian emperors, as well as canons of the Church, show that it was very strictly

## THE HOLLY AND THE IVY.

Old French Carol Tune.

1. The Hol-ly and the I-vy, Now both are full well grown; Of all the trees that spring in wood, The hol-ly bears the crown. The hol-ly bears a blos-som As white as a li-ly flow'r; And Ma-ry bore sweet Jesus Christ To be our sweet Sav-iour, To be our sweet Sav-iour.

2. The hol-ly bears a ber-ry, As red as an-y blood, And Ma-ry bore sweet Je-sus Christ, To do poor sin-ners good. The hol-ly bears a prick-le As sharp as an-y thorn, And Ma-ry bore sweet Jesus Christ, On Christmas Day in the morn, On Christmas Day in the morn.

3. The hol-ly bears a bark, As bit-ter as an-y gall, And Ma-ry bore sweet Je-sus Christ, For to redeem us all. The hol-ly and the i-vy Now are both well-grown, Of ris-ing of the sun, The run-ning of the deer, The all the trees that are in the wood, The hol-ly bears the crown, The playing of the or-gan, The sing-ing of the choir, The singing of the choir.

observed as a time of rest from labor, of divine worship, and of Christian hilarity, and that it is most fit that the season so marked out by angels by songs of joy such as had not been heard on earth since the Creation, should also be observed as a time of festive gladness by the Church, and in the social life of Christians." This hilarity and festive gladness—the marked peculiarity of an old English Christmas—once included sundry pageants and religious shows, which, in an age less cultivated than our own, combined for the people instruc- tion and amusement, the clergy in them, as it were, teaching the multitude by a sort of parables. After the invention of printing, however, when better means of popular instruction became possible, these mysteries and moralities gradually degenerated into mere burlesques, masks, or mummeries, which frequently, it appears, proved to be more or less objectionable, and against which the Puritanism of the sixteenth and seventeenth centuries maintained an unceasing and destructive warfare; nevertheless there still survives in these prosaic days,

## THE KING OF SEASONS ALL.

STEPHEN ADAMS.

1. Oh! we love the Spring! on his del'rous wing The scent of bloom is borne; For he woos the flowers with his laughing show'rs, Tho' he scatter them ere morn. An inconstant elf, he ne'er knows himself; His mind doth change. Now a smiling face, then a wry grimace, And he withers ev'ry flower, And he withers ev'ry flower.

2. Let the Summer sun to his bright home run He too is fair to see; But when dimmed by cloud we laugh aloud, For a fiery lord is he; And the Autumn night by the tranquil light Of mild September moon Has a sweeter sheen for us all, I ween, Than the broad unblushing noon, Than broad unblushing morn.

3. But our song rings out for the Christmas stout, The hearty, true and bold; We resound the strain, and with might and main, Give three cheers for Christmas old, And again we sing till the roof doth ring Its echo, wall to wall, To the stout old wight whom we greet to-night, As the King of Seasons all, As the King of Seasons all.

especially in those hospitable mansions wherein "Christmas yearly dwells," and

> Numerous guests and viands dainty
> Fill the hall, and grace the board,

much of that hilarity which, indeed, is the essential part of the festival.

The bringing in and placing of the ponderous Christmas block, or Yule-log, on the hearth of the wide chimney of the old English hall, was the most joyous of the ceremonies observed on Christmas eve. This mode of rejoicing at the winter solstice appears to have originated with the Danes and pagan Saxons, and was intended to be emblematical of the return of the sun, and its increasing light and heat. But on the introduction of Christianity, the illuminations of the *Eve of Yule* were continued as representative of the *True Light*, which was then ushered into the world, in the person of our Saviour, the "Day-spring from on high." "This venerable Yule-log, destined to crackle a welcome to all comers, was drawn," says Mr. Chambers, "in triumph from its resting place at the feet of its living brethren of the woods. Each wayfarer raised his hat as it passed, for he well knew it was full of good promises, and that its flame would burn out old wrongs and heart-burnings." The towns of England have been described by Stowe and other old writers as presenting at this season a sylvan appearance; the houses dressed with branches of ivy and of holly; the churches converted into leafy tabernacles, and standards bedecked with evergreens set up in the street, while the young of both sexes danced around them. It is interesting to observe, from such descriptions, the close resemblance between these manners and customs and those described in the passages quoted from Smith and Brady; when, in accordance with Scripture injunctions, the people of Israel went forth into the mount and brought thence "olive-branches, and pine-branches, and myrtle-branches, and palm-branches, and branches of thick trees, and made themselves booths, every one upon the roof of his house, and in their courts, and in the courts of the

## THE TIME DRAWS NIGH.

FESTAL SONGS.

1. The Christmas time draws nigh, The crowds go up and down, There's joy and hope in
2. I sit a-lone and dream Of those who loved the day, Friends gone to fair-er
3. And thoughts still deeper go: I pon-der if a-bove Thou hear'st, 'mid heav'nly

D. C.—The Christmas time draws nigh, The Christmas greeting dear; Be there no pause for

Fine.

all the town; And bright in childhood's eye A look of ex-pec-ta-tion sweet That
realms for aye To-night be-side me seem; They smile that thus in hap-py ways, As
peace and love, Our talk-ing to and fro; And if, beyond this verge of time We

tear or sigh, The Christ-mas joy so near.

D.C.

comes of mus-ing oft and long On what the day of gift and song Shall bring as offering meet.
oft-en as the year goes round, We mark the feast whose joys abound, O rarest day of days!
know Thee bet-ter as Thou art, Thou'lt one day clasp us heart to heart, As swells the Christmas chime!

house of God, and in the street of the watergate, and in the street of the gate of Ephraim." Says a writer in the "Gentleman's Magazine" for 1765: "The ancient custom of dressing our churches and houses at Christmas with evergreens, appears to be not only thus traceable to the Feast of Tabernacles, but is also supposed to have been derived from certain expressions in the following prophecies of the coming of our Saviour: Behold the days come, saith the Lord, that I will raise unto David a right-eous Branch; For behold I will bring forth my servant the Branch; Thus speaketh the Lord of Hosts, saying behold the Man whose name is The Branch, and He shall grow up out of his place; At that time will I cause the Branch of Righteousness to grow up unto David; Thus saith the Lord God, I will also take of the highest Branch of the high cedar, and will set it, I will crop off from the top of his young twigs a tender one, and will plant it upon an high mountain and eminent, in the mountain of the height of Israel will I plant it, and it shall bring forth boughs, and bear fruit, and it shall be a goodly cedar; In that day shall the Branch of the Lord be beautiful and glorious; For He shall grow up before Him as a tender plant, and as a root out of a dry ground; and the Lord shall reign over them in Mount Zion from henceforth even for ever; There shall come forth a rod out of the stem of Jesse, and a branch shall grow out of his roots, which shall stand for an ensign of the people, and my servant David shall be their Prince for ever. For it must be confessed that those passages and expressions in which our Saviour is represented under the type of a Branch, a Righteous Branch, a Bough, the Branch of Right-eousness, who will reign for ever, etc., in the above-quoted clear and eminent prophecies of his first appearance in the flesh upon earth, are in a most lively manner brought to our memories, and unmistakably alluded to by those *branches* and *boughs* of evergreens with which our churches and houses are adorned, whose gay appearance and perpetual verdure, in that dead season of the year, when all Nature looks comfortless, dark, and dreary, and when the rest of the vegetable world has shed its honors, does agreeably charm the unwearied beholder and make a very suitable accompaniment of the universal joy which always attends the annual commemoration of that holy festival." Another quaint old writer thus

## CHRISTMAS DAY IN THE MORNING.:

TRADITIONAL.

1. I saw three ships come sail-ing in, On Christmas day, on Christmas day; I
2. And what was in those ships all three, On Christmas day, on Christmas day? And
3. Our Saviour Christ and his la-die, On Christmas day, on Christmas day; Our

saw three ships come sail-ing in, On Christ-mas day in the morn-ing.
what was in those ships all three, On Christ-mas day in the morn-ing?
Sav-iour Christ and his la-die, On Christ-mas day in the morn-ing.

4. Pray whither sailed those ships all three?
5. Oh, they sailed into Bethlehem,
6. And all the bells on earth shall ring,
7. And all the angels in Heaven shall sing,
8. And all the souls on earth shall sing,
9. Then let us all rejoice amain,

spiritualizes the practice of Christmas decoration: "So our churches and houses, decked with bayes and rosemary, holly and ivy, and other plants which are always green, winter and summer, signify and put us in mind of His Deity; that the Child who now was born was God and Man, who should spring up like a tender plant, should always be green and flourishing, and live for evermore." In this custom there appears to be also a reference to those passages of the prophet Isaiah, which foretell the felicities attending the coming of Christ, namely: "The glory of Lebanon shall come unto thee, the fir-tree, the pine-tree, and the box, together, to beautify the place of my sanctuary." (Isaiah lx. 13.) "Instead of the thorn, shall come up the fir-tree, and instead of the brier shall come up the myrtle-tree, and it shall be to the Lord for a name, for an everlasting sign that shall not be cut off." In an old English custom described by Thomas Millar, we find a happy response to this prophecy of Isaiah: "The hundreds of silver-toned bells of London ring loud, deep, and clear, from tower and spire, to welcome in Christmas. The far-stretching suburbs, like glad children, take up and fling back the sound over hill and valley, marsh and meadow, while steeple calls to steeple across the winding arms of the mast-crowded river, proclaiming to the heathen voyager who has brought his treasures from afar to our coast, and who is ignorant of our religion, the near approach of some great Christian festival."

Carol singing appears to have originated in a usage of the primitive Church, for " In the early ages the bishops were accustomed to sing carols on Christmas day with their clergy." Jeremy Taylor, referring to this custom in his Great Exemplar, says of the Gloria in Excelsis, "As soon as those blessed choristers had sung their Christmas Carol, and taught the church a hymn to put into her offices for ever in the anniversary of this Festivity, the angels returned into heaven." The term "carol" is supposed to be derived either from the Italian "caroli"—a song

of devotion, or carol, properly "a round dance," from the French *carole, querole*; Breton *keroll*, a dance; or the Welsh *caroli*, to reel, to dance. *Chanson de carole* was a song accompanying a dance which as the French *balade*, from Italian *ballare*, to dance, applied to the song itself. Carols, it is said, were early introduced by the clergy into England from Italy, probably soon after the Norman Conquest, as a substitute for the Yule and wassail songs of heathen origin, which, until then, had been in use among the vulgar. The custom of singing these "caroli" is still maintained in Italy; indeed, on the continent, caroling at Christmas is almost universal, and particularly in Rome, where, during the season of Advent, the

## AS JOSEPH WAS A-WALKING.

TRADITIONAL. (Somersetshire.)

1. As Jo-seph was a-walk-ing, He heard an an-gel sing, This night shall be the birth-time Of Christ the heav'n-ly King.
2. He neith-er shall be born In hous-en nor in hall Nor in the place of Pa-ra-dise, But in an ox's stall.
3. He neith-er shall be cloth-ed In pur-ple nor in pall, But in the fair white lin-en That us-en ba-bies all.

| He neither shall be rocked, | As Joseph was a-walking. | Then be ye glad, good people, |
| In silver nor in gold, | There did an angel sing; | This night of all the year, |
| But in a wooden manger | And Mary's child at midnight | And light ye up your candles, |
| That resteth on the mould. | Was born to be our King. | For His star it shineth clear. |

Pifferari may be seen and heard performing their Novena before the shrine of the Madonna and Bambino. These pilgrims, who, by the way, are shepherds from the Calabrian mountains, annually flock to Rome at this season. Their picturesque costume is thus described: "On their heads they wear conical felt hats adorned with a frayed peacock's feather, or a faded band of red cords and tassels; their bodies are clad in red waistcoats, blue jackets, and small clothes of skin or yellowish homespun cloth; skin sandals are bound to their feet with cords that interlace each other up the leg as far as the knee,—and over all is worn a long brown or blue cloak with a short cape,

buckled closely round the neck. Sometimes, but rarely, this cloak is of a deep red with a scalloped cape. As they stand before the pictures of the Madonna, their hats placed on the ground before them, and their thick disheveled hair covering their sunburnt brows, blowing away on their instruments or pausing to sing their *novena*, they form a picture which every artist desires to paint. These Pifferari always go in couples, one playing on the zampogna or bagpipe, the base and treble accompaniment, and the other on the piffero, or pastoral pipe, which carries the air. Sometimes one of them varies the performance by singing, in a strong peasant voice, verse after verse of the *novena* to the accompaniment of the bagpipe." The old English Yule songs before referred to, are mentioned by Brady in his Calendaria (1808). He says that in his time they were still sung by the people about the church-yards after service on Christmas day. The example given by him is identical with that in the Christmas of Washington Irving's Sketch Book.

> Ule, Ule, Ule, Ule,
> Three puddings in a pule,
> Crack nuts and cry Ule.

These Yule songs, it appears, were sung at the bringing in of the Christmas block, or Yule-Log, which was anciently introduced into the old English baronial hall with much pomp and circumstance, the minstrels saluting its appearance with a song. The custom of carol singing formerly prevailed over the greater part of the British Isles, and there are still in use in many places, especially among the peasantry of Derbyshire and Lancashire, Yorkshire, Northumberland, and Durham, carols of

## THE WASSAIL SONG.

TRADITIONAL.

1. Here we come a wassailing Among the leaves so green, Here we come a
2. We are not daily beggars That beg from door to door, But we are neighbor's
3. Good Master and good Mistress, As you sit by the fire, Pray think of us poor

wand'ring, So fair to be seen, Love and joy come to you, And to you your wassail
children Whom you have seen before, Love and joy come to you, And to you your wassail
children As wand'ring in the mire, Love and joy come to you, And to you your wassail

too, And God bless you and send you a happy new year, And God send you a happy new year.

We have a little purse
  Made of ratching leather skin;
We want some of your small change
  To line it well within. *Cho.*

Bring us out a table,
  And spread it with a cloth;
Bring us out a moldy cheese,
  And some of your Christmas loaf.

God bless the Master of this house,
  Likewise the Mistress too;
And all the little children
  That round the table go. *Cho.*

undoubted antiquity, illustrative of the manners and sentiments of the Middle Ages, some of which are said to be fragments of the Mystery and Miracle Plays, formerly enacted at this season. "As Joseph was a-walking," may be taken as a specimen of these curious old Carols. Numeral hymns were common in the olden time. One of the most ancient of all these popular carols, the original of which is preserved among the Sloane manuscripts, is of a date not later than the fourteenth century, and is entitled "Joyes Five," or the Five Joys of Mary. Another popular carol, from a Kentish version, is entitled "Christmas Day in the Morning." Ritson thinks that the different versions of this carol may have had their origin in the following curious fragment found by him in Scotland:

> There comes a ship far sailing then,
> Saint Michel was the stieres-man ;
> Saint John sate in the horn :
> Our Lord harped, our Lady sang,
> And all the bells of heaven they rang,
> On Christ's Sonday at morn.

SEE-SAW, MARGERY DAW.

The carol entitled The Holly and the Ivy, is from Sylvester's collection, and is derived from an old broadside printed more than a century and a half ago. The holly, from time immemorial, has been the favorite Christmas evergreen. Dr. Turner, an early English writer on plants, calls it "holy-tree;" which appellation was given it most probably from its being used in holy places. It has a great variety of names in Germany, amongst which is *Christdorn;* in Danish it is also called *Christhorn;* and in Swedish *Christtorn,* amongst other appellations; from whence it appears that it is considered a holy plant by many people in those countries. So popular had carols such as these become in the fifteenth century, that Wynkyn de Worde, one of the earliest printers, published a collection of them in 1521, containing among others, the celebrated "Boar's Head Carol," the best in the collection; for, besides the devotional carols in use at the season, there were those of a convivial character. These "jolie carols," as old Tusser calls them, were sung by the company or by itinerant minstrels who attended the feasts for this especial purpose. The origin of this old-time ceremony of

## THE BOAR'S-HEAD CAROL.

bringing in the Boar's Head, with singing, to the high table in the hall of Queen's College, Oxford, England, on Christmas Day, is unknown; but it may reasonably be inferred, says the author of the "Holiday Book," that the custom has been observed since the foundation of the college in 1340. The Boar's Head, highly decorated with bay, holly, rosemary, etc., in a large pewter dish, is slowly borne into the hall by two strong servants of the college, who hold it up as high as they can, that it may be seen by the visitors ranged on either side of the hall. The gentleman who sings the ancient carol, or "Boar's Head Carol," as it is called, and which is here given,—generally one of the members of the college, though sometimes one of the choir of Magdalen College—immediately precedes the Boar's Head, and as he commences the song with, "The Boar's Head in hand bear I," touches the dish with his right hand. Two young choristers from Magdalen College follow, to sing conjointly with many of the junior members of Queen's College, the chorus, "Caput apri defero," etc. The dish is carried, as before stated, to the high table, where sit the Provost, Bursar, Fellows, and others connected with the College, and at which many visitors are congregated.

The Reformation, it appears, did not by any means impair the popularity of the Christmas Carol in England. Says an old writer of 1631: "Suppose Christmas now approaching, the evergreen ivy trimming and adorning the portals and partcloses of so frequented a building; the *usual carols* to observe antiquity cheerfully sounding, and that which is the complement of his inferior comforts, his neighbors, whom he tenders as members of his own family, join with him in this consort of mirth and melody." Mr. Davies Gilbert has, in a collection of ancient Christmas carols, said, that "Till recently in the west of England on Christmas eve, about seven or eight o'clock in the evening, cakes were drawn hot from the oven; cider or beer exhilarated the spirits in every house; and the singing of carols was continued late in the night. On Christmas day these carols took the place of psalms in all the churches, especially at afternoon service, the whole congregation joining; and at the end it was usual for the parish clerk to declare, in a loud voice, his wishes for a merry Christmas and a happy New Year, to all the parishioners." In Wales Christmas caroling is still kept up, perhaps

## OLD CHRISTMAS.

F. ROMER.
J. BRIDGEMAN.

1. Once more the rap - id fleet-ing year Has brought old Christmas to our door; Come, let us
2. Up - on the hearth pile up the fire, And, that it may burn clear and bright, Cast in it
3. And you, fair Sovereign of our isle, Who love to deck the Christmas tree, So that the

treat him with such cheer As folks were wont in days of yore, As folks were wont in days of
ev - 'ry base de - sire, All en - vy, hatred, vengeance, spite, All en - vy, hatred, vengeance,
mas-sy, re - gal pile Resound with mirth and jol - li - ty, Resound with mirth and jol - li -

old fa - mil-iar sprite, And at his bid - ding banish'd care, And at his bid - ding banish'd
be the ge-nial glow, That dan-ces thro' each swelling vein, That dan-ces thro' each swelling
Christmas fir - tree, too, Send blessings far thro' all the land, Send blessings far thro' all the

yore, When burgher grave, and belt-ed knight, And cot-tage maid and la - dy
spite; Be sure, dear friend, the end will 'show That on - ly this will prove your
ty,— Re - mem-ber that the stem a - new Must thrive, if prun'd with careful

care. O - bey'd the old fa - mil - iar sprite, And at his bid-ding banish'd care;
vein. And yours will be the gen - ial glow That dan-ces thro' each swell-ing vein;
land. And from your Christmas fir - tree, too, Send blessings far thro' all the land;

to a greater extent even than in England. After the turn of midnight on Christmas eve, divine service is celebrated, followed by the singing of carols to the harp ; and they are also with similar accompaniment sung in the houses, during the continuance of the Christmas holidays.   The instruments used by the waits at Christmas in old times, consisted ordinarily of hautboys of four different sizes, although Morley's "Consort Lessons," dedicated to the Lord Mayor and Aldermen of London, 1529, speak of the treble and bass viols, the flute, the cittern or English guitar, the treble lute, and the pandora.   This ancient custom of carol-singing at Christmas, is one of those which of late years has greatly revived and become generally popular both in Europe and America.   The usage, however, in regard to their performance, has been made to conform in great measure to our modern notions of propriety and convenience. Itinerant minstrels, during the season of Advent, do not now often awaken people from their slumbers at midnight with a carol similar to that of

> God rest you, merry gentlemen,
> Let nothing you dismay !

Nor do the "waits," those famous bands of vocal and instrumental performers, go now as they once did, from house to house, and from hamlet to hamlet, "all the night long, chanting such carols as our pious forefathers loved well to listen to."   Noc-

## CRADLE-SONG OF VIRGIN.

turnes such as these with pastoral symphonies, performed by such shepherd-like swains, are altogether too romantic for these more prosaic days.   And yet the sacred singer Keble, who is one of the most popular of our modern poets, has piously sung,

> Wake me that I, the twelvemonth long,
>   May bear the song
> About me in the world's great throng ;
> That treasured joys of Christmas tide
> May with mine hour of gloom abide ;
>   The Christmas Carol ring
> Deep in my heart, when I would sing,
> Each of the twelve good days,
> Its earnest yield of duteous love and praise,
> Ensuring happy months, and hallowing common ways.

In France, "Noel" is the term used to express Christmas songs or carols, as well as the tide of Yule itself.   This word *noel*, or *nowell*, is commonly understood to be derived from the Latin *natalis* (the *dies natalis* of Our Lord), and it is said by Mr. Wright to have been introduced into England at the time of the Norman Conquest.

Christmas Carols, as already observed, were divided into two classes ; the more serious of them, those of a religious character, were sung morning and evening ; and those which were convivial in their nature, at those bountiful and stately banquets in which our English ancestors so greatly delighted, and which were indeed the especial glory of the Christmas holidays. Some account of those Gothic halls in which these Christmas festivities were held, will be found of interest. The following facts are derived chiefly from Thomas Wright's learned work, entitled "Domestic Manners and Sentiments of the Middle Ages." First we learn that the most important part of the Saxon house was the hall. It was the place where the household collected round their lord and protector; and where the visits of a stranger were first received—the scene of hospitality. These Saxon dwellings appear to have been of wood, of which material houses continued very generally to be built, until comparatively modern times. A great change, however, was wrought in England by the entrance of the Normans. Some time after that period, or about the middle of the twelfth century, we begin to become better acquainted with the domestic manners of our forefathers, and from this time to the end of the fourteenth century the change was very gradual, and in many respects the manners and customs remained nearly the same. The "hall," or, according to the Norman word, the "salle," was still the principal part of the building; but its old Saxon character seems to have been so universally acknowledged that the first or Saxon name prevailed over the other. The name at this time usually given to the whole dwelling-house, was the Norman word "manoir," or manor, and we find this

## ALL PRAISE TO THEE.

MARTIN LUTHER.
COSTELLO. "LEYDEN."

1. All praise to Thee, e-ternal Lord! Clothed in a garb of flesh and blood; Choosing a manger
2. A little child, Thou art our guest, That weary ones in Thee may rest; Forlorn and low - ly
3. Thou comest in the darksome night, To make us children of the light, To make us, in the
4. All this for us Thy love hath done; By this to Thee our love is won: For this we tune our

for Thy throne, While worlds on worlds are Thine alone, While worlds on worlds are Thine alone.
is Thy birth, That we may rise to heaven from earth, That we may rise to heaven from earth.
realms divine, Like Thine own angels round Thee shine, Like Thine own an - gels round Thee shine.
cheerful lays, To Thee our thanks in ceaseless praise, To Thee our thanks in ceaseless praise.

applied popularly to the houses of all classes, excepting only the cottages of laboring people. In houses of the twelfth century, the hall, situated on the ground floor, and open to the roof, continued to form the principal feature of the building. A chamber generally adjoined one end, and at the other was usually a stable. The whole building stood within a small inclosure, consisting, in front, of a yard or court, called in Norman "aire" (area); and in the rear, of a garden which was surrounded with a hedge and ditch. In front the house had generally one door, which was the main entrance into the hall, from which apartment there was a door into the chamber at one end; and one into the "croiche," or stable, at the other end, and a back door into the garden. The stable, as a matter of course, would have a large door, or outlet into the yard. The chief windows were those of the hall. Alexander Neckam, Abbot of Cirencester, who died in 1217, has left us a sufficiently clear description of the Norman hall. He says that it had a vestibule or screen (vestibulum), and was entered through a porch (porticus), and that it had a court (atrium). In the interior of the hall, there were posts (or columns) placed at regular distances. The few examples of Norman halls which remain are thus divided internally by two rows of these columns. He enumerates the materials required in the construction of the hall, which shows that he is speaking of a building constructed of wood. A fine example of one of these halls, though of a later period, is, or was recently, standing in the city of Gloucester, with its internal posts as here described. There appears, also, to have been an inner court-yard, in which Neckam intimates that poultry was kept. The whole building and the two court-yards were surrounded by a wall, outside of which were the garden and orchard. At the close of the fourteenth century the middle classes of England had made great advances in wealth and independence. This increase of wealth appears in the multiplication of articles of furniture and house-hold implements, especially those of a more valuable description. There was also a great increase both in the number and magnitude of the houses which intervened between the castle and the cottage. Instead of having one or two bedrooms only, and turning people at night into the hall to sleep, as in earlier times, we now find whole suites of chambers; while, where before the family lived chiefly in the hall, privacy was now sought by the addition of parlors, of which

## GOD REST YE.

OLD ENGLISH.
Words by D. M. MULOCK.

1. God rest ye, mer-ry gen-tle-men, let nothing you dis-may, For Jesus Christ, our
2. God rest ye, lit-tle chil-dren, let nothing you af-fright, For Jesus Christ, your
3. God rest ye, all good Chris-tians; up-on this blessed morn The Lord of all good

Sav-iour, was born on Christmas day; The dawn rose red on Beth-le-hem, the
Sav-iour, was born this hap-py night; A-long the hills of Gal-i-lee the
Chris-tians was of a wom-an born; Now all your sor-rows He doth heal, your

stars shone thro' the gray, When Je-sus Christ, our Sav-iour, was born on Christmas Day.
white flocks sleeping lay, When Christ, the child of Naz-a-reth, was born on Christmas Day.
sins He takes a-way, For Jesus Christ, your Sav-iour, was born on Christmas Day.

there were often more than one in a house of ordinary size. The hall was, in fact, already beginning to diminish in relative importance to the rest of the mansion. Whether in town or country, houses of any magnitude were now generally built round an interior court, into which the rooms almost invariably looked, only small and unimportant windows looking toward the street or country. This arrangement, of course, originated in the necessity of studying security, a necessity which was never felt in England more severely than during the fifteenth century. The hall was still but scantily furnished. The permanent furniture consisted chiefly of benches and of a seat with a back to it, for the superior members of the family. The head table, at least, which stood on a dais, or raised platform, at the upper end of the hall, was often a permanent one; and there were in general other permanent tables, or "tables dormants;" but still the majority of the tables in the hall were made up for each meal, by placing boards upon trestles. Cushions with ornamental cloths called "bankers" and "dorsers," for placing over the benches and backs of the seats of the better persons at the table, were also in general use. On special occasions tapestry was suspended on the walls of the hall. Another article of furniture also had now become common, the "buffet," or stand on which the plate and other vessels were arranged. A vocabulary of the fifteenth century enumerates as the ordinary furniture of the hall: "A board, a trestle, a banker, a dorser, a natte (table cloth), a table dormant, a basin, a laver, fire on a hearth, a brand or torch, a Yule block, an andiron, tongs, a pair of bellows,

wood for the fire, a long settle, a chair, a bench, a stool, a cushion, and a screen." There were also "waits," or trumpeters, in olden time always attached to the halls of great people, to announce the commencement of the dinner. Only persons of a certain rank were allowed this piece of ostentation; but everybody who could obtain it had minstrelsy at dinner. The wandering minstrel was welcome in every hall; and for this very reason the class of ambulatory musicians was very numerous. In the sixteenth century the hall still continued to hold its position as the great public apart-

## MOURNER'S CHRISTMAS.

H. K. Reeder.

1. The old familiar Christmas songs, the bells that gaily ring, Have each an undertone of woe beyond imagining; For every joyful note awakes, with longings all untold, Some mem'ry of the joys we shared in those dear days of old, Some mem'ry of the joys we shared in those dear days of old.

2. Sweet chimes, your music thrills us thro' we know not why we weep; Earth's melody or discord ne'er can break our loved ones' sleep, For us the burdened days will come, the trials and the cares Of life shall press upon our hearts, but endless peace is theirs, Of life shall press upon our hearts, but endless peace is theirs.

3. Poor mourning heart, not all in vain, thy lonely grief shall be, For Christmas hath a joy in store, a gift reserved for thee—The deep, unchanging love of those whom death has purified, The "peace that passeth knowledge" comes to us at Christmas-tide, The "peace that passeth knowledge" comes to us at Christmas-tide.

4. The treasured soul that passed away hath left a shining light To guide us o'er the stormy seas, to steer our course aright, And when the links that bind our souls to earth are wholly riven, God grant us all to meet and know our precious ones in Heaven! God grant us all to meet and know our precious ones in Heaven!

ment of the house, and in its arrangements it differed slightly from those of an earlier date; it was, indeed, now the only part of the house which had not been affected by the increasing taste for domestic privacy. We have many examples of the old Gothic hall of this period in England, not only as it existed and was used in the sixteenth century, but in some cases, especially in colleges, still used for its original purposes. One of the simplest, and at the same time best examples of these halls, is found in the Hospital of St. Cross near Winchester, which has been described as follows: " The principal entrance to the main building from the first or outer court, opened into a thorough lobby, having on one side several doors or arches leading to the buttery, kitchen, and domestic offices; on the other side, the hall, parted off by a screen, generally of wood elaborately carved, and enriched with shields and with a variety of ornament, and pierced with several arches having folding doors. Above the screen and over the lobby,

## THREE KINGS OF ORIENT.

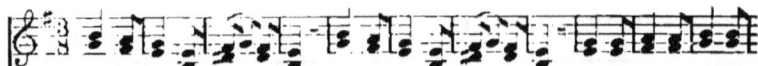

1. We three kings of Orient are, Bearing gifts we traverse far Field and fountain, moor and
2. Born a babe on Bethlehem's plain, Gold we bring to crown Him again; King for ever— ceasing
3. Frankincense to offer have I; Incense owns a Deity nigh; Prayer and praising all men
4. Myrrh is mine; its bitter perfume Breathes a life of gath'ring gloom; Sorrowing, sighing, bleeding,
5. Glorious now behold Him rise, King and God and Sacrifice; Heaven sings "Hallelujah!"

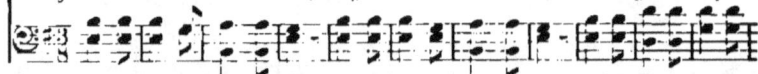

*Chorus.*

mountain, Following yonder Star.    Oh, star of wonder, star of might, Star with roy-al
never— Over us all to reign.    Oh, star of wonder, star of might, Star with roy-al
raising, Worship Him, God on high.    Oh, star of wonder, star of might, Star with roy-al
dying, Seal'd in the stone-cold tomb.    Oh, star of wonder, star of might, Star with roy-al
"Hal-le-lu-jah!" earth replies,    Oh, star of wonder, star of might, Star with roy-al

beau-ty bright, Westward lead-ing, still proceed-ing, Guide us to the perfect light.

The last three verses may be sung each by a different voice, to represent the Wise Men.

was the minstrels' gallery, and on its front were usually hung armor, antlers, and similar memorials of the family exploits. The hall itself was a large and lofty room, in the shape of a parallelogram; the roof, the timbers of which were framed with pendents, richly carved and emblazoned with heraldic insignia, formed one of its most striking features. 'The topbeam of the hall'—in allusion to the position of his coat of arms—was a symbolical manner of drinking the health of the master of the house. At the upper end of this chamber —farthest from the entrance—the floor was usually raised a step, and this part was styled the 'dais,' or 'high place.' On one side of the dais was a deep embayed window, reaching nearly down to the floor; the other windows ranged along one or both sides of the hall, at a considerable height above the ground, so as to leave room for wainscoting or arras below them. They were enriched with stained glass, representing the armorial bearings of the family, their connections, and royal patrons, and between the windows were hung full length portraits of the same persons. The royal arms, also, usually occupied a conspicuous station at either end of the room. The head table was laid for the lord and principal guests on the raised place, parallel with the upper end wall, and other tables were ranged along the sides for inferior visitors and retainers. Tables so placed were said to stand 'banquet-wise.' In the centre of the hall was the rere-dosse, or fire-iron, against which fagots were piled, and burnt upon the stone floor; the smoke passing through an aperture in the roof immediately overhead, which was generally formed into an elevated lantern, a conspicuous ornament to the exterior of the building. In latter times a wide arched fire-place was formed in the wall on one side of the room.''

The earlier half of the sixteenth century was the period when the pageantry of feasting in these halls was carried to its greatest degree of splendor, especially at Christmas.

## IN BETHLEHEM.

OLD ENGLISH.
F. A. G. OUSELEY.

1. In Beth - le - hem, that no - ble place, As by the pro - phet said it was, Of the Vir - gin Ma - ry. filled with grace, "Sal - va - tor mun - di na - tus est."
2. On Christ - mas night an an - gel told The shepherds watch - ing by their fold, In Beth - le - hem, full nigh the wold, "Sal - va - tor mun - di na - tus est."
3. The shep - herds were en - compassed right, A - bout them shone a glo - rious light, "Dread ye naught," said the angel bright, "Sal - va - tor mun - di na - tus est."
4. "No cause have ye to be a - fraid, For why? this day is Je - sus laid On Ma - ry's lap, that gentle maid:" "Sal - va - tor mun - di na - tus est."

*Chorus.*

Be we mer - ry in this feast, "In quo Sal - va - tor na - tus est."

"In the houses of the noble and wealthy, the dinner itself was laid out with great pomp, was almost always accompanied with music, and not unfrequently interrupted with dances, mummings, and masquerades." It is not difficult, therefore, to form an idea of those domestic establishments in which our forefathers used to keep their Christmas. We say *our* forefathers, for although the old manorial residences belonged to the nobility and gentry of the land, yet the whole population may in a manner be said to have kept their Christmas there. Everywhere, indeed, during the twelve days of Christmas, these old halls were the centres of holiday festivities. From time to time it appears that the gentry and nobility of the realm were admonished by royal authority of their duty to go down to their country seats, and then and there to entertain their friends and neighbors with liberal hospitality. Aubrey says of these times: "In the days of yore, lords and gentlemen lived in the country like petty kings; had jura regalia belonging

17

to their seignories; had their castles and boroughs; seldom went to London but in Parliament time, or once a year to do homage to the king. They always ate in Gothic halls at the high table or *orielle* (which is a little room at the upper end of the hall, where stands a table), with the folks at the side-tables. The meat was served up by watchwords. Jacks are but a late inven-

tion." Here in the hall the mumming, and the loaf-stealing, and other Christmas sports, were performed. The hearth was commonly in the middle, whence the saying, "Round about our sea-coal fire." Noblemen and gentlemen of fair estates had their heralds, who wore their coat-of-arms at Christmas, and at other solemn times, and cried "Largesse," thrice. The halls in fact, of all the

## WHEN CHRIST WAS BORN.

OLD MANUSCRIPT.
ARTHUR H. BROWN.

1. When Christ was born of Ma-ry free, In Beth-le-hem, that fair ci-tie,
2. Herdsmen be-held these An-gels bright, To them ap-pear-ing with great light,
3. The King is come to save mankind, As in Scrip-ture truths we find,
4. Then, dear Lord, for Thy great grace, Grant us in bliss to see Thy face,

An-gels sang there with mirth and glee, In ex-cel-sis Glo-ri-a.
Who said, "God's Son is born to-night, In ex-cel-sis Glo-ri-a."
There-fore this song we have in mind, "In ex-cel-sis Glo-ri-a."
That we may sing to Thy sol-ace, "In ex-cel-sis Glo-ri-a."

*ff* Chorus.

In ex-cel-sis Glo-ri-a, In ex-cel-sis Glo-ri-a,

In ex-cel-sis Glo-ri-a, In ex-cel-sis Glo-ri-a.

colleges, at the Universities of Oxford and Cambridge, and in the Inns of Court, still remain, as in Aubrey's time, accurate examples of the ancient baronial and conventual halls; preserving not merely their original form and appearance, but the identical arrangement and service of the tables. It is said that at Houghton Chapel, Notting-

hamshire, "the good Sir William Hollis," that example of the "Fine old English gentleman, all of the olden time," who kept his house in great splendor and hospitality, began Christmas at All-Hallow-tide (October 31), and continued it till Candlemas (February 2); during which time *any man* was permitted to stay three days, without being asked who he was or whence he came. In the diary of the Rev. John Ward, Vicar of Stratford-upon-Avon, extending from 1648 to 1679, it is stated that the Duke of Norfolk expended £20,000 in keeping Christmas. Charles II. gave over keeping this festival on account, it is said, of its expense. The Duke of Norfolk's profuse hospitality gave great offence at court, where it appears to have been more the fashion to keep disorderly households than to keep Christmas; and from about the above period of degeneracy, it is said, this good old custom of keeping Christmas began to decline. Indeed it appears that the decline of Christmas customs was really as much owing to the general corruption of manners introduced into England by a profligate king

## THY STORY BIDES FOR AYE.

E. C. PHELPS.
MARY DOUGLAS

1. The lit-tle child of summers three Comes climbing to his mother's knee, In-to her lap to bear her tell The Christmas tale he loves so well, The dear old tale of skies that rang When of good-will the an-gels sang, That matchless host, se-rene and white, The shepherds saw one win-ter night. The mighty deeds that men have told In state-ly tome or flu-ent rhyme, Like mis-ty shadows fade away, But thy sweet story bides for aye, O Christmas day! glad Christmas day!

2. This sto-ry of the hallowed years Tells too of sac-ri-fice and tears, Of One who prayed a-lone and wept While His a-wea-ried foll'wers slept: But soft the dar-ling at her side Hears ech-oes sweet of dis-tant chimes That bring the sto-ry back to me Of Beth-le-hem and Cal-va-ry. The mighty deeds that men have told In state-ly tome or flu-ent rhyme, Like

---

and court, as it was to any influence exercised upon them by the severe Puritanism of Cromwell's time. The picturesque and poetical custom of bringing in the Yule-log, elsewhere described, though shorn of the "pomp and circumstance" which formerly attended it, is still maintained in various parts of the country. Anciently a Yule song was sung on these occasions. The poet Herrick furnishes an example—which was written, probably, for this express purpose:

> With the last year's brand
> Light the new block, and
> For good success in his spending,
> On your psalteries play
> That sweet luck may
> Come while the log is a-teending (burning).

Then, it is said, went round the spicy wassail bowl, drowning every former grudge and animosity; an example it would seem, worthy of modern imitation. "Wassail!" was the word; "Wassail!" every guest returned, as he took the circling goblet from his friend. A fine specimen of a wassail bowl of undoubted Anglo-Saxon work, formerly belonging to the Abbey of Glastonbury, is now in the possession of Lord Arundel of Wardour; it holds two quarts, and formerly had eight pegs inside, dividing the liquor into half pints; on the lid is carved the Crucifixion, with the Virgin and John, one on each side; and round the cup are carved the twelve apostles. The spicy wassail, by the way, besides being sweetened, was also "augmented" by the addition of a toast and apples stuck full of cloves;

## SING, JOYOUSLY SING.

CHARLOTTE PIERSOL.

1. All hail! bright was the dawn - ing! Sing, sing, joy - ous - ly sing! Peace, peace! list to the
2. See, see, there in a man - ger Wise Men kneel to their King! Day - star o - ver them
3. Lo! now shepherds in won - der Haste from hill - side a - far, Where beamed ra - di - ant
4. All hail! brighter than morn - ing! Sing, sing, joy - ous - ly sing! Peace, peace! list to the

message, Sweet of the bells as they ring! Sing, sing, joyously sing, Sing with the bells as they ring.
blaz - ing, leads to adoration bring, Day star glo - rious, Light to the nations must bring.
glo - ry, The wondrous star of promise! Haste, speed - ing, They too have followed the Star!
message, Sweet of the bells as they ring! Sing, sing, joyously sing, Sing with the bells as they ring.

the liquor might be wine, cider, or ale, and was served smoking hot. According to traditional authority, the origin of this wassailing is traced to Rowena, the daughter of the Saxon Hengist. Richard Verstegan (1605) says: "As this lady was very beautiful, so was she of a very comely deportment; and Hingistus, having invited King Vortiger to a supper at his new builded castle, caused that after supper she came forth of her chamber into the king's presence, with a cup of gold filled with wine in her hand, and making in very seemly manner a low reverence unto the king, said with a pleasing grace and countenance, 'Waesheal, hlaford Cyning'—'Be of health, Lord King.' Of the beauty of this lady the king took so great liking, that he became exceed-

ingly inamored with her, and desired to have her in marriage, which Hingistus agreed unto, upon condition that the king should give unto him the whole country of Kent, whereunto he willingly condescended, and divorcing himself from his former married wife, married with the Saxon Lady Rowena." Perhaps in the "loving cup," still in use in London at the state dinners of the Lord Mayor, there is an allusion to this historical event. Bishop Cox in his "Impressions of England," describing one of these dinners given in 1851, says: "The toastmaster appeared behind his lordship's chair, and began: 'My Lord Archbishop of Canterbury, my Lord Bishop of London,' and so on through the roll of bishops—'my lords, ladies, and gentlemen, the Lord Mayor

HOME FOR THE HOLIDAYS.

and Lady Mayoress greet you in a loving cup and give you a hearty welcome.' The Mayor and Mayoress then rose, and taking the loving cup in hand, she uncovered it for him, with a graceful courtesy, to which he returned a bow, and then drank, wiped the chalice with his napkin, allowed it to be covered, and then sat down, while the lady, turning to the Archbishop, who rose accordingly, repeated the ceremony, save that he uncovered the cup, and it was her turn to taste the draught. Thus the cup went round.'' The mystic mistletoe, or kissing-bush, however, appears to have reg-ulated the custom of wassailing at Christmas, for with the disappearance of its white berries, one of which was to be plucked at each kiss, this innocent sport came to an end. The following imaginary scene gives us a very good idea of the appearance of one of these old English halls on a Christmas eve : '' A fire on the wide hearth-stone ; an oaken table; with a goodly company; closed doors; the mistletoe aloft upon a mighty beam ; evergreens abundant ; the Minstrels in the tapestried gallery ; quaint figures of Mummers, drolly attired, peep from behind the half drawn curtains, dependent before the

## O VOICES OF THE SKY.

W. MOZART.
FELICIA HEMANS.

mp

1. O love-ly voi-ces of the sky, Which hymned the Saviour's birth, Are ye not sing-ing
2. O clear and shining light, whose beams Awhile Heaven's glory shed Around the palms, and
3. O star which led to Him whose love Brought down man's ransom free, Where art thou?—'midst the

still on high, That once sang, '' Peace on earth?'' To us yet speak the hallowed strains Where-
o'er the streams, And on the shepherds' head,— Be near, thro' life, be near in death, As
host a-bove, May we still gaze on thee? In highest Heav'n thou art not set, Thy

with in times gone by, Ye blessed the wond'ring Syrian swains, O voices of the sky!
on that holiest night Of hope, and joy, and child-like faith, O clear and shining light!
rays earth may not dim: Send them to guide us on-ward yet, O star which led to Him!

recess of the deep bay-windows.'' As an accompaniment to the Yule-Log, a candle of monstrous size, called the Yule-candle, or Christmas candle, shed its light on the festive board during the evening. Brand in his '' Popular Antiquities,'' states that '' in the buttery of St. John's College, Oxford, an ancient candle socket of stone still remains, ornamented with the figure of the Holy Lamb. It was formerly used for holding the Christmas candle, which, during the twelve nights of the Christmas festival, was burned on the high table at supper.'' The Mysteries, Miracle Plays, and Moralities, formerly enacted during the Christmas holidays, have in modern times gradually disappeared, or degenerated from their pristine splendor and magnificence into mere burlesques, such as the mock play of St. George and the Dragon. This demoralization, however, does not seem to have extended to the Christmas tree, the most picturesque of the mediæval pageants, which, with undiminished glory towering aloft, festooned by garlands of gold and silver paper, and sparkling with its myriad lights, still presents an enchanting vision to thousands of happy children here as well as abroad. The custom of decorating the Christmas tree, although of German origin and of great antiquity, has recently been introduced into England and America. Indeed, it would seem to have been naturalized with us at a much earlier period even than in England. For in Pennsylvania, where many of the settlers are of German descent, Christmas Eve is observed with many of the ceremonies practiced in the Fatherland. The Christmas tree branches forth in all its splendor, and the Christ-Child—according to the German legend—comes through the air on golden wings, and causes the bough to produce in the night all manner of fruit, gilt sweetmeats, apples, nuts, etc., for the good children. Bunsen is thought by some to have contributed to Christianize a custom derived from pagan times, by placing a picture of the Madonna della Seggiola amid the tapers, so as to illuminate the loveliest infant representation of Him who brought good gifts unto men ; and thus to sanctify

## MANGER ALL-GLORIOUS.

JOHN SELWYN.

1. Man - ger all - glo - rious! let the joy - ous cho - rus
   Join - ing the songs of a - ges gone be - fore us,
2. Birth - day of won - der, Time's first Christmas morning,
   Once were they sands of gold Time's glass adorn - ing,—

Burst from all lips in one glad
Voic - ing the joy of an - gels
Long waited for by saints in
That day by ho - ly prophets

hymn of mirth;
at His birth.
days of old!
long fore - told.

Down from the heav'ns He long a - go de - scend - ed,

High to those heav'ns our glad song we raise! An - gels and men, their

might - y cho - rus blend - ed, Swell the grand har - mo - ny, resound His praise, Re-

sound His praise, resound His praise, Resound His praise, resound His praise!

the ancient German custom of hanging gifts on a tree, dating from the time of heathen life in a forest. It is said that Luther in his family celebrated Christmas Eve according to this German custom. In an engraving published in Leipsic, the great Reformer, who was very fond of children and music, is represented in the midst of the little ones, playing upon a zittern, an instrument not unlike the modern guitar.

It is not, however, our well-known Christmas tree and its customs which it is our especial purpose here to notice, but rather those half-forgotten Christmas Mummeries, Plays, and Moralities which once formed the most intellectual part of the sports and

## ONCE UPON A TIME.

CLARA WALLACE.
MRS. CHAS. BARNARD.

*Allegretto.*

*mf*

1. 'Twas once up-on a time, dear, The tale you've heard me tell; 'Twas grandma told it
2. The gold-en stars they sang, dear, That wondrous, wondrous night; All Heaven with music
3. And then we saw the Star, dear, That led the Wise Men on; For fan-cy calls from

me, dear, We loved it pass-ing well—How skies were filled with song, dear, Where-
rang, dear, An an-them of de-light. The sim-ple shepherds list, dear, The
far, dear, The glo-ry a-ges gone. We saw the gifts they gave, dear, And

of the bells yet chime, A hallow'd sto-ry sweet, dear, Of "Once up-on a time," A
an-gel choir sub-lime, Eyes filled with wonder-mist, dear; 'Twas once up-on a time, Eyes
told in gladsome rhyme, The gold and myrrh and in-cense Of "Once up-on a time," The

*1st and 2d verses.* *3d verse.*

hal-low'd sto-ry sweet, dear, Of "Once up-on a time."
filled with won-der mist, dear; 'Twas once up-on a time.
gold and myrrh and in-cense Of "Once up - - - on a time."

pastimes of our ancestors. The custom of representing at every solemn festival of the church some event recorded in Scripture, became very general in Christendom at an early period. Gregory Nazianzen, patriarch of Constantinople, and others eminent in the church, had dramatized portions of the Old and New Testament, and substituted them for the Greek plays still publicly represented in their day. These sacred dramas were modeled on those of the ancient Greek tragedy, the choruses being turned into Christian hymns. One only of the Patriarch's plays, a tragedy called "Christ's Passion," is extant. The Christians found in the wit and elegance of his writings, all that they could desire in the heathen poets. Farces, also, such as the Feast of Fools and of the Ass were enacted, with the design, it is said, of weaning the people from the ancient heathen spectacles, particularly those of the licentious Bacchanalian and Calendary solemnities. The more modern mysteries, miracle plays, and moralities, were also devised by the clergy in later times, doubtless with the same good intention of withdrawing their people at this season of the Nativity from a participation in the traditional games of the Roman Saturnalia. These were composed of Scriptural incidents, or, as Fitz-Stephen informs us, of "Representations of those miracles that were wrought

## HAIL! EVER-BLESSED MORN.

GOLLMICK.

1. See, a - mid the winter's snow, Born for us on earth be - low, See the ten - der Lamb ap - pears, Promised from e - ter - nal years. Hail, thou ev - er - bles - sed morn! Hail, Redemption's happy dawn! Sing thro' all Je - ru - sa - lem, "Christ is born in Beth - le - hem!"

2. Lo, with - in a man - ger lies He who built the star - ry skies; See the He who throned in height sub - lime, Sits a - mid the cher - u - bim! Say, ye ho - ly shep - herds, say, What your joy - ful news to - day; Wherefore have ye left your sheep On the lone - ly mountain steep? "Christ is born! Christ is born! Christ is born in Beth - le - hem!"

3. "As we watched at dead of night, Lo, we saw a wondrous light, An - gels sing - ing 'Peace on Earth' Told us of a Saviour's birth." Teach, oh, teach us, Ho - ly Child, By thy - self so meek and mild, Teach us to be more like Thee In thy sweet hu - mil - i - ty! Christ is born! Christ is born! Christ is born in Beth - le - hem!

by holy confessors; or those passions and sufferings in which the martyrs so signally displayed their fortitude. The actors were the scholars of the clergy; the church itself was frequently used as a place of exhibition; and the rich vestments and sacred furniture employed in the church service were sometimes permitted to be used by the performers, to give superior truth and lustre to their representations. The "ludi," or Christmas plays, formerly exhibited at court, were of quite a different character from those described here. It is said they can be traced back certainly as far as the reign of Edward III.; and they are by some thought to be much older. The dresses appropriated in 1348 to one of these plays, show that they were mummeries, and not theatrical divertisements. The King (Edward III.) then kept his Christmas at his castle at Guilford, the "keep" of which remains to this day. The dresses on that occasion, it is said, consisted of eighty tunics of buckram of various colors; forty-two vizors; fourteen faces of women; four-teen of men; and fourteen heads of angels made with silver; twenty-eight crests; fourteen mantels embroidered with heads of dragons; fourteen white tunics, wrought with the heads aud wings of peacocks; fourteen with the heads and wings of swans; fourteen tunics, painted with the eyes of peacocks; fourteen tunics of English linen, painted; and fourteen other tunics embroid-

## THE STORY OF A STAR.

WILHELM GANZ.

1. It was midnight in the cit y, Silence had its peaceful reign, Heavy eyes were
2. They were watching by the cit y, Watching quiet flocks by night, When the air was
3. So they haste to greet the stranger, In the silence of the night, And are guided

sunk in slumber When the an-gel anthem came; Shepherds on-ly saw the splendor
filled with mu-sic, And the darkness took its flight; For the hosts of choiring an-gels
to his manger By the star's re-fulgent light. Clear above the low-ly dwelling

From the Heav'nly gates a-far, Shepherds were the first to hear it.—Wondrous sto-ry
From their home in Heaven a-far, Chanting in ma-jes-tic sweetness, Told the sto-ry
The bright radiance gleams a-far, And they find Him "with his mother," This the sto-ry

of a star, Wondrous sto-ry of a star. Story of His na-tal star! Wonder star,

wonder star, Sto-ry of His na-tal star! Wonder star, wonder star, Story of His na-tal star.

ered with stars of gold. The magnificent pageants and disguisings frequently exhibited at court, in succeeding reigns, and especially in the reign of Henry VIII., were but a species of mummeries destitute of character and humor; their chief aim being to surprise the spectators "by the ridiculous and exaggerated oddity of the vizors, and by the singularity and splendor of the dresses;—everything was out of nature and propriety." Stowe thus describes a remarkable mummery made by the citizens of London in 1377, for the disport of the young Prince Richard, son to the Black Prince: "They rode, disguised and well horsed, 130 in number, with minstrels and torch-lights of wax, to Kennington beside Lambeth, where the young Prince remained

## HEIGH-HO, THE HOLLY.

W. CRAWFORD.
EDITH M. THOMAS.

1. As dreaming by the fire I sat, I heard a mer-ry din; The door I o-pened wide; at that A stran-ger child stepped in, He wore a flee-cy, warm white hat, Tied round his dim-pled chin, Tra la la la, tra la la, Tra la la la la la, Tra la la, la la la, la la la la la, Tra la la, tra la la, tra la la, tra la la, Tra la la, tra la la la la la la la la, la la la la la la la la la.

2. Green leaves and ber-ries red he brought, His face and voice were jolly, "I have no flowers, but these I thought Would cure your melanchol-y. I'll sing a song that I've been taught—It's called "Heigh-ho, the Holly!" Tra la la la, tra la la,

with his mother. These maskers alighted, entered the palace hall, and set to the Prince and his mother and lords, cups and rings of gold, which they won at a cast; after which they feasted, and the Prince and lords danced with the mummers, which jollity being ended, they were made to drink," etc. The plays exhibited in the country at this season appear to have been of a more mixed character. Such were the Cornish mummeries or miracle plays; which were not performed as elsewhere in churches, but in an earthen amphitheatre in some open field. These continued to be exhibited long after the abolition of the miracle plays and moralities in other parts of the kingdom. Accordingly we find them lingering in Cornwall even to the present time; and there, as also in Devonshire and Staffordshire, the old spirit of Christmas is kept up with great earnestness. There is also in the northern part of England a species of mumming called

## ONCE IN ROYAL DAVID'S CITY.

*Allegro moderato.*                                                 GAUNTLETT

1. Once in roy - al Da - vid's ci - ty, Stood a low - ly cattle - shed,
2. He came down to earth from Heaven, Who was God and Lord of all;
3. And thro' all His wondrous childhood, He would hon - or and o - bey,
4. For He is our childhood's pattern, Day by day like us He grew;
5. And at last our eyes shall see Him, Thro' His own re - deem - ing love;

Where a moth - er laid her Ba - by In a man - ger for a bed.
And His shel - ter was a sta - ble, And His cra - dle was a stall.
Love and watch the low - ly moth - er, In whose gen - tle arms He lay.
He was lit - tle, weak, and helpless, Tears and smiles like us He knew;
For that child, so dear and gen - tle, Is our Lord in Heaven a - bove.

Ma - ry was that moth - er mild, Je - sus Christ her on - ly child.
With the poor, and mean, and lowly, Lived on earth the Saviour holy.
Christian chil - dren all must be Mild, o - be - dient, good as He.
And He feeleth for our sad - ness, And He shareth in our glad - ness.
And He leads His chil - dren on To the place where He has gone.

the sword dance, and, says Mr. Henderson, "this may yet be looked for in most towns from the Humber to the Cheviot Hills." There are some trifling local variations both in dance and song; the latter has altered with the times; the former is plainly a relic of the war dances of our Danish and Saxon ancestors. Tacitus thus describes a sword dance among the ancient Germans: "One public diversion was constantly exhibited at all their meetings; young men, who by frequent exercise have attained to great perfection in that pastime, strip themselves, and dance among the points of swords and spears, with most wonderful agility, and even with the most elegant and graceful motions. They do not perform this dance for hire, but for the entertainment of the spectators, esteeming their applause a sufficient reward." Mr. Brand also tells us that he has seen this dance frequently performed in the northern part of England, about Christmas, with little or no variation from the ancient method. Washington Irving also refers to the custom in the " Sketch Book." There is a relic of the ancient mystery and miracle plays to be found in the more modern Christmas mummeries ; especially in that popular play of " St. George and the Dragon." This is still represented in some parts of England by a sort of dramatic corps headed by " Father Christmas." These mummers go abroad and about the country on Christmas Eve, performing this mock play in the halls of the gentry and in the kitchens of farm-houses. According to the " Golden Legend," on which this old play is founded, the city of Sylene, being infested with a dragon in the marsh, and the sheep failing — which had been given, two a day, to prevent his hurting the people — an ordinance substituted children and young peo-

## GOOD NEWS.

Stirling.

1. Good news on Christmas morning, Good news, O children dear! For Christ, once born in Bethl'em, Is
2. Good news on Christmas morning, Good news, O children glad! Rare gifts are yours to give Him, As

liv - ing now and here, Good news on Christmas morning, Good news, O children sweet! The
ev - er Wise Men had, Good news on Christmas morning, Good news, O children fair! Still

way to find the Christ-child Is light-ed for your feet. O wondrous Christmas morning, Thrice
holds the one Good Shepherd, The feeblest in His care. O wondrous Christmas morning, Thrice

wondrous, children dear, That He who came to Bethl'em Is liv - ing now, and here.

ple, to be chosen by lot, whether rich or poor. The king's daughter was drawn, and St. George happening to pass by when she was on her way to be devoured, fought and killed the dragon. In this legend there seems to be an allusion to the spiritual combat against "that old serpent the Devil," or the dragon mentioned in the Apocalypse. In 1849 this still very popular drama of St. George and the Dragon was acted on the floor of the Free Trade Hall in Manchester, where it is customary to celebrate the Epiphany, called Old Christmas or Twelfth Day, with many ancient forms and ceremonies. The programme for each year varies slightly; sometimes there is a procession of the Months ; sometimes of the Seasons, etc. ; but there never fail to be the presentation and carrying of the Boar's Head, with the necessary glees and choruses attending this ceremony.

Among the religious shows which, like those of the Mysteries and Miracle Plays, gave life and animation to the Christmas festivities of our forefathers, was that of the Boy-Bishop. "The accounts of the origin of this curious custom have been," says Mr. Fosbrooke, "elucidated into obscurity." It is said to have been founded on this story in the Legend of St. Nicholas: "A bishop who had been elected to a vacant see, was warned by a dream to go to the doors of the church at the hour of matins, and 'hym that sholde fyrste come to the chyrche, and have the name of Nicholas, they sholde sacre hym Bissop,'—that is, one bishop was superseded by another." Hone, on the subject of the Boy-Bishop, writes: "Anciently, on the 6th of December (St. Nicholas' Day), the choir-boys in cathedral and collegiate churches chose one of their number to maintain the state and authority of a bishop; for which purpose he was habited

## HOLLY GREEN WITH BERRIES RED.

1. Of all the trees in for-est vast The oak seems king to me; How proud he flings his boughs abroad, A
2. Strong the oak, but sweet the pine, And soft it sings to me, Thro' summer hours when 'neath its shade I
3. Oak and pine be strong and sweet, Still mine the Christmas tree, For fruitage rare we gather there From

stur-dy gi-ant he! His good tough heart brave ships hath made, To sail the seas I ween, But
dream what life may be; Its spi-cy wood in ma-ny forms O'er all the land is seen; But
boughs most fair to see, Oh, for-est green in Christmas glow, Oh, leaf of lustrous sheen, Oh,

*Chorus.*

there's a tree more dear to me, The Christmas hol-ly green. The hol-ly tree, the hol-ly tree, Our
give to me the hol-ly tree, The Christmas hol-ly green. The hol-ly tree, the hol-ly tree, Our
tree of trees, most dear to me, Thou Christmas hol-ly green. The hol-ly tree, the hol-ly tree, Our

Christmas green when snow's o'erhead, The holly tree, the hol-ly tree, The holly green, with berries red.

in rich episcopal robes, wore a mitre on his head, and bore a crozier in his hand; his fellows for the time being assuming the character and dress of priests, yielding him canonical obedience, taking possession of the church, and, except mass, performing all the ceremonies and offices, and on Holy Innocents' day, actually preaching a sermon to the assembled congregation." There is a monument of such a child-bishop who died while in office, standing on the north side of Salisbury Cathedral, on which is sculptured the figure of a youth clad in episcopal robes, with his foot on a lion-headed and dragon-tailed monster, in allusion to the expression of the psalmist, "Thou shalt tread on the lion and the dragon." Although there resulted much actual profanity from the above prescribed ritualistic observances, yet there seems to have been nothing irreverent intended by them, for we find that whatever was strictly sacramental in its nature, or that properly belonged to the priestly office, was not originally permitted or exercised by these mimic prelates. "But our ancestors," says Fosbrooke, "used all these mummeries, as we now do the catechism, to impress principles upon the minds of their children." The election of this Episcopus Puerorum, or Episcopus Choristorum, always took place on St. Nicholas' Day (December 6), and as St. Nicholas was the patron saint of schoolboys and choristers, the Boy-Bishop naturally became identified in name with his patron saint. Thus St. Nicholas as he was called, became a person of great consequence, perambulating both town and country, habited as a bishop, "in pontificalibus," with his fellow choristers also in appro-

## CHRISTMAS AGAIN.

JOHN SELWYN

Moderato.

1. Christ - mas a - gain! sing as of old, Tra la la la la, Tra la la
2. Wake, all ye bells, mu - sic that tells, Tra la la la la, Tra la la
3. Blaze, ruddy fires, whose flame aspires! Tra la la la la, Tra la la

la, Think not of storm, care not for cold, Tra la la la la, Tra la la la.
la, How in our glee we're happy and free, Tra la la la la, Tra la la la.
la, Nev - er a pause, good Santa Claus! Tra la la la la, Tra la la la.

Gai - ly sing! Tra la la la la, la la la, Tra la la la la, Voi - ces ring,

Tra la la la la, la la la la, From hill - side and val - ley, Tra

la la la la la, From hill - side and val - ley, Tra la la la la la, la la la la.

priate vestments, singing carols, etc., being in fact Christmas personified, or "Old Father Christmas." From a printed church-book containing the service of the Boy-Bishop set to music, we learn that on the eve of Innocents' day, the Boy-Bishop and his youthful clergy, in their copes, and with burning tapers in their hands, went in solemn procession, chanting and singing versicles as they walked, into the choir by the west door, in such order that the dean and canons went foremost, the chaplains next, and the Boy-Bishop, with his priests, in the last and highest place. He then took his seat, and the rest of the children disposed them selves upon each side of the choir, upon

## MERRY BELLS OF LONG AGO.

A. Reichardt.
Archibald Douglas.

1. Now the win - ter sun is sink - ing, Soon the night, the night his face will
2. Years a - go! and flakes were fall - ing Thro' the frost - y, frost - y win - ter
3. Oh, the bells my heart re - mem - bers With their chim - ing, chim-ing loud or

hills re - peat the prom - ise, 'Tis the eve, the eve of Christ - mas dear; And the
hear them gai - ly sing - ing As the hour, the hour of glad - ness tells, Clearly
mem - ber eyes that glis - tened When the snow, the snow was in the dells, I re-

the uppermost ascent; the canons resident, reversing the usual order, bearing the incense and the book, and the petit-canons the tapers, according to the Rubric. Afterwards he proceeded to the altar of the Holy Trinity and All Saints, which he first censed, and next the Image of the Holy Trinity, his priests all the while singing.

Then they all chanted a service with prayers and responses, and, in the like manner taking his seat, the Boy-Bishop repeated salutations, prayers, and versicles; and, in conclusion, gave his benediction to the people, the full chorus answering, *Deo Gratias!* After he received his crozier from the cross-bearer, other ceremonies were performed,

## SEE AMID THE SNOW.

Sir John Goss.

*Moderato.*

*Solo. (Treble or Tenor alternately.)*

1. See a - mid the win - ter's snow, Born for us on earth be - low,
2. Lo, with - in a man - ger lies He who built the star - ry skies;
3. Say, ye ho - ly shep - herds, say, What your joy - ful news to - day;

See the ten - der Lamb ap - pears, Prom - ised from e - ter - nal years.
He, who throned in height sub - lime, Sits a - mid the Cher - u - bim!
Where - fore have ye left your sheep On the lone - ly moun - tain steep?

*Chorus. ff*

Hail! Thou ev - er - bless - ed morn! Hail, Re - demp - tion's hap - py dawn!

Sing through all Je - ru - sa - lem, Christ is born in Beth - le - hem.

"As we watched at dead of night, Lo, we saw a wondrous light; Angels singing peace on earth, Told us of the Saviour's birth."

Sacred Infant, all divine, What a tender love was Thine; Thus to come from highest bliss Down to such a world as this!

Teach, O teach us, Holy Child, By Thy face so meek and mild, Teach us to resemble Thee, In Thy sweet humility!

18

and he chanted the compline; turning toward the choir he delivered an exhortation, and last of all pronounced the benediction. In process of time, however, all this seemingly orderly behavior was changed for the worse. It appeared that boys would be boys, and that they mixed up with their regularly-appointed services the buffooneries of the so-called "Feast of Fools," and of "The Ass," and instead of psalms and hymns, were now "sung or said" indecent songs and jests; and in place of the fragrance of incense, there were substituted all sorts of unsavory abominations. These enormities had reached such a pitch at the time of the Reformation in the reign of Henry VIII., that we are not surprised to find the ceremonies of the Boy-Bishop installation abrogated by royal authority. Nevertheless, according to Strype: "In the reacting times which followed, an edict was issued November 13, 1554, by the Bishop

## GOOD KING WENCESLAS.

J. M. Neale *tr.*
From the Latin.

1. Good King Wen-ces-las looked out, On the feast of Stephen, When the snow lay round about, Deep, and crisp and even: Brightly shone the moon that night, Tho' the frost was cru-el, When a poor man came in sight, Gathering winter fu-el.
2. "Hith-er,* page, and stand by me, If thou know'st it, tell-ing, Yon-der peasant, who is he? Where and what his dwelling?" "Sire,† he lives a good league hence, Underneath the mountain; Right against the for-est fence, By Saint Agnes' foun-tain."
3. "Bring me* flesh, and bring me wine, Bring me pine-logs hith-er; Thou and I will see him dine, When we bear them thither." Page and monarch forth they went, Forth they went to-geth-er; Thro' the rude wind's wild la-ment And the bit-ter weath-er.
4. "Sire,† the night is dark-er now, And the wind blows stronger; Fails my heart, I know not how, I can go no longer." "Mark* my footsteps, good my page; Tread thou in them bold-ly: Thou shalt find the win-ter's rage Freeze thy blood less cold-ly."
5. In his mas-ter's steps he trod, Where the snow lay dint-ed; Heat was in the ve-ry sod Which the saint had printed. Therefore, Christian men, be sure, Wealth or rank pos-sess-ing, Ye who now will bless the poor, Shall yourselves find bless-ing.

*Tenor Solos, if preferred. †Soprano Solos.

of London, to all the clergy of his diocese, to have the procession of a Boy-Bishop." And again, "On the 5th of December, or St. Nicholas' eve, of the same year, 'at even song,' came a commandment that St. Nicholas should not go abroad or about; but notwithstanding, it seems, so much were the citizens taken with the 'mask' of St. Nicholas (that is, Boy-Bishop), that there went about these St. Nicholases in divers parishes." Again, Strype informs us, that "In 1556, on the eve of his day, St. Nicholas, that is, a boy habited like a bishop, 'in pontificalibus,' went abroad in most parts of London, singing after the old fashion and was received by many ignorant but well-disposed people into their houses, and had as much good cheer as ever was wont to be had before, at least in many places." But with the final establishment of the Reformation under Elizabeth, this pastime or pageant of the Boy-Bishop disappears;

and henceforth he is not to be found in England, excepting, perhaps, under an alias as "Old Father Christmas." Ben Jonson appears to have attempted a partial revival of the pageant in his "Masque" presented at court in 1616; in which Christmas is represented in the novel character of an ardent professor of Protestantism. He says: "Ha! would you have kept *me out?* Christmas, Old Christmas, Christmas of London, and Captaine Christmas! Why, I am no dangerous person, and so I told my friends o' the guard. I am old Gregory Christmas still; and as good a Protestant as any in my Parish." This plea of his Protestantism, however, did not satisfy the suspicious Puritanical spirit of that age; for at a subsequent period, during the civil wars of the seventeenth century, we find him and his children solemnly banished the land by act of Parliament! Needham, in his "History of the Rebellion" (1661), bewailing sadly

## THE FIRST NOWELL.

TRADITIONAL.

*mf*

1. The first Now-ell the Angel did say, Was to certain poor shepherds in fields as they
2. They looked up and saw a Star, Shining in the East, beyond them
3. And by the light of that same Star, Three wise men came from country a-
4. This Star drew nigh to the north-west, O'er Bethlehem it took its

lay; In fields where they lay keeping their sheep, On a cold winter's night that was so deep.
far, And to the earth it gave great light, And so it contin-ued both day and night.
far; To seek for a King was their in-tent, And to follow the Star wherever it went.
rest, And there it did both stop and stay, Right o-ver the place where Je-sus lay.

*Chorus.* ff

Now-ell, Now-ell, Now-ell, Now-ell, Born is the King of Is-ra-el.

Then entered in those wise men three,
Full reverently upon their knee,
And offered there, in His presence,
Their gold, and myrrh, and frankincense.—*Cho.*

Then let us all with one accord,
Sing praises to our Heavenly Lord,
That hath made Heaven and earth of naught,
And with His blood mankind hath bought.—*Cho.*

the decline of Christmas, in consequence of Puritanism and of similar legislation, says,

Gone are those golden days of yore,
When Christmas was a High-Day,
Whose sports we now shall see no more;
'Tis turned into Good-Friday.

But if the Long Parliament could expel him from England, it could not prevent his taking up his abode among the more tolerant Dutch in the "New Netherlands," and where, according to Knickerbocker's "History of New York," "he has continued to flourish at Christmas in spite of the 'Blue laws' of the neighboring puritanical state of Connecticut." He does not now, however, go any more abroad, habited "in pontificalibus." Having turned Presbyterian, he contents himself with the ordinary guise of a Dutchman, heavily furred, and has also exchanged his wassail-bowl for the "bowl" of a short Dutch pipe, with which he has completely mystified and befogged the intellect of his former enemies. In addition to the Christmas mummeries and plays noticed above a brief account perhaps should be given of some of the other old English games and amusements appropriate to this season, and especially of the Lord of Misrule, whose authority in some places extended not only over the Christmas holidays, but from the time of his election at Halloween (31st October) even until Whitsuntide. Brand, in his Popular Antiquities speaking of these games, says, " I find in a tract entitled Round about our Coal-fire, or Christmas Entertainments, published in the early part of the last century, the following : ' Then comes mumming or masquerading, when the squire's wardrobe is ransacked for dresses of all kinds. Corks are burnt to black the faces of the fair, or make deputy mustachios, and every one of the family, except the squire himself, must be transformed.' " This account further says: " The time of the year being cold and frosty, the diversions are within doors, either in exercise, or by the fireside. Dancing is one of the chief exercises ; or else there is a match at Blindman's-buff or Puss in the Corner. The next game is Questions and Commands, when the commander may oblige his subjects to answer any lawful

## HOLLY CROWNS THE GREEN.

G. ROSSINI.
CLARA WALLACE.

*Lively.*

1. Hol - ly crowns the Christ - mas green, Pine and box with it we weave;
2. Sing-ing waits, a hap - py throng, 'Neath the eaves with sim - ple skill,
3. 'Mid the storm that dies and swells, Fit - ful chim - ing faint - ly steals,

Comes the yule - log on the scene, Glows the hearth on Christmas eve. Children all, sing
Mind - ful of the an - gel song, Chant their Christmas car - ols still. Children all, sing
Mu - sic of the vil - lage bells, Ring - ing out their mer - ry peals. Children all, sing

mer-ri - ly your Christmas songs with glee; Children all, sing merri - ly Christmas songs with glee.

question, and make the same obey him instantly, under the penalty of being smutted, or paying such forfeit as may be laid on the aggressor. Most of the other diversions are cards and dice." Although there appears to have been a considerable falling off in modern times in the number and variety of these Christmas games and amusements, still we gather from the above that the sports on a Christmas eve, a hundred and fifty years ago, were not very much unlike those at present in vogue. The names of almost all the pastimes above mentioned must be familiar to every reader, who has probably participated in some of them. One of these favorite Christmas sports, once generally played on Christmas eve, has been handed down to us from time immemorial, under the name of Snap-dragon. In England this amusement is familiar to many people, but as it is not so well known elsewhere, we subjoin from the Book of Days a description of the game : " A quantity of raisins is deposited in a large bowl or dish (the broader and shallower this is, the better), and brandy or some other spirit is poured over the fruit and ignited. The bystanders now endeavor, by turns, to grasp a raisin, by plunging their hands through the flames; and as this is somewhat of an arduous feat, requiring both courage and rapidity of action, a considerable amount of laughter and merriment is evoked at the expense of the unsuccessful competitors. While the sport of Snap-dragon is going on, it is usual to extinguish all the lights in the room, so that the lurid glare from the flaming spirits may exercise to the full its weird-like effect." Christmas gambols such as these, and indeed holiday festivities of all kinds, were formerly presided over by an officer of great consequence, entitled the Lord of Misrule or Christmas Prince. The rights and privileges of this potentate are, it appears, derived from the Roman Saturnalia, a festival instituted in commemoration of the freedom and equality which once prevailed on earth in the golden reign of Saturn, or, as it has been suggested, from even a still higher origin. For the ancient Jews had among them a sort of Lord of Misrule, or "Symposiarch," as he was called, at their merry-makings, whose duty it was to promote the general hilarity. "If thou be made the master of the feast," says the author of Ecclesiasticus, "take diligent care for them, and when thou hast done all thy office, take thy place that thou mayest be

## SO NOW IS COME OUR FEAST.

George Wither, 1635.

1. So now is come our joy-ful feast, Let ev-'ry soul be jol-ly! Each room with i-vy
2. Now all our neighbors' chimneys smoke, And Christmas blocks are burning, Their ovens with baked

leaves is drest, And ev-'ry post with hol-ly. Tho' some churls at our mirth re-pine, Your
meat do choke, And all their spits are turning. With-out the door let sor-row lie, And,

brows let gar-lands twine, Drown sorrow—why should we repine? And let us all be merry!
if for cold it die, We'll bu-ry it in Christmas pie, And ev-er more be merry!

merry with them, and receive a crown for thy well ordering of the feast." But whatever may have been the origin of the office, his authority seems to have been pretty generally acknowledged in England previous to the civil wars of the seventeenth century. A good idea of the merry-makings of our ancestors, and of the nature of the duties of the Lord of Misrule, or master of ceremonies, may be formed from a consideration of the will of the Right Worshipful Richard Evelyn, Esq., of the sixteenth century, father of the author of "The Diary," and deputy lieutenant of the counties of Surrey and Sussex, thus appointing and defining the functions of a Christmas Lord of Misrule, over his estate at Wotton: "*Imprimis.* — I give free leave to Owen Flood, my trumpeter, gentleman, to be Lord of Misrule of all good orders during the twelve days. And also I give free leave to the said Owen Flood, to command all and every person or persons whatsoever, as well servants as others, to be at his command whensoever he shall sound his trumpet or music, and to do him service, as though I were present myself, at their perils . . . I give full power and authority to his lordship to break up all locks, bolts, bars, doors, and latches, and to fling up all doors out of hinges, to come at those who presume to disobey his lordship's commands. God save the king!'' Sir Richard's son did not depart from the economy and hospitality of the old house, but "*more veterum*," kept a Christmas in which they had no fewer than three hundred bumpkins every holiday. Hollingshed also informs us that, "What time there is always one appointed to make sporte at Courte, called commonly Lord of Misrule, whose office is not unknowne to such as have been brought up in noblemen's houses, and among great housekeepers, which use liberal feasting in the season." Again, Stowe says, "At the Feast of Christmas, in the king's court, wherever he chanced to reside, there was appointed a Lord of Misrule, or master of merry disports; the same merryfellow made his appearance at the house of every nobleman and person of distinction, and among the rest the Lord Mayor of London, and the sheriffs, had severally of them their Lord of Misrule; ever contending, without quarrel or offense, who should make the rarest pastimes to delight the beholders; this pageant potentate began his rule at All-hallow Eve, and continued the same till the morrow after the Feast of the Purification, in which space there were fine and subtle disguisings, masks, and mummeries." The sway of this officer, the Master of Merry Disports, was not confined to the court, nor to the houses of the opulent; but

## CHRISTMAS AS IT COMES.

HELEN MATHER.

he was also elected in various towns and parishes, where, however, his reign seems to have been of short duration. The practical result of this facetious and popular species of misrule perhaps may be gathered in part from the graphic description left by Stubbs, who, from all accounts, was himself a notable rebel not only against "misrule," but also against all "right rule." In the Anatomy of Abuses, he says; "First of all, the wilde heads of the parish flocking togither, chuse them a graund captaine of mischiefe, whom they innoble with the title of Lorde of Misrule; and him they crowne with great solemnity, and adopt for their king. This king annoynted chooseth forth twentie, fourty, threescore, or an hundred, lustie fellows, like to himself, to waite upon his lordly majesty, and to guarde his noble person. Then every one of these men he investeth with his liveries of greene, yellow, or some other light wanton colour, and as though they were not gaudy ynaugh, they bedecke themselves with scarffes, ribbons and laces, hanged all over with gold ringes, pretious stones, and other jewels. This done, they tie about either legge twentie, or fourtie belles, with rich handkerchiefes in their handes, and sometimes laide across over their shoulders and neckes, borrowed, for the most part, of their pretie Mopsies and loving Bessies. Thus all thinges set in order, then have they their hobby-horses, their dragons, and other antiques, together with their baudie pipers, and thundring drummers to strike up the

THE MASTER OF MERRY DISPORTS.

devils' daunce withal. Then march this heathen company towards the church, their pypers pyping, their drummers thundring, their stumpes dauncing, their belles jyngling, their handkerchiefes fluttering aboute their heades like madde men, their hobbyhorses and other monsters skirmishing amongst the throng: and in this state they go to the church though the minister be at prayer or preaching, dauncing and singing like devils incarnate, with such a confused noise that no man can heare his owne voyce.

Then the foolish people they looke, they stare, they laugh, they fleere, and mount upon the formes and pewes, to see these goodly pageants solemnized. Then after this, aboute the church they go againe and againe, and so fourthe into the churche-yard, where they have commonly their summer halls, their bowers, arbours, and banqueting houses set up, wherein they feaste, banquette, and daunce all that day, and peradventure all that night too; and thus these terrestrial furies spend the Sabbath-day. Then, for

## DAINTY WEE STOCKINGS.

I. B. Woodbury.

1. Dain - ty wee stockings hang all in    a    row,  Blue, gray and scar-let   in firelight's faint glow;
2. Fun - ny wee stockings hang all in    a    row,  Stuffed with surpris - es from top down to   toe;

Sleep - ers with cur - ly pates tucked in their beds, Dreaming of toyshops that dance thro' their heads.
Skates, balls and trumpets, and whips, tops and drums, Books, dolls, and candies, with sweet sugar plums.

mf

Dain - ty wee stockings that hang in   a   row    San - ta Claus coming the children well know,

With on - ly such treasure as   he can de - vise, To quicken their love and to gladden their eyes.

the further innobling of this honourable lordane — lord, I should say — they have certaine papers wherein is painted some babelerie or other of imagerie worke, and these they call my Lorde of Misrule's badges or cognizances. These they give to every one that will give to them money to maintaine them in this their heathenish develrie; and who will not show himself buxome to them and give them money, they shall be mocked and flouted shamefully; yea, and many times carried upon a cowlstaffe, and dived over heade and eares in water, or otherwise most horribly abused. And so besotted are some, that they not only give them money, but weare their badges or cognizances in their hattes or cappes openly. Another sorte of fantasticall fooles bring to these hounds of evil, the Lord of Misrule and his complices, some bread, some good ale, some new cheese, some old cheese, some custardes, some cracknels, some cakes, some flauns, some tartes, some creame, some meate, some one thing and some another."

It would seem from this account, although Strutt appears to have inferred in his Sports and Pastimes that Stubbs was speaking of the Christmas holidays, that the Lord of Misrule was sometimes also president over the summer sports ; and that his authority appears to have been occasionally extended over the whole period, from All-hallows till Whitsuntide. Stubbs speak of this revel being on the Sabbath-day, and also of their erecting summer-halls, etc., in the church-yard, from which we may infer that the Sab-bath-day mentioned was a Whitsunday, be-cause, the "belles that were tied about either legge," indicate the morris-dance, a dance peculiar to Whitsuntide. But the amusing account by Stubbs of the Lord of Misrule, and his alleged evil doings, does not convey to us so truthful an impression of this mighty potentate as may be derived from other less prejudiced sources. In con-

## THE SLEIGH RIDE.

J. C. JOHNSON.

1. Swiftly, swiftly o'er the snow, Merrily, merrily, cheerily, cheerily, Do we merry rid - ers go,
2. Sweetly, sweetly ring the bells, Merrily, merrily, cheerily, cheerily, Sweetly, sweetly music swells,
3. Onward, onward o'er the snow, Merrily, merrily, cheerily, cheerily, Do we merry rid - ers go,

La la la la  la  la la,  la  la la,  la  la la,  la la la la  la  la la,

Singing all so merrily. How bright and cold! what frosty air! But we are warm and do not care, With
Sing we all so merrily. How pleasant thus, with cheerful friends, To know the joy that winter sends, O
Singing all so merrily. How bright and cold! what frosty air! But we are warm and do not care, With

la la la  la  la la la.  Merrily, merrily, merrily, merrily, merrily, merrily,  merrily, merrily, O

mirth and song, we bound along, We laugh and sing so merrily, merrily, Laugh and sing so merrily.
winter days, we sing and praise! We laugh and sing so merrily, merrily, Laugh and sing so merrily.
mirth and song, we bound along, We laugh and sing so merrily, merrily, Laugh and sing so merrily.

trast with the above, we subjoin an account of certain stately proceedings by the law-yers of the Inner Temple. In 1561, a Lord of Misrule, having with him a train of one hundred horsemen, richly appareled, rode through London to the Inner Temple, where there was great reveling throughout the Christmas. Lord Robert Dudley, after-wards Earl of Leicester, being the constable and marshal, under the name of Palaphilos, and Christopher Hatton, afterwards Chan-cellor, master of the game. A sort of Par-liament had been previously held on St. Thomas's eve, to decide whether the society should keep Christmas, and if so, the old-est bencher should deliver a speech on the occasion, and the oldest butler publish the officers' names, and then—"in token of joy and good liking, the bench and company pass beneath the hearth, and sing a carol, and so to *boyer*" (collation). Again, in 1629, we read that, "The Templars chose

Bulstrode Whitelocke as Master of the Revels; and as soon as the evening was come, enterred the hall followed by sixteen revellers. They were proper handsome young gentlemen, habited in rich suits, shoes and stockings, hats and great feathers. The Master led them in his bar gown, with a white staff in his hand, the music playing before them. They began with the old masques; after which they daunced the brawls, and then the master took his seat, while the revellers flaunted through galliards, corantos, French and country dances, till it grew very late. As might be expected, the reputation of this dancing soon brought a store of other gentlemen and ladies, some

## A FUNNY OLD FELLOW.

HELEN MARTIN.
FRANCIS H. BROWN.

1. A fun-ny old fel-low, as we have heard say, Comes round once a year in the
   With bag light-ly swung on his shoulder, they tell, How he ur-ges his rein-deer that

2. His po-nies the rein-deer that tra-vel by night, No sun ev-er saw them,—they
   In his furs speeds he on thro' the moon ray so cold, And his sleigh is quite gone ere its

3. He's nev-er a stran-ger, but al-ways at home, 'Neath the cotter's low roof or the
   His welcome is heart-y where'er he may call, But the children they greet him the

u-su-al way; } "Brave Pran-cer! Gay Dash-er! Like an arrow, arrow, arrow, arrow! Now,
children love well; }

know not its light; } "Brave Pran-cer! Gay Dash-er! Like an arrow, arrow, arrow, arrow! Now,
presence is told; }

earl's loft-y dome; } "Brave Pran-cer! Gay Dash-er! Like an arrow, arrow, arrow, arrow! Now,
gladdest of all: }

Com-et! now, Vix-en! On, Donnern und Blitz-en! Brave Prancer! Gay Dash-er Like an

ar-row, ar-row, ar-row, ar-row! Now, Com-et! now, Vix-en! On, Donnern und Blitzen!"

of whom were of great quality. To crown the ambition and vanity of all, a great German lord had a desire to witness the revels, then making such a sensation at court, and the Templars entertained him at great cost to themselves, receiving in exchange that which cost the great noble very little,—his avowal that 'Dere vas no such nople gollege in Ghristendom as deirs.'" The Templars, according to Hone, also formerly held in their hall at Christmas, around about their coal fire, a species of hunt with hound and horn, conducted by the Lord of Misrule; a fox and cat being the game pursued.

This hunt seems at one time to have been general in great houses, and to have had a sort of symbolic signification. There was also, it appears, a very splendid Christmas at the Middle Temple in 1635, when Francis Vivian of Cornwall was the Christmas Prince, and expended £2,000 out of his own pocket, beyond the allowance of the society, in order to support his state with sufficient dignity. He had his lord keeper, lord treasurer, eight white staves, captain of pensioners, and his guard, and two chaplains, who, when they preached before him, saluted him on ascending the pulpit, with three low bows, as was then done to the king. Sandys says: "Towards the end of the seventeenth

## OLD SANTA CLAUS.

JOHN READ.

1. Old Santa Claus sat all alone, his pipe up-on his knee, A funny look about his eyes for
2. He had been busy as a bee, had stuffed his pack with toys; Had gathered worlds of odds and ends, his
3. Of candies too, or clear or striped, he had a bounteous store, And raisins, figs, and prunes, and grapes, but
4. He clapped his specs upon his nose, picked up his rusty pen; And wrote more lines in one short hour than

fun-ny chap was he; His queer old cap was twisted, torn, his wig was all awry; He sat and mused, as
gifts for girls and boys, Had dolls for girls, and whips for boys, with harrows, horses, drays, Bureaus and trunks for
wanted something more, I'm almost ready now, he said, and Christmas nearly here; But one thing more, I
you could write in ten; Then, Christmas eve and all in bed, Quick down the chimney flew, And left, beside the

lost in thought, while time went flying by. Santa Claus, who fears no danger, Over all the world a ranger,
Dolly's clothes: all these his pack displays. Santa Claus, who fears no danger, Over all the world a ranger,
need a book, for little folks this year." Santa Claus, who fears no danger, Over all the world a ranger,
stocking filled, the book he meant for you. Santa Claus, who fears no danger, Over all the world a ranger,

Ev'rywhere a welcome stranger, Speeds afar on Christmas eve! Santa Claus, who fears no danger,

O - ver all the world a ranger, Ev'rywhere a welcome stranger, Speeds afar on Christmas eve!

century these revels ceased, having gradually fallen off ; and the dignity of Master of the revels instead of being eagerly sought for, as in former times, needed a bribe or premium to induce any member to take it upon him."

The custom of serving the boar's head with minstrelsy at the Christmas dinner, with more or less of the ceremonies still used at Queen's College, Oxford, was very general in England previous to the civil wars of the seventeenth century, not only in the halls of the Universities, but also in the houses of the nobility and gentry. According to Aubrey, "The first dish that was served up in the old baronial halls was the boar's head, which was brought in with great state, and with minstrelsy ; and, between the flourishes of the heralds' trumpets, carols were chanted forth." Perhaps the most splendid example of Christmas

## DEAR SANTA CLAUS.

L. V. Crosby.
Clara Wallace.

1. Oh, Santa Claus, dear Santa! Come, make another call. Al ready we have hoped it long, We children large and small. Dear San-ta Claus, you surely Our house will not for-get! And bring along your Christmas pack, The table's read-y set. Dear San-ta Claus, you're kind as kind can be, When from the North you hurry down, To deck each Christmas tree.

2. Oh, Santa Claus, dear Santa! Trim ev'ry tree to-night With candies, nuts, and pretty toys, And ta-pers blazing bright; We'll be so ve-ry happy, And grateful more and more! Oh, best and dearest Santa Claus, Why pass by an-y door? Dear San-ta Claus, you're

3. We give thee happy greeting For all thy Christmas cheer, For all the joy thy coming brings In ev-'ry pass-ing year; We love thee all so dearly We dream of thee at night, In fan-cy see thy Christmas glee And hail it with de-light, Dear San-ta Claus, you're

*Chorus.*

banqueting of this kind of which we have read, is that recently illustrated by Gilbert, which took place in the reign of Henry VII., in the great hall of Westminster. To this feast the mayor and aldermen of London were invited, and all the sports of the time were exhibited before them in the great hall which was hung with tapestry, the which sports being ended *in the morning*, the king, queen and court sat down at a table of stone, to one hundred and twenty dishes, placed by as many knights and esquires ; while the mayor was served with twenty-four dishes and abundance of wine. And finally, the king and queen being conveyed with great lights into the palace, the mayor with his company, in barges, returned to London by break of next day." It is this royal Christmas which Mr. Gilbert has represented with such truthfulness. The artist has selected the upper end of the hall, showing the great stone table, with the king and queen seated beneath a canopy of state, emblazoned with the royal arms ; the dais wall is hung with tapestry, and wreathed with Christmas evergreens, and the banners above are surmounted with laurel crowns. The servitors are bringing in the royal dishes, conspicu-ous amongst which is the peacock in all its glory of gaudy plumage, and the boar's head dressed with holly, bay, and rosemary. Another celebrated account of a Christmas dinner, at the time of the famous Christmas Prince (or Lord of Misrule) who presided over the festivities at St. John's, Oxford, in 1607, is given us by Aubrey: "The first messe was a boar's head, which was carried by the tallest and lustiest of all the guard,

## WITH JOYOUS HEARTS.

*Allegretto marsial.*

CATHARINE WILSON.

1. Come with joy-ous hearts to-day, Christmas carols gai-ly sing; Holly twines with fragrant bay,
2. Tune-ful bells more loudly ring, Vo-cal all the ambient air, Thus earth greets her Infant King,

And the merry church bells ring } Hearing joyous, free from care, } Tidings glad that once the angels sang To shepherds on the plain, That

Tra la Tra la

Christmas morn so long a - go, That hap - py Christmas morn. La la la la la la la la

Tra la la la la la

la la la la la la la la la la, That hap - py Christmas morn.

before whom (as attendants) wente first, one attired in a horseman's coate, with a boar's spear in his hande ; next to him another huntsman in greene with a bloody faulcion drawne ; next to him two pages in tafatye sarcenet, each of them with a messe of mustard ; next to whome came hee that carried the boar's head crost with a greene silke scarfe, by which hunge the empty scabbard of the faulcion which was carried before him. As these entered the hall, he sange this Christmas Caroll, the last three verses (lines) of every staffe being repeated after him by the whole companye." The ceremony now observed in Queen's College, Oxford, differs but little from the above. Brawn, decorated with bay and rosemary, has been substituted for the boar's head, but otherwise the dish is brought in with very much of the same state and ceremony, the choir in their surplices singing in procession, by way of grace, the famous carol of those days,

Caput apri defero,
Reddens laudes Domino.

Various accounts have been given of the origin of this ancient custom. By some it is said to have originated with the Romans, who were accustomed to serve up the wild boar, sometimes in parts, sometimes the animal, as the first dish at their feasts. The following is the traditional receipt as given by an English lady for the brawn used, in the absence of the wild boar of more ancient times : "Soak the head in salt and water all night, scrape and clean it well, removing brain and eyes; boil until tender enough to remove the bones easily ; when quite tender pick meat from bones, chop fine, seasoning to taste, with red and black pepper, cloves, mace, nutmeg, and salt; mix well together and put in a press, letting it remain until cold." The boar's head was also an established Yule-tide dish of the North in the old heathen times. The whole boar

## OLD CHRISTMAS.

MOZART.
MARY HOWITT.

1. Now he who knows Old Christmas, He knows a wight of worth, For he's as good a
2. He comes with voice most cor - dial, It does one good to hear; For all the lit - tle
3. He tells us wit - ty sto - ries, He sings with might and main; We ne'er for - get his
4. Oh, he's a rare old fel - low, What gifts he gives a - way! There's not a lord in

fel - low As an - y on the earth; He comes warm-cloaked and coat - ed, And
chil - dren He asks each pass - ing year; His heart is warm and gladsome, Not
vis - it, Till he comes back a - gain; With lau - rel green and hol - ly We
En - gland Could e - qual him to - day! Good luck un - to Old Christmas, Long

buttoned to the chin; And ere he is a - nigh the door, We ope to let him in.
like your grip-ing elves, Who, with their wealth in plen - ty, Think on - ly of themselves.
make the house look gay; We know that it will please him, It was his an - cient way.
life now let us sing, He is more kind unto the poor Than an - y crown-ed king.

and boar's head, gorgeously ornamented. gilt, and painted, was also a favorite festival dish in England during the Norman era. Perhaps, as the wild boar was anciently accounted a public enemy, ferocious and destructive, a successful encounter with him was in those days considered an achievement worthy the valor of an accomplished knight, entitling him to the lasting gratitude of the country. The curious custom called the Rhyne Toll of Chetwode Manor, may be cited by way of illustration. The tradition is, that, at a very early period of English history, a lord of Chetwode, the ancestor of the present proprietor, slew in single combat an enormous wild boar, the terror of the surrounding country. For this good service, he and his heirs had conferred on them by royal authority certain valuable manorial rights and privileges, which the family enjoy to this day. This tradition received, about half a century since, a remarkable confirmation. Within a mile of Chetwode Manor house there existed a large

SHRINE OF ST. NICHOLAS: "WE ARE ALL GOOD CHILDREN."

mound, surrounded by a ditch, and bearing the name of the Boar's Pond. About the year 1810, the tenant to whose farm it belonged, wishing to bring it into cultivation, began to fill up the ditch by leveling the mound, when having lowered the latter about four feet, he came on the skeleton of an enormous boar, lying flat on its side, and at full length. The field containing it, as stated in Chambers' Book of Days, is still called the Boar's Head Field. There is, however, a very different account of the origin of the custom of serving the boar's head at Christmas, given by Dean Wade, in his Walks about Oxford: "Tradition presents this usage as a commemoration of an act of valor, performed by a student of a college, who, walking in a neighboring forest of Shotover, and reading 'Aristotle,' was suddenly attacked by a wild boar. The

## MERRILY RING THE BELLS.

"MANDOLINATA."
CHARLOTTE PIERSOL.

furious beast came open-mouthed upon the youth, who, however, very courageously and with happy presence of mind, is said to have rammed in the volume and cried, ' Græcum est' (it is Greek); fairly," adds the Dean, "choking the savage with the sage." Perhaps this manner of disposing of two enemies at once was considered by the Oxonians of that day an event worthy of a particular commemoration. The places where now the boar's head ceremony is specially observed, by bringing in the gigantic dish in procession, with song and chorus, on Christmas Day, are Queen's College, Oxford; St. John's College, Cambridge; and the Inner Temple, London. There has been also elsewhere, and even in this country, a successful attempt at a revival of this ancient ceremony, especially at the Twelfth Night parties of the Century Club in New York, where, it is said, the traditional boar's head has been served at the supper in this manner. But to return to the subject, the Christmas of our forefathers, the banquet would have been thought very incomplete without the appearance of the Christmas-pie, which was also anciently served with minstrelsy, but without the carol, the peculiar honor reserved for the boar's head—that "chiefest dish in all the land." This Christmas-pie was, it appears, quite a bill of fare in itself. Indeed fish, flesh, and fowl were to be found beneath its ample crust. We read that, "In the 26th year of Henry III., the Sheriff of Gloucester was ordered by that monarch to procure twenty salmon to be put into pies at Christmas ; and the Sheriff of Sussex, ten brawns, ten peacocks, and other items for the same purpose." The peacock was only produced at solemn and

## ON CHRISTMAS MORN.

HENRY PHILIPS.

1. Good news on Christmas morn, Good news, O children dear! No sweeter joy e'er born Than that which greets us here. Gai - ly we hail the joy-ous sea - son, Gai - ly we see the hap - py day draw nigh. La, la, la, la, la, la, la, la, la, la, la, la, la, la, la, La, la, la, la, la, la, la, la, la, la, la, la, la, la, la, la, la,

2. Good news on Christmas morn, Good news, O children glad! Rare gifts our lives a - dorn As Wise Men ev - er had. Mer - ry we sing the Christmas car - ol, Mer - ry with friends the songs of Christmas raise. La, la, la, la, la, la, la, la, la, la, la, la, la, la, la,

3. Good news on Christmas morn, Good news, O children fair! That e'en the most for - lorn And fee - blest are His care. Grate-ful we share the Christmas ban - quet, Grate - ful we spread a - far the Christmas cheer. La, la, la, la, la, la, la, la, la, la, la, la, la, la, la,

chivalric banquets, such as that of Christmas, and when thus served up, with gilded beak and plumed crest, his head appearing at one end of the pie, and his tail at the other, spread out in all its glory, was carried in state into the hall to the sound of minstrelsy, by the lady most distinguished for birth and beauty, the other ladies following in due order. Some of the dishes of the olden time do not appear to us to be very inviting ; yet others have stood the test of ages, as we see in the instance of a Christmas-pie, the receipt to make which is preserved in the books of the Salters' Company, in London. "For to make a moost choyce Paaste of Gamys to be eten at ye Feste of Chrystemasse (17th Richard II. A. D. 1394)." A pie so made by the Company's cook in 1836, was found excellent. It consisted of a pheasant, hare, and capon ; two partridges, two pigeons, and two rabbits; all boned and put into paste in the shape of a bird, with the livers and hearts, two mutton kidneys, forcemeats, and egg-balls, seasoning, spice, catsup, and pickled mushrooms, filled up with gravy made from the various bones. The North of England in more modern times continued to maintain a reputation for its Christmas-pies, composed of birds and game. In the Newcastle Chronicle of January 6, 1770, there is a description of a giant of this race, nearly nine feet in circumference. The learned Dr. Parr says of the mince-pie, which under its changed name continues to maintain its celebrity, that it should more properly be called *The Christmas-pie*, the term *mince* having been given to it in derision by the Puritans; indeed, in the seventeenth century, the eating of this pie became a test of orthodoxy. Bunyan, when in confinement and in distress for a comfortable meal, is

## CHRISTMAS WAITS.

BELLINI.
JEAN INGELOW.

1. God's great Gift to man for - lorn In a win-ter night was born; An - gels tell the
2. Wake, you friends and neighbors, wake, Thank our God for this Child's sake, Sing, my heart, the

glo - rious tale; Let not, Earth, thy welcome fail. Hail to the Manger-born, all hail!
an - them swell Since that bless-ed birth be - fell. Hail to the Manger-born, all hail!

Let not thy welcome fail. Hail! Lit - tle Child, how sunk Thy lot! Thy great might Thou
Let not thy welcome fail. Hail! Now is won the gift that we Lost be - neath the

hast for - got; Guider of all the stars that shone, Sleep, Thy glo - ry it is gone.
ap - ple - tree, Now is won the heav - en - ly shore, No more light wanes, or life gives o'er.

said to have refused to injure his morals by eating it, the Puritans of his day holding it to be a superstitious abomination. Anciently this pie was baked in the form of a *crache* or *manger*, the crossed bands at the top being traditionally considered to resemble the manner in which a child is secured in its crib. Its various savory contents had, it is supposed, some reference to the offerings of the Magi in the manger at Bethlehem.

In the primitive Church the feast of the Nativity appears to have been observed by the Eastern and Western Churches on different days; the Oriental Church keeping it on the 6th of January, calling it the Epiphany, and the Western Church, from the earliest time, on the 25th of December. According to the change of the style, made in England by act of Parliament, in 1752, "Old Christmas Day," as it is called, in contradistinction to that of the new style, falls on the eve of Epiphany or Twelfth-Day, and in some places, it is said, " is still observed as the festival of the Nativity." Bingham says that this day was kept as our Saviour's birthday for several ages by the churches of Egypt, Jerusalem, Antioch, Cyprus, and other churches of the East. In the fourth century, Chrysostom, in one of his homilies to the people of Antioch, tells them that, "Ten years were not yet passed since they came to the true knowledge of the day of Christ's birth, which they kept before on Epiphany, till the Western Church gave them better information." From that time it appears that the Nativity and Epiphany were kept as distinct festivals. Both Cassian and Jerome say : " The Nativity and Epiphany were kept on different days in all the Western Churches, and both these were indifferently called *Theophania et Epiphania, et prima et secunda Na-*

## BEAUTIFUL BELLS.

E. O. Lyte.

*Moderato.*

1. 2. Ring a-gain, Ring a-gain, Beauti-ful bells, beau-ti-ful bells;

Ring-ing, Ring-ing, Ring-ing, Ring-ing,

Ring a-gain, Ring a-gain, Beau-ti-ful bells, beau-ti-ful bells.

Ring-ing, Ring-ing, Ring-ing, Ring-ing.

1. On the breeze of ev'-ning steal-ing, Hark! the bells are slow-ly peal-ing, Wak-ing
2. As the toil of day is end-ing, Thro' the vales the bells are send-ing Tones with

ev-'ry ten-der feel-ing, Beautiful bells, beauti-ful bells, bells, beautiful bells.
ev-'ry mur-mur blending, Beautiful bells, beauti-ful bells, bells, beautiful bells.

*tivitas,*—the 'Epiphany' or 'Manifestation of God,' and his first and second Nativity ; that being the first, whereon he was born in the flesh, and that his second Nativity, or Epiphany, whereon he was baptized, and manifested by a star to the Gentiles." In the fourth century, however, the Easterns changed their festival of the Nativity, and united with the Westerns in observing the 25th of December. This variation in the early usage of the Greek and Latin Churches may have originated the custom of observing twelve days as the Christmas holidays. The Epiphany is said to denote Christ's manifestation to the world in four several respects, which at first were all commemorated upon this day, namely : 1. By his Nativity or Incarnation. 2. By the appearance of the Star which guided the Wise Men unto Christ at his birth. 3. By the glorious appearance that was made at his baptism. 4. By the manifestation of his Divinity, when by his first miracle He turned the water into wine, at the marriage of Cana in Galilee. In England the twelve days of Christmas were certainly observed as early as the time of Alfred the Great, and probably from a much earlier period. Collier, in his ecclesiastical History of Britain, cites an old law, of the time of Alfred, in which, "the twelve days after the Nativity of our Saviour are made holy days."

The Magi, or "Wise Men of the East,"

commemorated at the Epiphany, are supposed to have been Persians. These Magi in their own country were philosophers or priests, and besides were sometimes royal counselors, physicians, astrologers, or mathematicians. In fact they were similar to the Brahmins of India, the Philosophers among the Greeks, and the Druids among the Gauls. Zoroaster, one of their number and King of Bactria, the great reformer of the sect of the Magi, has left on record a curious prophecy relating to the future birth of a Saviour, and its announcement by a Star,

## IT CAME UPON THE MIDNIGHT.

J. B. Dykes.
E. H. Sears, 1800.

1. It came up-on the mid-night clear, That glorious song of old, From angels bend-ing
2. Still thro' the cloven skies they come, With peaceful wings unfurled; And still ce-les-tial
3. O ye, beneath life's crush-ing load, Whose forms are bending low, Who toil a-long the
4. For lo, the days are hast-'ning on, By prophet-bards fore-told, When with the ev-er-

near the earth   To touch their harps of gold: "Peace to the earth, good-will to man,
mu-sic floats   O'er all the wea-ry world; A-bove its sad and low-ly plains
climb-ing way,   With painful steps and slow, Look up! for glad and gold-en hours
cir-cling years   Comes round the age of gold! When peace shall o-ver all the earth

From Heaven's all-gracious King:" The earth in solemn stillness lay, To hear the an-gels sing.
They bend on heavenly wing, And ev-er o'er its Babel sounds, The bless-ed an-gels sing!
Come swiftly on the wing: Oh, rest be-side the wea-ry road, And hear the an-gels sing!
Its fin-al splendors fling, And the whole world send back the song Which now the an-gels sing!

which seems to agree in a remarkable manner with that of Balaam: "There shall come a star out of Jacob, and a sceptre shall rise out of Israel." Says Abul Pharajius, speaking of Zoroaster: "He taught the Persians the manifestation of the Lord Christ, commanding that they should bring him gifts; and revealed to them that it would happen in the latter time that a virgin would conceive without contact with a man, and that when her child was born, a star would appear and shine by day, in the

midst of which would be seen the figure of a virgin. 'But you, my children, will see its rising before all the nations. When, therefore, ye shall behold it, go whither the star shall guide ye and adore the child, and offer up to him your gifts, seeing that he is the word, which has created the Heavens.'" The Wise Men who came to Jerusalem in the days of Herod, are traditionally believed to have been three in number, and of the rank of kings or princes. The Venerable Bede, in the seventh century, was the first writer in England who gave a description of them, which he is supposed to have taken from some earlier account. According to Bede, "Melchior was old, with gray hair and long beard, and offered gold to our Saviour in acknowledgment of his sovereignty; Jaspar was young, without any beard, and offered frankincense in recognition of the Divinity; and Balthasar was of a dark complexion as a Moor, with a large spreading beard, and offered myrrh to our Saviour's humanity." The tradition is that they were baptized by St. Thomas, and afterwards themselves preached the gospel. In the fourth century their bodies were said to have been discovered by the Empress Helena, and taken to Constantinople; from thence to Milan; and when that city was taken by the Emperor Frederick in 1164, he gave these relics to Reinaldus, Archbishop of Cologne, whence they are commonly called "The Three Kings of Cologne." In England, a striking memorial of the offerings of the Magi is kept up by the sovereigns, who make an oblation of gold, frankincense, and myrrh, at the altar of the

## THE BABE OF BETHLEHEM.

1. The Babe in Bethl'em's manger laid, In humble form so low, By wond'ring angels is surveyed Thro' all His scenes of woe.
2. A Saviour! sinners all around! Sing, shout the wondrous word; Let ev'ry bosom hail the sound, A Saviour! Christ the Lord.
3. For not to sit on David's throne With worldly pomp and joy, He came for sinners to atone, And Satan to destroy.
4. Well may we sing a Saviour's birth, Who need the grace so given, And hail His coming down to earth, Who raises us to Heaven.

Noel, Noel, Now

sing a Saviour's birth, All hail, All hail, His coming down to earth, Who raises us to Heaven!

Chapel Royal in the Palace of St. James, on this festival. The story of the Three Kings of Cologne forms the subject of many of the early "mysteries," formerly so popular. There are, indeed, said to have been representations of the Magi in the French churches as early as the fifth century, and there are French mysteries relating to them in the eleventh century, and also a Latin one, wherein Virgil (who appears to have usually taken a conspicuous part in mediæval pageantry, and was supposed to have been a magician), accompanies the kings on their journey, and at the end of the adoration joins them very devoutly in the "benedicamus." The Adoration of the Magi was a favorite subject in our early English mysteries. In "Dives and Pauper," 1406, we read: "For to represente in playnge at Crystmasse Herodes and the Thre Kynges and other processes of the gospelles both then and at Ester, and at other times also, it is befull and comendable." These mysteries were suppressed early in the time of

James the First; but the Adoration of the Magi was afterwards introduced as a puppet show at Bartholomew Fair, as late as the time of Queen Anne. This representation of the Adoration of the Magi has given place in more modern times, at least in France and England, to the still popular game of drawing for king and queen on Twelfth-Night. This custom has generally been supposed to be in honor of the Three

## FROM FAR AWAY.

J. B. DYKES.
WILLIAM MORRIS.

1. From far a - way we come to you, The snow in the street, and the wind on the door, To
2. For as we wandered far and wide, The snow in the street, and the wind on the door, What
3. Un - der a tent when the night was deep, The snow in the street, and the wind on the door, There

tell of great tidings strange and true, Minstrels and maids, stand forth on the floor, Stand forth on the
hap do you deem there should us betide? Minstrels and maids, stand forth on the floor, Stand forth on the
lay three shepherds tending their sheep, Minstrels and maids, stand forth on the floor, Stand forth on the

floor. From far a - way we come to you, To tell of great tidings strange and true, From
floor. For as we wandered far and wide, What hap do you deem there should us betide? For
floor. Under a tent when the night was deep, There lay three shepherds tending their sheep, Un-

far away we come to you, To tell of great tidings strange . . . and true. . . .
as we wandered far and wide, What hap do you deem there should us be - tide? . . .
der a tent when the night was deep, There lay three shepherds tending their sheep. . . .

* 2nd and 4th and 5th lines may be sung as a response in each verse.

"O ye shepherds, what have ye seen,
   The snow in the street, etc.
To slay your sorrow and heal your teen?"
   Minstrels and maids, etc.

"In an ox-stall this night we saw,
   The snow in the street, etc.
A Babe and a Maid without a flaw,
   Minstrels and maids, etc.

"There was an old man there beside;
   The snow in the street, etc.
His hair was white, and his hood was wide,
   Minstrels and maids, etc.

"And as we gazed this thing upon,
   The snow in the street, etc.
Those twain knelt down to the little One,
   Minstrels and maids, etc.

"And a marvellous song we straight did hear,
   The snow in the street, etc.
That slew our sorrow and healed our care,"
   Minstrels and maids, etc.

News of a fair and a marvellous thing,
   The snow in the street, etc.
Nowell, Nowell, Nowell, we sing!
   Minstrels and maids, etc.

Kings of Cologne; although Mr. Soane thinks that in all probability it owes its origin to a Greek and Roman custom of casting lots at their banquets for who should be the *Rex Convivii*, or, as Horace calls him, the *Arbiter Bibendi*. An old calendar says: "On the 5th of January—the Vigil of the Epiphany—the Kings of the Bean are created, and on the 6th the feast of the Kings shall be held, and also of the Queen,

## CHRISTMAS VESPER HYMN.

J. HUGHES.
D. F. E. AUBER.

*Andantino.*

1. De-part a-while, each thought of care, Be earth-ly things for-got-ten all; And speak, my soul, thy ves-per prayer, O-be-dient to that sa-cred call. For hark! the peal-ing cho-rus swells, De-vo-tion chants the hymn of praise, And now of joy and hope it tells, Till fainting on the ear it says, Glo-ria ti-bi, Dom-i-ne!

2. Thine, wondrous Babe of Ga-li-lee! Fond theme of Da-vid's harp and song, Thine are the notes of min-strel-sy: To thee its ransomed chords be-long. And hark! a-gain the cho-rus swells, The song is waft-ed on the breeze, And to the listen-ing earth it tells, In accents soft and sweet as these, Glo-ria ti-bi, Dom-i-ne!

3. My heart doth feel that still He's near, To meet the soul in hours like this; Else why, oh, why that fall-ing tear, When all is peace and love and bliss? But hark! that peal-ing cho-rus swells A-new its thrill-ing ves-per strain, And still of joy and hope it tells, And bids Cre-a-tion sing a-gain, Glo-ria ti-bi, Dom-i-ne!

and let the banqueting be continued for many days." The usage now in regard to this game—particularly in France and England—is to place a bean and pea (or ring) in a Twelfth-cake, which, being divided, is distributed, and the persons finding the bean and pea, are the King and Queen of Twelfth-Night. Two hundred years ago the ingredients of the bean-cake were flour, honey, ginger, and pepper. "But it would not compete," says Mr. Sandys, ",with that beautiful, frosted, festooned, bedizened, and ornamented piece of confectionery, now called, *par eminence*, 'Twelfth-cake,' with its splendid waxen or plaster-of-paris kings and queens, the delight and admiration of school-boys and girls." In some parts of France the Bean-King is elected by another process. A child is placed under a table where he can see nothing ; and the master of the feast, holding up a piece of cake, demands whose portion it is to be. The child replies according to his own fancy, and this game continues till the piece which contains the bean has been allotted. A whole court is thus formed, and every time either of these magistrates is seen to drink, the company are bound to cry out under pain

## OVER LAND AND SEA.

of forfeit, "The King (or the Queen) drinks." Before concluding it should be mentioned that during the whole of the twelve days of Christmas, most of the social usages and observances thus far noticed were continued with more or less variation. The Yule-log and Christmas candle were burnt until Twelfth-Night. A small portion of the old log was carefully preserved to light that of the following year, and on the last day of its being in use, which in some places was even as late as Candlemas-Day (February 2), which festival in popular estimation was the conclusion of the Christmas holidays, a small piece of the Christmas block or log, having been kept on purpose for such burning, the practice was to

Kindle the Christmas brand, and then
  Till sunset let it burne ;
Which quenched, then lay it up agen,
  Till Christmas next returne.
Part must be kept, wherewith to teend
  The Christmas log next yeare ;
And where it is safely kept, the fiend
  Can do no mischief there.

Many curious superstitions are connected with the Yule-log. In France it was believed to keep away pestilence all the year from those seated around it.—*Nathan B. Warren.*

From "The Holidays : Christmas, Easter and Whitsuntide," by permission Dr. N. B Warren.

## THE GLAD BELLS ALL SAY.

A. G. Crowe.
Clara Wallace.

Ring, bells! swing, bells! Far o'er hill and plain! Ring, bells! swing, bells! Christ - mas time is come a - gain! Ring, bells! swing, bells! Far o'er dis - tant hill and plain! Ring, bells! swing, bells! The Child is come to reign!

1. "All hail! Far away," so the glad bells all say, "Comes bounding the sleigh, with its coursers so gay; And soon will the joy, born of gift and of toy, Make glad the warm heart of dear girl and brave boy." Ye glad bells of the Christmas so near, All hail! Ye glad bells of the Christmas so near, All hail!

2. "Rejoice we to-day!" so the glad bells all say, "Put ev - 'ry sad care that so vex - es a - way; Let Christmastide cheer find a warm welcome here, And bless this best day of the swift - passing year." Ye glad bells of the

3. "'Tis on this bright day," so the glad bells all say, "De - cember grows brighter than ev - er was May; When freedom from care makes the round world so fair, And greeting and welcome are heard ev'ry - where." Ye glad bells of the

## THE KERRY DANCE.

J. L. Mollot.

*Verse.*

1. Oh, the days of the Ker-ry danc-ing, Oh, the ring of the pip-er's tune! Oh, for one of those
2. Was there ev-er a sweet-er col-leen In the dance than Ei-ly More! Or a proud-er
4. Lov-ing voi-ces of old com-pan-ions, Stealing out of the past once more, And the sound of the

hours of gladness, Gone, a-las! like our youth, too soon; When the boys be-gan to gath-er
lad than Tha-dy, As he bold-ly took the floor; "Lads and lass-es, to your plac-es,
dear old mu-sic, Soft and sweet as in days of yore; When the boys be-gan to gath-er

In the glen, of a summer night, And the Kerry pip-er's tuning made us long with wild de-light.
Up the middle and down again;" Ah! the merry-hearted laughter ringing through the hap-py glen.
In the glen, of a summer night, And the Kerry pip-er's tuning made us long with wild de-light.

*rit.*

O to think of it, O to dream of it, fills my heart with tears! O the days of the Ker-ry dancing!

O the ring of the piper's tune! O for one of those hours of gladness, Gone, alas! like our youth, too

*Fine.*  *piu lento.*  *After 3d verse.*

soon!  3. Time goes on, and the hap-py years are dead, And one by one the merry hearts are fled; Si-lent now is the wild and lonely glen, Where the bright, glad

*rall.* (*To 4th verse.*)

laugh will ech - o ne'er a - gain. On - ly dreaming of days gone by, in my heart I hear

## THE CHRISTMAS TREE.

J. C. LOWRY.
CLARA WALLACE.

1. Hur - rah! and hur-rah for the Christ - mas tree! Oh, long may it wave in its
2. There are things full of won-der far o - ver the sea, But what are they all to the
3. When the birds are all fled, and the leaves are all dead, Then old San-ta Claus decks its

green - er - y! When the winter comes with its whitening snow, How proudly doth it grow!
Christ - mas tree! In its beauty bright with its fruit so fair, What can with it com-pare?
boughs, as 'tis said, But he comes at night and ere morning ray, He speeds him on his way.

Hur - rah! hur - rah for the Christ - mas tree, Its boughs all fresh, and its

wealth all free! Tho' the stur - dy oak for - sake the land, This, ev - er green, shall stand.

## CHRISTMAS IS COMING.

Henry Phillips.

1. "I want for-ty doz-en of fine wax-en dolls, And for-ty-four thousand be-
2. "There's Malcolm, and Har-ry, and Clarence, and John, Hope no end of hol-i-day
3. "And wonder-ful pic-tures, books, mu-sic, and flowers, And birds singing gai-ly in

side them; I've a tel-e-phone or-der for good bouncing balls, So ma-ny I nev-er can
treas-ure; Of San-ta Claus' vis-it from evening till dawn They talk or they dream without
ca-ges, Ten thousand good things to make happy the hours Of folks of all sta-tions and

hide them! Toys needed by millions, and trumpets, and drums, With cargoes of candies as-
meas-ure. There's Nellie, and Jennie, and Mary, and Bess, What rare things they'd have me go
a-ges. Move lively, my lads, with full boxes and trays, Kind people will ev-'ry-where

sort-ed, And oranges, almonds, and sweet su-gar plums, Quick pack them or have them im-
hunt-ing! The darlings I love them, and always can guess Silks, ribbons, furs, jewels they're
hail them, The time is fast speeding and it would a-maze If San-ta Claus ev-er should

port-ed. )
want-ing. )  For Christmas is coming, a week from to-morrow, And all must be read-y, be-
fail them. )

lieve me; If Santa Claus missed it, ah! there would be sorrow, From blame none could ever relieve me."

## MISTRESS SANTA CLAUS.

ALEX. LEE.
ADA S. SHELTON.

*Spirited.*

1. Of all the bu-sy people round, This bu-sy Christmas-tide, None works like Mis-tress
2. The North Star brightly shining down Gives all the light they need, For "How to Climb a
3. They've dolls in ev-'ry cor-ner there, They've dolls on all the chairs; Piled high on ev-'ry
4. The reindeer now are harnessed fast, The toys packed in the sleigh; And San-ta Claus wrapped

San-ta Claus For days and nights be-side; The good old man, her stur-dy spouse, Has
Chimney" is The on-ly book they read. But Mis-tress Claus is work-ing hard On
cupboard shelf, And all the way up-stairs; But not a stitch of cloth-ing would On
up in furs, Soon dashes on his way, But, as he goes, cries, smil-ing back, "I

so much now to do, If Madame Claus did not take hold He nev-er would get thro'. Oh! a
dresses, bonnets, sacks. And there are lots of clothes to make For all the jumping-jacks. Oh! a
an-y doll be seen, Un-less his wife were there, for he Can't sew on a ma-chine. For a
nev-er in my life Could do so much for boys and girls Without so good a wife!" So, a

helpmeet wise is his wife, In their home at Reindeer Hall, 'Mid icebergs cold her

heart is warm, Planning hap-pi-ness for all! A helpmeet wise is his wife

In their home at Reindeer Hall, Warm her heart for aye To the "Merry Christ-mas!" call.

"IT EVERYWHERE SPARKLED AND GLITTERED."

# A CHRISTMAS TREE.

I HAVE been looking on, this evening, at a merry company of children assembled round that pretty German toy, a Christmas Tree. The tree was planted in the middle of a great round table, and towered high above their heads. It was brilliantly lighted by a multitude of little tapers; and everywhere sparkled and glittered with bright objects. There were rosy-cheeked dolls, hiding behind the green leaves; there were real watches (with movable hands, at least, and an endless capacity of being wound up) dangling from innumerable twigs; there were French polished tables, chairs, bedsteads, wardrobes, eight-day clocks, and various other articles of domestic furniture (wonderfully made, in tin, at Wolverhampton), all perched among the boughs, as if in preparation for some fairy housekeeping; there were jolly, broad faced little men, much more agreeable in appearance than many real men—and no wonder, for their heads took off, and showed them to be full of sugar-plums; there were fiddles and drums; there were tambourines, books, work-boxes, paint-boxes, sweetmeat-boxes, peep-show-boxes, all kinds of boxes; there were trinkets for the elder girls, far brighter than any grown-up gold and jewels; there were baskets and pincushions in all devices; there were guns, swords, and banners; there were witches standing in enchanted rings of pasteboard, to tell fortunes; there were teetotums, humming-tops, and needle-cases; pen-wipers, smelling-bottles, conversation-cards, and bouquet-holders; real fruit, made artificially dazzling with gold leaf; imitation apples, pears, and walnuts, crammed with surprises; in short, as a pretty child, before me, delightedly whispered to another pretty child, her bosom friend, "There was everything and more."

This motley collection of odd objects clustering on the tree like magic fruit, and flashing back the bright looks directed towards it from every side—some of the diamond-eyes admiring it were hardly on a level with the table, and a few were languishing in timid wonder on the bosoms of pretty mothers, aunts, and nurses—made a lively realization of the fancies of childhood; and set me thinking how all the trees that grow and all the things that come into existence on the earth, have their wild adornments at that well-remembered time.

Being now at home again, and alone, the only person in the house awake, my thoughts are drawn back, by a fascination which I do not care to resist, to my own childhood. I begin to consider, what do we all remember best upon the branches of the Christmas Tree of our own young Christmas days, by which we climbed to real life?

Straight, in the middle of the room, cramped in the freedom of its growth by no encircling walls or soon-reached ceiling, a shadowy tree arises; and, looking up into the dreamy brightness of its top—for I observe in this tree the singular property that it appears to grow downwards toward the earth—I look into my youngest Christmas recollections!

All toys at first, I find. Up yonder among the green holly and red berries, is the Tumbler with his hands in his pockets, who wouldn't lie down, but whenever he was put upon the floor, persisted in rolling his fat body about until he rolled himself still, and brought those lobster eyes of his to bear upon me—when I affected to laugh very much, but in my heart of hearts was extremely doubtful of him. Close beside him is that infernal snuff-box, out of which there sprang a demoniacal Counsellor in a black gown, with an obnoxious head of hair, and a red cloth mouth, wide open, who was not to be endured on any terms, but could not be put away either; for he used suddenly, in a highly magnified state, to fly out of mammoth Snuff-boxes, in dreams, when least expected. Nor is the frog, with cobbler's wax on his tail, far off; for there was no knowing where he would not jump; and when he flew over the candle, and came upon one's hand with that spotted back—red on a green ground—he was horrible. The cardboard lady in a blue-silk skirt, who was stood up against the candlestick to dance, and whom I see on the same branch, was milder, and was beautiful; but I can't say as much for the larger cardboard man, who used to be hung against the wall and pulled by a string; there was a sinister expression in that nose of his; and when he got his legs round his neck (which he very often did), he was ghastly, and not a creature to be alone with. When did that dreadful Mask first look at me? Who put it on, and why was I so frightened that the sight of it is an era in my life? It is not a hideous visage in itself; it is even meant to be droll; why, then, were its stolid features so intolerable? Surely not because it hid the wearer's face. An apron would have done as much; and though I should have preferred even the

## LET OLD SANTA CLAUS COME IN.

HOWARD.

*Allegretto.*

1. Let old San-ta Claus come in, With his grisly-bearded chin, And his wondrous pack of toys For good little girls and boys, { Dear kind San-ta Claus, you'll see What good Here's for you a cup of whey, And children we can be; So we'd like it, please, to do Something in re-turn for you. bun-dle of sweet hay For the rein-deer four-in-hand That you drive from Christmas-land.

2. "Mer-ry Christmas!" he will say, "All who willingly o-bey, Good at school and fair at play, Shall have something fine to-day." { What care we for ice and snow, Or how By the fire-side warm and bright, We will cold the wind may blow? Let the temp-est beat and roar, We know it can-not pass the door. mer-ry be to-night, For the Christmas Child is near Bringing pleasure and good-cheer!

apron away, it would not have been absolutely insupportable, like the mask. Was it the immovability of the mask? The doll's face was immovable, but I was not afraid of *her*. Perhaps that fixed and set change coming over a real face, infused into my quickened heart some remote suggestion and dread of the universal change that is to come on every face, and make it still? Nothing reconciled me to it. No drummers, from whom proceeded a melancholy chirping on the turning of a handle; no regiment of soldiers, with a mute band, taken out of a box, and fitted, one by one, upon a stiff and lazy little set of lazy-tongs; no old woman, made of wires and a brown-paper composition, cutting up a pie for two small children, could give me permanent comfort for a long time. Nor was it any satisfaction to be shown the Mask, and see that it was made of paper, or to have it locked up, and be assured that no one wore it. The mere recollection of that fixed face, the mere knowledge of its existence anywhere, was sufficient to awake me in the night, all perspiration and horror, with, "Oh, I know it's coming! Oh, the Mask!" I never wondered what the dear old donkey with the panniers—there he is!—was made of, then. His hide was real to the touch, I recollect. And the great black horse with round red spots all over him—the horse that I could even get upon—I never wondered what had brought him to that strange condition, or thought that such a horse was not commonly seen at Newmarket. The four horses of no color, next to him, that went into the wagon of cheeses, and could be taken out and stabled under the piano, appear to have bits of fur-tippet for their tails, and other bits for their mares, and to stand on pegs instead of legs, but it was not so when they were brought home for a Christmas present. They were all right then; neither was their harness unceremoniously nailed into their chests, as appears to be the case now. The tinkling works of the music cart, I *did* find out to be made of quill toothpicks and wire; and I always thought that little tumbler in his

## CHRISTMAS AFTERMATH.

ANDERSON.
MARGARET E. SANGSTER.

1. The dear-est thing of all, dears, About the Christmas time, So full of mirth and mu-sic, Of sto-ry, song, and rhyme, Is that to lit-tle chil-dren, It brings e-nough of cheer, In homes that else were drear-y, To last them all the year.

2. You hung a dain-ty stock-ing Within the hearth-fire's glow, That sent a trail of splen-dor A-cross the drift-ed snow. But in the crowded ci-ty Are many children sweet, Who scarce have shoes and stock-ings For chill-y lit-tle feet.

3. Does San-ta Claus for-get them? The brave old Saint—not he! He heaps their pret-ty pres-ents On the mission Christmas tree. And af-ter-Christ-mas hours, In many an at-tic dim, Are glad to grate-ful chil-dren Who send their love to him.

4. The dear-est thing of all, dears, Go search the world a-bout, Is that the Christmas an-gels Find all the children out. And oft to lit-tle dar-lings In homes for-lorn of cheer, They bring such store of sun-shine, It lasts the whole round year.

shirt-sleeves, perpetually swarming up one side of a wooden frame, and coming down, head-foremost, on the other, rather a weak-minded person—though good-natured; but the Jacob's Ladder, next to him, made of little squares of red wood, that went flapping and clattering over one another, each developing a different picture, and the whole enlivened by small bells, was a mighty marvel and a great delight. Ah! The Doll's house!—of which I was not proprietor, but where I visited. I don't admire the Houses of Parliament half so much as that stone-fronted mansion with real glass windows, and doorsteps, and a real balcony—greener than I ever see now, except at watering-places; and even they afford but a poor imitation. And though it *did* open all at once, the entire house-front (which was a blow, I admit, as cancelling the fiction of a staircase; it was but to shut it up again, and I could believe. Even open, there were three distinct rooms in it: a sitting-room and bed-room, elegantly furnished, and,

20

best of all, a kitchen with uncommonly soft fire-irons, and a plentiful assortment of diminutive utensils—oh, the warming-pan!— and a tin man-cook in profile, who was always going to fry two fish. What Barmecide justice have I done to the noble feasts wherein the set of wooden platters figured, each with its own peculiar delicacy, as a ham or turkey, glued tight on to it, and garnished with something green, which I recollect as moss! Could all the Temperance Societies of these later days, united, give me such a tea-drinking as I have had through the means of yonder little set of blue crockery, which really would hold liquid (it ran out of the small wooden cask, I recollect, and tasted of matches), and which made tea, nectar. And if the two legs of the ineffectual little sugar-tongs did tumble over one another, and want purpose, like Punch's hands, what does it matter? And if I did once shriek out, as a poisoned child, and strike the fashionable company with consternation, by reason of having drunk a little teaspoon, inadvertently dissolved in too hot tea, I was never the worse for it, except by a powder!

Upon the next branches of the tree, lower down, hard by the green roller and miniature gardening-tools, how thick the books

## LO! NOW HE IS COME.

ELLEN DOUGLAS.

1. All hail! ring the bells, as they joyously chime, "All hail!" is the song of the dear Christmas time.
2. Lo! now He is come, Prince longed for of old, To Him we give welcome, our great joy untold.
3. Our voi-ces we raise in songs to His praise, His birthday we car-ol, the best of all days.
4. "All hail!" to the Presence full sweetly be-nign, With "peace and good-will," His message divine.

Car - ol, chil - dren, car - ol glad - ly, Car - ol, chil - dren, al - way,

Lo! the Christ child, born of Ma - ry, We greet Him to - day.

begin to hang. Thin books, in themselves, at first, but many of them, and with deliciously smooth covers of bright red or green. What fat black letters to begin with! "A was an archer and shot at a frog." Of course he was. He was an apple-pie also, and there he is! He was a good many things in his time, was A, and so were most of his friends, except X, who had so little versatility, that I never knew him to get beyond Xerxes or Xantippe, like Y, who was always confined to a Yacht or a Yew-tree; and Z, condemned forever to be a Zebra or a Zany. But now, the very tree itself changes, and becomes a bean-stalk—the marvellous bean-stalk up which Jack climbed to the Giant's house! And now, those dreadfully interesting double-headed Giants, with their clubs over their shoulders, began to stride along the boughs in a perfect throng, dragging knights and ladies home for dinner by the hair of their heads. And Jack—how noble, with his sword of sharpness, and his shoes of swiftness! Again those old meditations come upon me as I gaze up at him; and I debate within myself whether there was more than one Jack (which I am loath to believe possible), or only one genuine original admirable Jack, who achieved all the recorded exploits. Good for Christmas time is the ruddy color of the cloak in which —the tree making a forest of itself for her to trip through with her basket—Little Red Riding-Hood comes to me one Christmas Eve to give me information of the cruelty and treachery of that dissembling Wolf, who ate her grandmother, without making any impression on his appetite, and then ate her, after making that ferocious joke about his teeth. She was my first love. I felt that if I could have married Little Red Riding Hood, I should have known perfect bliss. But it was not to be ; and there was nothing for it but to look out the Wolf in the Noah's Ark there, and put him late in the procession on the table, as a monster who was to be degraded. Oh, the wonderful Noah's Ark! It was not found seaworthy when put in a washing-tub, and the animals were crammed in at the roof, and needed to have their legs well shaken down before they could be got in, even there— and then, ten to one but they began to tumble out at the door, which was but imperfectly fastened with a wire latch—but what was *that* against it! Consider the noble fly, a size or two smaller than the elephant; the lady-bird, the butterfly—all triumphs of art! Consider the goose, whose feet were so small, and whose balance was so indiffer-

## GLORY OF CHRISTMAS.

F, CAMPANA.
REV. J. M. NEALE *tr.*

1. A day, a day of glo - ry! A day that ends our woe! A day that tells of tri - umph
2. With " Glory in the highest " Archangels tell their mirth ; With songs of praise ascending
3 He comes, His throne the manger, He comes, His shrine the stall ; The ox and ass His courtiers,

Against the vanquished foe! Yield, summer's brightest sunrise, To this December morn : Lift up your gates, ye
Men answer from the earth : Glad angels swell the triumph, And mortals raise the horn, Lift up your gates, ye
Who made and governs all. Let earth, and sky, and ocean, His mighty way adorn; Lift up your gates, ye

*Chorus.*

prin - ces, And let the Child be born! A day, a day of glo - ry! A day that ends our woe!

A day that tells of tri - umph Against the vanquished foe! Yield, summer's brightest sunrise,

To this December morn : Lift up your gates, ye princes, And let the Child be born!

ent, that he usually tumbled forward, and knocked down all the animal creation. Consider Noah and his family, like idiotic tobacco-stoppers; how the leopard stuck to warm little fingers; and how the tails of the larger animals used gradually to resolve themselves into frayed bits of string!

Hush! Again a forest, and somebody up in a tree—not Robin Hood, not Valentine, not the Yellow Dwarf (I have passed him and all Mother Bunch's wonders, without mention), but an Eastern King with a glittering cimeter and turban. By Allah! two Eastern Kings, for I see another, looking over his shoulder! Down upon the grass at the tree's foot, lies the full length of a

coal-black Giant, stretched asleep, with his head in a lady's lap; and near them is a glass box, fastened with four locks of shining steel, in which he keeps the lady prisoner when he is awake. I see the four keys at his girdle now. The lady makes signs to the two kings in the tree, who softly descend. It is the setting-in of the bright Arabian Nights. Oh, now all common things become uncommon and enchanted to me! All lamps are wonderful; all rings are talismans. Common flower-pots are full of treasure, with a little earth scattered on the top; trees are for Ali Baba to hide in; beefsteaks are to throw down into the Valley of Diamonds, that the precious stones

## LITTLE CHILDREN, CAN YOU TELL?

1. Lit-tle children, can you tell? Do you know the sto-ry well? Ev-'ry girl and
2. Yes, we know the sto-ry well; Lis-ten now, and hear us tell, Ev-'ry girl and
3. Shepherds sat upon the ground, Fleecy flocks were scattered round, When a brightness
4. "Joy and peace," the angels sang, Far the pleasant echoes rang; "Peace on earth! to

every boy, Why the an-gels sing for joy On the Christmas morn-ing?
every boy, Why the an-gels sing for joy On the Christmas morn-ing.
filled the sky. And a song was heard on high On the Christmas morn-ing.
men good-will!" Hark! the angels sing it still On the Christmas morn-ing.

5. For a little babe that day
Cradled in a manger lay;
Born on earth our Lord to be;
This the wondering angels see
On the Christmas morning.

6. Joy our little hearts shall fill,
Peace and love, and all good-will;
This fair babe of Bethlehem
Children loves, and blesses them
On the Christmas morning.

may stick to them, and be carried by the eagles to their nests, whence the traders, with loud cries, will scare them. Tarts are made, according to the recipe of the Vizier's son of Bussorah, who turned pastry-cook after he was set down in his drawers at the gate of Damascus; cobblers are all Mustaphas, and in the habit of sewing up people cut into four pieces, to whom they are taken blindfold. Any iron ring let into stone is the entrance to a cave which only waits for the magician, and the little fire, and the necromancy, that will make the earth shake. All the dates imported come from the same tree as that unlucky date, with whose shell

the merchant knocked out the eye of the genie's invisible son. All olives are of the stock of that fresh fruit concerning which the Commander of the Faithful overheard the boy conduct the fictitious trial of the fraudulent olive-merchant; all apples are akin to the apple purchased (with two others) from the Sultan's gardener for three sequins, and which the tall black slave stole from the child. All dogs are associated with the dog, really a transformed man, who jumped upon the baker's counter, and put his paw on the piece of bad money. All rice recalls the rice which the awful lady, who was a ghoul, could only peck by grains, because of her nightly feasts in the burial-place. My very-rocking-horse—there he is, with his nostrils turned completely inside out, indicative of Blood!—should have a peg in his neck, by virtue thereof to fly away with me, as the wooden horse did with the Prince of Persia, in the sight of all his father's court. Yes, on every object that I recognize among those upper branches of my Christmas Tree, I see this fairy light! When I wake in bed, at daybreak, on the cold dark winter mornings, the white snow dimly beheld, outside, through the frost on the window-pane, I hear Dinarzade: "Sister, sister, if you are yet awake, I pray you to finish the his-tory of the young King of the Black Islands." Scheherazade replies, "If my lord the Sultan will suffer me to live another day, sister, I will not only finish that, but tell you a more wonderful story yet." Then the gracious Sultan goes out, giving no orders for the execution, and we all three breathe again. At this height of my tree I begin to see, cowering among the leaves—it may be born of turkey, or of pudding, or mince-pie, or of these many fancies, jumbled with Robinson Crusoe on his desert island, Philip Quarll among the monkeys, Sanford and Merton with Mr. Barlow, Mother Bunch, and the Mask—or it may be the result of indigestion, assisted by imagination and

## 'TWAS CLEAR AND COLD.

H. R. Bishop.

*Allegretto.*

1. 'Twas clear and cold that winter night; The stars all in the sky, As filled with ho - ly,
2. A - bove the plains beyond the hills, Be - yond the dis - tant seas, Rang mu - sic that still

new de - light, Sang sweet his lul - la - by; Out of the East the full moon came, White -
shapes and fills The na - tions' des - ti - nies; For out of love a Child was born, To

*Sing grace note 1st time.*

robed with light, a bride! Her face aglow with inward flame Could not its gladness hide.
man a Son was given, And ev - 'ry year His natal morn Fills all the world with Heaven.

over-doctoring—a prodigious nightmare. It is so exceedingly indistinct, that I don't know why it's frightful—but I know it is. I can only make out that it is an immense array of shapeless things, which appear to be planted on a vast exaggeration of the lazy-tongs that used to bear the toy soldiers, and to be slowly coming close to my eyes, and receding to an immeasurable distance. When it comes closest, it is worst. In connection with it, I descry remembrances of winter nights incredibly long; of being sent early to bed, as punishment for some offense, of waking in two hours, with a sensation of having been asleep two nights; of the leaden hopelessness of morning ever dawning, and the oppression of a weight of remorse.

And now, I see a wonderful row of little lights rise smoothly out of the ground, before a vast green curtain. Now, a bell rings—a magic bell, which still sounds in my ears, unlike all other bells—and music plays, amidst a buzz of voices, and a fragrant smell of orange-peel and oil. Anon, the magic bell commands the music to cease, and the great green curtain rolls itself up majestically, and The Play begins! The devoted dog of Montargis avenges the death of his master, foully murdered in the Forest of Bondy; and a humorous Peasant with a red nose and a very little hat, whom I take from this hour forth to my bosom as a friend (I think he was a Waiter or an Hostler at a village Inn, but many years have passed since he and I have met), remarks that the sassigassity of that dog is indeed surprising; and evermore this jocular conceit will live in my remembrance fresh and unfading, overtopping all possible jokes, unto the end of time. Or now, I learn with bitter tears how poor Jane Shore, dressed all in white, and with her brown hair hanging down, went starving through the streets ; or how George Barnwell killed the worthiest uncle that ever man had, and was afterwards so sorry for it that he ought to have been let

## ALL SILVER THE ROOFS.

off. Comes swift to comfort me, the Pantomime—stupendous Phenomenon!—when Clowns are shot from loaded mortars into the great chandelier, bright constellation that it is; when Harlequins, covered all over with scales of pure gold, twist and sparkle, like amazing fish ; when Pantaloon (whom I deem it no irreverence to compare in my own mind to my grandfather) puts red-hot pokers in his pocket, and cries, "Here's somebody coming!" or taxes the Clown with petty larceny, by saying, "Now, I sawed you do it!" when Everything is capable, with the greatest ease, of being changed into Anything; and "Nothing is, but thinking makes it so." Now, too, I perceive my first experience of the dreary sensation—often to return in after-life—of being unable, next day, to get back to the dull settled world; of wanting to live forever in the bright atmosphere I have quitted; of doting on the little Fairy, with the wand like a celestial Barber's Pole, and pining for a Fairy immortality along with her. Ah, she comes back, in many shapes, as my eye wanders down the branches of my Christmas Tree, and goes as often, and has never yet stayed by me! Out of this delight springs the toy-theatre—there it is, with its familiar proscenium, and ladies in feathers,

## CHRISTMAS ONCE A YEAR.

JOAQUIN MILLER.

*Andante semplice.*

*mf*

1. Those Christ - mas bells as sweet - ly chime As on the day when
2. Then he came sing - ing thro' the woods, And plucked the hol - ly
3. What tho' up - on his hoar - y head Has fallen man - y a

first they rung So mer - ri - ly in old - en time, And far and wide their
bright and green, Pulled here and there the i - vy buds; Was some - times hid - den,
win - ter's snow, His wreath is still as green and red As 'twas a thou-sand

mu - sic flung; Shaking the tall, gray, i - vied tower With all their deep me - lo-dious
sometimes seen,—Half bur - ied 'neath the mis - tle - toe His long beard hung with flakes of
years a - go; A - gain we're hap - py all day long, We smile, and lis - ten to the

power They still pro - claim to ev - 'ry ear, "Old Christmas comes but once a year!"
snow, And still he ev - er carolled clear, "Old Christmas comes but once a year!"
song Its bur - den still re - mote or near, "Old Christmas comes but once a year!"

in the boxes!—and all its attendant occupation with paste and glue, and gum, and water-colors, in the getting-up of The Miller and his Men, and Elizabeth, or the Exile of Siberia. In spite of a few besetting accidents and failures (particularly an unreasonable disposition in the respectable Kelmar, and some others, to become faint in the legs, and to double up, at exciting points of the drama), a teeming world of fancies so suggestive and all-embracing, that far below it on my Christmas Tree, I see dark, dirty, real theatres in the daytime, adorned with these associations as with the freshest garlands of the rarest flowers, and charming me yet.

But hark! The Waits are playing, and they break my childish sleep! What images do I associate with the Christmas music as I see them set forth on the Christmas Tree? Known before all the others, keeping far apart from all the others, they gather round my little bed. An angel, speaking to a group of shepherds in a field; some travelers with eyes uplifted, following a star; a baby in a manger; a child in a spacious temple, talking with grave men; a solemn figure, with a mild and beautiful face, raising a dead girl by the hand; again, near a city gate calling back the son of a widow, on

## AVE MARIA.

FRANZ SCHUBERT.

*Adagio.*

1. A - ve, Ma - ri - a!   Ho - ly Maid! Oh, deign to hear a maiden's
2. A - ve, Ma - ri - a!   Moth - er dear! The heath on which we now lie
3. A - ve, Ma - ri - a!   Hear our prayer! If still by thy protection

vow,      To thee we humbly look for aid,   To thee, to thee in sup - pli -
sleeping,  A down bed seems if thou art near,  To guard us in thy ho - ly
blest,     No spir - its of the earth or air   Shall dare, shall dare to break our

ca - tion bow. The heart with sin and sorrow laden, Beneath thy care shall find repose; Then
keep - ing, When thy soft smile creation cheer - eth, To rest is lull'd the stormy gale; The
peace - ful rest, Thy child with care and sorrow la - den, In lowly supplication bows; He

hear, oh, hear a lowly maiden, And soothe the anguish of her woes! A - ve, Ma - ri - a!
moon more silv'ry white appeareth; The dew shines brighter o'er the vale! A - ve, Ma - ri - a!
near, we pray thee, Holy Maiden, O Virgin Mother, hear our vows! A - ve, Ma - ri - a!

his bier, to life; a crowd of people looking through the open roof of a chamber where he sits, and letting down a sick person on a bed, with ropes; the same in a tempest, walking on the water to a ship; again, on a sea-shore, teaching a great multitude; again, with a child upon his knee, and other children round; again, restoring sight to the blind, speech to the dumb, hearing to the deaf, health to the sick, strength to the lame, knowledge to the ignorant; again, dying upon a Cross, watched by armed soldiers, a thick darkness coming on, the earth beginning to shake, and only one voice heard, "Forgive them, for they know not what they do!"

Still on the lower and maturer branches of the Tree Christmas associations cluster thick. School-books shut up; Ovid and Virgil silenced; the Rule of Three with its cool, impertinent inquiries, long disposed of; Terence and Plautus acted no more, in an arena of huddled desks and forms, all chipped and notched, and inked; cricket-bats, stumps, and balls, left higher up, with the smell of trodden grass and the softened noise of shouts in the evening air; the tree is still fresh, still gay. If I no more come home at Christmas time, there will be girls and boys (thank Heaven!) while the world lasts; and they do! Yonder they dance and play upon the branches of my Tree,

## CHRISTMAS TIME IS COME AGAIN.

1. Christ-mas time is come a-gain, Christ-mas plea-sures bring-ing;
2. An-gels sang, let men re-ply, And chil-dren join their voi-ces;

Let us join our voic-es now, And Christmas songs be singing. Years a-go, one
Raise the cho-rus loud and high, Earth and heav'n re-joic-es. When we reach that

star-ry night, Thus the sto-ry's giv-en, An-gel bands o'er Bethlehem's plains,
hap-py place Joy-ous prais-es bringing, Then, be-fore our Father's face,

*Chorus.*

Sang the songs of heaven.
We shall still be singing. } Glo-ry be to God on high! Peace, goodwill to

mor-tals! Christ, the Lord, is born to-night, Heav'n throws wide its por-tals.

God bless them, merrily, and my heart dances and plays too! And I *do* come home at Christmas. We all do, or we all should. We all come home, or ought to come home, for a short holiday—the longer, the better —from the great boarding-school, where we are forever working at our arithmetical slates, to take and give a rest. As to going a-visiting, where can we not go, if we will; where have we not been, when we would; starting our fancy from our Christmas Tree! Away into the winter prospect. There are many such upon the tree! On, by low-lying misty grounds, through fens and fogs, up long hills, winding dark as caverns between thick plantations, almost shutting out the sparkling stars; so out on broad heights, until we stop at last, with sudden silence, at an avenue. The gate-bell has a deep, half-awful sound in the frosty air; the gate swings open on its hinges; and, as we drive up to a great house, the glancing lights grow larger in the windows, and the opposing rows of trees seem to fall solemnly back on either side, to give us place. At intervals, all day, a frightened hare has shot across this whitened turf; or the distant clatter of a herd of deer trampling the hard frost, has, for the minute, crushed the silence too. Their watchful eyes beneath the fern

## THE MAGIC TREE.

CLARA MORTON.

*Spirited.*

1. Come, the mag·ic tree is lad·en with treasure; Come, its gifts so free are here in full
2. Come where holly green with berries red blending, Come where pine and bay, their fragrance at-

*D. C.* Come, the mag·ic tree is lad·en with treasure; Come, its gifts so free are here in full

*Fine.*

meas·ure; Here we gath·er fruits that, nowhere else growing, Ripen to Winter winds' blow·ing.
tending, Twin'd by loving hands, give Christmas day greeting, To welcome our thrice happy meeting!

meas·ure; Here we gath·er fruits that, nowhere else growing, Ripen to Winter winds' blow·ing.

*D.C.*

Tra la la la la la la la la la, Tra la la la la la la la la.

may be shining now, if we could see them, like the icy dew-drops on the leaves; but they are still, and all is still. And so, the lights growing larger, and the trees falling back before us, and closing up again behind us, as if to forbid retreat, we come to the house. There is probably a smell of roasted chestnuts and other good comfortable things all the time, for we are telling Winter Stories—or Ghost Stories, more shame for us—round the Christmas fire; and we have never stirred, except to draw a little nearer to it. But no matter for that. We came to the house, and it is an old house, full of great chimneys where wood is burnt on ancient dogs upon the hearth, and grim portraits (some of them with grim legends, too) lower distrustfully from the oaken panels of the walls. We are a middle-aged nobleman, and we make a generous supper with our host and hostess and their guests—it being Christmas-time, and the old house full of company—and then we go to bed. Our room is a very old room. It is hung with tapestry. We don't like the portrait of a cavalier in green, over the fireplace. There are great black beams in the ceiling, and there is a great black bedstead, supported at the foot by two great, black figures, who seem to have come off a couple of tombs in the old baronial church in the park, for our particular accommodation. But, we are not a superstitious nobleman, and we don't mind. Well! we dismiss our servant, lock the door, and sit before the fire in our dressing-gown, musing about a great many things. At length we go to bed. Well! we can't sleep. We toss and tumble and can't sleep. The embers on the hearth burn fitfully and make the room look ghostly. We can't help peeping out over the counterpane, at the two black figures and the cavalier—that wicked-looking cavalier—in green. In the flickering light they seem to advance and retire; which, though we are not by any means a superstitious nobleman, is not agreeable. Well! we get nervous—more and more nervous. We say "This is very foolish, but we can't stand this; we'll pretend to be ill, and knock up somebody." Well! we are just going to do it when the locked door

## HOME AGAIN.

MARSHALL S. PIKE.
Pet. Oliver Ditson & Co.

1. Home a - gain, home a - gain, From a for - eign shore! And oh, it fills my soul with joy, To meet my friends once more. Here I dropped the parting tear, To cross the o - cean's foam, But now I'm once again with those Who kindly greet me home. Home again, Home again, from a foreign shore, And oh, it fills my soul with joy, To meet my friends once more.

2. Hap - py hearts, hap - py hearts, With mine have laughed in glee, But oh, the friends I loved in youth Seem hap - pi - er to me; And if my guide should be the fate, Which bids me longer roam, But death a - lone can break the tie That binds my heart to home. Home again, Home again, from a foreign shore, And oh, it fills my soul with joy, To meet my friends once more.

3. Mu - sic sweet, mu - sic soft, Lin - gers round the place, And oh, I feel the childhood charm That time cannot ef - face. Then give me but my homestead roof, I'll ask no pal - ace dome, For I can live a hap - py life With those I love at home. Home again, Home again, from a foreign shore, And oh, it fills my soul with joy, To meet my friends once more.

opens, and there comes in a young woman, deadly pale, and with long, fair hair, who glides to the fire, and sits down in the chair we have left there, wringing her hands. Then, we notice that her clothes are wet. Our tongue cleaves to the roof of our mouth, and we can't speak ; but we observe her accurately. Her clothes are wet ; her long hair is dabbled with moist mud; she is dressed in the fashion of two hundred years ago ; and she has at her girdle a bunch of rusty keys. Well! there she sits, and we can't even faint, we are in such a state about it. Presently she gets up and tries all the locks in the room with the rusty keys, which won't fit one of them ; then she fixes her eyes on the portrait of the cavalier in green, and says, in a low, terrible voice, "The stags know it!" After that, she wrings her hands again, passes the bedside, and goes out at the door. We hurry on our dressing-gown, seize our pistols (we always travel with pistols), and are following, when we find the door locked. We turn the key, look out into the dark gallery ; no one there. We wander away, and try to find our servant. Can't be done. We pace the gallery till daybreak ; then return to our deserted room, fall asleep, and are awakened by our servant (nothing ever haunts *him*) and the shining sun. Well! we make a wretched breakfast, and all the company say we look queer. After breakfast, we go over the house with our host, and then we take him to the portrait of the cavalier in green, and then it all comes out. He was false to a

## CHRISTMAS IS HERE.

T. Andrews.

1. Sing we so mer - ri - ly, Lightly and cheer - i - ly, This hap - py day;
2. Far o'er the froz - en earth Sweetly the voice of mirth Ech - oes a - round;
3. Grateful and glad are we, Singing thus mer - ri - ly, Fond hearts so near;

Ban - ish all Cold winds are

sor - row, Ne'er let us bor - row Fears from to - mor - row To shadow to - day.
blow - ing, Fair cheeks are glow - ing, Joy is o'er - flow - ing, Pleasures a - bound.
sor - row, Why should we bor - row Fears for to - mor - row? Christmas is here.

young house-keeper once attached to that family, and famous for her beauty, who drowned herself in a pond, and whose body was discovered, after a long time, because the stags refused to drink of the water. Since which, it has been whispered that she traverses the house at midnight (but goes especially to that room where the cavalier in green was wont to sleep), trying the old locks with the rusty keys. Well! we tell our host of what we have seen, and a shade comes over his features, and he begs it may be hushed up ; and so it is. But it's all true, and we said so, before we died (we are dead now), to many responsible people. There is no end to the old houses, with re-sounding galleries, and dismal state-bed-chambers, and haunted wings shut up for many years, through which we may ramble, with an agreeable creeping up our back, and encounter any number of ghosts, but (it is worthy of remark, perhaps,) reducible to a very few general types and classes ; for ghosts have little originality, and "walk" in a beaten track. Thus, it comes to pass that a certain room in a certain old hall, where a certain bad lord, baronet, knight, or gentleman, shot himself, has certain planks in the floor from which the blood *will not* be taken out. You may scrape and scrape, as the present owner has done, or plane and plane, as his father did, or scrub and scrub, as his grandfather did, or burn and burn with strong acids, as his great-grandfather did, but there the blood will still be—no redder and no paler—no more and no less—always just the same. Thus, in such another house there is a haunted door, that never will keep open ; or another door that never will keep shut ; or a haunted sound of a spinning-wheel, or a hammer, or a footstep, or a cry, or a sigh, or a horse's tramp, or the rattling of a chain. Or else, there is a turret-clock, which, at the midnight hour, strikes thirteen when the head of the family is going to die ; or a shadowy, immovable black carriage, which at such a time is always seen by somebody, waiting near the great gates in the stable-yard. Or thus, it came to pass how Lady Mary went to pay a visit at a large wild house in the Scottish Highlands, and, being fatigued with her long journey, retired to bed early, and innocently said, next morning, at the breakfast-table, " How odd, to have so large a party last night, in this remote place, and not to tell me of it before I went to bed !" Then every one asked Lady Mary what she meant. Then Lady Mary replied, " Why, all night long the carriages were driving round and round the terrace, underneath my window!" Then the owner of the house turned pale, and so did his Lady, and Charles Macdoodle of Macdoodle signed to Lady Mary to say no more, and every one was silent. After breakfast, Charles Macdoodle told Lady Mary that it was a tradition in the family that those rumbling carriages on the terrace betokened death. And so it proved, for two months afterwards the lady of the mansion died. Lady Mary often told this story to the old Queen Charlotte ;

## THE SLEIGH RIDE.

JOHN DRAKE.

1. Jin - gle bells, jingle bells, In the misty moonlight; Jingle bells, jingle bells, On the frosty midnight;
2. Fast we glide, fast we glide, Snowflakes falling o'er us; Fast we glide, fast we glide, Christmas joy before us;
3. Hands are warm, eyes are bright, Welcome is December; Hearts aglow, cold the snow, Joys we well re-[member.

Speed along, speed along, 'Tis keen winter weather; Speed along, speed along, Light as any feather.
Mer - ry all, merry all, Ringing laughter hearty; Merry all, merry all, In our sleighing party!
Jin - gle bells, jingle bells, Far-off voices ringing, Jingle, bells, jingle, bells, Still I hear them singing.

by this token that the old King always said, "Eh, eh? What, what? Ghosts, ghosts? No such thing, no such thing !" And never left off saying so, until he went to bed. Or, a friend of somebody's, whom most of us know, had a particular friend, with whom he made the compact that, if it were possible for the spirit to return to this earth after its separation from the body, he of the twain who first died should reappear to the other. In course of time, this compact was forgotten by our friend : the two young men having progressed in life, and taken diverging paths that were wide asunder. But one night, years afterwards, our friend staying for the night in an inn, on the Yorkshire Moors, happened to look out of bed, and there, in the moonlight, leaning on a bureau near the window, steadfastly regarding him, saw his old college friend ! The appearance being solemnly addressed, replied, in a kind of whisper, but very audibly, " Do not come near me. I am dead. I am here to redeem my promise. I come from another world, but may not disclose its secrets !" Then the whole form, becoming paler, melted, as it were, into the moonlight, and faded away. Or, there was the daughter of the first occupier of the picturesque Elizabethan house, so famous in our neighborhood. You have heard about her? No! Why, she went out one summer evening, at twilight, when she was a beautiful girl, just seventeen years of age, to gather flowers in the garden ; and presently came running, terrified, into the hall to her father, saying, "Oh, dear father, I have met myself!" He took her in his arms, and told her it was fancy, but she said, "Oh, no! I met myself in the broad walk, and I was pale and gathering withered flowers, and I turned my head, and held them up!" And that night she died; and a picture of her that was begun, though it was never finished, they say is somewhere in the house to this day, with its face to the wall. Or, the uncle of my brother's wife was riding home on horseback, one mellow evening at sunset, when, in a green lane close to his own house, he saw a man standing before him, in the very centre of the narrow way. "Why does that man in the cloak stand there?" he thought. "Does he want me to ride over him?" But the figure never moved. He felt a strange sensation at seeing it so still, but slackened his trot and rode forward. When he was so close to it as almost to touch it with his stirrup, his horse shied, and the figure glided up the bank, in a curious, unearthly manner—backward, and without seeming to use its feet—and was gone. The uncle of my brother's wife, exclaiming, "Good Heaven! It's my cousin Harry, from Bombay!" put

## WELCOME CHRISTMAS CHEER.

1. Hark! the Christ-mas bells are ring-ing, Ring-ing thro' the fros-ty air,
2. Hark! the mer-ry peal is swell-ing From the gray old crumbling tower,
3. An-kle-deep the snow is ly-ing, Ev-'ry spray is clothed in white,

Hap-pi-ness to each one bring-ing, With re-lease from toil and care.
To the sim-plest crea-ture tell-ing Of Al-might-y love and power.
Yet a-broad the folk are hie-ing, Hands are bu-sy, hearts are light.

Ring ye bells mer-ri-ly, Ring ye bells cheer-i-ly, Wel-come sweet to Christmas cheer.

spurs to his horse, which was suddenly in a profuse sweat, and, wondering at such strange behavior, dashed round to the front of his house. There he saw the same figure, just passing in at the long French window of the drawing-room, opening on the ground. He threw his bridle to a servant, and hastened in after it. His sister was sitting there, alone. "Alice, where's my cousin Harry?" "Your cousin Harry, John?" "Yes. From Bombay. I met him in the lane just now, and saw him enter here, this instant." Not a creature had been seen by any one; and in that hour and minute, as it afterwards appeared, this cousin died in India. Or, it was a certain sensible old maiden lady, who died at ninety-nine, and retained her faculties to the last, who really did see the Orphan Boy; a story which has often been incorrectly told, but of which the real truth is this—because it is, in fact, a story belonging to our family—and she was a connection of our family. When she was about forty years of age, and still an uncommonly fine woman (her lover died young, which was the reason why she never married, though she had many offers), she went to stay at a place in Kent, which her brother, an Indian Merchant, had newly bought. There was a story that this place had once been held in trust, by the guardian of a young boy, who was himself the next heir, and who killed the young boy by harsh and cruel treatment. She knew nothing of that. It has been said that there was a cage in her bed-room in which the guardian used to put the boy. There was no such thing. There was only a closet. She went to bed, made no alarm whatever in the night, and in the morning said composedly to her maid when she came in, "Who is the pretty, forlorn-looking child who has been peeping out of that closet all night?" The maid replied by giving a loud scream, and instantly decamping. She was surprised ; but she was a woman of remarkable strength of mind, and she dressed herself and went downstairs, and closeted herself with her brother. "Now, Walter," she said, "I have been disturbed all night by a pretty, forlorn-looking boy, who has been constantly peeping out of that closet in my room, which I can't open. This is some trick." "I am

## GAILY BEATS THE DRUM.

German. Marching Song.

1. March on, march on, our way along, While gaily beats the drum, dum di dum ! With steady tramp and ringing song, The way will short become, dum di dum ! Tra la la la la, dum ! Tra la la la la, dum !
2. March on, march on, my comrades brave, With muskets flashing bright, dum di dum ! The stars and stripes above us wave, And flaunt the morning light, dum di dum! Tra la la la la, dum ! Tra la la la la, dum !
3. March on, march on, our steps are light, Our hearts from fear are free, dum di dum ! For freedom's sacred cause we fight, For law and lib-er-ty, dum di dum! Tra la la la, dum ! Tra la la la la, dum !

La la la la la la la, dum di dum ! With steady tramp and ringing song, The way will short become, dum di dum !

afraid not, Charlotte," said he, "for it is the legend of the house. It is the Orphan Boy. What did he do?" "He opened the door softly," said she, "and peeped out. Sometimes, he came a step or two into the room. Then I called to him to encourage him, and he shrunk, and shuddered, and crept in again, and shut the door." "The closet has no communication, Charlotte," said her brother, "with any other part of the house, and it's nailed up." This was undeniably true, and it took two carpenters a whole forenoon to get it open for examination. Then she was satisfied that she had seen the Orphan Boy. But, the wild and terrible part of the story is, that he was also seen by three of her brother's sons, in succession, who all died young. On the occasion of each child being taken ill, he came home in a heat, twelve hours before, and said, "Oh, mamma, I have been playing under a particular oak-tree, in a certain meadow, with a strange boy—a pretty, forlorn-looking boy, who was very timid, and made signs!" From fatal experience the parents came to know that this was the

Orphan Boy, and that the course of that child whom he chose for his little playmate was surely run. Legion is the name of the German castles, where we sit up alone to wait for the spectre—where we are shown into a room, made comparatively cheerful for our reception—where we glance round at the shadows, thrown on the blank walls by the crackling fire—where we feel very lonely when the village inn-keeper and his pretty daughter have retired, after laying down a fresh store of wood upon the hearth, and setting forth on the small table such supper-cheer as a cold roast capon, bread, grapes, and a flask of old Rhine wine— where the reverberating doors close on their retreat, one after another, like so many peals of sullen thunder—and where about the small hours of the night, we come into the knowledge of divers supernatural mysteries. Legion is the name of the haunted German students, in whose society we draw yet nearer to the fire, while the school-boy in the corner, opening his eyes wide and round, flies off the footstool he has chosen for his seat, when the door accidentally blows open. Vast is the crop of such fruit, shining on our Christmas Tree; in blossom, almost at the very top; ripening all down the boughs!

Among the later toys and fancies hanging there—as idle often and less pure—be the images once associated with the sweet

## CALM ON THE EAR OF NIGHT.

J. B. Dykes.
E. H. Sears, 1838.

1. Calm on the list - 'ning ear of night   Come Heaven's me - lo - dious strains,
2. Ce - les - tial choirs from courts a - bove   Shed sa - cred glo - ries there;
3. The answer-ing hills of Pal - es - tine   Send back the glad re - ply;
4. O'er the blue depths of Gal - i - lee   There comes a ho - lier calm,

Where wild Ju - de - a stretch - es far   Her sil - ver - man - tled plains.
And an - gels, with their spark - ling lyres,   Make mu - sic on the air.
And greet, from all their ho - ly heights,   The Day-Spring from on high.
And Shar - on waves, in sol - emn praise,   Her si - lent groves of palm.

"Glory to God!" the sounding skies
Loud with their anthems ring,
"Peace to the earth, good-will to men
From Heaven's eternal King!"

Light on thy hills, Jerusalem!
The Saviour now is born!
And bright on Bethlehem's joyous plains
Breaks the first Christmas morn.

old Waits, the softened music in the night, ever unalterable! Encircled by the social thoughts of Christmas time, still let the benignant Figure of my childhood stand unchanged! In every cheerful image and suggestion that the season brings, may the bright star that rested above the poor roof, be the star of all the Christian world! A moment's pause, O vanishing tree, of which the lower boughs are dark to me as yet, and let me look once more! I know there are blank spaces on thy branches, where eyes that I have loved, have shone and smiled; from which they are departed. But, far above, I see the raiser of the dead girl, and the Widow's Son; and God is good! If age be hiding for me in the unseen portion of thy downward growth, oh, may I, with a gray head, turn a child's heart to that Figure yet, and a child's trustfulness and confidence!

Now, the tree is decorated with bright merriment, and song, and dance, and cheerfulness. And they are welcome. Innocent and welcome be they ever held, beneath the branches of the Christmas Tree, which cast no gloomy shadow! But, as it sinks into the ground, I hear a whisper going through the leaves: "This, in commemoration of the law of love and kindness, mercy and compassion. . This is in remembrance of Me!"—*Charles Dickens.*